THE TRANSFORMATION
OF AMERICAN
RELIGION

ALSO BY ALAN WOLFE

School Choice: The Moral Debate

Moral Freedom: The Search for Virtue in a World of Choice

One Nation, After All: What Middle-Class Americans Really Think about God, Country, Family, Racism, Welfare, Immigration, Homosexuality, Work, the Right, the Left, and Each Other

Marginalized in the Middle

The Human Difference: Animals, Computers, and the Necessity of Social Science

America at Century's End

Whose Keeper?: Social Science and Moral Obligation

America's Impasse: The Rise and Fall of the Politics of Growth

The Rise and Fall of the "Soviet Threat": Domestic Sources of the Cold War Consensus

The Limits of Legitimacy: Political Contradictions of Contemporary Capitalism

The Politics and Society Reader (with Ira Katznelson, Philip Brenner, and Gordon Adams)

The Seamy Side of Democracy: Repression in America

Political Analysis: An Unorthodox Approach (with Charles A. McCoy)

An End to Political Science: The Caucus Papers (ed. with Marvin Surkin)

THE TRANSFORMATION OF AMERICAN RELIGION

HOW WE ACTUALLY LIVE OUR FAITH

ALAN WOLFE

THE UNIVERSITY OF CHICAGO PRESS

The University of Chicago Press, Chicago 60637
Copyright © 2003 by Alan Wolfe
All rights reserved. Published by arrangement with The Free Press,
a division of Simon & Schuster, Inc.
First published in 2003
University of Chicago Press paperback edition 2005

Printed in the United States of America

18 17 16 15 14 13 12 11 10   3 4 5 6 7

ISBN-13: 978-0-226-90518-1 (paper)
ISBN-10: 0-226-90518-7 (paper)

Library of Congress Cataloging-in-Publication Data

Wolfe, Alan, 1942–
     The transformation of American religion : how we actually live our faith
  / Alan Wolfe.
        p.   cm.
     Originally published: New York : Free Press, c2003.
     Includes bibliographical references and index.
     ISBN 0-226-90518-7 (pbk. : alk. paper)
     1. United States—Religion—1960–   I. Title.

BL2525 .W65 2005
200′.973′090511—dc22

                                                    2004062051

♾ The paper used in this publication meets the minimum requirements of the
American National Standard for Information Sciences—Permanence of Paper for
Printed Library Materials, ANSI Z39.48-1992.

CONTENTS

Acknowledgments vii

Introduction: THE PASSING OF THE OLD-TIME RELIGION *1*

Chapter 1. WORSHIP *7*

Chapter 2. FELLOWSHIP *37*

Chapter 3. DOCTRINE *67*

Chapter 4. TRADITION *97*

Chapter 5. MORALITY *127*

Chapter 6. SIN *155*

Chapter 7. WITNESS *185*

Chapter 8. IDENTITY *215*

Conclusion: IS DEMOCRACY SAFE FROM RELIGION? *245*

Notes *265*

Index *297*

TO MY FAMILY

ACKNOWLEDGMENTS

"What are you?," I was asked by a dinner guest to whom I had just been introduced at Wheaton College, a conservative Protestant institution located in suburban Chicago. (Her decidedly Dutch name in that particular setting gave me a pretty good idea that she was a member of the Christian Reformed Church.) She knew what she was asking, I knew what she was asking, and she probably already knew the answer. Nevertheless, trying my best to evade the question, I answered that my grandparents came from Budapest. (Besides being true, experience has taught me that most Americans have no idea what religion to attach to a Hungarian background.) Everyone around the table laughed, but politely, as evangelical Protestants nearly always are, they pressed the point. "You know, we are not going to let you eat until you answer her question," one of the other guests said.

When you write about religion, people want to know about you in ways that do not apply if you write about, say, housing. This is no doubt because religion—a subject that takes one simultaneously into the most private realms of the human heart and the most public, and hence conflictual, areas of human society—defies the social scientist's claim to objectivity. So let me confess right off that I do not write about religion out of religious conviction. Although raised to be proud of my Jewish ethnic heritage—I still remember the names of the Jewish major leaguers of my youth—I am not, and never have been, a person of faith. When it comes to religion, I hear no inner voices, am attracted to no supernatural explanations of everyday events, look neither upward to heaven nor downward to hell, identify with no particular tradition, and feel no untoward guilt in having married a Christian (by birth, though not by conviction) and having, together with her, raised three children without benefit of confirmations or bar and bat mitzvahs.

Yet nor do I write out of the kind of hostility to religion that has characterized so many academics, especially in the humanities and social sciences, who feel that they have an obligation, evangelical in its own way, to dismiss any kind of faith as hopelessly wrongheaded and anachronistic in a skeptical age. I am attracted to religion, and to religious people, out of a sense that one-way conversations with the like-minded are never very satisfying. Perhaps that is why my travels into the world of religion as well as my research into the sociology of religion have enabled me to cross paths with evangelical Protestants I have come to count among my friends. Or why I teach at a Catholic university whose Jesuit heritage is obvious to me, even as the local Jesuits bemoan its absence. Or why, although I am not a believer in the religion of my birth, I know that my Jewish background has influenced everything from the choice of subjects about which I write to the way I write about them.

Readers will have to judge for themselves whether I have been fair to the people whose experiences I recount. I can only say what my intentions are. Were I to write with hostility about people who spend their weekends in activities I personally find uncongenial, I would be joining a long tradition of intellectual snobbishness toward people of faith—a tradition, I have come to believe, that ends in forms of bigotry little different from religion at its worst moments. But were I to write with uncritical admiration, I would be doing no favors for anyone, least of all the faithful themselves, for my report would be as trustworthy as the accounts written by fellow travelers of the Soviet Union.

In writing this book, my greatest debt has been to the ethnographers who provided the data upon which my descriptions and interpretations have been built; they will recognize their names in the notes. I hope that this book stands as an example of the power of ethnographic research, for in reading the best of this literature, I found myself present at the scenes described, even if I was not able to be there in person.

A number of specialists were kind enough to read the entire manuscript and to offer comments. I owe a special debt to Paul Baumann,

Lynn Davidman, Marc Edwards, R. Marie Griffith, Richard J. Mouw, James O'Toole, and John Schmaltzbauer. William McKinney offered helpful suggestions about churches to visit.

The Smith Richardson Foundation, and especially Mark Steinmeyer, provided a grant that made it possible for me to travel in order to make my own observations, as well as a chance to find time for uninterrupted writing. Boston College gave me a perfect learning and teaching environment. I want to express particular thanks to Susan Richard for keeping me organized and on course and to Patricia Chang for helpful intellectual feedback. Tom DeNardo was indispensable.

Suzanne Gluck, my agent, showed great faith in the project, as did Phil Rappaport, my first editor, and Bruce Nichols, my second. Bruce adopted my book when it fell into his lap and made so many constructive suggestions to improve it that I lost count. Portions of Chapter 6 appeared originally in *The Atlantic*.

My family, as they have so often before, supported me throughout the process, and this book is dedicated to them.

THE PASSING OF
THE OLD-TIME RELIGION

"So . . . thus it is, that natural men are held in the hand of God over the pit of hell," thundered America's most famous theologian, Jonathan Edwards, in 1741. "They have deserved the fiery pit, and are already sentenced to it; and God is dreadfully provoked, his anger is as great towards them as to those that are actually suffering the executions of the fierceness of his wrath in hell." For Edwards, God is great, humans are meek, and our only recourse is to accept the arbitrariness of his inscrutable grace.

Much ink has been spilled about whether "Sinners in the Hands of an Angry God" is typical of the theology of Jonathan Edwards. There is no doubt, however, that Edwards, even when he speaks in far more rapturous language about the wonders of the divine, paints a picture of religious believers as a people apart—their eyes focused not on the mundane world around them but on the ultimate judgment that awaits them. From his day to ours, that image has shaped the ways in which we argue over faith. Fed up with the sinful character of American life, evangelical Protestants, conservative Catholics, Orthodox Jews, Mormons, and other adherents to strong forms of religious faith have withdrawn from the dominant society, choosing to live in subcommunities of their own, to send their children to schools entrusted to teach the truths of their tradition, and to vote for candidates pledged to uphold and support their values. So visible are they, so strong do their convictions appear to be, and (especially in recent years) so palpable has been their influence over public policy that the spirit of Jonathan Edwards, or others like him, seems very much alive in the land.

If strong religious believers view secular society as the enemy, at best to be converted and at worst to be ignored, liberal and secular Americans are only too happy to agree that the faithful are indeed a breed apart. Deeply entrenched religious truths, they routinely insist, are little more than dogmas reiterated without examination and self-criticism. When believers refuse to engage the culture, their opponents dismiss them as fanatics, frustrated people rendered insecure by the dilemmas and opportunities of modernity. When they do mix with everyone else, especially by trying to demonstrate the wonders of their faith, they are called sectarian, their efforts at witnessing requiring constitutional restraints designed to protect the privacy and dignity of their targets. Yes, Jonathan Edwards remains alive and well in America, skeptics of religion are likely to conclude, but that is cause for concern, not celebration. Like Edwards himself, who certainly had his authoritarian side, strong believers, in the skeptics' view, can easily turn into petty tyrants, invoking divine authority to limit the freedom of those they fear.

The American people, it would seem, cannot make up their minds whether religious fervor is essential for salvation or incompatible with the principles of modern liberal democracy. But what if religious belief has little in common with the images conveyed by Jonathan Edwards? American religion has never existed in practice the way it is supposed to exist in theory. Democratic in their political instincts, geographically and economically mobile, attracted to popular culture more than to the written word, Americans from the earliest times have shaped religion to account for their personal needs; even Edwards was ridden out of his pulpit by worshippers fed up with his pious sermonizing. Always in a state of transition, faith in the United States, especially in the last half century or so, has been further transformed with dazzling speed. Tracing the history of Christian thought from the New Testament to the twentieth century, the theologian H. Richard Niebuhr documented the many ways in which Christ could become a transformer of culture. But in the United States culture has transformed Christ, as well as all other religions found within these shores. In every aspect of the religious life, American faith has met American culture—and American culture has triumphed.

Whether or not the faithful ever were a people apart, they are so no longer; if they were singing the famous gospel hymn today, they would say that the old-time religion is no longer good enough for them. Talk of hell, damnation, and even sin has been replaced by a nonjudgmental language of understanding and empathy. Gone are the arguments over doctrine and theology; if most believers cannot for the life of them recall what makes Luther different from Calvin, there is no need for the disputation and schism in which those reformers, as well as other religious leaders throughout the centuries, engaged. More Americans than ever proclaim themselves born again in Christ, but the lord to whom they turn rarely gets angry and frequently strengthens self-esteem. Traditional forms of worship, from reliance on organ music to the mysteries of the liturgy, have given way to audience participation and contemporary tastes. Some believers are anxious to witness their faith to others, but they tend to avoid methods that would make them seem unfriendly or invasive. If Jonathan Edwards were alive and well, he would likely be appalled; far from living in a world elsewhere, the faithful in the United States are remarkably like everyone else.

The message of this book is that religion in the United States is being transformed in radically new directions. This conclusion is based on time spent among the faithful of many varieties, as well as engagement with the writings of ethnographers who have studied religion as it is lived by real people in real life. So diverse are American religions, however, that I have not been able to discuss each and every one of them; the reader will not find much in this book dealing with Eastern Orthodox Christians, Hindus, or many other faiths that certainly deserve mention. Still, enough religions have been examined by sufficient numbers of social scientists to establish one conclusion: The most exotic religion in the United States is also the most familiar, as strikingly similar to the society in which it flourishes as it is distant from the religion we once knew. It is time for Americans to stop discussing a religion that no longer exists and to concentrate their attention on the one that flourishes all around them.

When we begin to recognize religion as it actually is, we will, I believe, be less likely to see ourselves divided into implacable camps. Here is my advice to those who view people on the other side of the faith divide as their enemy.

To people of faith, I say this: You have shaped American culture far too much to insist that you remain countercultural. You do not want to admit the extent to which your religion has accommodated itself to modern life in the United States for fear that this would somehow detract from your piety. But is it really so awful to have moved closer to the culture around you? You could take umbrage at the descriptions I will offer in this book of the ways in which you have succumbed to the individualism, and even on occasion the narcissism, of American life. But I would urge you instead to take pride in your flexibility and adaptability. Like everyone else in the United States, you innovate and originate. You want your institutions to be responsive to your needs. You seek faiths that are authentic and alive. Sometimes you probably do go too far in the alacrity with which you borrow from American culture, and on those occasions you may—and probably should—have second thoughts. But there is nothing in the transformation of American religion in which you have been such active participants that ought to cause bitter anguish and apocalyptic rejection.

To all those who worry about faith's potential fanaticism, I also have some words: We are all mainstream now. Ordinary people who want nothing more than to serve their God and to be modern, American, and full participants in their society have more in common with you than you realize. Because they do, the time has come for you to stop using the faithful as targets to promote an understanding of religion's role in public life that discriminates against those who make belief central to the way they live. Their views may be different from yours on abortion or prayer in school, but we expect people in a democracy to have different views on major questions of public policy. As modern Americans with distinctly tolerant sensibilities, you pride yourselves on your willingness to change, yet religious believers, even the most conservative among them, have adopted themselves to modern society far more than you have changed your views about what they are really like. You have made the whole country more sensitive to the inequalities of race and gender. Now it is time to extend the same sympathy to those who are different in the sincerity of their belief.

Religions can be astonishingly different, while human beings can be surprisingly the same. Study theology, and one comes away impressed by differences. Study real people, and one is more likely to notice the similarities, not only among people of different faiths but also between those for whom religion matters greatly and those for whom it matters not at all. Believers in the United States are neither saviors nor sectarians. Once we know more about them, we will, or so I hope, be less likely to fear either the imminent establishment of a theocracy or the day of wrath in which God punishes us for our sins.

CHAPTER 1

WORSHIP

WORSHIP'S PRIORITY

Those who worship at the Church of the Redeemer, an Episcopal congregation in Chestnut Hill, Massachusetts, enter a lovely old stone building that looks as if it were lifted out of a novel by Anthony Trollope and set down in the New World. Not all that many worship on the particular day I attend—the seventh Sunday after Pentecost or, if one prefers, the first Sunday following Independence Day 2002, an occasion to reflect on the meaning of the September 11 attack of the previous year. It is midsummer, when many of the regular members of the congregation are on vacation. But the sparse audience of thirty people symbolizes the fate of mainline churches in the United States, which, in the face of stiff competition from both the secular world as well as from more enthusiastic approaches to faith, rarely fill all their pews. All-white, prosperously dressed, and polite in a somewhat reserved way, the members of the church, familiar with its liturgy, worship quietly. The prayer books in front of them give them directions on when they are expected to listen and when they are expected to speak, but they do not need them—many of them (or so it seems to me) having grown up, if not exactly in this church, then certainly in its tradition. When it comes time to receive communion, people take turns walking up to the altar and, when done, walking orderly back to their place. The entire service lasts less than an hour.

The church's rector, the Reverend Richard H. Downes, is as dignified in his manner as those who listen to him. Speaking about September 11, Rev. Downes skillfully intertwines Christian and American messages. Strongly defending the separation of church and state, although not without a comment that a bit of "legal overkill" is often applied to the problem, he points out how, in spite of their other differences, church and nation both require a strong sense of collective affirmation to bring out the meanings each embodies; patriotism and religion in that sense, when rightly understood, have the power to make otherwise weak institutions strong. Soft-spoken but confident of his views, Rev. Downes understands his vocation as possessing an element of instruction. His sermon, meant to raise questions and to probe issues, makes it clear that, in this congregation, worship is not just about honoring God; it also serves to mark off Sunday mornings as a time to ponder who we are and how we are obligated to each other.

There is also plenty of room in the pews when the eleven o'clock service begins one month later in another part of the country: the Allen Temple Baptist Church in Oakland, California. But fifteen minutes after a teenage boy steps up to a microphone to start the service, nearly all the places are taken, both in the pews and onstage, as people stop milling around and settle down. Because worship at Allen Temple begins with gospel music designed to bring people to their feet with shouts of joy and affirmation, however, "settle down" is not exactly the right phrase. Worship at Allen Temple has little in common with the hushed atmosphere of the Church of the Redeemer. The nearly two-and-a-half-hour service obviously features music; it is a sign of how much has changed in American religion that "Old-Time Religion," the hymn used to symbolize the inherent conservatism of Southern whites in the film *Inherit the Wind*, is more likely to be heard these days in a black church. Just as present are expressions of black pride and celebrations of black achievement, such as the acknowledgment of an Eagle Scout who has won a full scholarship to Howard University. Finally, there is time—actually significant amounts of time—set aside for prayer. During that time, nearly half the assembled congregation comes to the front, kneels down, and is held, hugged, and anointed by church ministers. No one appears to be in charge of the service as Rev. Downes is in Chestnut Hill. Two women—Rev. Cheryl Elliott and Rev. Martha Taylor—come as close as anyone to leading the service, but at one time or another members of the youth ministry, members of the choir, or one of the congregation's many ministers take over. Despite the overwhelming black composition of both the congregation and the neighborhood in which it is located, white visitors are made to feel at home, as people go out of their way to welcome them with handshakes and good tidings.

J. Alfred Smith Sr., the charismatic senior pastor of Allen Temple, is not present the day I attend. Preaching instead is one of his students from the American Baptist Seminary of the West, the Reverend Rogelio Ovalle, an Assembly of God pastor from Oakland's rapidly growing Latino community. Like other cities in the United States, Oakland has been experiencing a dramatic increase in violent crime, and Rev. Ovalle, whose own family background is filled with examples of drug addiction and violence, addresses himself to the epidemic that is obviously on the minds of the congregation. Shouting from the pulpit, Rev. Ovalle depicts one brutal act of violence after another, asking over and over again the same question: "What is man that you are mindful of him?" (Ps. 8:3–5; Heb. 2:5–7). "We have many explanations for violence," he tells the assembled crowd in ringing terms, "but too few solutions." There is, however, one hope, no matter how bleak the situation seems. "Jesus went to the cross for you," he preaches. "Let's take the streets of Oakland back for the honor and glory of Jesus Christ." Rev. Ovalle's dramatic homiletic style is designed to encourage shouts of "Amen" and "Hallelujah," and those it certainly does. Audience participation in the sermon is as vibrant as audience participation in the music. Of all the services I have attended, time flew fastest at this one.

Worship is what people most often do when they practice religion. As the experiences of these two congregations illustrate, there are as many ways of worship as there are ways of being human. Yet worship must respond to the real needs of real people, whether they are prosperous suburbanites or the devout of the inner-city struggling with the poverty around them. There is no better place to begin to understand the ways in which American religion has been transformed than with those activities of prayer and participation that come closest to providing what people seek from their faith. When they worship, Americans revere a God who is anything but distant, inscrutable, or angry. They are more likely to honor a God to whom they can pray in their own, self-chosen way. In the process, they have substantially altered the faiths in which they believe.

THE CHANGING CATHOLIC LITURGY

In 1570, the Catholic Church established the Tridentine Latin Mass as the basic form of Catholic worship. Many years later, and in another part of the world, Catholics continued to adhere to the liturgy as laid down at the Council of Trent. For American Catholics in the 1950s, the Mass, as one recent history comments, "was immutable. As far as most people knew, the Mass had never changed and never would." In both halves of the Mass—the liturgy of the Word, in which hymns are sung, portions of the Bible read, and homilies delivered, and the liturgy of the Eucharist, in which Christ's words at the Last Supper are repeated by the priest as he consecrates the bread and wine that Catholics believe is transformed into Christ's body and blood—Catholics participated in rituals that seemed timeless.

The Tridentine Mass persisted with remarkably few alterations—until the 1960s and Vatican II, when it was altered completely. Concerned that ordinary Catholic worshipers were engaged in unthinking regurgitation of rites that had lost meaning for them, the Second Vatican Council in documents such as *Sacrosanctum Concilium*, while reiterating the importance of the liturgy in Catholic life, called for active steps designed to make liturgical worship more accessible to and understandable by "the people of God," or ordinary Catholic worshipers. The resulting changes have been dramatic. It is not just that the language of the Mass has shifted from Latin to the vernacular; the priest now faces the parishioners, the hymns are accompanied by guitar as well as organ, and homilies are unlikely to resemble the one delivered by the fiery Dublin priest of James Joyce's *A Portrait of the Artist as a Young Man*. Throughout Catholic America, greater lay participation in the Mass has become a fact of life, whether it takes the form of deacons assisting the priest, more singing in general, or more exchanging of greetings and wishes for peace among the parishioners.

One feature of the Mass that remained unchanged for centuries was the placement of the tabernacle, which holds the wafer used for Holy Communion, in a visible place so that its sacred character would be obvious to all. But this, too, changed after Vatican II. The reforms of the 1960s gave birth to a class of professional liturgists, theologians who engage in the task of trying to provide guidance for the new rites of the Mass, and many of them believe that by moving the tabernacle either to a separate eucharistic chapel or to a side altar, parishioners will be more likely to emphasize that Christ is present in the congregation as well as in the bread and the wine. In this way, they hold, ordinary believers will feel a greater sense of participation in the liturgy than if they were to treat it as a purely magical spectacle. Vatican II, as one liturgist puts it, "called for a shift to assembly or congregational participation. Assembly is really the better term because that includes the priest. He is not just running the show anymore. He is an active participant in the liturgy like everyone else." Another applies this principle to the issue of the placement of the tabernacle this way: "The church is the people of God. How can we accentuate that reality, not the reality of Jesus in a box?" These reformers believe that Catholic worshipers these days want to feel that they are involved in the forms of worship in which they engage, and they are prepared to fine-tune centuries-old aspects of the liturgy to accommodate that desire.

At stake in the argument over the location of the tabernacle are different theories of what worship is and how it should be practiced. Critics of Vatican II's reforms believe that liturgical worship has a special importance due to its ritualistic nature. Ritualized worship has many distinctive characteristics, including its emphasis on drama and narrative, its reliance on symbols, and its bodily appeal to the senses more than to the mindful qualities of the intellect. But what distinguishes ritual above all else is the lack of space it makes available for individuals to decide for themselves methods of worship that fit their own dispositions. Protestantism, in the view of many Catholic traditionalists, puts its emphasis on an individual's sense of inner conviction, while Catholicism, at its core, stresses the magical power that flows from collective participation in sacramental worship. Alter the liturgy, as Vatican II did, and one runs the risk of transforming Catholicism into just another Protestant denomination.

Many Catholic worshipers, especially among the older generations, agree; they often find themselves bewildered by the reforms to which they are expected to adhere, including the removal of the tabernacle. "When I walk into a church," says a male Catholic believer from a parish located in suburban Detroit, "I want to be drawn into the sacred and that is done when I can focus on the tabernacle. Without the tabernacle in the center, I can't focus and so it seems different, not as special, you know." "Jesus is in the tabernacle," as another insists. "We worship Jesus. But now I come into church and I'm not sure where the tabernacle is so that I can pray." A third links the tabernacle issue to the whole trend toward modernization in the Catholic Church. "When they took away the crucifix that was one thing. Now they have taken away the tabernacle too. Now there is absolutely nothing to focus on and now it doesn't even look like a church. In fact what you see up there now are a bunch of plants. It's Jesus I want to see and pray to, not a bunch of plants."

It is, however, an indication of the extent to which Catholic worship has been transformed in recent years that even these more traditionalist believers speak in the first person when they describe the attractions of their faith, rather than place their emphasis on considerations of doctrinal truth or liturgical correctness. In so doing, they appeal to forms of worship that reflect the modern world around them, even as they argue for an unchanged liturgy. We will never know whether Vatican II opened a Pandora's box of changes in the Catholic liturgy or whether it effectively stopped changes that would have been even more dramatic if it had never taken place. But we do know that no one can say, as one could say a half century ago, that the liturgy never changes. It does, and because it does, forms of worship in the Catholic Church have moved closer to the culture of individual choice and participation that characterizes other religions in the United States.

Some sense of the reality of post–Vatican II forms of liturgical worship can be obtained from a visit to St. Catherine's, a parish also located in the Detroit area. Many elderly Catholics have special memories of First Holy Communion, the day on which the boys and girls put on their best clothes, formed a procession outside the church, and entered together as a special Mass was celebrated in their honor. First Holy Communion is now celebrated at St. Catherine's in very different ways. For one thing, children sit together with their parents in the pews and are called, one by one, to the altar, as if the experience is less the celebration of a sacrament and more a secular activity resembling a school graduation. As might be expected in a modern suburb, each child's trip to the altar is accompanied by the blinking of flashbulbs and frequent expressions of congratulations. "The craziest time in the liturgy was when the children gathered around the altar," one parishioner says. "I mean it was nuts; noise, kids, cameras, coughing, sneezing, talking. It was chaos." Some worshipers claim that they are unhappy with this new informality, which strikes them as lacking the reverential qualities that make worship sacred. But in this case, it is not the actions of professional liturgists who are responsible for the loss of ritualistic magic; it is instead the conflict existing within the minds of ordinary worshipers, who want their Mass to be both majestic, as tradition demands, and responsive to their needs, as modernity encourages.

However distracting it may be to have the worship at Mass disrupted by flashbulbs, these parishioners from St. Catherine's were at least in church. Attendance at the liturgy was once a requirement of the Catholic faith; in fact, the term *liturgy* comes from the Greek word for "public duty." Catholics continue to believe that attendance at Mass is one of the defining features of Catholicism, but this does not mean that all Catholics can be found there on any given Sunday. "Following Vatican II," as the writer Charles Morris notes, "skipping Sunday Mass was quietly, if unofficially, dropped from the Catholic catalog of mortal sins. . . . Rightly or wrongly, most Catholics apparently feel that once- or twice-a-month Mass attendance keeps them in sufficient touch with their religion." Despite frequent efforts to reach out to the people of God through liturgical reforms such as the movement of the tabernacle, surveys suggest that attendance at Mass dropped from 71 percent of Catholics before Vatican II to 43 percent throughout the 1990s. Whatever the cause, the liturgy is unlikely to work its magic on contemporary Catholic believers because fewer are there when it takes place.

Even when Catholics attend Mass, moreover, they pay homage to God in decidedly individualistic ways. "What is your reason for attending Mass?" one survey asked Catholic respondents. The single largest group—37 percent—said the "feeling of meditating and communicating with God," while only 20 percent spoke of the "need to receive the Sacrament of Holy Communion." As if the reforms of Vatican II did not go far enough in appealing to the active participation of the faithful, one believer complained about the passivity of the worshipers and the uninspiring qualities of the homilies she experienced at Mass. When she attended an evangelical Protestant service, by contrast, "it was like *The Wizard of Oz* where it just turns into color." Before that, she knew the facts about Jesus, but she did not know who he really was. "I had never been to a church where people went early to get a seat. I had never been to a church where people stayed even up to a half hour after church was over."

Facing such stiff competition from technicolor worship, Catholics have been transforming the black-and-white qualities of their worship practices more along Protestant lines. This "Protestantization" of American Catholicism takes its extreme form among those Catholics who claim to be born-again. "Mary was the first Pentecostal, you know," one charismatic Catholic believes. In praying to her, one bypasses all intermediaries and speaks to a God who, far from being an aloof and alien father figure, can take human form. "The God of the Charismatics is very different from the Old Testament God whose name could not be spoken. In testimony, in conversation, and interviews members refer to this God as 'Daddy,' to themselves as his children," the sociologist who observed them writes. "Or they refer to Jesus as a brother, described by one interviewee as 'seen' jogging along during his morning run, dressed in the latest fashion in running suits and wearing a bandanna around his long hair."

Charismatic Catholics are something of an exotic sect, but their emphasis on the personal aspects of religious practice has had an impact on the more typical forms of Catholic worship. Consider the influence of the Jesuits, a religious order once known for its authori-

tarian and disciplined approach to the faith. Jesuits are in serious decline in the United States, but one aspect of their religious practice is
not: the *Spiritual Exercises* formulated by Ignatius Loyola, the founder
of the order. At the Jesuit university in which I teach, spiritual exercises are attractive to students and staff because they resonate with
the language of self-discovery. One Jesuit expresses this spiritual dimension of Catholic religious practice in these terms: "The past five
years . . . have been an especially rich time for me as a contemplative.
I have entered into a new relationship with Mary. I do some center-
ing prayer in her presence each day. I have come to appreciate the
feminine side of God. . . . How forgiving God is. How deeply in love
God is with everything human."

Catholics seek personalized forms of worship in many ways.
While only 4 percent of Catholics claim to be charismatic, one-third
praise the kinds of personalized prayer associated with them, and 23
percent of Catholic parishes have Charismatic Renewal Groups.
Moreover, a significant number of Catholic believers have been too
influenced by the Jesus First practices of American Protestantism to
cede too much authority for the things they care about to intermediaries, including parish priests. One study found that an "evangelical
orientation is growing," especially among young adult Catholics, as
more believers put "the emphasis on a 'personal relationship with
the Lord,' rather than on traditional Catholic sacramentalism, com-
munalism, or on the mediational role of the Church." As one Latino
worshiper says, "Why would I want to speak with a priest and ask for
confession to a man? Maybe the priest is a good person, but for
something very personal and spiritual, God is here with me and he's
the only person who understands."

Then there is the case of small-group forms of worship among
Catholic parishioners. About one in twenty Catholics now attends
some form of small group—a small percentage, to be sure, but one
whose growth has begun to attract the attention of Church leaders.
Catholics who participate in small groups like them because they
lack the sense of symbolic grandeur often attributed to Catholic worship. "It's so different [than Mass]. It's more life-giving, more en-
riching," says one believer. Nor does participation in such groups
have much to do with any lingering sense that Catholicism is the one

true faith or that the Church, and its hierarchy, are to be respected as institutions. Instead, like the similar groups one finds in Protestant circles, these are places in which all believers are considered equal. "There's a set of rules that we established from the beginning," as one member of a Catholic small group explains. "No one is to preach and no one is to teach. We're only there to share, and whatever's said is acceptable. You don't have to believe it, but you have to accept . . . that that person believes it, and that's fine. So one person does not comment on another person's views, opinions, or sharing."

Small groups are extremely popular at St. Brigid's, a Long Island parish the journalist Robert Keeler portrayed in a Pulitzer Prize–winning series for *Newsday*. Catholic officials are wont to call these groups "small Christian communities" and to find precedents for them—such as the gatherings of early Christians and the Latin American *communidades de base,* or left-leaning resistance groups—within the Catholic tradition. At St. Brigid's—which, because of its informal and welcoming character could never be called "St. Rigid's"—parishioners do not care what they are called. "We're not a small church community," a parishioner named Isabel Lister points out. "We're just a small group that prays." Small groups work at St. Brigid's for the reason that everything works there; this is a community of believers that cares deeply—for each other and for a church that feels very much a part of their home and family. As in many Protestant congregations, small-group religious practices at the Catholic St. Brigid's lead to a de-emphasis on doctrine, including those doctrines that have made Catholicism distinct from Protestantism. "Even in the religious education program," writes Keeler, "the approach is relational and experiential, rather than based solely on rote teaching of dogma." Worship at St. Brigid's comes first, but it is a form of worship as much designed to make people feel comfortable as it is to fill them with the majesty of God.

None of this means that Catholicism has lost its distinctive forms of worship. Catholics, by large percentages, continue to believe in transubstantiation, that the bread and the wine are in reality the body and blood of Christ. However transformed, the liturgy still exists; one would never confuse any Catholic Mass, even the most modernized, with a megachurch service. Yet Catholicism, for all its history of ritual and collective expression, is not an exception to the tendency of Americans to seek personalized forms of faith. In 1965, a nun, Sister Marie Augusta Neal, wrote that Catholics in the United States displayed an "individual emphasis, found also in Protestant spirituality" that "focuses on a personal type of religious experience" and a "private spirituality." The only thing that has changed since Sister Marie wrote, and since the reforms of Vatican II began to take hold, is that we now have more of the same.

American society is a nonliturgical society, its pace of life too fast, its commitments to individualism too powerful, its treatment of authority too irreverent, and its craving for innovation too intense to tolerate religious practices that call on believers to repeat the same word or songs with little room for creative expression. In a recent book, the philosopher Charles Taylor writes that William James's focus on religion's inner qualities blinded him to faith traditions, such as Catholicism, that give pride of place to a "collective connection through a common way of being." But Taylor is also quick to recognize that modern religious life is also characterized by a "new individualism" in which personal expressiveness inevitably plays a role. Taylor leaves up in the air the question of whether the new individualism will triumph over older forms of collective religious expression, although he is guardedly optimistic that a place will be found for the latter. He may well be right, but there can also be little question that liturgical faiths in the United States such as Catholicism are no longer religions in which obedient people follow rituals over which they have little or no say.

LITURGY WITHOUT REVERENCE

Judaism is also a liturgical religion, and, like Catholicism, its worship practices have been moving away from ritual. Even more than Catholics, indeed even more than any other religious denomination in the United States, Jews view worship attendance as optional. For some, this means no attendance at all. Among nonobservant Jews, the ritualistic character of the religion in which they were raised is powerful enough to influence their identity years later; one nonobservant Jew sings *Adon Olam* to her child, an important prayer from the Jewish liturgy, even if she cannot quite remember its name, and others observe the Friday night Sabbath meal, not with kosher food but with ritualistically ordered pizza or Chinese takeout. Still, for nonobservant Jews—no one knows their exact number, but a recent estimate suggests 25 percent of the Jewish population—the liturgy is never experienced in ways similar to Catholics who do not attend Mass.

There are other American Jews who make observance part of their identity but for whom faith takes second place to the social and educational opportunities their religious participation provides. "I think our kids are growing up absolutely knowing they are Jewish, and delighted they are Jewish," says one member of a focus group sponsored by Hadassah Southern California. "We spend a lot of time at the J[ewish] C[ommunity] C[enter]. My kids love their Hebrew school—our Hebrew school is wonderful. Our rabbis are so warm and loving, they make it a really nice place to be." For this woman, the liturgy is there, but it is an option. "We don't always go to Shabbat services; we don't get there all the time, but when we do it is not a have-to-go. I think their Jewishness is good and positive even though we don't conform to all the rituals." What makes people good Jews is not whether they show up in shul, this person reasons; it is the fact that, for her and her family, "the intention is still there." While such an intention-is-all-that-matters approach to worship can make sense to a particular believer, it is incompatible with the whole point of liturgical worship, which is not only obligatory but insistent on putting communal expressions of faith ahead of individualistic inclinations.

Reform Jews who are observant (in the sense that they regularly attend synagogue) can also find themselves dissatisfied with the liturgical character of their tradition. At Temple Shalom, a liberal Reform synagogue on the West Coast, ritual worship often becomes impossible, undesirable, or both. "I could do away with reading much of the Torah," one of the rabbis explains. "I feel like an automaton, expected to show reverence for it, to read this jibberish. I find no redeeming significance in many of the portions. . . . I can't understand why enlightened people would want to do this." This is by no means the view of all the clergy at Temple Shalom. "I am not into the ritual experience," another rabbi says, not very happily; because Temple members wanted their worship services to be beautifully presented and well conducted, he feels that he has become "an officiant" and "a performer." But perhaps it is for the best, he muses, since the Reform tradition, because of its "self-consciousness and overintellectuality about what we do," is never going to be particularly ritualistic to begin with.

"Prayer," writes Rabbi L. A. Hoffman of the Union of American Hebrew Congregations (the Reform denomination), "is still the pretext, but the justification of the act, the real purpose, is now achievement of community, the sense of belonging." His comment on what takes place during worship services is evidenced in many ways at Temple Shalom. Symbols are frowned upon here; there is no Star of David in the sanctuary. The prayer book, which contains little Hebrew, opens from left to right, as books in the United States do, and not right to left, as is common in the Jewish tradition. The prayers themselves are translated in ways that put little emphasis on reverence to God and instead stress religion's universal truths. Worship at Temple Shalom, many members of the congregation attest, does build a sense of community. But it does not do so through specifically religious means. Going to services on Friday night or Saturday is sacred in the sense that it marks a break with the busyness of the work week, but it is not Sacred in the sense that it marks an occasion to honor God. Temple Shalom is somewhat extreme in its leftist views, but its practices are nonetheless tailored for many Reform and Conservative Jews who, as one study of their attitudes puts it, "do not focus on the content of the liturgy as such, and when asked about the meaning of the Sabbath rarely respond in terms of traditional themes such as creation or redemption."

The discomfort with ritual that is experienced by more liberal Jews is not matched by the Orthodox; for them, ritual is primarily what worship is about. But just because they appreciate ritual does not mean that liturgical religion for them involves the repetition of prayers whose meaning and modes of expression leave little or no room for individuality. At Kehillat Kodesh, a Modern Orthodox synagogue, members recognize that morning *(shacharis)*, afternoon *(min-*

cha), and evening *(ma'ariv)* prayers continue a tradition of sacrifice to God that began before the destruction of the Holy Temple of Jerusalem in 70 C.E. Yet even though their prayers are codified in the form of a liturgy, that very codification, writes the sociologist who lived and prayed with them, means that they "become the creations of everyone and the inspiration of no one." Jewish prayer requires sufficient *kavannah,* an untranslatable term that includes "a combination of devotion, concentration, intensity, and intention." Many Orthodox believers find that they cannot achieve *kavannah* in the presence of others. They therefore call what they do alone at home prayer, or *tefilah,* reserving for the experience of the liturgy what they call davening, the process by which prayer takes place.

Besides the need for authenticity of expression, there is another reason why Orthodox Jews bring individual creativity to their practice of the liturgy: No one knows exactly what the liturgy is. Consider *nusach,* the chant by which the liturgy is sung. Ask almost any observant Jew about *nusach,* and you will learn that singing the prayers the traditional way is the very essence of Judaism. It is not hard to discover why. Outside of the more liberal congregations, and there only sometimes, prayers are conducted in Hebrew, and not everyone—in fact, only a minority—can read and speak the language. But the language of music is universal; everyone can learn to sing the right words properly, even if they do not fully understand their meaning. "Why is *nusach* so important to you?" observant Jews were asked. "Identification with tradition," one Modern Orthodox congregant immediately responded. "So what's traditional about you?" he asked rhetorically of a hypothetical believer. "Well," he gave a typical Orthodox answer, "I go to a synagogue where it's done right. . . . We do the tunes in the correct way."

Yet it turns out there is no correct way to chant *nusach.* At Shaarei Tefillah, the Modern Orthodox synagogue this person attends, only a few people—one member guesses 10 percent—actually know what it is. In three other synagogues in the Boston area, members, irrespective of denomination, have discovered that *nusach* is open to considerable interpretation. At B'nai Or, a countercultural *havurah,* or informal worship group originating outside of a synagogue, people speak of how *nusach* provides a sense of tradition that they desperately need: "It makes me feel like I'm really doing Jewish and that I'm not just being a New Age hippie," as one member puts it. But members also chant in English, and the singing itself has little in common with traditional Jewish chanting. Temple Israel, the Reform congregation, also insists on the importance of *nusach,* but its services rely on guitar music and they shift aspects of the liturgy around. Even at Beth Pinchas, an Ultra-Orthodox congregation, each member, as the rebbe explains, "has their little *kvetch* [twist], their little *drey* [ornamental turn]." As if to demonstrate how contemporary he could be, the rebbe's son, Rav Naftali Horowitz, points out that "We basically created the first rap music and that's called nusach."

When Orthodox Jews worship at their most liturgical, moreover, their practice is likely to shock Christians who think of worship as sacred moments of humble prayer before God. Joking, gossip, frequent interruptions—in short, just considerable amounts of noise— are present during most of the service. For the holiest of prayers, respectful devotion is expected, but during other portions of the liturgy, worshipers are permitted to be *mafsik,* to interrupt the ritual with questions or conversation, often disturbing others in the process. The sociologist who spent his time at Kehillat Kodesh observed many such examples; as he wrote in his field notes, "During the Torah scroll reading many people talk with one another. The gabbais [conductors of the prayer service] are trying to shush them, but small cliques and klatches defy this shushing and keep on talking. Indeed, in one or two cases the people being quieted engage the gabbai in conversation." Ritual one can find aplenty in Orthodox Jewish worship; reverence is something else.

Jews, like Catholics, are divided into those who insist on the power of an unchanged liturgy and those who are more experimental in the way they worship and pray. And, also like Catholics, those divisions often mean less in practice than they do in theory. Living in a non-Jewish society, often hesitant about their beliefs, and selective in their choice of ritual, Jews in the United States, whatever their degree of religious observance, are active creators of the liturgies they follow. They did not have the Jewish equivalent of a Second Vatican Council because they never needed it; their worship services, unlike the Tridentine Mass, have been changing with every movement of

Jewish people to new places of residence. Like other religious believers in the United States, Jews contribute to the transformation of their faith by becoming participants in the liturgies and rituals that define it.

NARCISSISM'S REACH

Protestant denominations in the United States differ among themselves with respect to liturgical worship. Some, especially the Episcopal, Lutheran, and Methodist churches, adhere to worship traditions not unlike Catholics and Jews, codified in prayer books and handed down from generation to generation. Others, like the Society of Friends, de-emphasize communal forms of worship, like Bible reading and music, in favor of silent prayer. And still others, such as Baptists and other conservative Protestants, consider themselves explicitly antisacramental and nonliturgical, as if such "high church" and Catholic forms of worship are too draped in mystery to allow much of a role for the individual to express her faith in ways that have meaning for her. This conservative Protestant distaste for liturgy is fairly common in all parts of the United States, including African American churches like Allen Temple. Evidence of faith, conservative Protestants believe, should not require memorization and emphasize rule following, but should instead flow directly out of the worshiper's need to honor God.

At Southside, a fundamentalist Protestant congregation in the Northeast, antiliturgical worship can be found at its most representative. "Throughout the service, although everything is led by those on the platform, there is a feeling of spontaneity and participation," the sociologist who observed its religious practices writes. "There are no recited prayers or responses, no prayer of confession or words of assurance, no formal call to worship or prayer for the world. The primary components of the service are singing, unrehearsed prayers by the ministers, and preaching. Even the pastor's sermon is not written out in advance." At conservative Protestant churches like Southside, we find ourselves worlds away from liturgical religions like Catholicism and Judaism.

No matter how different Protestant and Catholic worship may be, however, both take place in the same society. Because they are already nonliturgical in intention, conservative Protestant forms of worship do not adapt themselves to American culture by modifying age-old religious practices to accommodate individual tastes. Instead, they transform already individualistic worship styles into ones even more capable of helping believers with the mundane practicalities of modern life. At Southside, for example, "almost anything, good or bad, can be explained as God's doing. God keeps dishes from breaking and locates things that are lost. He supplies friends and offspring. He makes sure cars get fixed at affordable prices. He arranges convenient overtime work schedules and makes hiring and firing more pleasant. He provides clothes and food when they are needed, as well as less essential items like tickets to a rodeo or a pet dog for the children." The religion of these believers may be old-fashioned in its prophetic sensibility and its conservative orientation to the world, but the prayers offered are as down to earth as prayers can be.

Practical prayer is the norm throughout much of the world of conservative Protestantism. "Lord, give me a clean X-ray when I go for a mammogram next week" or "God, help the search committee find a new pastor for the church" are two of the forms taken by prayer at one Baptist church in New Jersey. At an evangelical church in an exurb of New York City, one women's group follows *Robert's Rules of Order* in the half hour devoted to prayer. First, there is old business—follow-up and, where possible, closure from the prayers of the previous week. (Closure is achieved when a particular request has been granted, enabling the prayer to be moved from the "petition" column into the "praise" column on the large tablet that serves as "God's scorecard.") When the meeting turns to new business, each participant has a chance to ask God to respond to her concerns, and as she does, others take notes so that they can pray for their friends during the week. Those concerns, moreover, are anything but otherworldly; most involve the health and healing of members, financial difficulties, and real estate, along with issues facing the church. We should not doubt the meaning that worship has for conservative Christians. But nor should we ignore the practical side, for the concerns that so many believers express in prayer suggest that, in their minds, God helps those who focus on themselves.

Not all religious leaders are happy about prayer that focuses on individual needs. "Christian worship," writes the Lutheran theologian Marva J. Dawn, "is about offerings or sacrifice." In her view, proper worship, which reflects the liturgical traditions of her denomination, requires an appreciation of God's power to punish us if we fail to take seriously the demands he makes upon us. But because we live in a culture of narcissism that makes us want to feel good about ourselves, Dawn argues, we make ourselves, and not God, the centerpiece of our worship. At a regional convention of one denomination, Dawn heard the assembled crowd sing this hymn:

> I will celebrate, sing unto the Lord.
>   I will sing to God a new song. (repeat)
>   I will praise God, I will sing to God a new song. (repeat)
>   Hallelujah, hallelujah, hallelujah,
>   Hallelujah, I will sing to God a new song. (repeat)
> I will celebrate, sing unto the Lord.
>   I will sing to God a new song. (repeat)
>   (Repeat all)

God is certainly being praised in this song, but there is also little doubt who is doing the praising; by the time the song is over, the subjective "I" is repeated twenty-eight times.

In some ways, such narcissism, if that is what it should be called, is simply a product of Protestant individualism; the Psalms, upon which the prayer she heard is based, has its share of first-person pronouns, and evangelical revivalism has always focused on individuals and their needs. But with the decline of mainline religion and the rise of evangelicalism, there has taken place a considerable increase in the number of people who seek forms of worship that downplay the foreign in favor of the familiar. Consider what happened at California's Mendocino Presbyterian Church in the 1970s. Once a mainline congregation associated with a historically liberal denomination, Mendocino Presbyterian was transformed into an evangelical institution by religious conservatives who found mainline religious styles lacking in vitality and commitment to Jesus. There is reason to believe that the United States throughout the 1970s and 1980s never had a full-scale culture war. But in one congregation after another, real battles were fought over what kind of worship is appropriate.

Every aspect of worship style was up for grabs at Mendocino Presbyterian. The more mainline Protestants, in the words of the social scientist who observed them:

> wear their Sunday best to attend services on a holy day in a sacred place. Within the sacred place, some spaces are more sacred than others, the altar, for example. Leadership in worship is monopolized by religious professionals, whose supramundane attire is a badge of their status. They speak with an intonation that would sound strange outside the sacred walls, and they follow a formal and explicit order of worship. They treat the religious artifacts—the pulpit Bible, the cross, the communion elements, the offering plate—with solemn respect. Aside from any words that are uttered in such an hour of worship, the entire ritual itself expresses the idea of the persistence and majesty of an extraordinary realm, the sacred world, which is set off from the business of this world, the secular world.

Mainline Protestant worship, in other words, has certain similarities to the liturgical aspects of Catholicism and Judaism. It is reverent. It follows routines. And it seeks considerable distance between the ordinary world and the world of worship.

The evangelicals could not have been more different:

> The mode of dress was cleaned-up everyday, not Sunday best: wool or flannel shirts and jeans for the men; shirtwaist dresses or sweaters and skirts for the women. Genders were distinct. Some women brought knitting or embroidery to work on, and a couple of the men brought guitars and tambourines. There were no hymnals on the chairs and no one handed out bulletins as you entered the room, so the only way you could know that this was to be a religious event,

rather than a meeting of the Grange, was that most people carried Bibles and the literature table featured titles such as *Mere Christianity, The Holy Spirit and You, The Cross and the Switchblade, The Total Woman,* and *Dare to Discipline.* The religiousness of the event had to be announced explicitly, since it was not implicit in the form, which was purely nascent.

For the evangelicals at Mendocino Presbyterian, worship was personal, enthusiastic, unstructured, and informal. In particular, the charismatics among them, who belonged to a group called the Antioch Fellowship, were the most down to earth. "In their prayers and testimonies, fellowship members asserted that God is approachable, familiar, and involved in their daily lives. Prayers were always addressed in sweet, colloquial tones to 'Lord,' or 'Jesus,' or 'Father.' Sometimes all three names were used, in an ingenious trinitarianism."

The worship wars found in Mendocino in the mid-1970s foreshadowed the rise of megachurches—sprawling edifices that, in their efforts to reach the "unchurched," offer not only family-friendly sermons but also a wide variety of services, from day care to athletic clubs, designed to make their environments attractive. Of all the factors that have contributed to the rapid membership growth of such churches, none has been more important than worship; megachurch leaders are unanimously convinced that too many Protestant churches turn people off with their predictable liturgies, unmemorable music, and didactic sermonizing. Instead of building a church around worship and then attracting an audience, they want to attract an audience and then find the appropriate forms of worship that will keep them in their seats. "People today crave intimacy," as the pastor of a growth-oriented church in the Southwest puts it. "They want to be known and loved for who they are. They come to church in the hope that someone will love them, that someone will accept them just as they are. They value a warm, open environment. Worship services that promote intimacy will win them over." It is no easy task achieving that sense of intimacy in the gigantic chapels located in even more gigantic megachurches, but these new religious entrepreneurs are determined nonetheless to do so.

There is little doubting their success. Some sense of how significant their growth has become can be gleaned from a study of 1,266 congregations associated with a wide variety of religious traditions, including Catholics and Jews. Two major kinds of worship were identified: ceremonial, in which the emphasis is placed on organ music, responsive reading, choir singing, and sermons; and enthusiastic, which features jumping and shouting, applause, electric guitar music, and personal testimony. Liturgical religions dominate the former category, evangelical and Pentecostal ones the latter. The study then examined the factors that were identified with each particular worship style. Some of the resulting findings are clearly the products of long-established historical forces; African American churches, not surprisingly, are more enthusiastic than ceremonial. Other findings, however, suggest future trends. Congregations in which more than 40 percent of the adults were under thirty-five are more likely to be enthusiastic, to take one example, than congregations with fewer than 20 percent of their members under that age. Along similar lines, newer congregations, those founded since 1970, are also far more likely to lean in the enthusiastic direction. The lessons for church leaders could hardly be clearer: If you want to reach those most likely to be members for decades, tailor your worship to the young and enthusiastic, not the old-fashioned and the advanced in age.

One consequence of the rise of enthusiastic worship is that it has turned American Protestantism topsy-turvy. Arriving at a large West Coast university as a freshman, Phil McGarey, a biomedical engineering major, checked out various campus-based religious organizations, including the mainline Campus Ministry Center and the more evangelically oriented Campus Crusade for Christ and the InterVarsity Christian Fellowship. The first of these he finds too "conservative" because "we sing hymns and stuff." InterVarsity, by contrast, "is more liberal because we sing contemporary Christian songs instead of hymns." While this college freshman can be criticized for confusing the terms by which religions are commonly described in America—mainline religions are invariably portrayed as more liberal than evangelical ones—he has touched on an important truth: In matters of worship style, mainline churches are the ones that seem stuffy and out of date, while evangelical movements capture the prize for an ability to blend seamlessly with the most contemporary trends in American popular culture.

Precisely because the forms of worship evangelicals offer are so contemporary, so intimate, and so upbeat, there is some question whether they should properly be called worship at all. Marva Dawn does not think so; "it is a misnomer," she writes, "to call services 'worship' if their purpose is to attract people rather than to adore God." Since attracting people is what megachurches do, Dawn raises an important question by asking what exactly is taking place in the sanctuaries they fill. ("Sanctuary" may not be the appropriate term here; Janie Sjogren, wife of the pastor of the Cincinnati Vineyard Fellowship, explained to me on my visit there that they do not use that term because of its strong religious connotations.)

One thing that certainly takes place there, as Phil McGarey's experience suggests, is music. About half of the time devoted to Sunday worship at the Cincinnati Vineyard Fellowship, as at many other growth-oriented evangelical churches throughout the United States, is devoted to musical performance. But it is not the music of traditional Protestant hymns, let alone the soaring melodies of Mendelssohn's *Elijah* or Bach's Mass in B minor. Rock music—or, as it is frequently called, contemporary Christian music—is now a featured part of Sunday services at evangelical churches throughout the United States. Leaders of these churches believe that the secret to their success is winning the allegiance of the young, and for that kind of purpose, the right kind of music can help. (One hardly ever sees senior citizens attending worship services at America's megachurches; young couples featuring young children predominate.) Just as comfortable chairs—some with holders on the side to accommodate the Coke purchased at the McDonald's, which has been given in a franchise in the church lobby—have replaced pews, loudspeakers and digital mixers have replaced choruses and organs. So that the audience will not be embarrassed by not knowing the lyrics, the words to the songs being played are projected onto huge screens on either side of the stage. Christian rock can even figure in church literature; indeed, one church puts its commitment to contemporary music into its statement of faith.

Wanting to be absolutely certain that no one will turn away and leave the moment they see an organ or hear something unfamiliar, megachurches give considerable thought to the music they feature. And they do so in ways deeply reflective of the culture of contemporary advertising, even polling members, as happens at Saddleback Church in Orange County, California, to find out from them their favorite radio stations so that they can model church music accordingly. (The pastor at another California church used market research to identify different contemporary musical styles and chose one with "a little bit more edge to it" when he realized that this was the kind of popular music most listened to in his area.) The whole idea behind this approach is that secular culture, for all its faults, knows something about getting and retaining an audience. Yet it is not clear that the people attracted by music they already know will remain in the churches to which they have been attracted. The typical praise song found in megachurches, according to a professor of preaching at Emory University, is "simplistic, repetitive, and, finally, boring. . . . In the short run, it gets you on your feet clapping your hands, but in the long run it cultivates a monotonic, downsized faith, a faith too naïve and simple to handle complexity, too repetitive to deal with real change."

The choice of contemporary music means that worshipers sacrifice another kind of music in return. One form of music typically ignored in evangelical circles is the classical variety. To some musical tastes, Handel and Bach may be "difficult," but that is often due to lack of familiarity rather than any technicalities of composition; one could hardly imagine music more accessible than *Israel in Egypt* or "Jesu, Joy of Man's Desiring." Worshipers who are never introduced to such music can never be led to the truly sublime—"Können Tränen meiner Wangen" from Bach's *St. Matthew Passion,* for example, or the "Agnus Dei" from Verdi's *Requiem*—where the composer really seems to have been inspired by a divine presence.

Classical music is by no means the only kind of music sacrificed in the interests of appealing to popular taste. Accompanying me on visits to a number of evangelical churches in Southern California was the music critic Martha Bayles, a great admirer of African American musical traditions. "In my view," she tells me, "there is something powerfully sacred about the best Afro-American gospel music, precisely *because* it gets you on your feet clapping. It rouses a degree of enthusiasm—jubilation—beyond anything in the European tradition. These are different modes of worship, and I would be the first to admit that gospel does not achieve the same degree of contemplative or emotional profundity as, say, a Mozart requiem. But neither does Mozart achieve what Mahalia Jackson achieves." The problem with contemporary Christian music, she continues, "is that it does *neither* of these things. It certainly does not get *me* on my feet clapping." The most intransigent battles in the worship wars of American Protestantism take place over music. And it is clear who is losing: those who believe that there are standards of musical excellence that, when reached, are capable of inducing moments of genuine transcendence.

Sermons in evangelical churches can be as contemporary as the music. Are they similarly disappointing, or at least disappointing to those, religious or not, who hope that the experience of going to church can provide believers with a deeper, more demanding, and ultimately more satisfying experience than they can obtain by listening to a Top 40 radio station? One close observer of American religion, Stephen Haynes, a professor of religious studies at Rhodes College in Memphis, tells me of his experiences with contemporary worship in his hometown. Haynes is impressed by Hope Presbyterian, one of the fastest growing congregations in the area, which his fiancée Alyce attends. He goes to Saturday services there with her, while, on Sundays, she comes to Idlewild Presbyterian (IPC), his downtown, and more traditional, church. Unlike Idlewild, which has more than its share of old Memphis families, Hope is informal and welcoming. "I would not think about attending worship without a tie at IPC," Haynes recounts. "Nor would I think about wearing one at Hope."

Reflecting its informal dress code, Hope Presbyterian is also relaxed in the theology it offers. Aware that not many of those who attend its services are comfortable turning to the right places in their prayer books, Hope Presbyterian uses the same PowerPoint approach to sermons that many megachurches use for the lyrics of their songs; an oversize screen highlights the two or three simple conclusions to be gotten from each sermon. And the resulting sermons, Haynes believes, "are theologically very thin." Scripture is cited but not very often, and when it is, preachers use it to buttress conclusions they have already made, which Haynes views as a conservative Christian version of the use of religion by liberal pastors to support their political views. When all is said and done, Haynes concludes that religion at Hope Presbyterian, in contrast to religion at Idlewild, is more of a spectacle. "There is some participation in terms of singing, but worship is basically something you witness, something that happens around you," he says.

Haynes's observations, with one significant caveat, correspond with my own experiences. Generally speaking, preaching in evangelically oriented growth churches, however dynamic in delivery, has remarkably little actual content. Scripture is invariably cited but only as a launching pad to reinforce the message of the salvation that Jesus can offer. Rarely is the congregation challenged to do anything other than give itself over to Christ, and even the pursuit of that objective is not accompanied by any sense of complexity or difficulty. In nearly all the sermons I heard, considerable time is devoted, as one would expect in a corporate boardroom, to statements emphasizing the church's success in mission or growth. The world outside the church is usually not acknowledged, and in one case in which it was—at the Harvest Christian Fellowship in Riverside, California—the result was not encouraging. For when the Reverend Jeff Lasseigne discussed contemporary events, he did so in ways that conformed to the script of contemporary conservative Protestantism, taking swipes at the theory of evolution, for example, or combining his strong statement in support of Israel with a comment on the need to save Jews by converting them to the Christian faith. If religion is understood as combining reason with revelation, a substantial amount of the preaching in evangelical America has a good deal of the latter and very little of the former.

Still, at its best, some forms of contemporary worship will reach, just as its advocates insist, people who might otherwise spend Sundays in front of their television sets. For four weeks in March 2002, Dave Workman, the senior pastor of Cincinnati Vineyard Fellowship, addresses himself to the question of what makes someone a good Christian. His answer consists of four things: passion, compassion, joy, and perseverance, and he devoted one Sunday to an exploration of each of them. On one level, Workman's sermons could be considered lessons in self-help, for each of the qualities he identified makes for not only a good Christian life but also a good life for anyone. Yet for all of its PowerPoint qualities, Workman's sermons are religious in a way that his church's often insipid music is not. In his discussion of passion, for example, Rev. Workman points out the difficulty in understanding other people's passions; can we really know what goes on in the mind of a football fan who paints his body in the colors of the team for whom he is rooting? Still, he goes on, there is a difference between religious passion and other kinds of passion. "Would the guy with the foam-rubber cheese head give his life for his passion?" Workman asks, with the obvious implication that Jesus did for his. The sermon does not at that point turn into an argument for martyrdom; Vineyard churches are too upbeat for that. But Workman's message is, in its own way, a serious effort to raise important questions about religious obligations for an audience not theologically inclined.

As churches find themselves seeking out worship styles that feel intimate and comfortable rather than imposing and distant, it is not clear that even the best forms of contemporary worship can survive. Indeed, there is reason to believe that the way evangelicals borrow from the culture surrounding them is blowing back into the sermons offered in the evangelical world. Evangelicals have long found ways to reconcile their version of Christianity with the materialistic, consumption-driven American culture, whether reflected in the ostentatious lifestyles of the televangelists, the success-oriented preaching of a Robert Schuller, or the explicitly procapitalist prosperity theology of the Kenneth Hagin Ministries of Tulsa, Oklahoma. Critics have found such tendencies disturbing, not only because they seem to turn their backs on the poor and needy but also because prosperity theology makes so few demands on those who practice it. As historian Randall Balmer writes of the appeal of such groups, "Jesus will save your soul and your marriage, make you happy, heal your body, and even make you rich. Who wouldn't look twice at that offer?"

The answer to Balmer's question, if we pay attention to the books that Americans buy, must be many people indeed. In 2000,

Americans were reminded of the excesses of prosperity theology when a slim little book called *The Prayer of Jabez* appeared on the best-seller lists, ultimately registering more than nine million copies sold. *The Prayer of Jabez* came right out of the heartland of American evangelicalism, indeed out of its most conservative precincts. Its author, Bruce Wilkinson, runs the Walk Thru the Bible Ministries. The chairman of the Center for Christian Leadership at the ultraconservative Dallas Theological Seminary offers a blurb on the back cover of the book. Dr. James Dobson of Focus on the Family featured the book on his website and interviewed the author on his radio station. Whatever else one thinks of such dyed-in-the-wool religious conservatives, they at least ought to be people who take their Christianity seriously. And yet what is offered in Wilkinson's book is a conception of religion so narcissistic that it makes prosperity theology look demanding by contrast.

Wilkinson's book uncovers the only two sentences in the entire Bible devoted to a man named Jabez, so named because his mother bore him in pain. His prayer, in its entirety, runs as follows:

> Oh, that You would bless me indeed,
>   and enlarge my territory,
>   that Your hand would be with me,
>   and that You would keep me from evil.

Like the prayer of celebration that so upset Marva Dawn, the prayer of Jabez, with a reference to the petitioner in each of its lines, focuses on the individual who is uttering it. There are, nonetheless, ways in which the prayer might be interpreted that would play down its narcissism in favor of honoring God; to be kept from evil, for example, suggests that one has been put on earth to serve some larger purpose. Wilkinson hints in this direction. "I want to show you," he writes, "that such a prayer is not the self-centered act it might appear, but a supremely spiritual one and exactly the kind of request our Father longs to hear."

But evidently what God wants most to hear are the ambitions of highly driven individuals. "If Jabez had worked on Wall Street," Wilkinson continues, "he might have prayed, 'Lord, increase the value of my investment portfolios.'" Christian executives, he tells his readers, ask him whether they can properly ask God for more business, and his answer is "Absolutely!" Wilkinson himself has recited the prayer for years, and it certainly has increased his opportunities; he has enlarged his Jabez territory with offshoots for children and women, cassettes, self-help guides, and every other marketable device he and his publisher could think of. One searches this exceptionally thin book in vain for any statement indicating that Christian prayer is an act of sacrifice. In Wilkinson's form of Christianity, you get far more than you give.

So simplistic is the message of *The Prayer of Jabez* that, with the exception of organizations like Focus on the Family, it has been subjected to considerable criticism by many evangelical leaders, who no doubt perceive the book as an embarrassing reminder of their religion's unsophisticated past. Still there is no denying that its millions of readers find something of value in it nor that what they find in it is help for themselves. Jon from North Carolina, a forty-one-year-old father of three, who has undergone six chemotherapy treatments for testicular cancer, experienced open-heart surgery, and lost his job as a sports executive, discovered the book and before long learned that his cancer was in remission and found himself with a new job. Another reader, Kathy, claims that as a result of the prayer, "I was pointed to an old life insurance [policy,] which I was able to cash out and send to my mortgage company. . . . I have always believed, but felt more like a grain of sand in a huge sandbox. Now I feel more important in God's eyes." Whatever tendencies that already exist in American religion to pray for very practical things are strengthened when prayer is offered in the name of Jabez.

Reactions such as these should not be too surprising. In the way they shape their worship services to attract new members, down to consulting surveys on the right kind of music to feature, evangelical megachurches have already prepared believers for a faith that puts their own needs first. As Pastor Workman's sermons indicate, simplistic sermonizing need not automatically follow when churches become so obsessed with gaining and keeping members that they modify every aspect of religious life within reach, including worship, to account for contemporary taste. But, then again, once popular taste rules, there are no barriers to the success of a book as focused on individuals and their desire for material success and personal recovery as *The Prayer of Jabez*. Worship in evangelical America may serve many needs, but otherworldly reverence is unlikely to be one of them, so determined are these churches to respond to the everyday concerns of those who attend them.

CONVERGENCE

At the height of the Cold War, some scholars argued that, for all the differences between capitalism and socialism, there would take place a convergence between the United States and the Soviet Union, since both were industrial powers guided by bureaucratic states. As fate would have it, that prediction turned out to be incorrect. But convergence, however inappropriate to states, may be true of religions. Despite the widespread diversity of worship styles throughout a society as divided by race, ethnicity, and class as the United States, one common thread can nonetheless be detected. Attempting to attract or to keep congregations whose members have been so strongly influenced by a common American culture, all of America's religions face the same imperative: Personalize or die. Each does so in different ways. Catholics, while retaining the liturgy, are also likely to borrow from Protestants the tendency to pray directly to Jesus without the help of intermediaries such as priests—a trend that will only intensify in the aftermath of the pedophilia scandals of 2002. Jews, as two students of their attitudes write, "may be moving toward Protestant constructions—individualistic, moralist, universal—of religious identity." And Protestants themselves have become even more Protestant, shifting away from denominations with strong liturgical and credal traditions to those that emphasize getting the intimate and personal sides of faith.

As all of the religions in the United States begin to resemble each other in practice, they do so by resembling most those of the evangelicals. For a religious sensibility that emerged among the dispossessed, evangelical patterns of worship—joyful, emotional, personal, and emphatic on the one hand, impatient with liturgy and theologically broad to the point of incoherence on the other—have increasingly become the dominant worship style in the United States. Even while fully acknowledging the distinctiveness of each American religious tradition, there is also a sense in which we are all evangelicals now. American religion survives and even flourishes not so much because it instructs people in the right ways to honor God but because people have taken so many aspects of religion into their own hands.

Because evangelicals describe themselves, and are described by others, as conservative Protestants, the increasing popularity of their worship styles ought to mean a return to the fiery preaching of Jonathan Edwards. But those who fear the consequences for the United States of a return to strong religious belief should not be fooled by evangelicalism's rapid growth. On the contrary, evangelicalism's popularity is due as much to its populistic and democratic urges—its determination to find out exactly what believers want and to offer it to them—as it is to certainties of the faith. The biggest challenge posed to American society by the popularity of megachurches and other forms of growth-oriented Protestantism is not bigotry but bathos. Television, publishing, political campaigning, education, self-help advice—all increasingly tell Americans what they already want to hear. Religion, it would seem, should now be added to that list.

CHAPTER 2

FELLOWSHIP

THE ANTI-INSTITUTIONAL BELIEVER

Fellowship, as it is commonly called among religious believers, is one of the prized rewards of religious practice. Christians recalling the ways in which Jesus gathered his flock, as well as Jews reflecting on their exile, have long sustained religions with strong communal characteristics. Only through fellowship with others, both religious traditions insist, is it possible for rituals to have significance, for obligations and duties to be fulfilled, and for both joy and piety to be shared. To worship is to worship together. Faith and fellowship are inextricably linked.

If believers praise the feeling of fellowship they receive from their faith, skeptics often treat fellowship as synonymous with narrowness. Of course religious people join together with others, they are likely to argue, but the others with whom they join tend to be remarkably like themselves. There is, in truth, grounds for their claim; evangelicals have been historically divided by race, Catholics were once organized into ethnic parishes, and denominational divisions among Jews overlapped with socioeconomic ones. If fellowship comes at the cost of never exposing believers to people whose viewpoints and lifestyles are different from their own, there may be no reason to encourage it.

Each of these positions assumes that religion continues to be capable of providing a sense of belonging. Can it? Americans have always been suspicious of institutions, or at least those that become national in scope and bureaucratic in nature. Those suspicions have often spilled over into the religious realm, as evidenced by nine-teenth-century sects hostile to existing denominations as well as by frequent criticism of religions that organize themselves hierarchi-cally. The practice of contemporary American religion shares some of these anti-institutional proclivities; a recent survey of baby boomers found that 54 percent of them believe that "churches and synagogues have lost the real spiritual part of religion" and that one-third sub-scribe to the proposition that "people have God within them, so churches aren't necessary." Fellowship may remain an important as-pect of religious practice in America, but we can take for granted nei-ther the forms in which it is embodied nor the kinds of rewards it offers. In the way they relate to the institutional aspects of religion, especially to the role of denominations and congregations, Ameri-cans are practicing their faith in ways so personal and individualistic that their practices blend seamlessly into the culture around them.

BEYOND THE DENOMINATIONAL SOCIETY

Denominations stand midway between two potential dangers. On the one hand, they serve, symbolically and organizationally, as evi-dence that the United States has no established church capable of en-forcing its doctrinal truths. Denominationalism and pluralism are inextricably linked; the ideal of religious pluralism achieves reality in an organizational system that resembles the competitive market more than the monopolistic state. At the same time, denomination-alism avoids the potential chaos of unchanneled religious enthusi-asm. A society committed to religious freedom can easily find itself in the grip of believers so pure in their faith that they come to dis-trust authority of any kind, a form of zealotry often attractive to reli-gious leaders in its initial stages but also one that, in their view, eventually requires direction. Denominations permit structure with-out centralization. Believers find themselves linked together with others and, in so doing, will have their anarchic instincts tempered, yet they are not forced against their will to join with strangers whose views are completely different from their own and thus will have their suspicions reduced. For all these reasons and others, sociologist Andrew Greeley has argued that Americans live in a "denominational society."

Greeley, however, was writing in the early 1970s, and much has changed in the practice of American religion since then. Sixteen years after he made his observation, another sociologist, Robert Wuthnow, surveyed the religious landscape and concluded that "denominational barriers have ceased to function as hermetic categories of religious identification." Although Wuthnow's argument that we are witnessing "the decline of denominationalism" has been challenged, the preponderance of the evidence suggests that he is correct.

To obtain a sense of the changing nature of denominations, one can do worse than to look at the most studied community in the United States. Muncie, Indiana—often called Middletown, the name used to (barely) disguise its identity—is no longer typical of much of anything in an increasingly diverse United States. Yet precisely because it has been studied so often and in such depth, Muncie is one of the few places in American society where one can obtain a solid sense of how denominations have changed through time.

In the 1920s, officials at John D. Rockefeller Jr.'s Institute of Social and Religious Research approached Robert Lynd to help them understand changing values in the United States, and he persuaded them that the best way to do so would be by examining the impact of industrialization on a predominantly Protestant small city. What Lynd and his wife Helen reported back to them, and to readers ever since, was not, from the point of view of official Protestantism, good news. Here, in the heartland of America, they uncovered evidence that Muncie was no longer as religious as it had been in 1890. Daily prayer and Bible reading within families were disappearing, and religious values were also being abandoned by other nonchurch institutions such as clubs and civic and social groups. Pastors continued to reach out to their flock, but "overt religious behavior," such as "kneeling and praying and reading from the Bible," was decreasingly part of their mission. Residents of Muncie were expected to return 10 percent of their earnings to the church through tithing, but very few of them did so. Church attendance was decreasing. And those who attended were not particularly engaged with the Lord: "My people seem to sit through the sermon in a kind of dazed, comatose state," one minister said. "They don't seem to be wrestling with my thought."

For all the evidence of religious decline in Muncie, however, the organizational life of the churches seemed healthy enough. The churches themselves were, in many cases, "imposing structures of stone and brick." And just as solid were their connections to the denominations of which they were a part. Increasingly critical of organized religion, the Lynds were disturbed by a tendency of Muncie's churches to put denominational considerations at the heart of their activities. Barely able to control their disdain, the Lynds tell of how, in 1925, a resolution from the national council of one of Muncie's leading denominations—their own—expressed "thanksgiving" for "the fact that Presbyterians are responding liberally in support of a great variety of religious, philanthropic, and educational causes." But, the document went on to suggest, it was also important for Presbyterian generosity to be reserved for Presbyterians: "We urge upon Presbyterian churches . . . that full measure of loyalty which inspires the fulfillment of obligations contracted by denominational agencies, before Presbyterian beneficence is poured upon causes outside the Church."

Such denomination-first prioritizing actually represented a change from a more open past; in the 1890s, Baptists would call off Sunday services if a new Methodist church were opening. But by the 1920s, denominational lines had tightened, largely in response to financial pressures. And as they hardened, so did the loyalties of individual members. While even at that time denominational doctrine meant little to the residents of Muncie—the Lynds despaired that the Quaker Church "has so far forgotten its historic traditions as to use a popular book of revival songs"—denominations were still important sociologically. "People cling from force of habit to the church into which they were born," they wrote, and a Protestant in particular is "born into one of the twenty-eight denominational groups and tends to remain in it throughout life." When the Lynds came back to Muncie during the Great Depression, moreover, they did not notice anything especially different. Despite the fact that hard economic times ought to bring out a more capacious sense of Christian charity, the Depression actually seemed to cause what one minister they interviewed called "a loss in cooperation among our churches." The Ministerial Association of Muncie, which once had tried to promote cooperation among the different denominations, "is *just dead wood,*" one pastor said. "It has done nothing about the depression. Some of the leading ministers in town do not even bother to go."

Did Muncie's believers ever consider switching from one Protestant denomination to another? The Lynds did not say because they did not ask. While one can fault them for shoddy research, the truth is that no one in their time would have thought of asking. Throughout the first half of the twentieth century, religion possessed what sociologists called an "ascribed" rather than an "achieved" status. Certain aspects of an individual's identity were determined by circumstances of birth and others were the result of what one chose to do with one's life. Race, region, class, and religion were generally held to belong to the former category, while, with luck, income and career could belong to the latter. This tendency to treat religion as an ascribed aspect of individual identity existed for the simple reason that it had roots in reality; a Gallup Poll taken in 1955 found that only 4 percent of Americans—one in twenty-five—did not adhere to the religion of their childhood. Religious switching was not the focus of the Lynds' work because so little religious switching actually took place.

By the mid-1980s, by contrast, another Gallup Poll revealed that one in three Americans had switched from the faith of their upbringing. There were many reasons for this change, including rising rates of intermarriage, a dramatic decline in the appeal of liberal churches and a corresponding growth of conservative ones, rapid geographic and social mobility, and public unhappiness with the kinds of self-interested bureaucratic behavior of national denominational headquarters that so disturbed the Lynds. Switching also varied dramatically among denominations, with some, especially "ethnic" faiths such as Catholics and Lutherans, facing lower rates of disaffection than others, such as Methodists and Episcopalians. For whatever reason and to whatever degree, religion had, by the 1970s and 1980s, increasingly become "achieved," a chosen identity that will not always, or even not often, be the same as the religious identity of one's parents or of one's upbringing. Survey researchers still want to know whether Catholics vote Democratic or Southern Baptists Republican, and so they ask people about the denominations to which they belong, as if families, and even sometimes individuals, are not torn apart by competing attractions to competing faiths. But it is now widely recognized, as it was not at the time that Middletown was published, that religion in the United States is as much about choice and personal autonomy as it is about belonging and community.

When a team of sociologists went back to Muncie in the 1970s, they quite naturally wanted to discover whether the national rates of switching uncovered by polling data applied to this once denominationally stable city. And, except for a somewhat higher switching rate than the national average among Catholics, they found that Muncie had indeed become like the rest of the United States. The city was still overwhelmingly Protestant. But compared to the 1920s and 1930s, more Muncie Protestants were leaving historically mainline denominations for "Southern" ones with evangelical or Pentecostal roots, such as the Church of God, the Church of the Nazarene, and other holiness churches. "The major denominational division in the community," they wrote, "is no longer the traditional Catholic-Protestant dichotomy; in many ways, Middletown's Catholics and Protestants are indistinguishable. The major division is now between the 'southern' Protestants and the more affluent and better-educated 'northern' Protestants and Catholics." And even this division had become porous. Perhaps as a result of extensive switching, Muncie residents were simply no longer interested in the specific denominational membership of their congregations. "The boundaries between Protestant denominations have become so permeable that husband and wife may belong to churches of different denominations without inviting censure in either place. Many people who belong to a church of one denomination regularly attend services at a church of another denomination and contribute to its support. . . . Every Catholic church has a few ex-Protestants, and all the large Protestant churches have a few ex-Catholics whose presence is taken for granted."

What is Muncie like now? Fortunately, the city was studied one more (surely not the last) time in the last decade of the twentieth century. As it happens, a continued shift away from specific denominational identity turns out to be one of the most striking features of its religious landscape. One of Muncie's congregations, Spirited Church, is part of the wave toward "Southern" forms of religious expression that had become popular in the 1970s. Spirited Church attracts individuals who care not a whit for denominational affiliation. "I am who I am spiritually no matter what church I am going to," says one member, while another claims that, although her parents thought it important to put one's name on a piece of paper to signify membership, for her, paper means nothing because "your heart has to be in the right place." Church officials are quite sympathetic to such talk. Although ostensibly Methodist, Spirited Church does not mention its denominational affiliation on its sign. Nor does its pastor care much for specific doctrine: "Good people argue about the meaning and method of baptism. Do we immerse? Do we sprinkle? We don't get uptight about it," he asks rhetorically. Spirited Church has been growing by leaps and bounds. In 1981, this church, small and rural, had eighty members. By 1996, now contemporary and charismatic, fourteen hundred regular churchgoers were attending its spirit-filled services every Sunday. As the experience of Spirited Church indicates, Muncie had, in the course of the twentieth century, been transformed from a community in which faith was a given to one in which faith is a choice. And the most popular choice proved to be one that, in demonstrating a willingness to cross denominational boundaries, strikes many believers as accepting and inclusive rather than as doctrinaire and sectarian.

Muncie's experience suggests that the decline of denominationalism is real, for if people switch with some frequency from one to another, denominations lose their capacity to convey any sense of fellowship. Some argue, however, that religious switching is not as destabilizing as it might at first seem. Many believers have switched from liberal churches to conservative ones, for example, which suggests that not all denominations are in decline. As the ranks of liberal churches become depleted, moreover, the remaining switching tends to be between one conservative denomination and another.

People may be acting rationally; having already invested their resources in a particular approach to religion, they stay with one roughly similar, even when they change. What looks like religious switching, especially within the conservative Christian camp, can therefore best be described as "the circulation of the saints"—people moving around among denominations but not really changing their outlook on the world.

The problem with this line of reasoning is that, appearances to the contrary, not all of the seemingly conservative churches within which the saints circulate are similar. The experience of one of Muncie's believers illustrates why. Teri was raised Baptist in a very conservative church. She moved away from Muncie for a while, and when she returned, it was the Baptist church of her childhood that she immediately joined. But not for long. Describing her experience there, she says that she "felt dead. I felt every time I walked into the church I felt I was a horrible sinner, which we are all sinners, but I felt like I didn't deserve to be in God's presence at God's church." Teri, it seems, had gotten a divorce, and because divorce was considered a sin among her Baptist congregants, she felt "guilt-ridden, guilt-ridden, guilt-ridden." Teri finally decided that she was "tired of being condemned" because, even in church, "you need some hugs." And so she left her church—strict discipline, enforced dress code, and all—and looked for another.

The one Teri found was Spirited Church. Here she feels accepted and at peace. Leaders at Spirited Church have themselves been divorced; indeed, one of them started a small group for divorced members. No longer stigmatized as a fallen woman, Teri was encouraged to attend the church's counseling services, which helped her begin the process of putting her life back together. Unlike the Baptist church to which she had once belonged, her new church accepts that people make mistakes; "people are not perfect," reads one of the church's publications, "and for the most part are very much aware of that fact. Therefore, people respond to being loved and lifted into shape rather than pounded."

As church practices go, it would be difficult to find two much farther apart than pounding at people and loving them. By switching from one church to another, this particular believer experienced a radically new environment, one that corresponded with her own sense of self-worth. Yet both the church that Teri left because of its strictness and the church that she joined because of its acceptance would be classified by any sociologist as "conservative Christian." Indeed, in some ways, the Pentecostal church, because of its historic identification with one of the more extreme sects in American religious history, could even be classified as more conservative than the Baptist church, since Baptists have been for so long one of the more established religions in American life. Had Teri been asked by the General Social Survey—the University of Chicago–based sample of Americans upon which estimates of religious switching generally rely—to identify her former and current religious affiliation, she would have become an example of a circulating saint. But her actual experience suggests an entirely different conclusion; although ostensibly remaining within the conservative orbit, Teri has in fact changed from one religious sensibility to another that is completely different.

Far from representing little more than an inherently temporary movement out of liberal churches in favor of conservative ones, religious switching, if Teri's experiences are at all representative, is much better understood as a byproduct of the same emphasis on meeting individual needs that has transformed their worship styles. The leaders of major denominations in the United States may know what differentiates a Baptist from a Methodist or John Calvin from Martin Luther, but those who join their churches, even when they happen to be comparison shopping, are not usually comparing denominational histories and theologies. ("I haven't the slightest idea," says one Presbyterian to the question of whether he believes what others of his denomination believe.) Ever on the lookout for a church and a pastor that feels somehow right for them, churchgoers put the denominations to which churches belong in the position of shedding whatever stands in the way of appealing to the greatest number of potential believers. The more the saints circulate, the more the building blocks upon which American Protestantism has been constructed begin to crumble.

This process of continued religious circulation is given additional impetus by the popularity of megachurches. It is widely known that megachurches recruit new members from a wide variety of Christian backgrounds. But it is a bit sobering to discover from a survey of megachurch *pastors* that more than half of them were serving in a ministry other than the one that provided their seminary training. And even when pastors of megachurches remain faithful to their denomination of origin, their very success at recruiting new members increases their leverage with respect to denominational headquarters. Hebron Baptist, a megachurch in exurban Atlanta, began its rapid growth with financial subsidies from the Southern Baptist Convention (SBC). Now that it attracts thousands of Georgians to its youth programs, its Starlight Crusades in the local football stadium, and its vacation bible schools, its pastor speaks of the "neutral environment" he likes to create between denominations and brags openly in his sermons of how he saves more people in a month than most SBC churches do in a decade.

Just as important in encouraging individuals to search out a religious denomination that makes sense for them is the attraction of small groups devoted to exploring not only the spiritual but also the personal needs of their members. Obviously pleased to see so many individuals willing to show up and participate in such groups, church officials, especially those affiliated with a denomination, cannot be completely happy with the switching such groups encourage. "American religion has long been known for its denominational and confessional pluralism," sociologist Robert Wuthnow has written. "Small groups take this pluralism one step further. A person is no longer limited simply to deciding whether to be a Baptist, a Lutheran, or a Catholic. . . . With dozens of small groups meeting in their neighborhoods, individuals trying to identify a comfortable spiritual niche can shop around more easily." To denominational leaders, small-group worship must seem uncomfortably like focus-group research in advertising: One can easily learn what members like about the denomination to which their church belongs, but one can just as easily learn what they dislike. Like megachurches, small groups sustain the vibrancy of American religion, but they do so at the expense of the denominational character of American society.

If the organizational Protestant infrastructure is slowly weakening under the influence of personal choice, much the same is true in

Judaism. When they switch, Jews tend not to leave their faith but instead to move to another Jewish denomination. Despite high rates of intermarriage, 85.1 percent of American Jews throughout the 1990s retained the Judaism of their upbringing, the highest rate of any American religious group. (Mormons were second with 81.4 percent.) At the same time, Jews have considerably higher rates of switching *within* their denominations than Protestants; only 56 percent continued to belong to the Jewish denomination in which they were raised. Unlike Protestants, interdenominational switching among Jews is from conservative to liberal rather than the other way around. Because Jews consider anyone born of a Jewish mother to be Jewish, Judaism is, by definition, an "ascribed" religion. This makes it all the more remarkable that the form of Judaism in which the majority of Jewish Americans believe is "achieved."

One form that change takes is an increase in the number of Jews who decide for themselves what denominational affiliation ought to mean. Typical of those who feel this way is a physician named Molly. Unlike Jews whose relationship to their tradition is more ethnic than religious, Molly has a strong sense of Jewish identity—she subscribes to at least one Jewish monthly—and she is conversant with those theological beliefs that make a person a Jew. Married to a non-Jew who converted, Molly is attracted to her religion because of its long-standing traditions, and she wants her children to be raised in the faith. Yet unlike Jews of her parents' and grandparents' generations, Molly, although Reform, avoids defining herself by denomination; indeed, Molly resists identifying with other aspects of organized Jewish life, such as community organizations, watchdogs against anti-Semitism such as the Anti-Defamation League, and the state of Israel. In a weak denominational universe, American Jews like Molly are linked to their traditions by individual choice rather than by communal attachment.

Even though her denominational ties are weak, Molly would have to be considered a success story in the world of contemporary American Jewry. For one thing, she still retains a denominational tie, however attenuated, which not all Jews do; such labels are rejected by between 20 and 30 percent of Jews living in New York, Los Angeles, Miami, Chicago, and Philadelphia, cities that contain 60 percent of the American Jewish population. In addition, Molly sends her children to a Reform day school and attends synagogue services, at least occasionally, which is not necessarily true of many Jewish believers, who tend to be less regular in their synagogue attendance than Protestants are in their churchgoing. A more communal religion in Europe, Judaism has become a more individualistic religion in the United States. "Perhaps more than Jewish professional leaders would wish," as one close observer of American Jews writes, "the voluntaristic nature of American society has been thoroughly incorporated into the Jewish communal world."

In the absence of denominations within their religion, Catholics, when they switch, have to switch to another religion entirely, which explains why Catholics have lower rates of switching than Protestants (although marginally higher rates than Jews or Mormons). But the fact that many Catholics remain Catholic can be deceptive. It is fairly common to find individuals who were born to Catholic parents, attended parochial schools, and were confirmed, and who then left the Church, stopped believing in God, or joined other religious traditions—only once again to discover Catholicism later in life. Measured quantitatively, such individuals would never be counted as switchers for they would be in the same designation as adults as they were as sixteen year olds. Yet because they were exposed to other religions in a serious way, or even to nonbelief, they are also Catholics by choice even if they had once been Catholics by birth.

In addition to the kinds of "virtual switching" that takes place when Catholics explore other faiths only to return to the Church, it is also the case that some never do return. Because Catholicism in America has become a mainline religion, one would assume that those Catholics who switch join mainline Protestant denominations. This expectation is further reinforced by the fact that conservative Protestant churches were the last to drop their conviction that Catholics were not proper Christians. (If Bob Jones University is representative of anything, not all conservative Protestants have dropped those convictions.) Yet a surprising amount of the switching that takes place among Catholics is to conservative Protestantism. Certainly the attraction of evangelicalism to Latinos is responsible for some of this. But even non-Latino Catholic switchers are more likely to switch to conservative than to mainline churches. Evidence for this point comes less from quantitative studies of religious switching than from qualitative ones; nearly every ethnographic account of conservative Protestantism shows significant numbers of former Catholics among them.

If these trends continue, America will no longer be the "denominational society" for the same reason that its (male) workers will no longer be "organization men." Some people will continue to work for one firm their entire lives, just as some denominations will continue to provide a sense of identity for ever-loyal churchgoers. But denominations will increasingly come after, not before, the phenomenon of belief. It is not that people begin with a denominational template and then decide what church to attend. It is much more likely that they will decide what kind of faith best suits their needs and in so doing select the appropriate denomination, if any, that comes with it. Whatever role denominations have played in sustaining the voluntary character of American religion in the past, they are less likely to serve in the future as effective intermediaries between the needs of ordinary believers and the imperatives of national religious organizations.

THE ANTI-INSTITUTIONAL CONGREGATION

Denominations offer a sense of belonging in the same way the American Association of Retired Persons and the National Association of Railroad Passengers do; one joins them only in the most passive, coupon-clipping, sorts of ways. That is why Americans, in search of the more intimate and personal sense of belonging called fellowship, tend to view themselves as belonging to the church around the corner, not the denominational headquarters in New York or Nashville. All politics, former Speaker of the House Tip O'Neill famously said, is local; so, it turns out, is religion. A preference for localism that has led Americans to create a federal system of government and to disdain cities has also caused them to be suspicious of the idea of a national church, or even of national churches.

Of all religions in the United States, spirit-filled Pentecostal ones have been in the forefront of efforts to capture the enthusiasm that comes when worship is warm and personal. It is therefore worth noting that there are some believers who find even Pentecostal church practices, despite their singing and shouting, too institutionally stultifying. "It was so dead for me," writes a believer named Jenny Orr about her experiences in one such church. "I watched as people were going nuts and dancing and shouting and I felt like I was looking at this thru some kind of soundproof and feeling-proof glass. . . . I was dying more and more each time I went. . . . I could feel the flow become a trickle, and then nothing at all." One day as she was praying, and being prayed over, her five-year-old daughter Katy came up to her and handed her a cup filled with dirt, which she took as a sign that the faith she had been practicing was impure. "That was enough for me," Jenny declared, for she knew at that moment that God had released her to find her own way of worshiping him.

When Jenny thinks back on what she calls "that climate controlled sanctuary" with its "big Sunday morning dog and pony show," she wonders how she ever could have been a regular churchgoer. "9 o'clock," she now realizes, "is no holier or apt to put you in touch with God than any other hour of the day." God does not want his believers to be "weak and codependent on a structure or a man to tell us how to think or what to say or to DEFINE WHO WE ARE IN CHRIST." There is, in Jenny's view, something fundamentally wrong with the idea that belief in Christ requires some form of instruction from a person in authority. "Guardian, schoolmaster, put in charge, supervision . . . these are all things of the old law," exclaims another believer named Leta van Duin. "But . . . this is not what leadership is supposed to be now. Fatherly leadership is hard to come by. Don't be a policeman."

Jenny Orr and Leta van Duin are adherents of the house church movement; like the early Christians of the New Testament, they believe they should worship in the sanctuary of their homes. Although home churching has not been widely studied by social scientists, it has a strong appeal to certain kinds of religious believers for whom authenticity of experience is more important than congregational affiliation, which they are likely to dismiss as mere "churchianity." As

Roger Upton, a former Southern Baptist pastor, explains in "Grace Abounding," his website devoted to the house church movement, "there simply is no scriptural basis for the church meeting in a specially constructed religious building." Institutions corrupt, he believes, and the church, understood bureaucratically, can corrupt absolutely. The house church movement aims to practice what one believer, Glenn Heller, calls "relational Christianity" rather than "accomplishment Christianity." In his view, "it is more important to focus on the being than on the doing" and "the doing will come without any effort if one learns the being." For Glenn, like Americans attracted to the ecology movement, simpler is better. "I've found the Lord is so good and guiding and directing in such a natural way with minimum effort on our part. Don't be in a hurry like the rest of the world."

House churchers resemble home-schoolers, many of whom are also conservative Christians distrustful of public worlds from which they feel alienated. Both groups reflect a strong, and possibly growing, anti-institutional strain in American culture. Resentful of restraint and routine, they search for experience uncontaminated by what they see as the inevitable compromises that have to be made when public life is shared with others one knows little and trusts even less. In these down-to-earth forms of religious expression, representing the ultimate in Protestant individualism, one can see echoes of both the frontier that dominated the rugged West and the transcendentalism that characterized the effete East. House churchers treat even the more evangelical Protestant churches the way Luther treated Catholics, denouncing them as more interested in protecting their privileges than in expressing their piety. Jesus, after all, reached out to all who would follow him without, in the words of one believer, "pyramid structures, programs, gimmicks, marketing, psychology, advertising, titles, schedules, [and] meetings."

So deep can this anti-institutionalism run that some house churches worry about the potential corruption of their own movement. "It seems that in all our newfound freedom in Christ to be a priesthood of believers," says one of them, a woman named Tracey Amino, "there are those who by stealth are attempting to put us into bondage again." House churches have to be wary of what she calls "the Old Testament prophet trying to operate and function within the New Testament church," by which she means those who "end up breaking fellowship over something as trivial as a small point of doctrine that you don't happen to agree with." Responding to an issue that has stirred great controversy within the house church movement, Tracey is particularly wary of "church planters," people trained by one faction of the movement to go out and help start new house churches. She urges her fellow believers to read the books of the person responsible for these efforts at church planting, for "he is a brother who the Lord has used to bring a lot of revelation to the body about many things." But don't trust him, because "the control and manipulation" of his efforts are "terrible" and have "caused a tremendous amount of offense and division within the house church community."

Compared to other countries, especially those in Western Europe, Americans remain a nation of churchgoers, a statement meant to express not only their hostility to nonbelievers but also their reluctance to join an antichurch movement that, however faithful its adherents may be to God, would be viewed by most of them as extreme. In writing about the house church movement, I do not wish to imply that it represents anything other than a very small movement unlikely to dissuade churchgoing Americans from their regular Sunday habits. But the suspicions such believers manifest toward established institutions do constitute a subcurrent in American religious practice to which nearly all congregations have to be responsive. Just as virtual switchers can influence religious institutions even when they never switch—the possibility that they might is sufficient for many churches to reach out to them—the anti-institutionalism latent in American culture influences a surprising number of churches in the United States as they struggle to retain members who could become alienated from the churches' formal requirements.

One example is provided by home fellowship. Some churches encourage Bible study and spiritual discussion outside the church, if not explicitly to discourage house churching, then certainly to respond to a widespread desire for forms of religious expression more personal and informal than church settings can provide. One such home-fellowship group is associated with the Hamden Assembly of God Church outside Philadelphia. Although Assemblies of God churches are usually classified as conservative, as most believers in this one would classify themselves, the members of this church have developed a suspicion of leadership resembling the counterculture movements of the 1960s. Like the educational reformers of those years who insisted that teachers ought to shed their pedagogical authority, Hamden's Pastor Vince goes to great lengths to assure those who gather to hear his sermons that his words are not the final word. "Your pathway in following Christ will be different from my pathway," he tells the home-fellowship group, as if his leadership role were purely advisory. Formally, the church's activities are organized around Sunday-morning worship, and the evening study sessions are meant to flesh out what takes place there. But Pastor Vince seems to suggest the opposite; home fellowship, he says at one point, "is not a part of the church, it *is* the church." Such anti-institutional talk pleases many of Hamden's parishioners. Paul and Carla Christianson, active members of the home-fellowship group, are among them. Catholics by birth—as in other conservative Protestant churches, there are a large number of former Catholics in this one—they came to detest the liberalism of their parish and switched to a fundamentalist Protestant church to find something solid to anchor their faith. There they discovered how rigid and doctrinaire a Baptist church can be, and chafing at the authoritarianism of its preacher, they switched out of that one as well. Now, having joined a Pentecostal church, they love Pastor Vince because he "is not one who has the authority thing."

Conservative Christians are not the only religious believers attracted to nonchurch settings; liberal Jews can be as well. Jews have always worshiped at home; it is the place where the Sabbath candles are lit and the prayers are chanted. But throughout the twentieth century, Jewish leaders have tried to create large synagogue centers—the "shul with a pool," as one historian has called them, where, as Mordecai Kaplan, the founder of Reconstructionist Judaism, put it, Jews "might find a far wider scope for expression and enjoyment than is possible in the home." Yet despite this effort to bring faith into institutions, recent developments in Judaism have taken faith back out of them. Decreasing rates of attendance at synagogue testify to the limited success of the synagogue-center movement. And so do various efforts, inspired by the upheavals of the 1960s, to create *havurot* (singular: *havurah*)—the Jewish equivalent of home-fellowship worship, which takes its origins from the Hebrew word for a group of friends. Part countercultural, part feminist, part communitarian, *havurot* reproduce the exodus from Egypt, as participants leave behind the formal trappings of synagogue membership in favor of a more immediate and direct spirituality. An example is offered by Kelton Minyan, a (since-disbanded) prayer group in the Los Angeles area in the 1970s. Distrustful of rabbinical authority, the group designated a variety of people to lead the prayer services at different times. The psalms to be read and the melodies to be sung were chosen based more on personal preference than on the rules of the liturgy. And most of the group's members rejected any interpretation of prayer emphasizing that Jews were somehow a "chosen people" different from others. The left-wing Jews attracted to Kelton Minyan would no doubt have felt out of place in Pastor Vince's Assembly of God Church, yet underlying both was a common feeling of dissatisfaction with top-down forms of religious organization.

Small-group worship, intimate and personal as it may be, cannot do away with the institutional priorities of congregations entirely. Thus Kelton Minyan, as it began to attract new members, became institutionalized by moving into the religious center of a nearby university. And the experiences of a Portland, Oregon, *havurah* is even more indicative of the inevitable pressures toward institutionalization that can sprout in even the most anti-institutional environments. Wanting at least some spiritual direction, the group advertised for a new rabbi in 1987. But afraid to use the *c* word (for congregation), *havurah* members insisted that the ad emphasize a teacher and resource person, not a religious leader, bringing forth a stinging letter of rebuke from the Union of American Hebrew Congregations (the Reform denomination). An appropriate rabbi was eventually found (causing some of the more anti-institutional members to quit), but the *havurah* continued to rent space, unwilling to take the next step in institutionalization: creating its own building. Insisting on its countercultural affinities, the group holds fast to a system of governance by committee, yet as the group grows in size, each member feels less influential and the committees themselves become increasingly oligarchic. "Our institutions haven't necessarily caught up with our size," one member says, trying to capture the frustrations of a group of people who want to worship together and who distrust institutional authority but who find themselves nonetheless in the reluctant role of institution builders.

Even those congregations that grow out of revivalist traditions and continue to appeal to the emotional rather than the organizational needs of their flock have not found a way to bypass institutional requirements. Pastor Vince of the Hamden Assembly of God Church, for example, is not quite so anti-institutional as his advocacy of home fellowship makes him appear to be. The function of such fellowship, in his view, is not to question the church's teachings but to bring waverers back to the truth; home fellowship is not a seminar and he is not Socrates. Along similar lines, the Pentecostally inclined Spirited Church of Muncie recognizes that the enthusiasm it encourages will go for naught if it spins off in anarchic directions; as one church document puts it, "An ongoing struggle is in *maintaining spiritual balance* in the worship services. We allow the Spirit freedom to move and work in our midst, and yet maintain an orderly service, full of integrity and sincere worship. . . . The key to maintaining spiritual balance in the worship services is in the pastor maintaining control and staying in authority during the worship services."

If anti-institutional movements within churches cannot fully do away with organization, however, organized churches cannot ignore the anti-institutional inclinations of their members. The best example is provided by the experience of many American Catholics. Faithful Catholics are not only expected to belong to a particular parish and to participate actively in the Catholic subculture of schools, charities, and voluntary associations but also to respect the authority embodied in a series of institutions ranging from the distant hierarchy to the local bishop. Yet practicing Catholics can hardly be immune to the anti-institutionalism existing everywhere around them. Consider those attracted to small groups. Like many religious leaders, Father Bernard Lee, who is the leading expert on small-group worship among Catholics, is encouraged by the seriousness of purpose such groups represent; these groups are, he writes, "genuine Christian communities with churchhood about them." Still, Father Lee may be trying to put the best face on a movement that will inevitably lead Catholics to question the institutional nature of their very institutional faith. While participation in small groups reinvigorates the faith of many Catholics, there is a tendency for their members, in coming to trust themselves more, to "become more critical of the institutional church."

Younger Catholics, moreover, are less likely to respect the institutional prerogatives of the Church than those of previous generations. Like Molly, the Reform Jewish physician, Mary Mallozzi is the kind of Catholic for whom the Church ought to be grateful. A cradle Catholic, she was raised in the institutional church and, as a thirty-year-old, remains loyal to it. "Church is a very big thing to me," says Mary. "I need to belong to a parish that is going to nurture me along and offer me the tools in the areas that I need." Fortunately for her, she found such a parish in Blessed Sacrament, where she met her husband Jim. Both remain active in parish affairs, yet, although Mary regularly attends Mass, she does not believe that she is obligated by her faith to do so. "I hate rules, such as 'you have to go to Mass,'" she adds. "I try to reframe it and say, 'It's part of our growth as religious people.'" Her Catholic identity is as strong as Catholic identity can be, and she says proudly that "I don't think there is anything that would drive me out of the Church." Yet she will make up her own mind on whether priests should be allowed to marry and whether birth control is permissible.

People like Mary Mallozzi are most likely in the minority among American Catholics between twenty and forty years old. Far more typical are individuals like Robert Wilkes, a twenty-seven-year-old graduate student. Asked whether he will be a lifelong Catholic, Robert, who has no interest in switching to any other religion, answers "definitely." But he does not view himself as a lifelong parishioner. He once found a parish in which he felt comfortable, particularly because the priest encouraged lay participation and an active concern with social justice. When the local bishop stepped in and stopped any experimentation, Robert dropped out and decided to keep his faith to himself rather than find another parish in which to worship. Unlike Catholics who retain only an ethnic identity with the Church, Robert is a believer and considers himself loyal in his own way. But unlike those active in particular parishes, he would like to see the Catholic Church become more like Protestant churches by altering what to him are outdated hierarchical and authoritarian forms of organization. His kind of Catholicism, however different from his faith in the past, may well come to represent his faith in the future. This is especially the case in the aftermath of the pedophilia and cover-up scandals of 2002 that rocked Catholicism in the United States. The decision by the Vatican to accept the resignation of Bernard Cardinal Law of Boston, after priests and faithful Catholics in the Boston area demanded it, suggests that the days of secrecy and unquestioned obedience are over for American Catholics.

These examples of alternative institutionalism on the part of believers from a variety of religious traditions suggest that Americans often want different rewards from their religious practice, and not all congregations (or parishes, synagogues, mosques, and temples) can provide them. On the one hand, Americans are attracted to faith because it brings them in touch with God's realm, a spiritual environment before which human beings stand in awe, perhaps expecting miracles or perhaps just a few quiet moments for solitude and reflection. On the other hand, they often find in their religious practice balm for the injured self, as church becomes a place in which believers pray to help find a cure for a loved one's cancer, join a support group for the strength to face a job layoff, or attend services to provide a sense of neighborly solidarity. Both realms—the majestically supreme and the crassly self-interested—can be easily corrupted by institutional requirements. The realm of God is too pure and powerful to tend to ordinary tasks of committee meetings or market analysis. And the realm of the self is too preoccupied with subjective meaning lying deep within the individual to equate it with mere church attendance or putting coins on a collection plate. As much as Americans tend to think of their local congregation as the one religious institution in which they have the greatest trust, the ways they practice their religion make it difficult for the local congregation to meet its own institutional needs.

To balance their often contradictory expectations, American believers are remarkably inventive in the experimental methods they
adopt to meet them. It is not that fellowship is missing in such nontraditional locales as home churching or *havurot;* on the contrary,
Americans seek out such venues precisely because they offer a sense
of connectedness to others. It is simply religious fellowship they
lack, or at least those forms of religious fellowship that require long-
term loyalties and institutional commitments.

THE PARACHURCH RESPONSE

Reggie Bryant met Jesus behind second base. In October 1999, he
missed a trip from his home in Mobile, Alabama, to St. Petersburg,
Florida, with a group of friends and decided instead to attend a
prayer meeting in Phoenix sponsored by Promise Keepers. With
thousands of other men—Promise Keeper revival meetings are usually very well attended—Reggie made his way out to Bank One Ball-
park, home of the Arizona Diamondbacks baseball team. There he
was led to the foot of the cross by a Native American preacher who
lifted him up in the air and told him how much Jesus loved him. "I
came back to Alabama a changed man," he testifies. "I have a Father
that has forgiven, cleansed and filled me."

In March 1990, University of Colorado football coach Bill Mc-
Cartney developed the idea of trying to fill an athletic stadium with
thousands of Christian men testifying to their promises to God and
to their wives, and within a few years, his idea had become one of the
most widely discussed religious movements in the United States.
(Because it restricted its appeal to men, and because Bill McCartney
had been involved in a campaign to repeal gay rights in Colorado, it
also became an extremely controversial one.) Promise Keepers is an
example of a "parachurch" organization, a movement that tries to
reach beyond denominations and congregations in search of ways of
reinforcing the faith. There is nothing particularly new about these
organizations. Jewish religious practice in the United States has
taken place not only in synagogues but also within and among a
whole series of organizations responsible for Hebrew teaching, com-

munity outreach, and support for Israel. Catholicism has likewise combined parish activities with the work of lodges, ethnic associations, educational institutions, and special purpose groups. And American Protestantism, especially of the evangelical variety, would find McCartney's efforts quite familiar; his conservative morality and his efforts to link sports with faith are a replay of the revivals led by Billy Sunday, a former baseball player.

Although not new, parachurch movements, especially among evangelicals, are more likely to challenge, rather than to sustain, the denominational character of American religious life. Appealing to charismatics and evangelicals who tend to be oblivious to denominational boundaries in the first place, they flourish in the same postdenominational universe as megachurches and small-group worship. Promise Keeper leaders insist that being postdenominational does not mean being antidenominational. "We're trying to show denominations we're not their enemy," one of them, Steve Chavis, says, and, to further that end, Promise Keepers has formed partnerships with a number of Protestant denominations, including the Assemblies of God, the Church of God (Cleveland, Tennessee), the International Pentecostal Holiness Church, and the Southern Baptist Convention, among others. Still, the organization makes little secret of its distaste for the kind of sectarian squabbling that has long characterized Protestant denominationalism. "No one is shooting over the walls at the real enemy," writes Glenn Wagner, another of the movement's leaders, presumably speaking about sin. "Rather, everyone is shooting at each other." By offering itself as broker intent on advancing Christian unity, Promise Keepers plays a prominent role in sustaining what has been called a "generic conservative Christianity" that cuts across all-existing denominational, doctrinal, and even cultural boundaries in search of an authentically rooted biblical faith.

At the same time, a parachurch movement like Promise Keepers also undermines denominational affiliations by encouraging religious switching. McCartney himself is a classic example of a religious switcher. Once a devout Catholic, he developed a reputation as a fierce, win-at-any-cost football coach, only to have a born-again experience after his career left behind a dysfunctional family—an alcoholic, work-addicted father, a seriously depressed mother, and an unmarried daughter impregnated by the quarterback of his football team. After he recognized that "God doesn't appraise my worth by my won-lost record," McCartney passed through a number of religious movements, including charismatic Catholic and Vineyard Fellowship ones, before resigning from his job at the University of Colorado to devote himself to Promise Keepers. His own experience has become a model for many of those who join his movement. The organization's charismatic excitement and confessional style are attractive to, and produce in turn, those kinds of religious seekers rarely satisfied to remain within one religious tradition through thick and thin.

Because its practices threaten existing denominational turf, Promise Keepers has not been well received by long-established denominations. Its often very successful efforts to attract Catholics prompted the United States Conference of Catholic Bishops to offer a 1996 "perspective" warning of possible conflicts between Promise Keeper theology and practice and those of the Catholic Church. Mainline denominations like the Methodists and Presbyterians are ambivalent about the movement, attracted by its success in tapping new sources of religious energy, yet worried about its treatment of women and homosexuals. And, although this may come as a surprise to liberals who view Promise Keepers as the embodiment of reaction, the organization is especially distrusted by fundamentalist churches and denominations, one of whose leaders, the late Ernest Pickering of the Baptist World Mission, condemned the movement as the most serious attack on fundamentalism since the rise of Billy Graham and predicted that "it is going to cause major problems for pastors who are trying to maintain a biblical position."

At the same time that Promise Keepers pays little attention to the proprieties of national denominations, the relationships it develops with local congregations also tend to be ambivalent. At its rallies, the organization no longer distributes "commitment cards" for adherents to sign, so as to dispel the worries of local pastors that their members might be poached. Its leaders repeatedly emphasize their desire to strengthen congregations, and many pastors, aware of its appeal, refrain from criticizing the movement, recognizing its power as a possible competitor for souls. "The goal of our organization is to

go out of business," one New York–based official of the movement
says, after which, presumably, men would be in better shape to participate in more traditional church-based activities. Yet tensions between the movement and local congregations nonetheless persist.
"We can't compete with all the fun and fanfare of a Promise Keepers
conference," exclaims one religious leader in Connecticut. "Besides,
some of the things that are considered appropriate in a stadium context don't always work well in the sanctuary."

Nor are religious practices that work in the sanctuary especially
appropriate for athletic venues. Speaking of his childhood, one member of the movement recalls that "the moral aspect was always
there," but that, "we didn't always go to church. In fact, there were
long periods of time when we didn't go at all, like two or three years
maybe." His not always positive experiences in church are typical of
men attracted to the movement; parachurch organizations like
Promise Keepers start with the premise that something about church
turns off many individuals whose souls might be saved in other
ways. In this they are no doubt correct. In some cases, it may be the
stiffness and formality of a pastor or the seemingly dogmatic nature
of the teachings. In others, it may be the prying eyes of neighbors. It
can even be the music. And in the case of Promise Keepers, it may involve the discomfort of being in a room surrounded by women, who
generally form the bulk of believers in most conservative Christian
churches. Whatever the reason, there can be little doubt that many
men who might feel uncomfortable in the intimate surroundings of
their local congregation have no problem being one among many in
the place they usually watch football.

Fully aware that those who come to a mass meeting in a football
stadium might lose their enthusiasm for religion once the excitement is over, Promise Keepers follows up its rallies with grassroots
"accountability groups," in which between five and fifteen men meet
regularly to discuss and reinforce their faith. Although Promise
Keeper accountability groups have some distinctive characteristics—
they are more likely to be racially integrated than most other small
groups, and because they are all male, they run counter to the tendency of women to dominate small-group forms of worship—they
share many of the characteristics of small-group worship in general.

Despite Bill McCartney's conservative political views, most of the accountability groups avoid discussions of any controversial topic; as one member warns, "you've got to be really careful trying to turn Christian values into political action," for if you do, "you have to enter the political arena, which is full of power games and dishonesty, and so on." There is, furthermore, a distinct tendency toward complete agreement on spiritual and religious matters. And Promise Keeper accountability groups rely on role playing and other often artificial means of getting discussion going. At one such group in Gary, Indiana, for example, the men use baseball metaphors to structure their discussion. "Heading for First" deals with the organizational aspects of the group, "Sliding into Second" discusses the nature of masculinity, and so on around the bases until "Coming Home" stresses the importance of teamwork and accountability. In these ways, accountability groups, ostensibly designed to keep men loyal to their local congregations, offer one more example of the tendency of contemporary religious believers to prefer intimate interaction to traditional Sunday forms of worship.

Even more importantly, Promise Keeper accountability groups share with other small groups an emphasis on emotionality. One might expect that a male-only group of conservative Christians meeting in football stadiums would promote forms of "muscular Christianity," which would put little if any emphasis on encouraging forms of emotional expression. Yet the organization cannot quite make up its mind about the proper roles that men should play. Some of the men attracted to it are traditionalists who believe that old-fashioned gender roles need to be reestablished. But others are strong adherents of a more "new age" consciousness associated with writers like the poet Robert Bly. In the latter view, accountability groups, as one member puts it, are "the kind of thing that is missing from a man's life today, the close ties with other men that are real, something that really means something." These men express a need to become more expressive of their feelings, even if such efforts are often scorned as "feminine." No wonder that groups verge off into discussions of impotency or child sexual abuse and see their share of weeping, hugging, and even rolling on the floor; indeed a participant in one such group in Texas tells his cobelievers of the time he shared his inability to keep himself from masturbating, a sin he was able to confess to his wife with the support of his group. One would have to be a therapist to determine the effects of such confessional practices on the individuals who engage in them. But it is not difficult, from a sociological point of view, to conclude that men who have begun to explore the inner child are not going to be the kind of individuals who stick loyally to an institution whether or not it serves their immediate need for self-gratification.

Promise Keeper accountability groups are, finally, structured in ways that cut directly across existing congregational lines. Although some of them meet in local churches, they are more likely to bring men together for breakfast or lunch in restaurants—a characteristic they share with other parachurch organizations such as Aglow International Fellowship, a self-help-oriented Pentecostal group that is in some ways the female equivalent of Promise Keepers, which, in its determination to avoid denominations and congregations, often meets in local hotels or in public places. And whether Promise Keeper meetings take place in or out of church, they go out of their way to include men from many different congregations. "We're not playin' church here," as one Promise Keeper leader insists. Were both the leaders and adherents to a movement like Promise Keepers satisfied with the performance and practices of local congregations, there would be no need for the movement in the first place.

There can be little doubt that Promise Keepers offers a powerful sense of fellowship not always available in church. Yet, as is also true of both megachurches and small groups, it is not always, specifically, religious fellowship that is being offered. Although people in groups like Promise Keepers do nearly all the things that people in churches do—they pray, hear sermons, testify, evangelize—they do so in radically different ways. Churches are best thought of as institutions rooted in a specific faith that try to reach out and attract people from all walks of life. Parachurch organizations reverse the process. They define a limited, and usually a nonreligious, category of people to whom they will appeal, such as athletes, businessmen, or prisoners, and then try to attract them to a nonspecific, if evangelical, form of faith. By restricting themselves to a defined category of people, organizations like Promise Keepers bring together persons who otherwise would never have met. Yet because the people they assemble together are chosen based on shared characteristics that are nonreligious in nature, it is never clear whether their motivations for belonging are emotional, secular, spiritual, or some uneasy, and perhaps unstable, combination of all three.

It would be incorrect to describe Promise Keepers as anti-institutional, for it is very much a national organization with field representatives and a large number of employed staff. But it would be correct to view it as one more way in which tendencies toward religious enthusiasm overflow already-existing institutional containers in favor of organizational forms that are as innovative as the worship practices associated with them. The tensions that frequently arise between congregations and Promise Keepers stem from the fact that there is a limited amount of time, energy, and money available to any religious believer, no matter how deep his or her faith. Denominations and congregations have already lost some of their institutional character as Americans demand forms of religious practice that speak to their own personal needs, and Promise Keepers does little to help them regain it. Unlike congregations, the relationship of Promise Keepers to local communities is fleeting; it arrives for giant rallies only to depart leaving an empty stadium or hotel behind, and even when it sponsors accountability groups, they lack the structure provided by houses of worship. Promise Keepers is a recent innovation with unstable finances and membership. Neither here nor there, but instead part of the flux and change of an ever-dynamic society, Promise Keepers testifies more to innovation than it does to permanence.

THE DARK SIDE OF FELLOWSHIP

In 1955, the sociologist Will Herberg published *Protestant, Catholic, Jew,* one of the most influential books ever written about American religion. Among his many conclusions was that Americans identify with their religions, not only for reasons of faith but also to give themselves a sense of membership. Americans, he wrote, "join churches as a way of naming and locating themselves socially." They believe in order to belong.

One can only wonder what Herberg would think of today's religious adherents, who frequently believe in order to be. Typical of their approach to faith is the widespread attitude among baby boomers—Americans born at the very time Herberg wrote his book—for whom denominations provide, in the words of one sociologist, "a psychological anchor of sorts" rather than "a strong basis of group belonging." Seeking but not always finding, impatient for results, anxious for authenticity, ever sensitive to hypocrisy, the religious life of the American people may not yet have experienced the turbulence of professional sports, where free agents search around for the team that will offer them the best contract, or the cut-your-own-best-deal retirement plans that increasingly characterize the benefits offered by American business firms. But it does seem to be heading in that direction.

This American propensity to reshape institutions to satisfy personal needs, while perhaps appropriate to consumer goods, seems to many observers to be out of place when matters of ultimate meaning and significance are at issue. They certainly have cause for concern. Denominational officials ought to worry about the unwillingness of believers to identify themselves with the histories and traditions that help structure belief. And congregations can and do offer a sense of ritual observance and participation in a collective endeavor that cannot be easily found in the home, or even in the stadium. Were religious institutions to join with secular ones in making it more difficult for people to develop long-term attachments with others, lost in the transition would not only be fellowship but also the kind of sensibility that reminds individuals that there exist duties and obligations to traditions and forces more permanent than their immediate wants and needs.

Still, there is one potential benefit to a form of faith that puts more emphasis on being than on belonging. "Denominationalism is the opposite of sectarianism," the historian Winthrop Hudson once observed, for a sect "claims the authority of Christ for itself alone," while a denomination implies that the group so formed "is but one member, called or *denominated* by a particular name, of a larger group—the Church—to which all denominations belong." Hudson's is an idealistic view that, alas, has little correspondence with reality.

Denominations and congregations were strongest in this country when Americans cared so much about the specifics of their faith that they formed ever more tightly bound communities hostile to people whose faith was different from their own. Like other aspects of religious practice in America, the inward-looking quality once associated with strong versions of faith has been transformed by the individualism and hedonism of American culture. That is not necessarily a bad thing. Against a historical pattern characterized by narrow sects—each persuaded that it had a monopoly on the truth—and parochial congregations that cared little for those outside the group, there is something to be said in favor of religious switching and transient congregational loyalties. In post-1960s America, institutions have to earn respect. Encouraging fellowship by disparaging others while reinforcing the prejudices of the like-minded may no longer be the best way to do so.

CHAPTER 3

DOCTRINE

THE STRANGE DISAPPEARANCE OF
DOCTRINE FROM CONSERVATIVE
PROTESTANTISM

Doctrine can be defined as a body of teachings specific to a particular religion that spells out an understanding of who God is and what he demands of human beings. Of all America's faithful, those who generally take doctrine the most seriously tend to be Protestant fundamentalists. Claiming to read the Bible as the literal word of God, fundamentalists are people who care very much what their faith is, whatever the cost in upward mobility, neighborly popularity, or alienation from public opinion, just as they care what your faith is, and mine.

Reflecting this passion for doctrine, fundamentalists tend to emphasize not only how they act but also how they think; doctrinal considerations devoted to expressing age-old considerations of man's relationship with God pepper their conversational style, as if Martin Luther were not some distant historical figure but a living presence in their lives. "There was no total turnabout in my worldview in a moment in time," Ralph Barnes, a fundamentalist student, says in explaining how the process of sanctification works. "You see, becoming a new creature in Christ—2 Corinthians 5:17—does not remove the indwelling sin that is part of our fallen human condition. That is part of our mortal being—sinful and corrupted. In redemption, God proclaims us righteous, objectively based on the finished work of

Christ. We can't add to it." Believers like Ralph Barnes are not particularly interested in debating their ideas; they tend to pronounce
them in ways that foreclose any intellectual give-and-take. But if one
went out looking for a place in the United States where individual
believers would mention scripture in ordinary conservation, down to
citations of chapter and verse, fundamentalist circles would be the
first to be explored.

This preoccupation with doctrine among fundamentalists is a
byproduct of the movement's history in the United States. Fundamentalists live in a world in which a great deal is at stake—nothing
less, in their view, than the fate of the human race. Although once accused of contributing to American anti-intellectualism, there has
been a decidedly intellectual side to fundamentalism; dissident theologians associated with the Princeton Theological Seminary such as
J. Gresham Machen, who was known for his dour pessimism and
strict teachings, gave fundamentalist ideas new life in the early years
of the twentieth century. Legacies of that tradition remain in the doctrine of "premillennialism" or "dispensationalism"—in essence, the
idea that Christ will return to earth in the not-too-distant future and
sweep soul-saved Christians into rapture, leaving nonbelievers to
face the horrors of the Apocalypse before the everlasting reign of
God is established. Wanting to be sure—desperately sure—that doctrines such as this one are sound, fundamentalists gather together
only the truly faithful and, in the process, turn their backs on believers seemingly close to them but not close enough to be fully trusted
because of some difference on a matter of biblical interpretation.

Closer examination of the actual beliefs and practices of fundamentalists, however, suggests two modifications to the notion that a
taste for ideas remains prominent in the way they think about God.
One is that the fundamentalist belief in biblical inerrancy produces
theology of a decidedly cut-and-paste quality, for if the truth is contained, loud and clear, in the words of the Bible—actually, not in any
Bible, but in the Scofield or Ryrie Reference Bibles—there is no need
for systematic thinking, techniques of exegesis, and canons of argumentation, all of which have been central to the kinds of theological
inquiry that have shaped other faiths. For all their Bible reading,
most fundamentalists familiarize themselves only with in-house

commentary. There are fundamentalists who buy and read the recondite theological works issued by conservative Protestant publishing houses. But ordinary believers—who, despite the impression their ideological opponents have of them, are often avid readers—are inclined toward prophecy, such as one finds in the novels of Hal Lindsey and Tim LaHaye. Doctrinaire they may be but interested in doctrine they are not.

When fundamentalist believers do read the Bible, moreover, they often do so in down-to-earth ways. At their least theological, fundamentalists play "Bible roulette," opening the text to a random passage in order to be guided by what they find. And even when they engage in more systematic study, their objective is not so much curiosity but immediate application. "Although they often read the Bible from cover to cover," sociologist Nancy Ammerman writes of the fundamentalist churchgoers she studied, "believers rarely refer to the themes of the whole Bible or even to whole books or stories. Rather, they 'search the scripture' to find the word or phrase that seems to answer the question at hand." Fundamentalists like to view themselves as descended from Jonathan Edwards, yet one does not find in the way they cite scripture anything like the never-ending, all-consuming qualities of mind with which Edwards was blessed. It is as if the Bible, considered as a body of ideas, is something of an afterthought, there to ratify ideas already so well formed that one need never puzzle over them. "The Bible can prove itself a flexible book," Ammerman writes about the fundamentalists' approach, "informing, shaping, and then ratifying decisions that need to be made."

Even though fundamentalists typically approach doctrine through secondary sources, their approach to faith tends to be more preoccupied with matters of theological substance than their close cousins, the evangelicals. Although they are often conflated, fundamentalists and evangelicals possess radically different religious temperaments—and, as a result, express quite different ideas about ideas. Since at least 1942, when the National Association of Evangelicals was founded, evangelicals have rejected extreme versions of dispensationalism, adopting more nuanced responses to modernity which, in turn, have led them away from the often aggressively doctrinaire pronouncements of fundamentalists. As their name implies—*evangelical* comes from the Greek word for the good news of the Gospel they seek to share—the primary obligation of evangelicals is to save as many souls as possible. Their confidence that they can do so—indeed, the optimistic determination they bring to the task—does not always sit well with fundamentalism's conviction that human beings can do little to save themselves in the face of God's dismay with the way we live now. This purposive and forward-looking side of evangelicalism is a refreshing contrast to the suspicious, often conspiratorial, side of fundamentalism. Evangelicals are more open to the world than fundamentalists. Less focused on texts and the words they contain, they are also quite willing to overlook fine points of theology in favor of broad-based coalitions that place greater emphasis on communicating doctrine than on developing and refining the doctrines they communicate.

It is not that evangelicals lack doctrine. Unlike fundamentalists who, in rebellion against mainline churches, often set up unaffiliated congregations, sects proliferate in the evangelical world, producing a bewildering variety of faith statements: the Assemblies of God have sixteen doctrinal standards dating back to 1916; Missouri Synod Lutherans have their "Doctrinal Position" of 1932; and Southern Baptists adhere to principles ranging from the 1659 "Declaration of Several People Called Anabaptists" to the "Baptist Faith and Message" first adopted in 1925 and revised three times since—the latest, dealing with religious liberty, in June 2000. Technically speaking, faith statements are not credal expressions; Baptists, for example, have many statements of faith but consider themselves a noncredal denomination. (Creeds, for many conservative Protestants, refer to the founding documents of Christianity, such as the Nicene Creed, and in that sense appear too "Catholic" for such strict Protestant temperaments.) Still, statements of faith are intended to specify the ideas in which conservative Christians are expected to believe and, in that sense, have significant doctrinal content. And for at least some of the churches included in the evangelical category, expressions of doctrine are not musty relics that play no role in everyday religious practice. The Christian Reformed Church, for one, requires that all people who hold office in the church, as well as all those who teach at church-related institutions such as Calvin College, in Grand

Rapids, Michigan, affirm the church's three great credal statements: the Heidelberg Catechism, the Belgic Confession, and the Canons of Dordt. In so doing, they affirm their belief in such fine points of theology as the notion of double predestination or the truth of limited, effectual atonement, not exactly the stuff of everyday conversation. (Double predestination means that both those who are saved and those who are not have been predetermined; limited or effectual atonement means that Christ died not to atone for all people but only for the elect.)

The care given to the writing of faith statements suggests a desire to take ideas seriously, since so much time and energy is spent putting them into words. But matters look quite different when, upon leaving behind institutions, one enters the world of actual evangelical practices. Evangelicals pay lip service to the quintessentially Protestant idea of a priesthood of all believers, a way of engaging in theological reflection that may have worked for Luther, who matched his distrust of received (Catholic) doctrine with an astonishing outpouring of scholarship and polemic. But few evangelical Protestants have that much confidence in their own priestly capacities. "Despite all the evangelical rhetoric about *sola scriptura* in the twentieth century," as one historian has written about conservative Christian reliance on scripture as the sole source of religious truth, "most evangelicals don't trust themselves to interpret the Bible, so they turn to others—local pastors, mendicant preachers and lecturers, authors of thousands of books, commentaries, and reference tools—for interpretative schemes." For all the vigor with which they ask others to join them in celebrating Jesus's dominion, ordinary evangelicals are unlikely to offer insights into such doctrinal statements as the Augsburg Confession, Keach's Catechism, or the Lausanne Covenant.

As a byproduct of this lack of confidence in doctrine, evangelical believers are sometimes hard pressed to explain exactly what, doctrinally speaking, their faith is. On her visits to a small town in Oregon, a sociologist found that "many of the most committed churchgoers couldn't even really tell me their church's denomination, a fact that suggested to me that feeling is believing." One minister called his a "Heinz 57 church," reflecting the wide variety of doctrines found

within, while another told her that "a lot of us call ourselves Christian but we don't know what we believe." This sociologist, a lesbian,
went to Oregon to study the efforts by conservative Christian
churches to oppose a gay-rights referendum. She found conservative
Christian activists intent on doing just that, but she also found religious Christians "far less certain of themselves and their beliefs than
I had anticipated, and the churches in which they placed their trust
much more fractious." These are people who believe, often passion-
ately, in God, even if they cannot tell others all that much about the
God in which they believe.

This lack of interest in dogma and doctrine is reinforced by the
tendency of evangelicals to come together in small groups. Because
their religious practices emphasize personal salvation, their political
style tends to be populist, and their tradition insists on the voluntary
character of faith, evangelicals are in the forefront of the small-group
movement. In one typical small-group meeting at an evangelical
church in the New York suburbs, the discussion material concerns
the hardships faced by the Israelites under the Pharaoh. But rather
than trying to focus the group's attention on the plight of people living at another time and in another place, the group's leader, determined to insure that the day's agenda would be relevant to the lives
of the women attending the session, instead asks each woman to reflect on "the most life-changing experience" she has had. Many
choose to speak of joyous events such as the birth of a child or a marriage, while others talk of the death of a loved one, but all agree that
God has helped through both good and bad times. "Sometimes you
feel heaven has a brass door and you just can't get through," the
leader says in response to some of the more harrowing personal stories that were offered. But, she goes on, just "the knowledge that
God is there" ought to be sufficient, even when God seems to be
withdrawing his help. Clearly, participants are more comfortable
speaking about personal problems than they are pondering the possibility of exile or discussing religious persecution.

The atmosphere in small groups encourages topics that promote
harmony and good feelings, not subjects that might lead to disagreement and discord. At Desert Evangelical, a three-thousand-member,
rapidly expanding church in an equally rapidly growing city in the

American Southwest, Lars and Ann run a group designed to "grow and go," a term used to express the idea that members should first be made to feel at home so that they might then engage more deeply in the church's many activities. "We don't really get into a lot of in-depth discussion," one group member says, because "[we] haven't approached a lot of subjects that could cause divisiveness." On one occasion, Lars wanted to bring up the issue of abortion. He did so, not by asking the group to discuss the topic, for that might have caused controversy, but by simply leaving a petition on a table for people to sign. Faith, for these believers, means walking with God; it does not mean arguing over theological (or moral and political) details. Indeed, Lars and Ann, like many evangelicals throughout the country, say that faith is so important to them that "religion"—which they associate with discord and disagreement and, therefore, if often in an unexpressed way, with doctrine—cannot be allowed to interfere with its exercise.

It has been argued that America has "an argument culture," but one finds little taste for argument among people so uncertain of their own views. After observing small-group practice among adherents to an Assembly of God congregation, a sociologist wrote that "for the most part . . . group members seemed to avoid rocking the boat; much of the discussion was one person after another adding a perspective that repeated the same basic point. People seemed to avoid making themselves vulnerable to criticism or correction by other group members by avoiding controversial topics and by not admitting the need for guidance in understanding or applying the Word of God." More popular than discussions of doctrine or politics in small groups like these are game-playing techniques designed to break down the walls that separate people. An evangelical fellowship in New Jersey, for example, starts some of its meetings by taping jigsaw puzzle pieces to people's foreheads to see to whom they might be connected, as well as by asking them to name the animal they most resemble or the movie that best captures their spiritual journey.

Small groups, by providing an informal and friendly environment, attract people to church who might otherwise carry images in their heads of unbending pastors. They give people who might have difficulty expressing themselves before a large audience the comfort of knowing that their listeners are likely to treat their confession with empathy and to relate similar stories of their own. They break down distinctions by treating all people as equally vulnerable before the Lord. They provide powerful emotional experiences for their members that are not unlike the emotions once unleashed through revivals and awakenings. What they tend not to do is to encourage any kind of doctrinal reflection. As supportive as such groups are for their members, they do not increase the understandings those members have of the doctrines associated with their faith. In one study, for example, those who said that their faith was deepened by their experience with small groups were just as likely as those who said the opposite to hold the incorrect views that Jesus was born in Jerusalem or that the Book of Acts can be found in the Old Testament. Whatever Bible study does, it does not seem to increase an already sketchy biblical familiarity that leads 80 percent of Americans to believe that Benjamin Franklin's aphorism "God helps those that help themselves" actually comes from scripture.

When they leave the security of the small group behind to worship in the cavernous cathedrals of megachurches, evangelicals face another powerful form of resistance to doctrine. Megachurches, whether or not they are affiliated with a specific denomination, tend to be eclectic in their theological commitments. It is not correct ideas they seek to find but what one observer calls "a more plausible model of Christianity—a model that fits with pervasive cultural understandings about choice, individualism, autonomy, the importance of the self, therapeutic sensibilities, and an anti-institutional inclination common today." To do so, they tend to think of themselves as postdenominational. Their pastors "do not aim to convince seekers of the truthfulness of a coherent doctrine or set of doctrines, such as Reformed theology or the Westminster Confession. Rather, they wish to persuade seekers to adopt the few core beliefs of evangelical theology."

By playing down doctrine in favor of feelings, evangelicalism far exceeds fundamentalism in its appeal to Christians impatient with disputation and disagreement. And yet distaste for doctrine does not stop there. For there has taken place within conservative Christian circles an explosive growth in yet another religious persuasion—a charismatic or Pentecostal one—that places even less emphasis on considerations of doctrinal truth than evangelicalism does.

Doctrines, whatever else one thinks of them, are statements of ideas, written down in texts, to be transmitted from one generation to another in ways that require a wide range of cognitive abilities, ranging from basic literacy to advanced interpretive understanding. Charismatic religious believers fully possess such cognitive abilities; just because they speak in tongues in church does not mean that they cannot provide, if asked, well-argued positions on behalf of their faith and its distinctive religious practices. Yet Pentecostals continue to look for "signs and wonders"—miraculous manifestations of God's presence among them—a disposition that assigns little or no priority to arguments rooted in traditions of philosophical or theological inquiry. Hence even when Pentecostals put aside the more exotic aspects of their traditions of their past to participate actively in the modern world, they do not do so in ways that encourage anything resembling systematic reflection about the nature of God and the duties people have to him.

Southern California religious movements with decidedly Pentecostal leanings, such as Calvary Chapel and the Vineyard Christian Fellowship, serve as graphic examples of the ways in which spirit-filled movements treat the doctrinal aspects of religious belief. These movements grew out of the Jesus People, young Californians who once may have been hippies or drug addicts but who, in the 1970s, found themselves attracted to Christianity, often outside of established churches and denominations. One close student of these movements calls them new-paradigm churches and argues that their growth and influence constitutes "a second reformation that is transforming the way Christianity will be experienced in the new millennium." That is surely something of an exaggeration, for in many ways these new Pentecostal movements resemble pietistic and heartfelt facets of earlier religious awakenings. But what seems unquestionably true is that religious movements like these are immensely popular. Calvary Chapel, which started in Pastor Chuck Smith's home, now has become a quasi denomination in its own right, sponsoring over six hundred churches, some of them attracting close to ten thousand worshipers each week. In 1994, the Vineyard Christian

Fellowship, which, under the leadership of John Wimber, had split off from Calvary Chapel in 1982, opened up as many new churches in the United States as the Methodists, even though it is far smaller in size. Greg Laurie, a preacher for the Harvest Christian Fellowship of Riverside, California, can expect audiences of twelve thousand people for his sermons. And no longer is the Vineyard movement an exclusively Southern California phenomenon; the largest such congregation, its founding pastor Steve Sjogren told me, is Vineyard Community Church in Cincinnati, not a city known for its attraction to Jesus freaks.

Popularity has its obvious benefits, especially for an evangelical form of religion. But popularity means bowing to, rather than resisting, popular culture, and since American popular culture is one that puts more emphasis on feeling good than thinking right, these movements tend to be especially hostile to potentially divisive doctrinal controversy. "Some people really like a high Episcopal type thing," as a pastor in one of the new-paradigm churches puts it, "and other people like to swing from chandeliers and leap out of windows," as if his job were to respond sympathetically to either inclination. Another pastor listens to tapes of the Bible-study classes led by Pastor Chuck and finds himself amazed at the degree to which Smith manages to avoid potentially divisive doctrinal controversies such as predestination and premillennialism. "The average student listening to Chuck will never even be faced with that stuff," he says. "You may not come out a theologian, but you'll be excited about God's love, you'll be excited about the reality, the possibility of a relationship with God, and you'll want to serve the Lord." One needs to point out that, in the diverse world of conservative Protestantism, judgments are nearly always relative; I have attended services at Calvary Chapel, as well as at Harvest and Vineyard Fellowship churches, and the sermons I heard, including one by Chuck Smith, have more doctrinal content and references to Biblical passages than one usually finds in, say, megachurches. But it is also the case that these churches attract their huge numbers of members not by complicating their lives with theological conundrums and complex moral reasoning but by offering them down-to-earth interpretations of scripture meant to convey the simplicity and directness of the teachings of Jesus.

The movers and shakers of these new-paradigm churches, conscious of the negative images many people have of "holy rollers," deemphasize their formal affiliations with Pentecostalism. Still, compared to the more staid forms of evangelical worship, they do not turn their backs on religious practices long popular among individuals in search of religious ecstasy. "I have seen people's legs grow out. I've seen blind and deaf people healed," says Oden Fong, a staff member at Calvary Chapel, by way of explaining the phenomenal popularity of his church. He has evidently seen a large number of them; just under half of the neo-Pentecostals polled in one survey said that they had been healed miraculously, and 65 percent had experienced one form or another of emotional healing. Although Chuck Smith himself downplays speaking in tongues during sermons, glossolalia—as it is technically called—is also a flourishing practice in these churches, especially in the many small groups they sponsor. It is, in any case, almost as common as faith healing; 41 percent of those surveyed said that they spoke frequently in tongues. One pastor says, "Tongues is an unlearned language. You don't understand what you're saying when you're speaking it." If a person does not understand what he is saying, another is not likely to understand his meaning. But this hardly matters in these churches, since their appeal has so much to do with being transported to a state of oneness with the holy spirit that lies somewhere on the other side of rationality. Doctrine is impossible to convey when one lacks a language of conveyance.

Pentecostalism is that rare American religion founded by both blacks and whites, although it was not long before patterns of racial segregation established themselves. From the start, African American Pentecostalism incorporated elements of folk spirituality, many of them with roots in Africa, into its worship practices, and it did so in ways that implicitly challenged the more established, but also more staid, black denominations, such as the African Methodist Episcopal (A.M.E.) Church or the National Baptist Convention. The past few years have seen a shift in popularity from the latter to the former; one of the Pentecostal denominations formed in the 1920s, Charles Harrison Mason's Church of God in Christ, has established nearly six hundred congregations a year since 1982 and is currently the fastest-growing religion among African Americans, second only to Baptists in its attraction to them, and it may well be the most rapidly expanding religious denomination in the United States as a whole.

As a consequence of its popularity, black Pentecostalism has begun to extend its reach into congregations that once disdained enthusiastic religion, such as the Ward A.M.E. Church in Los Angeles, Bridgestreet A.M.E. in Brooklyn, Payne Chapel in Nashville, and the Allen A.M.E. of Queens, New York. The fact that the pastor of the last of these, the Reverend Floyd Flake, was for a time a member of the U. S. House of Representatives suggests a significant change in the way African American Pentecostalism is practiced. In its early manifestations, Pentecostal faith focused more on expelling demons and diabolic spirits from the soul than it did on social and political action. That is no longer the case. In nearly all of the predominantly African American congregations in which Pentecostal influence has become important, educational programs and activities emphasizing black identity have assumed a place of significance, as have efforts at political mobilization. Anyone searching for ways by which African Americans can overcome self-destructive cycles of poverty, let alone a history of political passivity, ought to appreciate the positive benefits of Pentecostal Christianity.

Still there are ways in which the growth of Pentecostalism has had consequences among African Americans similar to the downplaying of doctrine among whites. An example is offered by Baltimore's Bethel A.M.E. Church, one of the oldest and most established black churches in the United States. One of Bethel's great leaders had been Daniel Payne, the founder of Wilberforce University in Ohio and Bethel's pastor from 1845 to 1849. (Floyd Flake served as president of Wilberforce in 2002–03.) Because the great majority of African Americans of his day were slaves and had no access to formal education, Payne strongly emphasized the need for education among black people and looked with disdain at the foot stomping and chanting he associated with the folk culture of slavery. As Bethel's historian has written, Payne "saw 'ring-shouts' and 'cornfield ditties' as manifestations of ignorance, not as aspects of African culture that should be preserved. Payne's major goal was an educational uplift of the clergy, laity, and the general A.M.E. Church so that they could become a part of the American mainstream."

Although an established feature of black life in Baltimore, Bethel A.M.E. Church stagnated over the course of the years; by 1975, it had roughly six hundred members. That figure grew dramatically, to over seven thousand in the following decade, and the major reason was the leadership of the Reverends John and Cecelia Williams-Bryant. John Bryant had once been a Peace Corps volunteer in Liberia, and when he returned to the United States for ministerial training, he brought with him a respect for African spirituality, incorporating drum music, African art, and African-inspired ritual into Bethel's services. In so doing, he launched eclectic and enthusiastic religious energy concerned with feeling the spirit. The Bryants, who had made their reputation by transforming St. Paul's A.M.E. of Cambridge, Massachusetts, into a "rocking church," were quite open to neo-Pentecostal religious practices, and before long, their efforts produced results. Although only 14 percent of Bethel's members reported speaking in tongues, 59 percent testified to receiving the gifts, including healing and prophecy.

Under John Bryant's leadership—he stayed until he became a bishop of the A.M.E. denomination in 1988—Bethel continued to emphasize the importance of education for African Americans—for example, by encouraging young people to attend divinity school. Still, at least some of the remarkable growth at Bethel A.M.E. was achieved by turning away from didactic approaches to faith. Whether one believes that Payne's views about the importance of education and decorum should be celebrated for their realism or denounced for their accommodation to white interests, they are unattractive to both a modern Pentecostal temperament *and* to an Afrocentric consciousness. Bryant considers himself someone who admires Payne, but he also rejects Payne's overly cerebral disposition. To separate mind from feeling, Bryant believes, is "to weaken and not to strengthen," and the A.M.E. Church "made its greatest strides when it was not ashamed of its feelings." The African Americans who come to Bethel are in search of black pride, a fairly widespread occurrence that is radically changing African American religious practice. That may explain why African Americans searching for a positive racial identity, although they may have little in common with the primarily white congregants at Calvary Chapel who come looking for spiritual replenishment, find themselves comfortable with religious practices that appeal to emotional release. Religious enthusiasm knows no inherent racial distinctions.

The gradual disappearance of doctrine that has taken place as religious energy has moved from fundamentalism to evangelicalism and on to Pentecostalism has important implications for the future of conservative Protestantism. Some of them were spelled out to me by Alan Jacobs, a professor of English at Wheaton College, Billy Graham's alma mater. Jacobs is an expert on the poet W. H. Auden and a frequent contributor to conservative magazines such as *First Things* and the *Weekly Standard*. Over breakfast near his campus, he explained to me that, at least doctrinally speaking, we are witnessing "the end of evangelicalism." Begun as a movement that set itself up, however brotherly, in opposition to fundamentalism, evangelical Christianity, he believes, has little place to turn now that fundamentalism has gone into decline. Jacobs, raised as a Southern Baptist, considers himself an evangelical in one sense, but in another he and his wife Teri have shifted their religious allegiance to a strict Episcopalian church. For them, as well as for some of their Wheaton colleagues, the doctrinal fuzziness and down-to-earth religious practices of evangelical churches leave little room for liturgy, symbolism, and mystery—all of which, they believe, are more likely to be found in a conservative version of Episcopalianism, evangelical Protestantism's substitute for Catholicism.

At the same time, however, the search for an authentic faith within the Jacobs family suggests why the choice made by Alan and his wife is unlikely to be widely shared. Teri Jacobs's brother Lynn, who was also raised a Southern Baptist, has become a Pentecostal; so strongly do Lynn and his wife feel about the matter that they moved to Pensacola, Florida, because that is where the Brownsville Assembly of God Church, to which they were determined to belong, is located. Although Pentecostalism is usually considered "low church" compared with the "high church" tradition of Episcopalianism, Jacobs pointed out to me that his decision and his brother-in-law's decision had one thing in common; both were moves "away from a denomination (the Southern Baptist) that defines itself by doctrine and eschews any physical manifestations of enthusiasm and toward denominations that place a strong emphasis on worship, that indeed define themselves by their form of worship." Yet if both Jacobs and his brother-in-law are searching for alternatives to faiths that assign a lower priority to doctrine, there is little doubt which choice is the more widespread among conservative Protestants in general. Pentecostal forms of religious expression have become popular because— like increasing numbers of school teachers, leaders of therapeutic communities, mental-health professionals, and even occasional academics who live in secular worlds—they seek authenticity through experience rather than through ideas.

"We're in the business of getting people to come to church," the leaders of a number of Southern California charismatic movements once told Richard Mouw, the president of Pasadena's Fuller Theology Seminary, after he pleaded with them to take the life of the mind more seriously, and "seminaries are no help at all in telling us how to do that." The consequences of this kind of attitude are obvious. Ralph Barnes, the fundamentalist student, talked about the conditions under which human beings could seek redemption. It is not clear that many contemporary evangelicals or Pentecostals would know what he was talking about. "If we use the words redemption or conversion," says the Reverend Jess Moody of the First Baptist Church of Van Nuys, California (which changed its name to Shepherd of the Hills Church in order to avoid too close an identification with any denomination), "they think we're talking about bonds."

MAINLINE RELIGION'S EQUALLY STRANGE MARGINALITY

Worlds away from the sun-drenched worshipers of both Calvary Chapel and the upbeat gospel singing of Bethel A.M.E. Church can be found the middle-class professionals who live in leafy suburbs like Oak Park just outside of Chicago. There, too, one can find religious believers who care little for doctrine. "We agree with the doctrine," says one believer in the town's Nazarene church. "But the people are more important than the doctrine." The same kind of approach marks the pastor of the evangelically oriented Oak Park Baptist Church, who does not want to draw sharp lines between his faithful and the faithful of other traditions. "It's alright to be different, as long as you're not different from the Lord," he explains; having a personal relationship with Jesus, in his view, is essential to being a Christian, but nearly everything else concerning doctrine is negotiable.

Yet there are also other religious traditions in this Chicago suburb that stand against the American tendency to shy away from doctrine; these can be found, not in conservative quarters but in liberal and mainline ones. Here pastors and rabbis, writes the sociologist who spoke with them, "were called to be stewards of the denominational, ritual, and doctrinal traditions of the congregation. And all of them conduct their role as public spokesperson for the congregation with great consciousness of their responsibility, not only to provide spiritual direction within the congregation but also to use the congregation's tradition and heritage to provide a rationale for outreach and leadership within the local context." In these congregations, "the process is not the point, and it is not viewed as moral in and of itself. The outcome is what matters, and the pastor or rabbi tries hard to lead the congregation to accept the outcome that he thinks is religiously correct."

It is common to think of mainline Protestants—and in more recent times Catholics and Reform Jews—as representing the American religious establishment. These are the denominations that have been most attractive to Americans who attend Ivy League colleges, work in Wall Street offices, join suburban country clubs, and spend time in Washington staffing commissions and bureaus. Mainline churches, furthermore, have conducted themselves like an establishment. If Episcopalian or Catholic, they have been organized in ways resembling a corporation. If Methodist or Presbyterian, they have had a headquarters with large staffs. And, crucial for any establishment, mainline churches, again until recent times, defined the culture of their society. Describing the situation as it existed before the 1960s, two sociologists wrote that "so wedded were the liberal, mainline churches to the dominant culture that their beliefs, values, and behavior were virtually indistinguishable from the culture."

In contrast to the mainline pattern, evangelical churches—whose members came primarily from rural areas, were less educated, and were less likely to pursue professional careers—have generally been viewed as representing the marginalized and the alienated. Evangelicals trace their roots to dissenting traditions in Great Britain and the United States. Suspicious of government, they either withdrew from politics or supported candidates pledged to return power from Washington to states and localities. In the two-party system that characterizes American Protestantism, mainline churches acted as if they were the establishment and conservative Christian churches conducted themselves as a party of opposition—and what they opposed most was the culture. From the point of view of evangelicals, liberal religion lacked the spiritual resources to combat a widespread drift to secular humanism, and the result was the nihilism plainly visible in the way popular culture celebrated sex and glorified violence.

When it comes to the ways in which contemporary denominations think about doctrine, however, these images confuse more than they clarify. For all their (often quite legitimate) denunciation of sex and violence in the popular media, evangelicals flourish amidst the celebrity-drenched, lowest-common-denominator, highly sentimentalized world of romance novels, daytime soaps, NASCAR races, and Opry-knockoff music that dominates America's entertainment industry. Let a book on a religious theme appear on a best-seller list, and it is evangelicals who are the likely purchasers. It is likewise impossible to tell where the immensely popular language of self-help therapy begins and the language of salvation through Jesus ends. Television producers once thought of evangelicals as a potential niche market that could be reached by religious programming aimed directly at them. But such efforts often failed, and one of the reasons why they failed was because there was no appreciable difference between the religious subculture and the general culture of popular media programming; conservative Christians are too busy watching the same sitcoms enjoyed by other Americans to support a highly profitable network of their own. Conservative Christians like to point out that Hollywood has a tendency to mock the religiously devout, but it also has a tendency to romanticize goodness and to present happy endings in a weepy style in ways that resonate with evangelical instincts.

In such an environment, mainline churches are left as distinctly marginalized holdouts for a way of life that insists on the importance of ideas written down in books meant to be read and digested. It is their members who constitute the dwindling audience for public television and talking-heads news programs. They are the ones who continue to believe that competing for "audience share" may not be the best way to serve God. It is here in the outreaches of liberal religion that one finds graduate students writing theses on such decidedly illiberal thinkers as Martin Luther and John Calvin. Mainline churches remain an establishment in the sense that they still attract disproportionate numbers of the rich and powerful, but like the establishment in Washington, they have also been losing members and influence consistently since the 1960s. And when it comes to the culture that they once did so much to shape, they often feel the same sense of alienation that once characterized evangelicals. The cultural situation in the United States, Bishop Richard Wilkie of the United Methodist Church once said, has become something of a "wasteland," echoing the criticism of television once made by Federal Communications Commission chairman Newton Minow. Like fundamentalists, with whom they have little else in common, liberal churches now find themselves among the last bastions of ideas in an American religious landscape increasingly characterized by empathic understanding on the one hand and emotional enthusiasm on the other.

In part to compensate for the wasteland of American culture, Bishop Wilkie, in 1987, took the lead in creating a Disciple Program designed to increase biblical and religious knowledge among Methodist believers. The program was quite demanding. Participants pledged to commit themselves to a thirty-two-week schedule of Bible study, which involved four to five hours of preparation each week, plus attendance at a two-and-a-half-hour small-group meeting. The idea was to read the entire Bible with the help of study guides and structured discussion questions. Despite the demanding nature of the commitment, the response to the program was overwhelmingly positive. Encouraged, the Board of Disciples of the Methodist Church in 1991 created a kind of advanced course that concentrated on four books: Genesis, Exodus, Luke, and Acts. For this part of the program, participants were also assigned readings such as Everett Fox's translations of Genesis and Exodus and Walter Harrelson and Randall Falk's *Jews and Christians: A Troubled Family*.

In actual practice, however, Bishop Wilkie's program did not quite work as planned. Participants at one church in a midsize Midwestern city undertook the more advanced Bible-study program. Called "Into the Word, Into the World," sessions begin with a video prepared by the Board of Disciples that provides background information on the evening's topic. Discussion of a biblical text follows, often relying on the questions that have been distributed in advance. Eventually, the group moves from the "word" to the "world"; the purpose here is to relate the specific religious materials under discussion to questions of how faith can make a difference, both in the personal lives of the members and in the community in which they live. Group meetings often take on a serious tone, more like a college classroom than a therapeutic encounter. Many participants come away with considerable biblical knowledge. A few even find themselves immersed in biblical esoterica. "Who is this Melchizedek guy, anyway?," one of them asked during one of the sessions. "Isn't he mentioned in Hebrews too?"

Still the bulk of the members of this Methodist bible group had a difficult time with the intellectual side of the program. Group discussions frequently wandered from the assigned topic. Sometimes questions were met by blank stares and embarrassing moments of silence, after which someone would say something like "Gee, that's a hard question. I don't know what to say." Opportunities to make wisecrack remarks were rarely passed over. Participants were much more likely to become engaged in relating themes to their personal lives than in debating abstractions; a discussion of Moses and the burning bush, for example, was organized around such questions as "Have you ever felt God is calling you to do something?" or "How have you responded to God?" And to the degree that the group moved closer to the world than to the word, its social attitudes took a conservative turn, one in direct opposition to the liberal church officials who drew up the program. The Disciple Program was a success but more for reasons of process than for reasons of purpose. "Many participants," writes the sociologist who observed the group in action, "told me that their experience with the group had changed their relationships with other people, helping them to be more accepting, forgiving, and willing to reach out." Although the leadership of a mainline denomination like Methodism encourages a more intellectual approach to the faith, ordinary members resemble evangelicals in the way they shape ideas to respond to the personal situations in which they find themselves.

Mainline denominations take on this resemblance to evangelicalism because their leaders are aware of the enormous cost Christianity has paid for its doctrinal strife. Given a choice between emphasizing doctrinal identity (and, with it, argumentation and discord) and accepting a broad range of competing faiths (and, with that, little doctrinal distinctiveness), mainline religious leaders invariably choose the latter. This is why the same kind of emotion-laden, support-giving dynamic found in evangelical circles reigns supreme among members of a mainline congregation outside Philadelphia, where weeping is plentiful, and "everyone agrees from the outset, overtly, that what is spoken in that circle is private; there is to be no criticism, no 'ridicule or embarrassment,' no competition, and all are welcome and invited to speak." And it also explains why one of the deacons active in the leadership of this congregation is unaware that predestination is one of the core tenets of Presbyterian doctrine—or that seventeen of the eighteen women in a Bible-study group never bring up the Calvinist idea of election in their conversations with the folklorist who interviewed them.

In one of the most comprehensive efforts to characterize Protestant religious beliefs, Nancy Ammerman found similar patterns of theological unpreparedness nationwide. She classified believers into three categories: activist, those who put considerations of social justice at the heart of their faith; evangelical, those who identify with born-again forms of conservative Christianity; and "Golden Rule Christians," for whom faith involves trying to lead a good life—and making the world a better place—by doing for others as they would do for you. Ammerman is persuaded that Golden Rule beliefs "may in fact be the dominant form of religiosity among middle-class suburban Americans," including many of those who might also be classified (by others) as evangelical. Yet even though such beliefs are meant to define the essence of faith for moderate Christians, Golden Rule principles are theologically fuzzy. They outline, not a set of correct assertions but a coterie of good practices. These ordinary Christians, much like the Methodists following Bishop Wilkie's program, view the Bible practically rather than doctrinally. "Their use of Scripture is defined more by choices and practice than by doctrine. They draw from Scripture their own inspiration and motivation and guidance for life in this world."

For all these fairly typical Protestant believers, the will to learn about one's tradition exists, but the will is also weak. Like the "Heinz 57 church" in Oregon, mainline congregations welcome people from a wide variety of religious backgrounds and interests; "our membership runs the spectrum from evangelical to Unitarian," says the former executive minister (otherwise known as Jeb Stuart Magruder of Watergate fame) of the comfortably mainline First Community Church of Columbus, Ohio. (In July 1990, Magruder became a senior pastor at the First Presbyterian Church of Lexington, Kentucky.) And in response to the diversity of faiths among their members, they go out of their way never to proclaim any kind of triumphal superiority of one over the others. Evangelical churches lack doctrine because they want to attract new members. Mainline churches lack doctrine because they want to hold on to those declining numbers of members they have.

CATHOLICS, JEWS, AND IDEAS

Developments similar to those involving mainline Protestants have also been taking place in the world of American Catholicism. Once dismissed by liberal Protestants and Jews as hopelessly dogmatic, Catholics, in America's short-attention-span culture, now seem highly intellectual; their colleges are generally held in high standing; despite the pedophilia crisis, the pronouncements of the Church's leadership on issues ranging from cloning to foreign policy cannot be ignored; and some of America's leading journalists and scholars do not hide their membership in the Church. Reflecting this appreciation for the life of the mind, Catholic religious practice, especially when compared to the evangelical insistence on a personal relationship with Jesus, treats matters of doctrine as the essence of the faith: the Nicene Creed is repeated at each Mass, the bread and the wine of the Eucharist are transformed into the body and blood of Christ, and prayers are offered to Mary in the belief that Mary is the mother of God. Asked by pollsters to list what they consider to be the essence of Catholicism, most Catholics dismiss regular church attendance or the obligation to obey the teachings of the hierarchy. But they do regard as essential the Real Presence, the belief that God is present in the sacraments. "The Catholic laity believes that creedal doctrines are more important than adherence to what they see as specific rules and moral teachings of the Church," write the authors of one widely cited study of Catholic attitudes.

At the same time, however, changes are taking place in American Catholicism that threaten to weaken the Church's doctrinal distinctiveness. The most significant is the decreasing importance of doctrine by generation: Asked a number of statements that emphasize whether Church teachings or the individual's own conscience ought to guide religious and moral views, the younger the Catholic, the more likely he or she holds the view that individuals are the appropriate decision makers. And young American Catholics are not familiar with the Church's position on issues involving social justice or the role of the Church in the modern world; in one survey, 79 percent of them had not heard of the American Bishop's 1986 statement of economic justice, half had not read or discussed any of the leading ideas associated with the Second Vatican Council, and 73 percent were not familiar with John Paul II's criticism of the culture of death. While no one can predict the future, such trends are likely to continue. For as the Church responds to ideas of gender equality and personal autonomy that have influenced all Americans since the 1960s, it can no longer assume that members will (if they ever did) compare Catholic religious teachings with those of Protestants and conclude that the former represent the truth. Doctrine is simply not that important to them. Hence, a recent study of young American

Catholics concluded that "their knowledge of the faith and of its traditional symbols and root metaphors is limited, fragmentary, or nonexistent."

American Catholics, consequently, are unlikely to share the views of more orthodox Catholic theologians such as Joseph Cardinal Ratzinger, the prefect of the Vatican's Congregation for the Doctrine of the Faith. Since Ratzinger is determined to preserve and protect core Catholic theological doctrines, it would be helpful to obtain some sense of how widely his views are accepted among ordinary Catholic believers. Fortunately, there is evidence on this point. The Notre Dame Study of Catholic Life, one of the more ambitious efforts to find out what was on the minds of American Catholics, surveyed "Core Catholics," people who were regular attenders of Mass and who took their Catholic identity seriously. Core Catholics were asked if, in their view, "God has sent his son, Jesus, who continues to live in the church" and that "as a result, the church teaches and sanctifies us for God." Twenty-one percent of those surveyed agreed with this statement, which was written to express one of the key points of Ratzinger's theology. By contrast, 48 percent of those polled agreed with two other statements expressing the point of view that individuals themselves can have direct access to God through Jesus, a theological interpretation closer to Protestantism than to the history of Catholic doctrine. "There is a great deal of confusion and diversity among Core Catholics as to precisely how God relates to the world and to their salvation," write the authors of the Notre Dame study. "In a sense, this should not be surprising, given the lack of theological education of most lay people and the sense of mystery surrounding God."

A study of a Catholic parish in a large Southern city undertaken in 1951 examined church teachings among active parishioners and found that their "Catholic mind" was "about two-thirds Catholic and one-third pagan." One can only wonder what the author of this study would make of today's Catholics. Consider one of the more controversial recent attempts by the Vatican to define a doctrinal point central to Catholicism's understanding of itself: *Dominus Iesus,* Cardinal Ratzinger's September 2000 declaration attacking relativism, which was widely interpreted as a defense of Catholicism as the one true faith. When Cardinal Ratzinger writes that "the Catholic faithful *are required to profess* that there is an historical continuity—rooted in the apostolic succession—between the Church founded by Christ and the Catholic Church," today's young Catholics are likely to reject any such formulation suggesting that non-Catholic Christians have the wrong doctrinal ideas. What does it mean to be a good Catholic, one young person is asked? "I just feel as long as you live a life without harming others or yourself and . . . you are just really living a good, decent life, then you really are living the way God intended you to live," he responds. This decidedly nondoctrinal sentiment is more and more the norm among contemporary Catholics; only a minority among post–Vatican II Catholics believes that the Catholic Church is the one true Church, and 45 percent say that they could be just as happy in some other religious tradition that was not Catholic. "It's *my* one true religion," another believer responds when asked if the Catholic Church is the one true church. "For me and for my children and my family, it's the one true church. But to God, I don't think it's the one true church. . . . I really believe that the God that I think is out there isn't really going to care that the Episcopalians do things one way and Catholics do it another way." As the authors of a recent survey of young Catholics conclude, "Significant numbers of young adult Catholics today no longer see the Roman Catholic Church as unique or essential, the pope as necessary, the Church's structures as important, or tradition as a source of objective truth."

Catholics who admire their religion's commitments to social justice and who appreciate its spirituality bear a strong resemblance to Golden Rule Christians. Like them, these Catholics are believers who insist more on having the right attitudes than possessing the right ideas. Differences between believers like them and Protestants remain, and they remain important, but, as Father Andrew Greeley has observed, such differences "are not doctrinal or ethical." In the way they put doctrinal considerations on the back burner, American Catholics, however distinctive their religious imaginations, are much like the rest of America's faithful.

No other religious group in the United States deserves a place among those dissidents from popular culture who continue to insist on the importance of ideas than Jews. Because of the emphasis Jews place on the interpretation of Talmudic law, and because Jews have been so successful in the intellectually oriented professions, the kind of twelve-step religious confessionalism so widespread among evangelical religious believers ought to be less popular among the Jews. To this day, rabbinical training involves deep knowledge of the tradition, Jewish studies departments flourish at nearly all of the major universities in the United States, and Jewish believers of all denominations are encouraged, if not required, to attend classes designed to teach the essentials of their tradition (and, in many cases, to teach the Hebrew language). Yet when it comes to ordinary Jews who consider themselves actively religious, especially those who identify with Conservative and Reform denominations, there, too, one finds a significant move away from doctrine.

Judaism puts more value on obedience to tradition than on matters of doctrine, and because it does, nothing in the Jewish tradition is quite comparable to the statement of faiths that characterize the evangelical kaleidoscope or the ominously sounding (from a Jewish point of view) Congregation for the Doctrine of the Faith located in the Vatican. Still, there has been a noticeable decline among Jews in the degree to which they are familiar with the doctrinal aspects of their faith. Interviews conducted among "moderately affiliated Jews" found that respondents express strong beliefs in God. They also insist on the importance of synagogue attendance. What they do not do is to express any clear connection between the two. "They told us time and again that they do not come to synagogue expecting to find God there, or stay away because they do not," the authors of this survey comment. "The words in the prayer book do not particularly interest them. The God described and invoked in those prayers is very different from the one in which they believe—too commanding, for one thing, and . . . too 'Jewish.'" Like Catholics unwilling to accept that theirs might be the one true faith, many contemporary Jews identify with their own tradition, but they also want a God who speaks to everyone, not just to them. "The God in whom our subjects believe is, in this sense, not a particularly Jewish God—or at least not a particular*ist* Jewish God," the study concludes. "Moderately affiliated Jews in America have rather embraced universalist and personalist elements of the tradition and of modern culture.

They have left aside or rejected those parts of Judaism that claim a special relation between God and the Jewish people."

That observant Jews are turned off by the idea of a God that is too Jewish says volumes about the kind of faith in which they believe. For one thing, their knowledge of doctrine is not very deep. Asked whether they believe that there is a Messiah and that he will come, only 31 percent of the non-Orthodox Jews in one study agree (and only 7 percent agree very strongly). To the question of whether the Torah was revealed by God to Moses at Sinai, a belief that comes close to defining Judaism as a religion, 50 percent agree, 13 percent very strongly. Even on the straightforward question of whether God exists, only half the non-Orthodox Jews answer "definitely." Uncommitted to a God identified with a specific religion and people, Jews express doubts on matters of theology at levels that Christians would most likely consider of crisis proportion.

In addition, American Jews, to the extent that they know about the doctrinal distinctiveness of their faith, tend to pick and choose from the details with which they are familiar, rejecting, for example, Jewish doctrines that seem excessively male chauvinistic or aggressively nationalistic in favor of those emphasizing social justice or spirituality. "Oh, man, this is like an essay in college," says a Jewish lawyer named Amy to a question about God, going on to stress that her relationship with the deity, "whatever it is, is personal." Another believer, Nancy, a convert from Catholicism, has this advice: "Keep it real simple. You don't have to literally pray . . . just check in consistently." Like Protestants and Catholics, large numbers of contemporary Jews make a distinction between faith, which is important to them, and religion, which they identify with obsolete theological ideas. "Few of the individuals to whom we spoke about God," write the authors of the most comprehensive survey, "seemed to draw on specific texts or ideas. Some had a minimal acquaintance with Jewish sources, but either were not confident enough to cite the sources with which they were familiar or felt that it would have been pretentious to do so. No one referred to religion courses they had had in college or the sources they had studied there."

Evangelical Christians, determined to spread the good news of the gospel, set a priority on reaching Americans where they are, and since where they are is submerged in the sensibility of self-help and recovery, that is where they bravely go. By contrast, mainline religions, including Catholics and Jews, tend to be more frankly elitist, a term meant not to suggest that they are antidemocratic but to call attention to a leadership structure in which a learned clergy is expected to teach and willing parishioners are expected to learn. Enough of the tutorial mission of mainline religions persists in the United States to produce marked differences between these mainline religions and more populistic styles of worship. Most mainline denominations, including non-Protestant ones, find, as did Bishop Wilkie of the Methodists, that one of their most important tasks is educational. If doctrine is lacking in mainline churches, it is not for lack of trying.

Yet trying can take the leaders of American mainline denominations only so far. Hindered in their efforts to teach doctrine by the anti-intellectualism of the culture around them, these leaders also have to deal with the consequences of their own liberalism. Consider the experience of a mainline believer named Betty Taylor. Betty is incredibly active in her Michigan church: "I'm doing vacation Bible school—I'm the director of that for the third year in a row. I'm on the Christian Education Committee. I just got off the Sunday Scheduling Committee." She is a Presbyterian, and proud to be one, but her pride has little to do with her denomination's beliefs. On the contrary, she likes her church because it allows "so much leeway" concerning doctrine. It is important to her that in a communicant's class she took, "the minister had encouraged questioning and arriving at your own conclusions about beliefs." Her experience illustrates the uncomfortable truth that encouraging people to think for themselves is usually not the best way to get them to think in doctrinally acceptable ways. If mainline religions insist that the great intellectual heroes of their traditions—the Calvins, the Luthers, the Knoxes, the Wesleys, the Ratzingers, the Murrays, the brothers Niebuhr, the Heschels—promulgated truths to which all believers should adhere, they will likely lose people with the energy and commitment of Betty Taylor. But if they want to keep people like her, they will have to make determined efforts to familiarize their members with their faith—and then prepare themselves for the inevitable disappointments that occur when Bible or Torah study becomes not a chance to engage with ideas but an opportunity to explore the self.

DEALING WITH DISAPPOINTMENT

When he studied American religion in the 1950s, Will Herberg came away disappointed. Citing, somewhat unfairly and decidedly out of context, President Eisenhower's 1952 declaration that "Our government makes no sense unless it is founded in a deeply felt religious faith—and I don't care what it is," Herberg asked if faith can matter if the content of faith matters so little. Losing all pretense of sociological objectivity, he answered that it could not. Practicing their religion in ways that allowed little room for "serious commitment" or "real inner conviction," Americans, Herberg wrote, could never understand the depth of passion that led so many of the faithful—Jesus, to be sure, but also Antigone or Thomas More—to die for their beliefs. "What should reach down to the core of existence, shattering and renewing, merely skims the surface of life," he concluded. "Religion thus becomes a kind of protection the self throws up against the radical demand of faith." Our faith in faith may have been strong, but our faiths themselves were not.

One can easily understand the frustration that Will Herberg felt as he observed Americans getting comfortable with their neighbors rather than right with God; in many contemporary American religious precincts, Antigone would have been asked if she wanted help in letting go of her obsession with her brother. Although I do not share Herberg's religious convictions, I do wonder why doctrine plays so little a role in the way Americans practice their faith. Belief, after all, should involve belief in something. It is not that I have come to admire fundamentalists, who insist on the priority of truth (as they see it) over all other considerations; most of them, in fact, send a chill up my spine. Yet, especially when compared to the religious practices of other conservative Christians, I do respect their willingness to stand against the emotionality of American culture in favor of ideas—strongly held ideas, to say the least—about who God is and why he asks so much of us. I just wish, even as I know that this is impossible, that they would be a lot more willing to engage in ideas with which they disagree instead of being so quick to proclaim them wrong or unchristian.

Fundamentalists will always be a minority, even among conservative Christians, and surely, given how disputatious they can be, this is not to be lamented. Nothing prevents Americans from deciding that their faith is so important to them that they are under an obligation to devote their lives to the study and application of their faith's particular teachings. But in overwhelming numbers, they have chosen not to do so, and despite frequent great awakenings, including the emergence of what has (confusingly) been called a "fourth great awakening" in contemporary times, they have chosen not to do so again and again. Each failure has resulted in jeremiads of disappointment from those who find, as if discovering the fact anew in each generation, that Americans prefer practical, commonsensical, and even materialistic concepts of religion to those driven by doctrinal or theological considerations. We need those jeremiads, for religion does command the pauses and reflections that make life meaningful. But, like ideologues in politics, there also comes a point at which the jeremiads turn sour and begin to tire. Will Herberg claimed that Americans were naïve to believe that they could create a religion "so innocently *man-centered.*" But he may have been naïve to think that people could continue to believe in the power of the religious doctrines that once inspired their ancestors when their society chews up ideas of any sort in order to digest them for widespread public consumption.

CHAPTER 4

TRADITION

WEAKEST LINKS

"The feeling one gets when they actually go up to read from the Torah is so intense," as one person who has been through the experience describes it. "It has to do with time. It has to do with connection from generation to generation. This is the book. This is the document that has been like the silver thread throughout the ages of Judaism. It's such a personal honor to stand before it and read a part." For this individual, to belong to a tradition is to become part of a chain, and the longer the chain, the more secure each individual link.

Tradition and religion have become so intertwined that the two words are often used as synonyms. Religion—a mighty fortress in some faiths, a rock of ages in others—stands there, impervious to change, a monument of transcendental truth. For those dismayed by the shallow glitter of the world around them, the traditionalism of religion is an anchor, while for those seeking to escape, it is more likely to resemble a prison. Love it or leave it—and many do both— tradition itself existed long before an individual comes into the world and will long survive that individual's death.

Yet the United States is a decidedly nontraditional society. It opens its doors to people fleeing from traditional countries. It contains only a minority of people living in what is nostalgically called the traditional family. It frequently rebuilds historical sites by equipping them with modern conveniences. Because Jews place such a

high value on tradition, they offer a particularly appropriate introduction to the ways in which all American religions try to honor
their past in a society that constantly looks to the future.

Consider the individual who found the experience of reading the
Torah so moving. As it happens, she made her comments while reflecting on her experience of an adult bat mitzvah, about as nontraditional a practice as one can find within Judaism. Where boys are
concerned, Jews can trace the ritual of reading from the Torah at age
thirteen, and then celebrating afterwards, to the thirteenth century—not all the way back to Moses, to be sure, but impressive
enough as the lengths of modern traditions go. To this day, the bar
mitzvah, for most Jews, is the one ritual that defines for them the
meaning of their tradition. Yet the bar mitzvah, at least as practiced
in the typically suburban Reform or Conservative synagogue, is a distinctly modern affair. There is, for one thing, no specific tradition for
celebrating the bar mitzvah on a Sabbath day during regular synagogue observance. In Europe, moreover, the bar mitzvah, primarily a
religious moment, was, in the words of one historian, "quiet, humble, . . . bereft of fanfare," hardly the often ostentatious celebration of
materialism it became in the United States. And it is not that regular
Sabbath worshipers witness, in the course of their observance, a
weekly bar mitzvah. It is more often the case that witnessing a bar
mitzvah is the reason for their Sabbath attendance. "Maintenance of
the bar and bat mitzvah monopoly," as one scholar of American
Jewry has written, "is a sine qua non for any synagogue movement,
and rabbis should accept the necessity of running 'birthday parties
for thirteen year olds.' The reality is that these events are the prime
reason for formal synagogue membership, as well as the major
source of Shabbat worshippers in many synagogues."

Even though contemporary bar mitzvahs are already less than
fully traditional, the woman who read from the Torah broke with tradition in two additional ways. First, she underwent a bat mitzvah, an
extension of the traditionally male bar mitzvah to women, and a
practice that dates only to 1922, when Mordecai Kaplan, the leader
of Reconstructionist Judaism, called his daughter Judith to the Torah.
Second, she performed the ritual as an adult, a wrinkle that has no
basis in Jewish tradition; this approach caught on after an episode of

The Dick Van Dyke Show in the 1960s featured a character longing for the ceremony he never had at age thirteen. Connected like a silver thread through the generations she may feel, but she feels it as she undergoes a ceremony whose connections to the past are fraying.

Traditions have always been important to Jews, so important that many Jews take considerable pains to adapt them to the circumstances of their modern lives. As this woman's experiences testify, modernity does not do away with traditions; if anything, a world in constant flux requires them. Traditions will always be with us. The interesting question is not whether religious traditions maintain themselves in the United States but how.

UNORTHODOX ORTHODOXY

If Jews emphasize the value of tradition among Americans, the Orthodox emphasize the importance of tradition among Jews. Orthodoxy appears in many forms in the United States, but it is common to divide it into two broad groups: the Modern Orthodox and the Haredi, or Ultra-Orthodox, a term that applies to sects like the Hasidim, the most well-known branch of which is known as the Lubavitchers. For both groups, the maintenance of Jewish traditions is their reason for being. Yet each, in its own way, reveals a distinctly nontraditional side.

The term Modern Orthodoxy testifies to the ways in which this particular approach to strict observance seeks to meet the world around it on relatively equal terms. Modern Orthodox Jews keep kosher, celebrate the holidays, observe the Sabbath, and attend synagogue, where the services are held in ways meant to conform to Jewish tradition. At the same time, they tend to live in neighborhoods that are open to people of other faiths, to include girls in school and study, to follow careers as professionals, and to encourage their young boys to wear colorful, knitted skullcaps instead of plain black ones. Modern Orthodox Jews can buy kosher TV dinners at their local supermarkets, sip vintage-dated kosher wines, enjoy soy-based products made to resemble bacon, and let their fingers do the walking through Yellow Pages tailored specifically for the Orthodox market. A religious denomination that began as a classic movement of the downtrodden—historically speaking, Reform Jews were upper and middle class, while Orthodoxy spread among the less well off—has been transformed into one capable of accommodating itself to the shopping-mall culture of suburban North America.

Such accommodations do not take place without raising difficult questions of interpretation. "Is Club Med Kosher?" asked an article in the Modern Orthodox magazine *Tradition* in 1985. Although modern techniques of food production and modern means of transportation make it possible for Orthodox Jews to take vacations much like the vacations of other Americans, the rules about what is permissible are ambiguous. For example, Modern Orthodox Jews in the late 1980s took to the idea of the Glatt Yacht, a cruise ship that circled Manhattan serving only kosher food. It was common for young people to dance together on these cruises. Reflecting a tendency among Orthodox Jews to interpret some traditions strongly (even while revising and transforming others), the agency responsible for the authenticity of the kosher designation withdrew certification. True, such social dancing had been permitted in Modern Orthodox synagogues, but now, the agency declared, "when we certify an establishment as kosher, it must meet all regulations of Jewish law, including the entertainment." Sometimes, in other words, the Modern Orthodox interpret the demands of tradition strongly, and sometimes those demands are relaxed. But however particular rules are interpreted, interpretation is always taking place.

Ultra-Orthodox Jews have little inclination to blend in with the society they see everywhere around them. This can take the form of turning their backs on gentiles, as happened when Ultra-Orthodox Jews opened a slaughterhouse in a rural Iowa town, but it can also take the form of conflicts—sometimes bitterly ugly conflicts—with Jews from other denominations, including the Modern Orthodox (who, in the view of the most Orthodox of American Jews, are insufficiently committed to *frumkeit,* or obedience to Jewish law). Yet for all its insistence on the power of tradition, Ultra-Orthodoxy, a product of eighteenth- and nineteenth-century romantic and nationalist movements in Eastern and Central Europe, is of recent historical vintage. So, consequently, are the rituals and practices that make it distinct. Jewish law is usually understood as codified in the Talmud, but the Ultra-Orthodox rely on a variety of other texts, including the Midrash, the Aggadah, the Jerusalem Talmud, and, for the more mystically inclined, the Kabbalah. Groups like the Lubavitchers have been led by charismatic leaders, whereas authority in Judaism has been traditionally been vested in words, not people. We are so used to seeing Ultra-Orthodox Jewish men dressed in black that we can be forgiven for not realizing that, in the interwar period, Orthodox Jews in Europe wore local garb—or for not knowing that the Talmud, which views black as a sign of mourning, specifies unstained white clothing. Most significant of all, Ultra-Orthodoxy, precisely because of its fundamentalist nature, searches for clear meanings in the Torah, when the entire tradition of Judaic learning—hence the not always complimentary adjective "Talmudic"—insists on the need for interpreting texts that often contain seemingly contradictory passages. Traditions, it has been said, are frequently invented, and one of those invented traditions, having as much to do with a reaction against liberalism and secularism among Jews as with unbroken links extending back to biblical times, was Ultra-Orthodox Judaism.

This should not be taken to mean that those who convert to Orthodox Judaism, in any of its versions, do so lightly; even when invented, traditions can impose heavy demands on those who honor them. There are, for the Ultra-Orthodox, the discomforts of wearing black clothes and dark fur hats (for men) or long-sleeve dresses (for women), even in the middle of summer. Then there are the requirements of keeping kosher, which, for all Orthodox Jews, is not just a matter of avoiding some foods in favor of others but of following elaborate rules about plates, silverware, dish washing, and restaurants. Then come the holidays, which can involve eating outside in a small hut even in inclement weather. Observing the Sabbath means refraining from travel or using electricity from sundown on Friday to sundown on Saturday; since dusk comes early during the winter, Orthodox Jews may find it impossible to hold regular nine-to-five jobs and thus to pursue anything resembling a career. And, for those who affiliate with it, Orthodoxy demands of its women that they undergo a ritual bath one week after their period ends before they can resume sexual activity with their husbands. This is not a tradition you join unless you are prepared to make the tradition central to every aspect of the way you live.

The traditions of Orthodoxy are not only demanding but also bereft of many of the rewards available to conservative believers of other faiths. Evangelical Christians have their own demanding restraints—from the regulation of sexuality to bans on dancing and drinking—but they also emphasize the "good news" associated with finding Jesus. Yet Orthodox Jews would find the weeping and therapeutic support-giving of evangelical and Pentecostal Christianity foreign to their religious practice. There is, in fact, little emotional release associated with Orthodox religious practice. Prayers, spoken in a foreign language, are mumbled and ritualistic. Little emphasis is placed on spiritual transformation; indeed, as one member of a Modern Orthodox congregation in Boston put it (through the use of a modern metaphor), "Spirituality does not compute in Orthodoxy. . . . It has a *goyish* [non-Jewish] ring to it." Evangelicals speak of how they leave church glowing with joy. It is not that Orthodox Jews necessarily leave synagogue sallow; singing and swaying—*shokeling,* in Yiddish—is part of their tradition. But the heart of Jewish religious practice is study, and for that task, the emotional aspects of Protestantism have little place.

Because the rituals are onerous and the immediate rewards few, many Jews turn away from Orthodoxy. For those who join or remain, the tradition offers an alternative to the hedonistic, freedom-filled world around them. At Bias Chana, a learning center for Lubavitcher women outside Minneapolis, female adherents clearly want an authoritative religion, one that the leaders of their movement are committed to providing. But nor is piety the sole source of their commitment to Ultra-Orthodoxy. "These women's explicit desire to get married," sociologist Lynn Davidman writes about them, "fits in with the agenda of the Lubavitch community, which in its zeal to promote the proliferation of Jewish religious families actually arranged marriages for its members." Although it seems like an ancient custom, moreover, arranging marriages can take on a modern flavor. Ultra-Orthodox Jews believe that there is a *bashert,* or destined one, that the matchmaker must make every effort to find. But there is also flexibility in the process. "You mean there can be more than one?" exclaims a Hasidic woman from Brooklyn. "Could be," replies the *shotkin*, or matchmaker. "Each person has a number of possible matches—the rabbis say three, or maybe ten—but there is always one who is the *richtige zivvug,* the optimal other half."

As the experiences of these women demonstrate, ultraconservative religions benefit from the ultraliberal nature of American society. Unwilling to participate in a culture of loose relationships and promiscuous sex, the women of Bias Chana and other Ultra-Orthodox communities choose not to have choices; their rabbis recognize that such freedom to choose, which can be a danger to any conservative religious movement, also enables the Lubavitch to grow. Yet it is also clear that Ultra-Orthodox women are often as much in search of community—a sense of belonging to an all-inclusive group—as they are in search of tradition. When the "tradition" of a society is constant change, as it is in the United States, it takes a certain decisiveness to find, and to be willing to justify, venerable practices that run so much against the grain of contemporary life.

The communal benefits of Orthodoxy help explain why the 1960s—a growth period for political radicalism and the counterculture—was also the period in which Orthodox Judaism shook off its lethargy and began to appeal to a whole new set of believers. Nor was this simultaneous growth of practices so seemingly at odds purely coincidental. In a study of one hundred and fifty new Modern Orthodox Jewish women, 70 percent of those who had been in their late teens or early twenties between 1966 and 1976 described themselves as attracted to the counterculture. (Another 10 percent were "red-diaper" babies, children of communist parents.) "I knew I had committed myself to Orthodoxy," one woman exclaims, "when I finally gave away my Bob Dylan records."

There are good reasons why so many Jews who breathed the radical air of the 1960s eventually turned Orthodox. Hippies, as a sociologist of American Orthodoxy has written, saw Orthodoxy "as one of several viable choices." In their quest for authenticity, these rebels believed that Orthodoxy shared much with Eastern religions: "its mysticism; its Chasidim and rebbes, whose relationship paralleled that of disciples and gurus; its special kosher diet, a parallel to the interest in macrobiotic diets and natural foods; a unique style of dress;

a far heavier emphasis on ritual than was found in established American religions." Many of these comparisons were in fact spurious; kosher food preparation, for example, is motivated neither by considerations of health nor by organic purity but by ritual. More importantly, most Orthodox leaders understood that seekers who lacked the commitment to Torah study had better seek elsewhere. Yet perhaps the countercultural acolytes who turned, however hesitatingly, to Orthodoxy, realized something about the movement that may have escaped its leaders: Even the most conservative religious movements in a liberal society become, willingly or not, rebels against an establishment they find complacent and cowardly, hardly a disposition that can rightly be labeled as traditional.

While it would be improper to include Orthodox Judaism as part of the counterculture, it would not be improper to suggest that strict religious movements have a countercultural side—and that it is precisely this distinctiveness from the dominant culture that constitutes one of their major sources of appeal. In many ways, this countercultural character is even more visible among the Ultra-Orthodox than among their Modern cousins. The Jews may be the chosen people, but by wearing clothing that stands out so radically from what everyone else around them is wearing, Ultra-Orthodox Jews let others know that they are choosing chosenness. Stigmas can be imposed by majorities on minorities, in which case they are a source of shame, but they can also be adopted by members of minority movements themselves and, as such, become a source of pride. In every aspect of their demeanor and comportment, Ultra-Orthodox Jews, whatever else they may be, are not assimilated Jews who have blended into the American mainstream, and they are not at all uncomfortable letting the rest of the world know that.

Ultra-Orthodoxy is countercultural in another way. Members of sectarian political groups, anxious to demonstrate their revolutionary credentials, often adopt a strategy of no enemies to the left (or right), as if only the extreme positions can be the genuine positions. A similar phenomenon takes place among the Ultra-Orthodox, as adherents aspire to be more traditional than the tradition requires. At times, the Ultra-Orthodox have separated men and women, not only in synagogue, which is required, but also at social events, which is not. A similar disposition is manifest in what has been called "exaggerated conformity," such as when converts lift their hands up over their heads during ritual washing, a practice traditionally restricted to rabbis. One historian describes a tendency in nineteenth-century Orthodoxy to "over justify" newly adopted, but seemingly traditional, religious practices, and one sees the same dynamic at work in these efforts by contemporary Ultra-Orthodox Jews, not only to mark themselves off from the rest of their society but also to distinguish themselves from other Orthodox Jews.

Although different in their choices, both Modern and Ultra-Orthodox Jews adapt to modernity, either by accepting many of its practices (as with the Modern Orthodox) or by engaging in deliberate choices to reject them (as with the Ultra-Orthodox). In so doing, they demonstrate the truth of the idea that the very concept of having a tradition is "a peculiarly modern notion" because in a truly traditional society, what we today call "tradition" would simply represent the natural order of doing things and, in that sense, would have no distinct existence. In the United States, it would seem, tradition never finds you. If you want it badly enough—and the Orthodox certainly do—you have to go out and find it yourself.

A MOVING TARGET

Because they try, however imperfectly, to invent traditions that run against the grain of modern society's emphasis on individual freedom, Orthodox Jews receive considerable sociological attention. But it is important to remember that they still represent the overwhelming minority of self-identified Jews, most of whom are Conservative or Reform (or who reject denominational labels entirely). The fact that these more popular denominations attach less importance to strict observance does not mean that they escape from the problem of how to honor tradition in a nontraditional society. It only means that the problem poses itself to them in a different way.

An important ritual for Jews involves kaddish, the memorial prayer for the dead. Like many requirements of Jewish observance, kaddish is governed by fairly strict rules: daily recital for eleven months after the death of a parent or child, thirty days of recital for other members of the family, and yearly markings of the death thereafter—all of which takes place in a minyan, or group of ten men (in some congregations, women can be included) over the age of thirteen. At Kehillath Achim, a somewhat typical Conservative synagogue, kaddish is extremely popular; in fact, members who do not come for regular synagogue service will come to kaddish, and some of them, through their experience, will become more observant Jews. There is no doubt that such significant moments as the death of a loved one lead people to appreciate the power of tradition and to want to be part of it.

At the same time, Kehillath Achim has its own nontraditional way of reciting kaddish. Not everyone understands the rules of observance, so some people recite it even when it is not required. The annual event is turned into a celebratory breakfast, complete with bagels and lox, to honor those who regularly met the other kaddish requirements, and "regularly" is given a broad definition by the rabbi to be as inclusive as possible. Although the kaddish prayer honors God in exalted terms, recital of the prayer can have important therapeutic benefits for those who have lost a loved one. Daily attendance, as one believer emphasizes, "helps set my day; it gives me a chance to shoot the breeze with a bunch of guys I see every day and feel close to, like family; it sets me straight, gives me a sense of rootedness." Kaddish works at Kehillath Achim, not because it carries forward an unchanging tradition, but because it becomes, in the words of the person who studied it, "a living social organism with its own life and its own evolving traditions."

Finding the right balance between tradition and innovation has proven to be difficult for Conservative Jews. For those who seek strong roots in tradition, Orthodoxy, especially in its modern forms, beckons. But for a far larger majority of Conservative Jews, innovation typically wins out; many Jews seek a faith that is, in one sociologist's words, "comfortable," which means that it generally possesses "a relaxed Jewish attachment, tied to both an untroubled sense of community and rootedness, as well as a tolerance of one's right to make religious and affiliational choices, to be attached by personal preference and not by obligation." Because it is under pressure from both a stricter and a looser side, sociologists now wonder, as they once did about the Orthodox, whether Conservative Judaism can survive. "We have found that a large fraction of Conservative homes and formal institutions are unable to pass along a vision of Jewish life that includes regular participation in public worship," one of them has written. "The result of these social processes is a steady decline in service attendance among Conservative Jews by generation in the United States and Canada." Among synagogue attenders, Conservatism retains its appeal; 47 percent of all households that join a congregation join a Conservative one, according to one estimate. Yet its location midway between Orthodoxy and Reform, once an advantage for Conservative Jewry, could turn into the disadvantage of lacking a firm enough sense of identity.

And then there is Reform Judaism, the least traditional of all. At Temple Shalom, the left-wing Reform synagogue on the West Coast, one of the rabbis refers to the wearing of the yarmulke as "mindless traditionalism." His comment was evoked by a controversy at the temple that originated when one member said she felt "shocked" to see the congregation's president wearing a yarmulke during high holiday service. Members of Temple Shalom were put in a bind because one of their leaders decided to return, however tentatively, to what was at one time a common, and decidedly harmless, Jewish tradition. On the one hand, the members associate traditional Jewish customs with forms of religion they wanted to reject; yarmulkes, from such a point of view, are, as one rabbi put it, "in the realm of *meshugas*," or crazy. On the other hand, they also believe in individual choice, and if a person wants to wear a yarmulke, can others rightly object? Searching for a solution, the congregation voted down a proposal to leave yarmulkes outside the sanctuary, for that proposal seemed too coercive, as if the Temple were endorsing their use. But nor did they forbid anyone from wearing a yarmulke if they felt strongly about it. "If someone wants to wear a yarmulke, let him bring his own," as one member concluded.

For Reform Jews like these, Judaism is not so much a religion as it is an ethical system. According to one of them, "the commitment of Jewish idealism to social change is the primary purpose of religion . . . otherwise religion is useless." Not all that certain what Judaism is—and even if they did know, not all that sure they wanted to be identified as religious Jews—these members of a Reform congregation honor tradition, but they honor it selectively. In the pick-and-choose form of religion so common in liberal Jewish circles, some members feel that the cruel treatment of animals in the Old Testament is "unJewish," another believes that the giving of the Ten Commandments by Moses was "counter to the democratic spirit of the Jewish tradition," and still another objects to the many priests in the Bible on the grounds that "Judaism invites the direct relationship of the individual with God."

Many Reform Jews have become more centrist in both their political and religious outlook since the 1970s, when Temple Shalom was in its heyday, and at least some of them would look back upon the attitudes expressed at that time with embarrassment. Still, selectivity with respect to tradition continues to be characteristic of many contemporary Jews. Those interviewed in one study, for example, are proud of their Jewish heritage, but they also take it for granted that the traditions associated with that heritage are options, there to be followed if they make sense, revised if they make only partial sense, and rejected entirely if they are perceived as antiquated or absurd. "The rules of tradition—which after all make ritual into ritual, separate it out from the flux of life—exist as guidelines or opportunities," write the authors of this study, "but exercise little compulsion or authority in and of themselves." To the traditionalist, this notion that tradition can be divorced from authority is absurd, for the whole point of binding yourself to a ritual is to make yourself part of something unchanging and therefore overpowering. But one woman, Suzanne, has an effective answer—or at least an answer that is effective for her. When she chooses a ritual, and when she then observes it, that ritual has a special meaning to her precisely because it stands out in a sea of nonobservance.

In a nontraditional society such as the United States, openness to change, which the Reform denomination certainly demonstrates, increases possibilities for increased market share. Unbound by a strict adherence to tradition, Reform Jews are especially well positioned to appeal to women—they took the lead in allowing them to become rabbis—and have been more receptive than other Jewish denominations to "outreach" programs designed to welcome non-Jewish spouses and the children of mixed marriages to Judaism. Unlike other Jews, moreover, Reform Jews have not rejected nontraditional marriage; in March 2000, the Central Conference of American Rabbis passed a resolution allowing Reform rabbis, if they wished, to perform same-sex weddings. ("Over the next few months," reads the newsletter of Beth Israel, a temple in West Hartford, Connecticut, "we hope that everyone will have the opportunity to meet Rabbi [Elissa] Kohen, Missy Sachs, her partner, and Bailey, their dog, and welcome them into our community," and this in a religion that once proclaimed that "the new is prohibited by the Torah.") Reform Judaism seems tailor-made for America's culture of choice; to cite just one example, San Francisco's Congregation Emanuel provides a "synaplex" experience: different Friday night services for different tastes, just as the nearby movie theaters offer many smaller screens instead of one large one. No wonder the appeal of Reform Judaism persists, and even grows, at a time when Christians tend to switch to more conservative denominations.

Although Reform Jews are the least traditional denomination within Judaism, their experiences complicate, rather than simplify, the relationship between tradition and modernity in the United States. Because Reform Jews exist in reaction to strict forms of the faith, those who reject tradition are paradoxically very much in the tradition of Reform Judaism; the dinner celebrating the first class of rabbis to graduate from the Reform Seminary of Cincinnati in 1883 deliberately featured such nonkosher food as shellfish and ice cream served after meat. And to the degree that Reform Jews turn and rediscover what they once rejected, they find themselves breaking with their tradition in order to become more traditional. Through the history of Reform Judaism, believers have discovered that their innovation has gone too far; at the beginning of the twentieth century, for example, Reform Jews brought back into prominence some traditions they had previously abandoned, such as the blowing of the *shofar* or celebrating the *succah*. The same process occurs today; the 1999 Statement of Principles for Reformed Judaism—only the third effort in the history of the denomination to define its mission—emphasized the teachings of the Torah, insisted on the importance of the Sabbath, and spoke of a special relationship to the Jewish people and to the state of Israel. It can hardly be surprising that in the aftermath of the Holocaust, Jews who live in an overwhelmingly Christian country and who witness up to half of their coreligionists marrying non-Jews, would want to preserve some aspects of their tradition, even if their religious beliefs are liberal ones. As pliable as traditions can be, there is a point beyond which reform has to stop or else there will be no traditions left to reinterpret.

The way Reform Jews walk the tightrope of tradition—leaning this way in the hope of attracting new members, even converts from other faiths, then leaning that way not to lose touch with Judaism altogether—suggests the problem all forms of Judaism have with tradition. Tradition is often viewed as a take-it-or-leave-it proposition; the tradition never changes, and the task of the individual believer is to link herself to it in the hopes of finding meaning or to remove herself from it in the expectation of finding freedom. But rarely do traditions work that way in the real world. Stricter denominations like the Ultra-Orthodox find that they sometimes have to move their traditions a bit closer to actual experience and at other times shift them a bit farther away. More accommodationist movements, like Reform Judaism, relax traditions in order to gain members, only to tighten them again so as not to lose them.

Tradition for contemporary American Jews is, in short, not a fixed but a moving target. The word *tradition* is a noun, but to do it justice, it should be imagined as a verb. One sociologist suggests the expression "traditioning" to capture the process by which individuals move in and out of traditions as they search for symbols and rituals that make sense out of their lives. As awkward as the term sounds, it does accurately convey the active role that Jews play in shaping the traditions that, in turn, shape them. The experiences of Jews in modern America teach everyone that traditions remain alive and well. And they also teach that traditions, in this day and age, take forms that people who once lived in traditional societies would barely be able to recognize.

BORN-AGAIN MAVERICKS

Jews sometimes adhere to their traditions even when they do not necessarily believe in God. The opposite is true of many of those Christians in the United States linked to evangelical Protestant churches. One does not become or remain an evangelical unless certainty of God's existence, tested, perhaps in more than one crisis, is reaffirmed and joyously proclaimed. Because of God's power to look directly into the human heart, faith, for evangelicals, requires neither bureaucratic outlets nor religious expertise. Protestantism began by challenging the religious authority of Catholicism, and ever since, its evangelical currents in particular have tended to emphasize sincerity of conviction over institutional fidelity, one reason why evangelical sects, especially Pentecostals, have been described by one historian as "mavericks at heart, careless of tradition, willing to drop old allegiances at the first hint of strain."

Evangelical Protestants are usually thought of as political conservatives, and those who lean toward fundamentalism will quickly add that they are theological conservatives as well. It seems a short step to conclude that the rise in the political influence of evangelicals since the 1970s reflects a determination to react against the corruptions of the modern world by reasserting the importance of traditional ways of life. There are some obvious truths to this conclusion, for the dislike and distrust of contemporary America's loose morality in evangelical circles is very real, even among the young. Yet any too-easy association between evangelicalism and traditionalism must be resisted. For if tradition means accepting the world into which you, and all your ancestors, were born, you can hardly rank tradition all that highly if you have to be born-again. Sometimes the faithful in the United States, like Orthodox Jews, have difficulty living the way their ancestors did because modernity and its seductions stand in their way. But for others, such as evangelicals, the way their ancestors lived could be the *wrong* way to live, especially if, in doing so, nothing is revived and little of worth is revealed. Traditionalism, for them, is not a moving target but barely a target at all. Jesus fills their hearts to live in the best way, which can be, but does not necessarily have to be, the oldest way.

To appreciate the rather limited role that tradition plays in America's evangelical subculture, it pays to visit Gwinnett County, outside Atlanta, for several years during the 1980s the fastest-growing county in the United States. With affordable land for housing developments and office parks, Gwinnett attracted upwardly mobile professionals, many of whom recently arrived in the Atlanta area in hopes of finding economic opportunities and a wholesome way of life for their children. No longer rural, certainly not urban, and not exactly suburban either, Gwinnett became a model for the ways in which Americans reject traditional ways of life in favor of an anarchic kind of sprawl that conforms to none of the rules by which communities are expected to organize themselves. In that sense, it also serves as an ideal place to investigate the way American Christians organize their religious lives. The American South is one region of the country in which evangelical Protestants are rapidly growing. But the religion growing in Gwinnett has little in common with any "old-time religion" that draws a line in the sand against change.

In 1929, reflecting its then-rural status, Dacula, one of Gwinnett's towns, could be said to contain well-established religious traditions: 65.8 percent of its residents were Baptist and 31.0 percent Methodist. Now, its denominations, in the words of a sociologist who studied the community, "included Christian and Missionary Alliance, Anglican, Assembly of God, Church of Christ, Christian Science, Episcopal, Nazarene, Presbyterian, numerous independent full gospel fellowships, Southern and independent Baptist, United Methodist, and African Methodist Episcopal," not counting the Eastern Orthodox, Unitarian, Roman Catholic, Jewish, and Hindu residents, nor those attracted to a Wiccan coven or to feminist spirituality groups. As if to demonstrate that exurban sprawl must be accompanied by its religious counterpart, the arrival of newcomers in Dacula unsettled all established patterns of religious allegiance, creating a congregation for each and every taste.

The conflicts over religion that take place in Dacula are not, as they were at the time of the Scopes trial, between civil libertarians and fundamentalists; they are between the more traditional religions of the town's old-timers and the more personalized religions of its newcomers. The former are likely to hold fast to the church of their upbringing. But the town's newer arrivals tend to be religious switchers. Some of the latter are searching for more casual approaches to faith, characteristic of time-starved commuters, while others gravitate towards charismatic forms of religious expression, including those inherited from the Pentecostal movements of the early twentieth century that speak to a deeper and more authentic experience than could be found in habitual Sunday worship. It is these more "conservative" evangelicals, and not the more "liberal" modernists, who pose the stronger challenge to the religious traditionalists among Dacula's old-timers. "When charismatics talked of being saved or 'born again' and baptized in the Holy Spirit, traditionalists felt threatened and condemned as religious illiterates by the charismatics," a sociologist reports. "In response, the traditionalists accentuated the actions that they had always seen as representing Christianity, in turn calling the charismatics hypocrites because their exclusionary language and practices did not demonstrate acceptance and love." It is as if the disdain for established forms of faith demonstrated by the founders of Pentecostalism extended its legacy straight into the cul de sacs of postmodern America.

Charismatics and old-timers played out their conflicts at Hebron Baptist, the largest and one of the most evangelical churches in Dacula, attracting more worshipers than there are people in the town. Megachurches like Hebron Baptist are, in their commitment to an evangelical understanding of faith, attractive to strict religious believers like Dacula's charismatics. But hoping to bring into worship the unchurched, they also are reluctant to identify with any of Protestantism's many traditions and, even to some degree, with Christianity itself. For example, Willow Creek, America's most famous megachurch, located outside Chicago, displays no cross on its building, but this does not mean it lacks one. "We do have a cross," as a tour guide explained. "We bring it out for special occasions, like baptism." This openly strategic way of thinking about religious identity is fairly common in evangelical circles; one survey of megachurches found that more than half of them refrain from placing religious symbols in prominent places.

Trying to combine appeals to both the very religious and the religiously suspicious, megachurches lean forward toward the experimental rather than backward toward the old-fashioned. "Tradition, according to many pastors," writes the author of the most authoritative examination of American megachurches, "poses an unnecessary barrier for seekers who are trying to bridge the gap between their relatively secular daily lives and the evangelical teachings of seeker churches." It is not that all traditions can be dispensed with; clearly the Bible and belief in the divinity of Jesus are retained. But leaders of these churches see no need to hold fast to the idea that the tradition in which a person was raised is, other things being equal, the best tradition for that person now. Nor do they put much stock in sticking by time-tested routines. Back in Dacula, the minister of Hebron Baptist, Bryant Quinn, is determined not to let tradition stand in the way of his efforts to recruit new members. Recognizing how busy some of the exurbanite commuters in Atlanta can be, he organized Saturday night services for them. "In doing this, we are showing that Hebron is willing to break with tradition," he says. "We have to understand that the message of Christ is the same, but the methods of delivering that message are not sacred."

The evangelical churches found in Gwinnett County, Georgia, are relatively conventional and appeal to newly prosperous white, middle-class, professional families. An even more dramatic example of the break with tradition among conservative Protestants can be found in churches that deliberately set themselves up to attract nontraditional members in nontraditional ways. One does not expect to find such a church affiliated with the Southern Baptist Convention, among the most conservative denominations in the United States, but, then again, Mosaic in Los Angeles is full of surprises. Mosaic is Baptist enough in its theology and practices to count as a conservative church; women, for example, cannot become church elders, receive ordination, or baptize believers, and the church takes conservative positions on the issue of homosexuality. Many of Mosaic's members, moreover, come from evangelical backgrounds and consider themselves obligated to spread the word of the Lord. Reflecting the historic patterns of racial segregation that divided Baptists, Mosaic has relatively few African Americans among its membership. But nothing else about the church resembles popular impressions of what a Southern Baptist congregation is like.

You cannot actually go to Mosaic because it does not have a building. It did have one—actually the high school made famous by *Stand and Deliver*, the story of exceptional teacher Jaime Escalante—but Mosaic now meets in two places: the auditorium of San Gabriel High School on Sunday mornings and, on Sunday evenings—of all places for Baptists to gather—the Los Angeles Entertainment Center, a nightclub once owned by the rock star Prince. (When not rented out to Mosaic, the nightclub is one of the favorite spots for parties hosted by Michael Jordan or Shaquille O'Neal.) Mosaic, despite its paucity of African Americans, may be the largest multiethnic church in the United States, its membership fairly evenly divided among whites, Latinos, and Asians. Roughly a third to a half of those attracted to the church work in the media and entertainment business. "We have people who lean toward innovation, toward change, toward invention, toward risk, toward adventure," says Mosaic's lead pastor Erwin McManus, an immigrant from El Salvador who preaches in flawless, idiomatic English. "We tend to filter out into other churches people who would like stability, security, and predictability."

In its desire to be relevant to young Angelinos who tend to lead a fast-paced life, Mosaic aims to give its religious practices a contemporary, rather than a traditional, feel. One Sunday service in April 2002, devoted to emphasizing the importance of opening up one's heart to Jesus, began with a welcome video, followed by periodic simulated heartbeats booming out of the sophisticated loudspeaker system, worship songs sung by a hard-driving rock band, a short dramatic presentation, the first part of Pastor Erwin's sermon, an audio presentation, the sermon's second part, a dance number, the conclusion of the sermon, and then the invitation and collection. Another session in the high school, designed to illustrate how human beings are earthly creatures and therefore not all that different under the skin, featured a dance in which four men jumped out on the stage all covered with mud, slowly revealing to the audience that each was of a different race. The service I attended in August 2002 was devoted to exploring the ways young people could "plug in" to the church and its many activities. After the usual contemporary Christian music, Pastor Erwin offered what can only be called a riff on Luke 9:61–62, actually a rather sober passage in which Jesus tells a potential follower who simply wants to say good-bye to his wife that he is therefore unfit for the Lord's service. As he finished, a group of young people dressed as cheerleaders jumped out onto the stage calling out the letters for "pluggie," a church member dressed as an electrical plug, all designed to illustrate the evening's theme. It was not quite avant-garde theater, but it did, from the response of the audience, seem to make the point.

"The move towards what is fresh, new, and popular is intended to increase legitimacy that any message heard at Mosaic is relevant to people today," writes one of the pastors at Mosaic. That objective is fulfilled not only by the ways in which members attempt to display their artistic talents—whether they lie in film, art and sculpture, or contemporary music—but also the ways in which ethnic customs are recognized. One Wednesday a month, some four hundred Mosaic members gather to celebrate the Lord's Supper. If someone is being sent on an overseas mission to India, nan instead of bread will be used to represent Christ's body; when the destination is Africa, drum music and woven prayer mats will be introduced. Unlike megachurches, where the pews have been made as comfortable as possible, Mosaic threw them out completely; couches, bean bags, love seats, and lounge chairs furnished the seating for Sunday-evening events at the building Mosaic no longer owns. Mosaic's culture is not for everyone; people seeking a more traditional religion usually leave, which means, among other things, that the church is more attractive to single people than to two-and three-generation families. Mosaic's leadership takes the word of the Lord seriously, but they also understand that to thrive in a nontraditional city like Los Angeles, they need to be responsive to the environment around them. (Mosaic, evangelical to its core, is in the process of planting churches in Manhattan and Seattle.)

Evangelicals can be accused of many things, including their relative failure (until recently) to take questions of social justice seriously, their flirtations with anti-Catholicism and anti-Semitism, and their suspicion of modern science, including Darwinism. But they cannot be accused of being stick-in-the-muds determined to turn their back on progress in favor of old-fashioned ways. Early in their history, evangelicals were prepared to abandon tradition for the sake of doctrinal purity. Now they are prepared to abandon tradition for the sake of organizational growth. Revivalism and traditionalism are, and probably always have been, incompatible. Megachurches, as well as innovative congregations like Mosaic, are the inevitable result. And no one knows where it will end. "No church, according to my research, had established guidelines regarding how much innovation, such as incorporating therapeutic categories into messages, is appropriate," writes sociologist Kimon Sargeant in his study of megachurches. As one pastor puts it, "We don't have a statement that says we'll only go this far. I think we'll do whatever it takes, as long as it's biblical."

To point out the innovative side of conservative Protestantism is not to undermine the importance of its appeal to traditional values; like Orthodox Jews, fundamentalists and evangelicals want to live a different kind of life than the rest of America and find in their faith a way to do so. The fact that evangelicals approach their faith in such innovative ways, however, simply underscores how dynamic conservative religion in the United States has become. Even the increasing political influence of conservative Protestantism's emphasis on moral traditionalism reflects this paradox. From its modern emergence in the 1920s, fundamentalism and evangelicalism distrusted active political participation. Had conservative Protestants adhered to this traditional preference for personal salvation over political activism, they would never have become involved in highly public protests against abortion, divorce, and other evils they associate with secular culture. Without their willingness to break with tradition, in other words, there would have been no mass movement against *Roe v. Wade,* no revitalization of the Republican Party, and, most likely, no presidency of George W. Bush. Conservative Protestants broke with their past to change the world around them, perhaps not realizing how much they themselves would be changed along the way.

BEYOND THE SCARIEST SACRAMENT

Catholics have roughly fifteen hundred more years of tradition to work with than Protestants. They have a time-tested organizational structure called the Papacy charged with the task of maintaining the credal teachings of the church. Explicitly linked to ideas about natural law, which posit timeless universal principles that do not depend upon circumstances of time and place to establish their truth, Catholics do not subject their teachings to popularity tests or the decisions of majorities. Those searching for traditionalists with sufficient resources to resist the hedonistic and relativistic temptations of modern American life often look to Catholics to provide a kind of ballast. As Peter Berger wrote in 1967, "Catholicism, for reasons intrinsic to its tradition, has tried hardest in maintaining a staunchly resistant stance in the face of secularization and pluralism, and indeed has tried down to our own century to engage in vigorous counterattacks designed to re-establish something like Christendom at least within limited territories." Or, as the theologian Stanley Hauerwas, a Methodist, puts it more succinctly, "Catholics, more than any other people, must resist the presumption of modernity."

In the United States, a society that places so little value on tradition, Catholics have often been treated as less likely than other religious groups to join the long march toward upward mobility and suburbanization. Whether described as "Polish peasants" or as "urban villagers," American Catholics—particularly the ethnic, working-class, machine-based ward heeling Catholics of Northeastern and Midwestern cities—were usually portrayed as more committed to what sociologists habitually call the gemeinschaft values of blood-based solidarity than to gesellschaft understandings of meritocratic advancement and impersonal standards of justice. There is some justice in that viewpoint; the urban parishes of 1950s Catholicism were more "old world" in their attitudes toward the traditions of the Church than the contemporary middle-class, suburbanized parishes of their children and grandchildren. In fact, an anthropologist who studied St. Thaddeus, a working-class parish in a primarily Polish section of Detroit in the 1970s, found at least some older parishioners more traditionalist than the hierarchy, especially after Vatican II. "Archdiocesan attempts to promote a re-examination of traditional religious beliefs and practices, to suggest that being a 'good Christian' is based more on 'putting Christianity into practice,' and less on fear or such traditional criteria as attending Sunday mass and receiving the sacraments," he writes, "were relatively unsuccessful. . . . To raise questions on what one was taught by nuns and priests was viewed as sinful if not sacrilegious. In short, you lived your faith; you didn't ask why."

The bewilderment this anthropologist found among older Catholics at St. Thaddeus illustrates the dilemmas facing all Catholics in the aftermath of Vatican II. Catholicism has long been a traditional religion in two senses of the term: It sought to hold fast to unchanging conceptions of worship, and it respected the authority of a hierarchy responsible for preserving the faith. Vatican II drove a wedge between these two forms of traditionalism. The reforms of the early 1960s overturned many of the traditional ways in which the liturgy was celebrated, often to the dismay of more conservative believers. But for conservative believers to reject those reforms in the name of continuity also meant rejecting the authority of the hierarchy that had endorsed them, indeed that had used its considerable power to put them into practice. At the same time, more liberal Catholics who found themselves appreciating the changes introduced by Vatican II also found themselves in the odd position of defending papal authority. When radical changes are supported by a long-established hierarchy, no one knows what it means to be either a traditionalist or a modernist. No wonder, then, that Catholic conservatives often find themselves in disagreement with the hierarchy on issues such as capital punishment, thereby relying on the same tendency to interpret seemingly authoritative teachings for their own purposes that they identify with the Catholic left, while Catholics who believe in abortion or gay rights, and in that sense are modern, often hold fast to their inherited identity as Catholics.

Despite such difficulties of interpretation, however, the Notre Dame Study of Catholic Life since Vatican II is correct to conclude that even active Catholics are "by no means 'traditional' in their attitude toward church teachings, policy, and priorities." Whether or not Catholics are charged with a special responsibility to oppose modernity—there does seem something off-kilter about one particular religion being assigned such a role—they themselves have chosen to be as modern as other religious believers in the United States.

So rapidly has tradition been abandoned within American Catholicism that many of the practices associated with the faith have been increasingly hollowed out from within. Historian Robert Orsi has written of the "intense devotional creativity and improvisation in American Catholic culture" that characterized the religious life of his parent's generation, but in today's world, one study found that 61 percent of religiously active Catholics never pray with a rosary, 76 percent never engage in the novena (nine consecutive evenings of prayer), 44 percent never participate in the Stations of the Cross, and 53 percent never attend Benediction. Another survey discovered that far more Catholics pray privately (77 percent) than say devotions to Mary or other saints (29 percent) or finger the rosary (20 percent). And among younger Catholics, the figures are even more striking; for both Latinos and non-Latinos, more said that they had participated in a meditation group or meditated on their own in the past year than had attended a Eucharistic adoration or Benediction.

Declining interest in, and practice of, the devotions has been accompanied by a decrease in the practice of the sacrament that, for an earlier generation, most seemed to characterize the faith—confession, or, as it is called after Vatican II, the Sacrament of Reconciliation. According to one estimate, 38 percent of American Catholics in 1965 said that they attended confession once a month, compared with 38 percent who, in 1975, said that they never went at all. It is not hard to understand why. One devout younger Catholic speaks of her dislike of "walking into a dark, quiet church and going into a booth." Her parish, Blessed Sacrament, had gone over to general confession during Lent, and she loved it. "There were so many young people it was wonderful. To me it was a whole different experience, going to confession. I really liked it. It was collective, but then you could go by yourself to a priest. . . . It was a way to feel welcome into the whole thing, calming you down before you go up to confession." Many Catholics share this believer's distaste for the confessional. In his account of St. Brigid's, a thriving Catholic church, the journalist Robert Keeler interviewed many older parishioners who viewed confession as "the scariest sacrament: a sweat-inducing ordeal in a dark, closetlike box, where the sinner kneels and waits for the sound of a small panel to be slid back, revealing behind a screen the fuzzy outline of a priest who may or may not act with compassion." Against the warmth that contemporary religious believers expect, traditional confession, associated as it is with the dark and the dismal, does not stand much of a chance.

Despite, or perhaps because of, the decline of traditional confession, the hopes of spiritual leaders at St. Brigid's are high. "What we call the quality of the confession is vastly improved," as the Reverend Francis X. Gaeta—Father Frank—puts it. People are no longer preoccupied by sin; instead, they use the opportunity provided by confession to examine their personal relationship with God. This seems like the typical pattern nationwide. "There seems to be movement away from a 'checklist' form of Confession in favor of longer personal discussions of guilt and healing," write the authors of the Notre Dame Study of Catholic Life. Confession remains one of the key aspects of religious practice that differentiates Catholics from other religious believers, but it is no longer surrounded by traditional rituals that reinforce the authority of the Church and accentuate the penance of the believer, despite John Paul II's apostolic letter of May 2002, "Misericordia Dei," which discouraged forms of group confession many believers find attractive. In the aftermath of the Church's pedophilia scandal, moreover, which has not only brought into question priestly authority but also has made Catholics even more reluctant to enter traditional confessionals, old-fashioned confession, in the words of one observer, is on its way to the "endangered species list."

Like many Catholic parishes in the years since Vatican II, St. Brigid's has also had to accommodate traditional Catholic teachings about marriage and the family—marriage is also a sacrament in the Catholic faith—to the realities of modern life. Mary and Ron Grossi speak of the experience they had in preparation for their 1969 marriage, especially the three-to-four-hour session dealing with the Church's teachings on marriage and sexuality. (Many older Catholics remember Cana Conferences, named after the site of a wedding in Galilee observed by Jesus.) "It seemed like a very long time—I mean, to be talked at," Mary says. "A young priest spoke for most of the afternoon, and then a doctor came in with some charts and talked about sexuality," Ron adds. "No dialogue at all." They don't do marriage counseling at St. Brigid's that way anymore; in fact, given the realities of dual-career jobs and commuting time from Long Island to

Manhattan, fewer and fewer couples show up. Those that do are asked not just to reflect on God's grace but to articulate what they plan to do with their credit cards once they are married. Meeting together with married couples (instead of with a priest), the newly engaged couples are treated as mature adults with views of their own. And church elders refuse to lecture to them on the fine points of church teachings. "We did not put our personal feelings or stands on abortion or birth control in front of them," the wife of one of the married couples says. "Unless we are asked directly about these matters, we don't really discuss them. I am, of course, anti-abortion, and so is my husband, but you can waste a lot of time and get into heated discussions about right to life."

Not all of the sacraments are in decline in American Catholicism; some are actually flourishing. Among Catholics who attend Mass, the proportion of those who receive communion has been increasing. As parishes become more involved with people dying of AIDS, moreover, the sacrament of annointing the sick—once called "Extreme Unction"—is regaining its popularity. Catholics who feel that their church is stern and unforgiving tend to shun its traditional practices, while those who feel it is caring and concerned participate with considerable enthusiasm, choosing among its various traditions and investing considerable energy in applying those that make sense to them to the realities of the world around them.

Despite the transformation of traditional attitudes on the part of middle-class Catholic believers, there is one ray of hope for Catholic traditionalism; in important ways, Latino immigration has given new life to forms of religious traditionalism that non-Latino Catholics have been abandoning. Compared to other Catholics, Latinos, conclude the authors of one important study of American Catholicism, "had greater participation in personal devotions of many kinds, including making the Stations of the Cross, saying the rosary, wearing medals and scapulars, keeping images of saints in the home, having altars in the home, having a car or home blessed, and carrying out *promesas* (promises) in return for divine favors." Immigration from Latin America to the United States swelled just after the reforms of Vatican II began to take effect, and there is reason to believe that just as non-Latino Catholics were absorbing the impact of those reforms,

Latinos were by and large ignoring them. Indeed, only 27 percent of the Latinos interviewed in one study had even heard of Vatican II, compared to 56 percent of other Catholics.

Some of the ways in which the religious practices of American Catholicism have been influenced by Latino immigration can be seen at St. Peter's, a parish in San Francisco's Mission District. "This is an Irish parish," said one member to one of her priests as Spanish-speaking parishioners began to arrive in the 1950s. "Not anymore, it isn't," the priest responded. He was right. St. Peter's retained its primarily Irish character until the mid-1960s, but eventually, new arrivals from Mexico, Nicaragua, and El Salvador transformed St. Peter's into a church having more in common with Third World religion than with suburban American Catholicism. Most of these arrivals, as well as Tagalog-speaking Filipinos, whose arrival gave St. Peter's a trilingual flavor, held fast to traditional Catholic devotions, such as novenas, triduums, and missions, and they gave the parish's piety a distinctly Marian cast. In the late 1970s, new copastors were appointed to St. Peter's, and they encouraged the trend. Under their leadership, a religious-goods store was opened at the church where members could buy their rosaries and holy pictures. On Ash Wednesday and Good Friday, parish leaders took the opportunity to emphasize the sufferings experienced by Jesus. Young people staged the Way of the Cross to large crowds. Statues of Our Lady of San Juan, originally from the Mexican state of Jalisco, spread throughout San Francisco's Mission District, attracting huge crowds that attended Mass and celebrated with a mariachi band. "If these things are important to these people," one of the parish's priests says, "then, first of all, let's find out what is of value in these things, and affirm them."

Although many Catholics from Latin America are more traditional in their religious practices than the grandchildren of the Irish and Polish immigrants that came before them, their traditionalism is also of a different sort. Earlier generations of Catholic immigrants tended to be conservative in their politics as well as in their religious practices; many Italian Americans became Republicans, and even though most Irish were Democrats, they were conservative on cultural matters and in their views on foreign policy. Immigrants from

Latin America, by contrast, have often experienced political repression in their home countries, and even when they have not, they are generally greeted in the United States by an activist clergy motivated by strong views about social justice. This was certainly the case at St. Peter's, which through the 1970s was identified with the left-wing causes that are so prominent a feature of politics in San Francisco. (In St. Peter's more radical days, its activist priests used traditional symbols and religious practices as part of their political protests, such as the effort by one priest to lead a Stations of the Cross that stopped to pray at sites chosen to represent the military-industrial complex.) But even more conventional communities witness considerable political activism on the part of Latino Catholics; San Antonio, Texas, for example, is the home base of Ernesto Cortes, a community organizer trained in the Saul Alinsky tradition, and Cortes anchors his activities in Texas's Latino Catholic parishes.

In some cases, moreover, Latinos contribute directly to the modernizing forces transforming all of America's religious traditions. St. Pius X, located in El Paso, Texas—which the liberal Catholic writer Paul Wilkes cites as "not only one of the most outstanding Hispanic parishes in America, but one of the best, *period*"—is anything but traditional in its religious practices. Members are strongly encouraged to become involved with the parish's many ministries that deal with issues ranging from AIDS counseling to personal enrichment to young singles groups. Members speak of their religion, not in terms of the church and its requirements, but in terms of their own spiritual quests; "Father Arturo," one member says of St. Pius X's priest Father Bañuelas, "didn't teach me to be a Catholic; he taught me how to have a faith." Perhaps because it appeals to second generation Latinos, who are generally not as religiously traditionalist as their parents, the impact of Vatican II can clearly be seen in this parish, especially in the ways in which lay involvement is encouraged. "We need to make changes, especially for Hispanic Catholics," says Father Bañuelas, because "we are losing them to other churches." His solution is to reject Eurocentric Catholicism, not in favor of old-fashioned Catholicism but a new mixture that combines Catholic teaching, elements of Latin American popular worship, and the typically North American language of religious seeking. This particular parish, excellent as it is, may not be typical of Latino worship in the United States, but it does serve as an interesting effort to be pre–Vatican II and post–Vatican II simultaneously, combining traditional and modern into something resembling both—and neither.

As the children and grandchildren of the wave of post-1965 immigrants from Latin America marry, achieve some degree of upward mobility, and raise families, their liberalism in politics is likely to influence their conservatism in religion rather than the other way around. Paul Wilkes recounts that when he visited St. Pius X, he heard many stories of conversion, "not conversions to Catholicism," as he puts it, "but conversions *within* Catholicism." All Catholics in the United States have eventually converted the religions they brought with them from abroad, and there is every reason to expect that the same will be true of those who have recently come from Latin America.

AN INNOVATIVE GOD

It remains an article of faith among many commentators on American politics that religious believers are in the forefront of a determined effort to restore traditional morality to the country. As the journalist Michael Barone interpreted the election of 2000, "The single greatest divide in American politics is that the Bush coalition consists of people who are religious and respect traditional morality while the Gore coalition consists of people who are not traditionally religious and favor a more relativistic morality." From such a perspective, believers are capable not only of saving their own souls but also of saving their society. Because they are so old-fashioned in their approach to tradition, they can help prevent the United States from careening in the wrong direction toward change at any price.

Yet Barone's conclusion takes insufficient cognizance of the realities of actual religious experience in the United States. "There is no conservative tradition in America," the late historian of religion William McLoughlin once wrote, "because God is not a conservative. God is an innovator. American culture is thus always in the making but never complete. It will be completed, according to one of our most cherished cultural myths, at the end of human time." McLoughlin is speaking of Christians, but his point holds for non-Christians as well, and it holds for all of them more now than at any time in America's past. The United States has conservatives aplenty, but it lacks traditionalists, if for no other reason that so many religious conservatives are the inventors of new forms of religious practice.

It is therefore incorrect to believe that, just because American politics has turned to the right in the years since Ronald Reagan occupied the White House, American culture will as well. In fact, the opposite may well turn out to be true; even voters attracted to the Republican Party because they believe that divorce rates are too high and pornography too easily available sustain through their religious practices a culture that continually upsets the old in favor of the new. The overwhelming majority of believers do not view their faith as requiring them to be against change. Inventive in the way they adapt their religions to the temptations and also the opportunities offered by the modern world, they have contributed far more to the dynamism that has long characterized their society than they have resisted it in the name of unchanging ways of life.

CHAPTER 5

MORALITY

FAITH AND PERSONAL MORALITY

"Citizens who are steeped in the strengths of their freely chosen religious beliefs," William L. Simon Jr., a Catholic businessman, unsuccessful candidate for governor of California, and the son of the former secretary of the treasury of the United States, told the Heritage Foundation in September 2000, are "people who, day-in and day-out, do their best to live responsibly, provide for their families, and respect the liberties and rights of their fellow-citizens." By emphasizing beliefs freely chosen, Simon rejected the view of those nineteenth-century Christians who insisted that, to be a moral society, America first had to be a Protestant one. But he did express a widely shared opinion that people must adhere to one religion or another, lest they slide off toward self-regarding, if not self-destructive, behavior.

Yet a moment's reflection ought to reveal how complicated the relationship between religion and moral behavior actually is. People who are saved are usually saved from something, which is why the confessions of those who have found God constitute a veritable catalog of immoral behaviors, and while we might want to believe, and they might want us to believe, that their discovery of God's power changed all that, their accounts, save those of saints such as Augustine, are not always persuasive. Everyone in the United States, religious or not, lives in a world in which moral choices can be bewildering and their outcomes not always predictable. Both morality and religion are too dynamic for any one-to-one relationship between them to remain stable for any long period of time.

FROM SUBMISSION TO EMPOWERMENT

Questions of gender offer one illustration of how complicated the relationship between faith and morality can be. Among religious conservatives, or at least among their leaders, no other change in the nature of American life is held to be as responsible for America's slide into moral despondency as the movement launched by large numbers of women for greater equality. Feminism, they believe, is immoral at its core, for it asks women to put their own needs ahead of their loved ones—as well as ahead of God's clear instructions. "The woman in the Garden of Eden," conservative activist Phyllis Schlafly has written, "freely decided to tamper with God's order and ignore His rules. She sought her own self-fulfillment. She decided to do things her way, independent of God's commandment." The only cure, therefore, is a return to traditional gender roles ordained by God. "Much of the conflict in the modern family," writes the astonishingly popular Christian author Tim LaHaye along similar lines, "is caused either by misunderstanding of or by the refusal to accept the role each member was designed by God to fulfill. . . . It is essential to family harmony that the wife submit to her husband's leadership." Faith, from the perspective of these writers, serves not only matters spiritual but also matters secular; in LaHaye's words, it can "insulate the Christian home against all evil forces." Women need to turn to Jesus in order to turn away from feminism; by paying more attention to their families, they will pay less to themselves, thereby moving American society from its dangerous preoccupation with the quest for individual liberation.

In June 1998, the Southern Baptist Convention, as if influenced by such conservative views, altered its "Faith and Message" to recommend that the wife should "submit herself graciously" to the husband. But no sooner did it adopt such a recommendation than Baptists throughout the country reacted by substituting the notion of "mutual submission" between husbands and wives for the "wifely

submission" emphasized by their denomination. Behind that reaction lies a story that has received too little attention; conservative religious devotion, in its own particular way, encourages women to
explore their own needs. Of course this does not happen the way it
does among liberals and feminists; in those quarters of American
life, political movements outside the church encourage women to
seek changes within it. In conservative religious circles, by contrast,
the process usually works the other way around: Encouraged by their
faith to witness and worship, conservative women develop sufficient
self-confidence to become dissatisfied with a purely submissive role
in society. In theory, or at least in Phyllis Schlafly's theory, faith is
supposed to reinforce a personal morality emphasizing obedience. In
practice, it gives the faithful a sense of empowerment.

Many of the churches to which conservative religious believers belong, unlike mainline and liberal congregations, do not permit women
to serve as clergy. Because such policies are so close to the very definition of conservative religiosity and its way of conducting its affairs,
women who belong to these churches typically find this kind of gender discrimination acceptable. Women need not be pastors, one conservative Protestant woman believes, because they are so active in
other forms of church activity: "We have a counseling ministry
here. . . . We have our pro-life group. We have our single parents
group—single parents who minister to other single parents. . . . We
have women counselors who counsel women in the prayer room."
Conservative Christian women are often quick to cite arguments
about "male headship"—the Biblically based idea that men should
properly rule over women—as the grounds for their support of distinct roles for men and women within the church. "We believe that a
woman cannot have spiritual authority over a man," as an evangelical
named Rhonda puts it, "because God has given that role to a man." In
their internal structure, conservative churches convey a picture of the
world as it looked before feminism made its appearance in the world:
Men preach, while their wives entertain and encourage volunteer
work. It is as if these churches, by resisting larger social trends to include women in the ministry, proudly identify themselves as anti-
dotes to the immorality they see everywhere around them.

Missed by this picture, however, is the fact that large numbers of conservative Christian women accept an all-male leadership of their churches not because they believe that men are natural leaders but because, as strong women, they find men too insecure to be directly challenged by assertive women. Consider Parkview Evangelical Free Church in Texas. Like so many conservative congregations, Parkview does not allow women to serve as pastors; indeed, it goes farther and excludes them from serving on the Elders Board and even from teaching Sunday-school classes. Yet Parkview does allow women-only Bible-study groups, one of which is led by a woman named Angela. "The male ego," Angela asserts, "is like a balloon with slow leaks, or like a bucket with holes in it. If wives don't build up their husbands, then their husbands' egos get soft and men become susceptible to the cute little girl next door or to the lady at work." As committed a conservative Christian as one can find, Angela nonetheless scoffs at the idea that a proper understanding of gender roles can be found through a literal reading of the Bible. In a Bible-study class, she tells the assembled women that "Many of the verses in Proverbs refer to a 'son.' I will often change those references to read 'daughter,' because I think it is important that God's message be personalized for us." Considering her outgoing personality and rhetorical abilities, women like Angela at churches like Parkview are clergy in everything but name.

As Angela's work indicates, it is not a rebellion against the empowerment of females that has enabled conservative Christianity to grow by leaps and bounds; it is the unleashing of female power itself. "Shoot, we do everything," says a conservative believer named Marisa. To be sure, the man is the overseer as God intended, another holds, "but none of these men would be anywhere without the support of their wives." Men do important things outside the church, like evangelization, she continues, but "the women, in my opinion, keep the church going." The more these women talk, the clearer it becomes that they are feminists of a particular sort.

In secular circles, feminists do not speak with one voice: There are radical feminists who denounce capitalism and patriarchy, liberal feminists who seek equality between men and women in wages or public life, and "difference" or "essentialist" feminists who argue that women's morality tends to be more caring and cooperative while men's morality is more principled and abstract. Conservative

Christian women are not radicals politically and, unconcerned about gender equality in the church leadership, neither are they liberals. But they do resemble difference feminists. Had they been given the opportunity to read feminist writers like Carol Gilligan, who argues that women approach morality more in terms of relationships than in terms of rules, many conservative Protestant women would find much with which they agree.

When Gilligan wrote about women's distinctive approaches to moral conduct, little did she know that transformations in the practice of American religion would strengthen her thesis. Nor could she have imagined that her ideas about women experiencing morality through personal relationships would in particular overlap with at least two of the more distinctive features of conservative Protestantism: an emphasis on the emotional side of faith and a preference for a direct relationship with the deity over more bureaucratic and institutional commitments. These changes can be seen most dramatically in Pentecostalism, which, unlike many other forms of conservative Protestantism, has had strong women in positions of leadership, such as the white evangelist Aimee Semple McPherson and the black preacher Lucy Smith. Contemporary Pentecostal churches attract those who look past sectarianism and dogma, which they associate with religion, to a personal relationship with Jesus, which they associate with faith. "It's emotional for me," one such believer feels. "It's like being with someone that you are totally, totally in love with and receiving that love back from them. In worship, relationship with the Lord goes far beyond . . . anything you can experience with a human being. Definitely." Implicit, if not always articulated, in this way of thinking is the idea that men are responsible for the organizational aspects of the church, for that is their way of being in the world, but women, because they know more about emotions and feelings, are really in charge of its spirituality.

When relationships with other human beings are required, women like these often seek a Bible-study group of their own, a place in which women can meet with other women to discuss their spirituality. While many of the women who attend such Bible-study groups would shudder at the comparison, their meetings bear a striking resemblance to the "consciousness raising" groups that

marked 1970s-style feminism. Like their secular counterparts, evangelical women often have jobs, raise children, and take care of elderly
parents; unlike them, they add to the pressures faced by nearly all
contemporary Americans the additional time-consuming components of frequent church and study-group attendance. "Jugglers for
Jesus," as they sometimes call themselves, they are not so much opposed to the changes that have overtaken American domestic life as
bewildered by them. These women find in their support groups advice from cobelievers that in any earlier age might have been provided by relatives—and that among more secular Americans can be
provided by mental-health professionals. The intent of such groups
may be spiritual, but their therapeutic effect is undeniable. This was
certainly true of the women who met for Bible study at the Spring-
field Evangelical Church in New Jersey. "My self-esteem is so much
better now," says one. "I'm more confident. I'll say what I feel. I
don't just 'yes' people to death. I used to be . . . a people pleaser. . . .
Now I've learned to know who I am, what I'm about, my likes, my
dislikes, and I can express those things, whereas before I didn't."

Having learned something about making one's voice heard in
church, conservative Christian women are not especially submissive
at home. The sociologist who studied Parkview Evangelical Free
Church in Texas could not find a single instance of the principle of female submission actually being put into practice. Rather, conservative Christian spouses, like nearly all contemporary Americans,
negotiate and renegotiate the terms of their marriage. What has been
called "gender inerrancy"—the idea that there is only one way for
men and women to interact, and that is by the man commanding the
woman—finds considerable support in words but very little support
in the practice of everyday life. To submit is not to let another person
boss you around. It is instead for individuals, including very strong-
willed people, to find ways to work together. As one believer makes
the point, the boss in any marriage is neither the husband nor the
wife but Christ. Each marriage partner is therefore under an obligation "to live up to the standards of a higher authority."

Even on an issue as sensitive as sex, conservative churches have
had to take cognizance of radical changes in gender roles since the
1960s that include a fuller appreciation of female sexuality. As early

as 1973, one religious studies scholar notes, "Marabel Morgan became the first evangelical Christian to tell women that they should have orgasms." Her book, *The Total Woman,* not only became a bestseller but also foreshadowed transformations in the way conservative Christians would come to treat sex—within marriage, of course—in their sermons and small groups. Sex within marriage, as Pastor Bill of Parkview says to the women in his ministry, "is a beautiful thing. You should anticipate it and you should enjoy it. Sexual desire is not evil." The problem with sex, he preaches, is not that it leads to temptation; the problem is that many of the men who attend his church do not know much about the sexual needs of their wives. And so he offers them instruction: "At the risk of sounding crass, men are microwaves and women are crockpots. It takes just seven seconds for men to become aroused. But for a woman, foreplay begins when you wake up in the morning. It takes all day long for a woman." Compared to the free-wheeling sexuality of the 1960s and 1970s, this emphasis on sex within marriage represents a distinctly conservative form of morality. But compared to the views of Christian saints like Augustine and Ambrose—who frowned upon sex even within marriage—let alone the censorious and puritanical side of twentieth-century fundamentalism, it is distinctly unconventional. A religious movement that once preached abstinence and restraint now conducts classes in the best way to achieve orgasm.

Only when we develop an appreciation for the complexities of gender relations as they actually exist in conservative Protestantism can we begin to understand the emergence of biblical feminists, women who try to combine their commitment to evangelical faith with an equally strong commitment to women's equality. Some women raised in evangelical traditions simply grow out of them or come to question practices that seem backward to their emerging sense of gender equality. "I've heard from others the fear that younger women will leave the church and go elsewhere," says a woman named Mary who was raised in a Reformed Protestant church. "Well, why not? . . . Men can go all the way for Jesus Christ. Women come up here and we're stopped with church doctrine." But others who develop a similar appreciation for gender equality choose to stay with their congregations and to struggle, however awkwardly, for feminist ideals. Grace, a friend of Mary's, is unwilling to allow her church to exclude her. "[I'm] in it for the long run," she says. But she is also determined to make her point of view known. "My commitment was such that I wouldn't back down. I mean, I couldn't. It is so wrapped up in my belief in what it means to be a Christian."

There are at least two national organizations devoted to advancing biblical feminism: the Evangelical and Ecumenical Women's Caucus (EEWC), first founded in 1970, and Christians for Biblical Equality (CBE), which, in a development all too common in evangelical circles, split off from EEWC in the late 1980s. (The issue that divided them was homosexuality; CBE believes that "Homosexuality is not endorsed by Scripture," its president, Mimi Haddad, told me.) Because of its more conservative stance on questions of sexuality, CBE has been more successful than EEWC in reaching conservative Christian women. Still, neither organization has successfully evangelized—that is, carried its message of equality to Christian women with the same fervor as more traditional evangelicals carry their message of God to the unchurched. Linda Bieze, coordinator of the executive council of EEWC, has watched the development of megachurches like Willow Creek with awe and wonders how feminists can have parallel influence on American culture. "There are lots of women who have to be reached" at places like Willow Creek, she told me, defining them as "women who are using their gifts but do not realize it."

The real influence of feminism on conservative Christianity can be found not in organizations like CBE and EEWC but in the fact that even the most conservative Christian activists have had to alter their once patriarchal views to take account of the real-life experiences and attitudes of evangelical women. For all the talk of wifely submission found in the movement's literature, one also finds frequent criticism of the strong silent husband who expects his wife to do all the housework and to take care of all the children's needs. An example is provided by, of all people, the Reverend Jerry Falwell, who argues that men who "spend little time at home and who take no interest in their wives and children" turn their wives into lonely creatures susceptible to the appeals of feminism. Precisely because women have become so important to the success of conservative

Christianity, leaders like Falwell have learned the risks of alienating them. Although he has never explicitly rejected the fundamentalist legacy that shaped him, Falwell has shied away from sounding like John R. Rice, whose 1941 book *Bobbed Hair, Bossy Wives, and Women Preachers* attacked all modern ideas about proper gender roles. Instead, Falwell goes so far as to reject the fundamentalist tradition of offering strict rules for personal conduct that all Christians are expected to follow. As one anthropologist has noted, just as Falwell was "calling on fathers and husbands to be more involved," he was also "calling on preachers to get out of the business of micromanaging family life."

Of all the changes in gender roles to which fundamentalists have learned to adjust, perhaps the most important is the fact of working women. Conservative Christianity had long appealed to less well-off Americans, and when it began to reach into the middle class, the families attracted to its message usually required two incomes to maintain their improved standard of living. Female participation in the labor force has not been met with cries of denunciation from conservative Christian leaders; on the contrary, they tend to avoid taking stands that would prove so unpopular among their members. "The decision to have a career or to be a homemaker," writes the Reverend James Dobson, founder of Focus on the Family, "is an intensely personal choice that can only be made by a woman and her husband." In the advice he gives to contemporary evangelical families, Dobson tends to be more practical than confessional, dealing, as he does, with managing money, finding time for romance, and communicating with children. And he makes his argument for female submission in words that almost sound inspired by feminism: "There is a vast difference," he writes, "between being a confident, spiritually submissive woman and being a doormat. People wipe their feet on doormats, as we know." When he talks, the language is certainly Christian, and no one would confuse Dr. Dobson with Dr. Spock. Yet when conservative Christianity clashes with contemporary gender realities, the latter barely budges while the former shifts ground significantly.

Lest one conclude that women's empowerment is a byproduct of something specifically Christian rather than something specifically conservative, gender relations have taken a similar form in Orthodox Judaism, especially among converts to stricter forms of religious obedience. Judaism is replete with symbols of women's second-class status, ranging from partitions in synagogues that divide the sexes to the laws of the *Niddah* dealing with menstrual impurity and sexual prohibition. Women attracted to Orthodoxy—because they are highly observant Jews who take halakah, or Jewish law, as binding—have no urge to serve as rabbis, let alone to lead protests against the sex segregation so prominent in their tradition. Yet because they also believe that women, as one believer puts it, "are more spiritual and better at [religious] things than men," they transform segregation by sex into what one sociologist calls "a tradition of female institution building, which, although it does not and cannot formally challenge male hegemony in synagogue and study, does establish nurturing, caring, and interconnected relationships as the primary basis for their everyday lives."

Indicative of the ways in which contemporary women's consciousness interacts with ancient ritual is what has happened in many Orthodox communities to the *mikveh,* or menstrual bath. To meet the requirements of the *Niddah,* Orthodox Jewish women refrain from sex with their husbands for seven days after their period ends and then undergo a bath in order to be purified. The *mikveh* ought not to be a ritual encouraging female solidarity. The Talmudic passages upon which the ritual bath are based, for one thing, leave little doubt that the practice originated in the belief that women who showed blood were unclean. In addition, the laws of *tzeniut,* or modesty, encourage women to immerse themselves in private. Still, as one also finds in Bible study among conservative Christians, there are some women who find themselves brought closer together to other women during menstrual bath. One woman, for example, speaks of "the whole secret sharing of it with other women" she finds there, as well as the *mikveh*'s importance in making new female friends. Women also find an enhanced appreciation of their own sexuality. "At this time of the month I am acutely aware of myself, everything is heightened because I am paying attention to what is happening inside of me," another Orthodox Jewish woman recounts. "Over the years it is building a cycle for me; it's a rhythm that is related to me and my body alone."

Besides the bath, the enforced withdrawal from sexual activity that follows can also have unexpected erotic benefits. A number of Orthodox women speak of the ways in which forced withdrawal heightens the anticipation of sex and thus improves it when it finally takes place. As one recent convert says, "We made a commitment to try this practice for at least one month. We got separate beds. I went to the mikveh and when next we made love it was wonderful."

For their opposite number, women who find themselves looking for ways to deter the sexual appetites of their husbands, the ritual bath plays a role as well. "It allows me a bed of my own," one comments, while another adds that "I can say no with no pretense of a headache if I wish." Even Ultra-Orthodox women speak these lines; as a Brooklyn woman named Nurit put it, "*mikvah* was the first *mitzvah* I found really exciting. It was such a different idea to me—to regulate intimacy—and I love it. I mean, who's always in the mood, you know? I like having some time to myself, and this way my husband isn't offended." Whatever ends it serves—sexual pleasure or sexual abstinence—the ancient tradition of the *mikveh* finds itself used in the contemporary war between the sexes. The often pronounced rejection of feminism as an ideology one finds among these women is accompanied in practice by an incorporation of some of feminism's important actual practices.

Conservative religious women are unlikely to be found demonstrating for the Equal Rights Amendment or joining the National Organization for Women, although among them one finds a surprising amount of support for the idea that qualified women should earn the same as qualified men. But this does not mean that they can be found sitting at home knitting bible cozies as they wait for their wage-earning husbands to come home and exercise male headship. Give people power, including the power of faith, and it can hardly be surprising that they come to feel empowered. What they do with that power is anyone's guess, although few could have guessed back in the 1970s, when conservative religions started their recent growth spurt, that so many women would use it not to submit themselves, graciously or otherwise, to their husbands but instead to learn the skills necessary for mastery and self-confidence.

FAITH-BASED ACCEPTANCE

The idea that religion can have positive benefits for personal morality would be something of a purely academic question were it not for efforts on behalf of faith-based initiatives: programs that enable churches and other religious organizations to use government money for charitable and social-welfare purposes. Where the welfare state failed, the reasoning behind these policies holds, religion might succeed; the best cure for poverty and its persistent social pathologies is not to throw money at people but to encourage them to turn around their lives by discovering the power of faith. "If government begins to partner with those [faith-based] organizations . . . ," writes Stephen Goldsmith, the former mayor of Indianapolis, "they will teach our youth about citizenship, civility, charity, and a host of other values more effectively than ever before."

Although faith-based initiatives have been supported by a diverse political coalition that includes white conservative evangelicals, religiously inspired community activists, and African American ministers, the clear thrust of these programs, especially after some prominent conservatives began to question whether they really wanted government support for their churches, has been an effort to improve the lives of inner-city residents, many of them African American. It seems safe to predict that over the next few decades, a national sociological experiment will be conducted to see if it is true that people who are devout religious believers are more likely to lead lives of greater moral responsibility.

Relying on faith to improve the conditions of inner-city life will certainly be no easy task. In poverty-stricken, inner-city black communities, ministers often feel themselves confronted by immorality all around them. Crime can be prevalent in the neighborhood. Gangs engage in turf struggles in and around church property, while prostitution and drug addiction are visible for all to see. For many inner-city black pastors, the streets of the community are fearful places, to be shunned at all cost. At Eastside Chapel, an A.M.E. church located in a black neighborhood of Charleston, South Carolina, the pastor talks about a ten-year-old girl who offered to sell him her body for ten dollars. "And the sad part about it is, the mothers sometime send their children out to sell themselves. 'Cause the mothers are hooked on that nasty dope. That filthy, nasty, low-down drug," he adds. Comparing Eastside Chapel to "a besieged military outpost struggling to survive behind enemy lines," the sociologist who studied it writes about how its preachers view their congregation "as a tiny piece of God's Kingdom, isolated in the midst of hostile territory."

The most determined effort to overcome obstacles such as these by using the black church on behalf of social activism involves Boston's Ten Point Coalition. Many of the ministers who have joined in this effort are affiliated with Pentecostal traditions that make a sharp distinction between the holiness inside the church and the evil lurking on the street. Yet the activists of the Ten Point Coalition reject such a Manichean view on behalf of efforts to promote social justice. The theory behind their efforts begins with the premise that people whose lives have been marked by poverty and dependency too often seek immediate gratification and hence lack such personal virtues as a sense of responsibility and an appreciation of discipline, precisely those attributes that would help them find and keep jobs. Religion can help because it offers a vision of a commanding God whose word is law. As a group of social scientists who have studied the work of the Ten Point Coalition writes, "the ministers advocate 'tough love' after the model of Jesus and of the prophets who presented stark choices and painted vivid pictures of what would happen with each choice." The power of religion, from this perspective, stems from its inherent opposition to the self-destructive culture of the ghetto. Religion can lead people out of cycles of poverty and dependency just as it led Moses out of Egypt.

Boston's Ten Point Coalition deserves much of the national praise it receives; its efforts to enlist religion on behalf of self-improvement is a much needed this-worldly corrective to the sense of exilic spirituality that led previous generations of black Pentecostals to downplay direct political action. Still, the actual activities of the ministers in Boston, impressive as they are, do not necessarily tell a story in which strengthened religious faith results in improvements in personal moral conduct.

One reason for this conclusion lies in the approach to salvation these ministers generally take. Especially for those whose lives are marked by lack of opportunity, the most appropriate response, one of the activists in the Ten Point Coalition argues, is a "whole person" approach to salvation, which consists not just in giving oneself over to Jesus, but in having one's physical and social needs met. "Before we get a person to really understand about salvation," he explains, "we first must reach the needs, whether it be homes, food, clothes, job, whatever an individual person might need. . . . And then I introduce him to salvation." This pastor's comment suggests that the relationship between faith and personal moral conduct is quite different from, if not diametrically opposed to, the relationship posited by theory. Advocates for faith-based approaches to social services argue that once people find God, they are more likely to lead responsible lives. But in real life, efforts are first made to bring people up to a sufficient economic level to enable them to accept responsibility, only after which efforts can be made to save their souls. Religion, in short, can be a byproduct, not a cause, of social improvement. In some cases, moreover, religion can stand in the way of saving the whole person. Boston's activist ministers are not shy about criticizing those who believe that salvation consists *only* in saving souls. One of them clearly seems to have his more conservative ministerial colleagues in mind when he says that "We get involved with the spirit too much and not dealing with the total man. How do I reach this guy and get him into a job, into a house and into some kind of structure, and let him know he has a reason to live?"

There is a second complication to the story of religion and morality as it emerges out of the experience of inner-city Boston. The theory behind faith-based initiatives posits two mutually exclusive worlds: the culture of the ghetto, with its often illegal and self-destructive behavior, and the world of faith, which promotes personal discipline and obedience to law. But in reality, these two realms exercise demonstrable influence on each other. Indeed, part of the success of a preacher like Eugene Rivers, pastor of the Azusa Christian Community in Boston, lies in his understanding of, and willingness to make use of, the culture of his surrounding neighborhood. No one who has seen or heard Rev. Rivers—my paths have crossed with his on many occasions—can doubt his commitment to God, yet recognizing that not all of those he wishes to reach have positive feelings toward his Christian faith, he frequently puts religion on the back burner in his effort to bring about personal transformation in the lives of those living in his community. In ways that are surely unintended, the Azusa Christian Community resembles suburban megachurches in the sense that it downplays its identity as a specifically religious institution. Inside the church, the visitor becomes immediately aware of its urban location, for the walls are adorned with scenes from the Four Corners neighborhood in which the church is located: police officers of both races, filthy alleyways, and abandoned storefronts. By placing gritty pictures of urban reality, and not just pictures of Jesus, on its walls, Azusa wants to make a statement: No sharp line will be drawn between the church and the street, for it is the job of the church to be in the street. And the church's minister certainly is. Rev. Rivers often can be found walking throughout the Four Corners neighborhood of Boston, as intent on spreading his ideas about black self-improvement to teenagers as he is flying to Washington to lobby on behalf of faith-based initiatives.

Spending so much time in the streets surrounding his church, Rev. Rivers understands that if he wants to have influence over the culture, he must be prepared to be influenced by it in return. "Drawing from the same *Godfather*-inspired lexicon that young Black self-styled 'gangsters' have sometimes appropriated," writes one sociologist who has observed him at close quarters, "Rivers has referred to himself as a *patroni* and claims to have enlisted his congregation in the Church of God in Christ denomination because it was becoming 'the biggest Black crime family.'" The charismatic style at which Rivers is so adept is a considerable advantage not only in preaching but also for reaching angry and alienated young people. When those young people engage with Rivers, they are not dealing with an aloof and foreign presence but with a man who has gone out of his way to learn how to communicate with them.

Activities like those associated with Eugene Rivers can also be found in Latino Pentecostalism. Alcance Victoria, or Victory Outreach, an extremely successful string of churches in the Los Angeles area, has grown by appealing to former gang members and drug addicts, and it does so by adopting their language and subculture. Alcance welcomes Christian hip-hop, even when it takes a violent form usually condemned by conservative Christians. ("The devil hates our guts, man," run the lyrics of one rapper who belongs to the church, "why should I miss a chance to stick him in the neck, man? When I preach and win souls . . . that's when I put a 9 millimeter in his chest.") Alcance also never strays far from the fashions popular among its members; church members affirm their faith in Jesus, even if they do so with slogans plastered on the baseball caps they wear backward on their heads. Christian graffiti is frowned on, especially when the writing is illegal, but church members often look the other way since it is a form of getting out the Lord's word. To reach the church's younger members through street dramas, the church created a youth ministry called God's Anointed Now Generation—or GANG, an appropriate reminder of the culture within which the church operates.

An especially striking example of the ways in which the culture can influence religion as much as the other way around involves not Christianity but Islam, and it takes place not among those who may, if their behavior does not change, someday find themselves in prison but among those already incarcerated. As many as 30 percent of the African Americans residing in prisons are Muslims, nearly all of them converts. Their religion stands in dramatically sharp contrast to the conditions of prison life; they typically refrain from all addictive substances, resist the buying and selling of sexual favors, and demonstrate remarkable self-discipline in the face of frequent provocation. The language used by Muslim converts among inmates is, by its very nature, non-Christian, but it does share with Christian language an emphasis on salvation. Honoring the *sharia,* or precepts of Islamic law, which includes such pronouncements as "the strongest is he who can control himself," offers to those attracted to Islam the strength to survive the often degrading conditions in which they find themselves.

Although Islam in many ways resists the culture of the prison, in other ways it copies it. "We have to deal with discipline in the ranks of the masjid [mosque]," as one life-term Sunni Muslim comments. To do so, Muslims, he points out, judge their own, and when mild punishment fails, "other methods can be invoked. In certain instances people have been severely beaten up or stabbed, depending upon the severity of the transgression and the threat it presents to security of the Muslim community." Islam among African American prisoners frequently takes the form of a total institution within a total institution; it offers an alternative to the immorality surrounding it by substituting a morality strikingly secular in its attachment to using discipline as a form of punishment. In both the world of the prison and the world of Islam, proper moral conduct is not viewed as a process of growth and development on the part of the individual so much as it is understood as a byproduct of obedience to strictly enforced rules.

Religion can indeed change the lives of the inner-city poor. At the Revival Center Church of God in Christ, located near the notorious Henry Horner Homes in Chicago—notorious because, as a best-selling book put it, there are no children there—a woman named Celia, upon discovering Jesus, was able to free herself from welfare, complete her education, and become a nurse; even the project drunk was able to get and keep a job after joining the church. But "whole person" salvation and the mutual interaction between faith and inner-city culture complicate the question of who or what is responsible for such changes. Salvation aimed at more than a person's soul is not all that different from traditional social-work efforts at improvement, although the fact that it comes accompanied by religious language may help make it more effective. And when ministers sound more like gangsters than gangsters sound like ministers—or, even more problematic, when imams act like gangsters to enforce obedience to religious tenets—it becomes difficult to attribute any changes in personal moral conduct to the influence of faith alone.

THE MORMON EXCEPTION

In a determined effort to create a personal morality that stands in sharp contrast to the immorality of the world, some religions set themselves off, physically or psychologically, from the rest of society. The most visible, paradoxically for reasons of their general invisibility, are small sects at the margins of American religious life such as the Amish or the pacifist Mennonites and the Church of the

Brethren. Yet even these religions have not been completely successful in protecting themselves from the temptations of the world. After
generations of relative success in preserving their religion unchanged, the Amish are beginning to experience increased juvenile
delinquency among the young. And even when crime and drug addiction are avoided, churches that withdraw from the world have a
hard time appealing to a new generation. One sociologist who studied Mennonites in Lancaster, Pennsylvania, found that many of them
"returned home . . . after going to college or doing missionary work
to find their Mennonite churches failing to provide resources or programs for them." Upset with dress codes and inflexible rules of religious authority, a number of younger Mennonites were attracted to
charismatic churches, thus entering a world of seeking that was anti-
thetical to the tradition in which they were raised. No religion can
stay old-fashioned forever in a society that constantly reinvents the
new.

There is, however, one American religion that not only has
shown a pronounced ability to reinforce strong conceptions of
morality among its members but also is one of the largest and
fastest-growing religions in the United States: the Church of Jesus
Christ of Latter-day Saints, also known as Mormons. (There are
more Mormons in the United States than there are members of the
Presbyterian, United Church of Christ, Disciples of Christ, and Episcopalian denominations.) Mormonism is the great exception to any
suggestion that faith and traditional moral conduct have little to do
with one another. Although not all Mormons subscribe to the Word
of Wisdom that forbids the consumption of alcohol and even coffee
and tea—"Jack Mormons" is the term that has been given to those
who claim membership but omit some required practices—enough
do to make Mormonism and abstention all but synonymous in the
eyes of those outside the faith. Once denounced by non-Mormons as
libertines for their practice of polygamy, Latter-day Saints are now
widely admired by large numbers of Americans for their strict personal conduct. From time to time, stories of continued adherence to
polygamy on the part of some Mormons emerge, and as they do,
some less than attractive forms of moral conduct that seem oppres-
sive to women and potentially abusive of children emerge along with

them. And not all evangelical Protestants are happy with what they perceive to be Mormon deviations from Christian teachings on sin and grace. Yet in the course of a century and a half, a religion that began by challenging the central religious and moral precepts of a predominantly Protestant society has come to stand in the public mind as the embodiment of old-fashioned Christian ideals.

Mormons, of course, are only human, which is why from time to time evidence of immoral behavior on the part of individual members of the Church comes to light. Still, considerable evidence exists that the Mormon reputation for moral probity is justified. A thorough review of survey data concludes that "more so than the average American, Mormons want children, marriage, and a more traditional division of labor; they are also less likely to have cohabited and more likely to disapprove of extramarital sex." Although some of the differences between Latter-day Saints and members of other conservative faiths with respect to marriage practices disappear when actual behavior, rather than attitudes, are compared, one study showed that nearly half of Mormon mothers are willing to accept the Church's instructions not to enter the labor force, which stands in sharp contrast to the ways in which conservative Protestant churches have shied away from offering advice in this area. Not surprisingly, given their code of conduct, Saints are also less likely than members of other faiths, including conservative ones, to smoke, drink, and take drugs.

If there is widespread agreement that Mormons live appreciably different moral lives from other Americans, there is little if any agreement why. One potential explanation, however, is surely wrong: Mormonism does not successfully teach conservative morality because it is an old-fashioned church. On the surface, Mormonism stands an exception to the patterns working to transform American religion. But in reality, Mormonism was one of the first American religions to be transformed—not with respect to its emphasis on personal morality but with respect to its approach to theology and doctrine.

Of all religions in the United States, Mormonism is, theologically speaking, one of the least demanding. Latter-day Saints downplay Adam's sin against God and view God and man as engaged in a mutually cooperative and generally beneficial relationship. Optimistic and forward-looking, Mormonism holds out the prospect of sainthood to all (male) believers. Hierarchical in the sense that the Church is governed by a council of elders, Mormonism nonetheless exists without a professional clergy and relies on lay leadership for the bulk of its ritual practice. Extremely modern in its adaptability to the world in which it finds itself, Mormons, when faced with the need to change unpopular aspects of their faith, such as polygamy or the exclusion of African Americans from the priesthood, will promptly change them. Compared to other faiths, Mormon religious practice gives little sense of God as a transcendent, omnipotent power guiding his obedient servants to their already-chosen destiny and instead elevates human beings to the status of the divine. Whatever else it may be, Mormonism is not fundamentalist. Its leadership and many of its members may be politically conservative, but theologically speaking, Mormonism stands as a rebuke to a Calvinist-like emphasis on original sin and man's degraded condition.

Nor have Latter-day Saints avoided a tendency among nearly all American religions to downplay doctrinal distinctiveness. Mormonism began as a Hebraic religion, drawing many of its practices, including polygamy and the construction of temples, from the Old Testament. Over time, however, the faith evolved into a more specifically Christian form, emphasizing the name of Jesus in its official title and increasingly referring to those outside the faith, including Protestants and Catholics, as non-Mormon rather than as gentile. Such changes inevitably dilute doctrine. The belief that Latter-day Saints carry the original blood of Israel could not survive the Mormon desire to grow, implying, as it did, that Mormonism was an ascribed faith, and eventually even birthright Saints no longer took the idea that seriously. Other doctrinal issues are similarly downplayed. Asked in 1998 if Mormons continue to believe that God was once a man, the Church's president, Gordon Hinckley, responded, "I wouldn't say that. . . . That gets into some deep theology we don't know very much about." Even more than other American religions, Mormonism, in the words of one anthropologist, "is all but creedless and stands completely without exegesis."

Because specific doctrine plays little role in propagating the faith,

Mormonism in practice, like other conservative American religions, tends to be thoroughly practical in its offerings to individuals. In Arizona, a high-school girl tells of how, after going to the movies with some friends, she came home so depressed that she "felt like dying." Picking up her "Patriarchal Blessing," a semipersonal church document dealing with her purpose in life, she realized that, because her future course was not yet determined, it would be wrong for her to take her own life. Members of the ward—the term Mormons use for a local congregation—received her warmly, enabling her to overcome her personal crisis. While similar on the surface to the therapeutic confessionalism of evangelical Protestantism, this young woman's experience was actually quite different. She never prayed and in that sense never asked God directly for help; on the contrary, she solved, with the help of the church, a problem for herself. The anthropologist who observed this incident describes the process as "do-it-yourself theology." Mormons, he writes, talk about faith and church "without a structure which actively prescribes the right answer to any question. Mormonism is thus a way of helping its members think out the solutions to problems with each other's help and in such a way that, when the problems change, the way to think about them does too. It allows for dynamic problem-solving by local, homogenous groups."

Reflecting its origins as a frontier religion, Mormon religious practice is democratic in a Jacksonian sense; it trusts in the down-to-earth wisdom of ordinary people, dislikes the kinds of expertise associated with trained theologians or philosophers, and insists on the validity of personal experience. "There may be sixteen different opinions on when the millennium is going to occur, but no one calls particular guesses unsound or doctrinally adventuresome," writes anthropologist Mark Leone. "Whatever is said, it is almost never contradicted, called wrong, or labeled as being opposed to church doctrine or policy." It is as if Latter-day Saints are too busy applying their faith to life's practical problems to be excessively bothered with assigning blame or overcoming guilt.

One reason why Mormon worship practices so rarely arouse internal controversy is because they tend to be so positive toward the Church and its leaders. Speaking of Joseph Smith, the church's founder, one retired man in 1999, at a ward whose location has been kept confidential, says that "there's never a time that I sit in a fast and testimony meeting . . . that I don't think about how grateful I am for a young boy who wanted to know which church to join." Another, the ward bishop, praises President Hinckley as "a wonderful man" and a "prophet of God" and gives thanks that "things are advancing more every year," even though "the devil's at work against us." Rarely are Mormons given to anguished confessions of disappointment or cries of woe that God has betrayed those who believe in him. Unlike small-group practices in other faith traditions, which often reach moments of emotional catharsis before harmony is achieved, Mormon testimonies tend to be harmonious from the start. There is little weeping because there is little to weep about.

These practical aspects of Mormonism make it especially attractive to switchers looking for a faith that can help them negotiate their way through a complicated world. At the Elkton Ward in Delaware, David Obzansky, thirty-one years old, was born and raised Catholic and converted to Mormonism shortly after taking a job with DuPont in 1982. First trying a local Unitarian church, he settled on the Mormons because he and his wife "felt very comfortable there. We liked the people we met. I don't think any revelation came over me during the discussions. . . . The Mormon church provided what we thought was a friendly atmosphere, a very practical atmosphere. It wasn't very ritualistic." Another member, twenty-eight year old Nancy Quinn, thanks the church for encouraging her to read, but while she has read the Bible, she has not quite gotten to *The Book of Mormon* and has only recently picked up *The Doctrine and Covenants*. "Before I worried about all the little details," she says. "Now I just do my best and then I don't worry about the rest." For her, as for so many others, faith makes it possible to get on with life. "At first it bothered me that we have meetings instead of a church service and that everything's set up like a corporation," Michael Wheeler admits. But, he continues, "that's the way our society is. It makes sense to set things up like that."

If it is not religious doctrine, at least as that term is usually understood, that unites Latter-day Saints around a common understanding of moral behavior, it may well be culture. Mormonism

began, as we would say today, as an explicitly countercultural movement. "In direct contrast to most Protestant parishes made up of
congregations whose members worshiped together on Sundays but
returned during the week to a pluralistic (albeit Protestant) culture,"
writes the historian Jan Shipps about Mormons living in the Great
Basin, "the Saints who attended sacrament meetings or heard sermons from less than imposing stands on Sundays lived out their ordinary weekday lives in close proximity to one another." Strong
personal ties made up in intensity what Mormon faith lacked in a
conception of an omnipotent God, since neighborly disapproval
could be just as effective as fears of eternal damnation in moving
people to improve their moral conduct. As blended in with the rest
of American culture as their religious practices have been, the cultural practices of the Mormons have made them, as they call themselves, "a particular people."

Mormonism has changed many times since that new civilization
was created, and no time may be more important than the past two
or three decades. Now secure and established, Mormonism is intent
on spreading the word. Its missionary activity produces converts in
Africa, Asia, and Latin America. And within the United States, Saints
live in all regions of the country, and the religion increasingly resembles more liberal faiths in its multicultural diversity: Polynesian
wards hold luaus, Hispanic ones celebrate Noche de Latina, and
Asian ones welcome Chinese New Year. While the Mormon leadership takes great pride in such missionary activity, expansion does
raise an awkward dilemma: Can the culture that originally sustained
the religion survive a diaspora that includes Saints living outside the
original Great Basin as well as accept the multicultural character of
the modern world? As one sociologist points out, too much "pecu-
liarity" can undermine Mormonism by making it obsolete in the face
of the need for new religions to adapt, while "too much assimilation
is just another form of oblivion, in which the social boundary between the new religion and its host society gradually disappears, and
along with it any unique sense of identity on the parts of the religious adherents."

Aware of the difficulties involved, the Church has taken steps to
avoid becoming a Sunday-only faith indistinguishable from other

versions of American Christianity. Every ward is considered to be, in
Shipps's words, "both a reflection and embodiment of a Mormon village on alien soil." Houses of worship are constructed according to a
standard plan, and "the teachings and activities are standardized so
that—as far as is feasible—Mormonism is the same wherever it is in
the world. Almost a religious franchise, the church remains a constant in a multicultural world." If the faithful are "scattered" rather
than "gathered," one can at least gather them together in ways that
emphasize not only the commonality of Mormons with each other
but also their collective distinctiveness from everyone else.

Yet it is not at all clear that Mormonism can survive its expansive
proclivities as both a distinct culture and as a distinct faith. Mormons around the United States continue to send their children to
Brigham Young University and to honor calls for church service and
missionary work in order to avoid being "inexorably (if slowly) assimilated into the great ecumenical blandness of today's mainline
denominations," as one observer of the church puts it. Yet one wonders how long the church can hold onto members like Sheila Anderson, who teaches preschool children in the Elkton Ward. "I went to a
Seventh-Day Adventist grammar school, a Catholic high school, a
Mormon college," she says. "I come from an Episcopalian and
Methodist background. My sister is a practicing Sufi." Mrs. Anderson is increasingly unhappy with her faith because she does not feel
that she can grow within it. "You hear the same kind of lessons over
and over again. Unless you keep your life among the Mormons, seeing the Mormon way, the church is not very interested in you."
Sheila Anderson believes that the Joseph Smith story is true, but it is
true for Mormons "as the White is for the Adventists, the Calvin is
for the Presbyterians, and the Luther is for the Lutherans." Mrs. Anderson is anything but a typical Mormon believer. But she recognizes
a fundamental truth when she says that as people like her are exposed to a world outside the church, Mormonism will have to expand its own horizons to keep them.

The problems posed by multicultural expansion are even more
acute for a religious movement that began with such a pronounced
cultural identity. In the 1970s, church leaders expressed a wariness
toward ethnic branches of the faith if they carried out their activities

in languages other than English. But oral histories collected among "people of color" by the Charles Redd Center for Western Studies at Brigham Young University show that many of those attracted to the faith prefer ethnically specific wards and branches; "I can communicate easily," testifies Kiyomi Patrick, a Japanese student, about her experience in a Japanese-speaking ward. "I can just become friends with Japanese people because we know each other. We don't have to explain everything we feel." Should Mormonism retain the kind of pragmatic, problem-solving approach to religion that has worked so well in its expansion to states besides Utah, it will allow a place for immigrants to retain their native language. But in so doing, efforts to standardize religious practices so that every ward resembles every other one, and all of them resemble those in Utah, will inevitably be undermined.

It is impossible to know how the dilemmas facing the Church of Jesus Christ of Latter-day Saints will be resolved. Mormonism, by retaining its peculiar culture, may well be able to preserve its success in successfully transmitting to its members standards of personal moral conduct at sharp odds with the more libertarian morality of American society. If, however, the Church of Jesus Christ of Latter-day Saints becomes one more version of an American mainline religion, Mormons will someday become morally indistinguishable from Americans of other faiths. Whatever the direction the religion takes, Mormonism's development to this point leads to two conclusions about the relationship between religion and personal moral conduct. One is that some religions can indeed have a strong and lasting impact on personal moral conduct. And the other is that what makes this possible are not always religious factors but can include sociological and cultural ones as well.

AN EXPERIMENT IN MORALITY

Intrigued by the question of whether religious faith can be positively associated with personal moral conduct, a sociologist tried out an experiment with one of his classes at a conservative Christian university. All 150 students were given an extra point on an exam they had taken. They were then told that some of the exams were graded in error and of those that were, some were undergraded while others were overgraded. Since only one point was involved, the students were also informed that the exams would not be collected and regraded; instead they should just let the instructor know whether their grade was one point too high, one point too low, or just right. The teacher wanted to know whether students who were more religious would be less likely to cheat than those who were less religious. And that is exactly what he found. Although everyone's grade was one point too high, the faithful, on every single measure of religiosity, were the ones more likely to say so.

This study was conducted to address one of the difficulties facing social scientists as they grapple with the relationship between religion and personal morality. A debate over the question can be traced to a widely cited 1969 article; expecting to find that such variables as church attendance and belief in an afterlife would be associated with low rates of juvenile delinquency, its authors discovered that religious belief had little or no relationship to what society labeled as deviant behavior. Since then, hosts of studies have tried to shed further light on the subject. The results are inconsistent and puzzling, depending, as is often the case with such research, on the wording of questions in surveys or the samples chosen for analysis. Sometimes researchers confirm the hypothesis that religion makes little difference with respect to moral conduct; there is, for example, if anything, a tendency for evangelicals to divorce in greater amounts, or to have more children out of wedlock, than other religious believers. On the other hand, many studies have found that people who attend church regularly and indicate a strong belief in God are less likely to report high rates of gambling, alcohol and drug consumption, tax cheating, and domestic violence. Perhaps the fairest way to summarize the empirical data is to say that religious faith has a slight, but nonetheless positive, effect on personal morality.

Despite this emerging consensus, however, the issue is far from settled. For one thing, it may be the case that, as with the Mormons, something other than religious faith narrowly understood could have an influence on morality; it has been suggested, for example, that participation in any kind of small-group activity, whether or not indi-

viduals are themselves religious, can reduce alcohol and drug consumption, and since small groups are increasingly popular in American religion, morality effects, as they might be called, may have more
to do with group psychology than with faith. For another, causality is
nearly impossible to ascertain in studies like these, so that it may be
that moral people are attracted to religion and not the other way
around. But the single most difficult problem with the sociological
literature is the one that the experiment at the conservative Christian university set out to correct. Nearly all of the associations that
have been found between religion and moral conduct are based on
what people say about their religiosity, not what they actually do.
People do not just have a tendency to exaggerate whether or not they
go to church; they also know what kinds of moral behavior are valued by their religion and by their society. Self-reporting is important,
but it is clearly preferable, where possible, to observe behavior rather
than to rely on secondhand accounts.

Because this experiment reported on what students actually did
rather than what they said, it makes an important contribution to the
literature dealing with religion and personal moral conduct. But it
does not make a contribution that will please those who believe that
religious faith causes people to deepen their moral sense. The true
importance of this little study lies in the fact that, given a chance to
cheat, the overwhelming majority of students, religious or not, in
fact took it. Whatever difference there was between the more and
less religious pales in the face of the fact that only forty-one of the
150 students honestly admitted receiving an extra point.

The prevalence of widespread cheating at a predominantly conservative Christian university would seem to confirm the views of
those who believe that religion, far from having a positive influence
on personal moral conduct, is more likely to produce hypocrisy than
honesty. For all the talk of faith-based initiatives and charitable
choice, they would point out, religion's record on personal morality
cannot be evaluated without considering such real-world events as
the financial scandals associated with Jimmy Swaggert and Jim and
Tammy Faye Bakker, the persistence of racism or anti-Semitism
among various religious denominations, or the all-too-frequent examples of pedophilia found in the Catholic priesthood and the im-

moral (by any standard) efforts of the Church hierarchy to keep them secret. If anything, people of this persuasion believe, faith is more likely to be associated with immorality than its opposite, since it causes so many people to close their eyes to the kind of self-examination that genuine morality requires.

Yet it is as wrong to gloat about religion's failure to live up to the highest standards of morality as it is to believe that religious belief by itself can transform a bad person into a good one. Religion and morality interact in ways that can rarely produce a one-to-one relationship in either direction. Religion cannot be treated in so functional a manner, as if one can wind it up like a clock—or bring it to a stop—in order to cure one's favorite social ills. We live, for better or worse, in a society in which people receive cues on how to act from many, often contradictory, sources. Against the seductions of careerism and conformism—and in the face of media-induced cynicism, the necessity of political compromise, the demands of children, and the simple human desire to live without perpetual crises of conscience—religion can play only a supporting role in transforming secular society into its own views of the good life.

None of this answers the question of whether the United States would be better off if it allowed more leeway for faith-based organizations to play more of a role in public policy; my personal view is that it probably would be. But to expect that religion can serve as a corrective to any one of a number of perceived moral flaws in the United States—that, for example, it can lead individuals to repudiate the lessons of the 1960s or to transform themselves from law-breaking to law-abiding citizens—reflects an outdated conception of what religion is actually like. Long ago and far away, faith may well have been strict enough, and its capacity to win obedience strong enough, for religion to offer a panacea for the world's miseries. But these days the world is no longer quite so miserable and religion is not quite so powerful. Most of the religious believers in the United States do not believe that God exists in order to balance the federal budget or lower the rate of recidivism. Blending religion and politics in such a manner is a temptation they have little trouble resisting.

CHAPTER 6

SIN

A DIFFERENT STANDARD

It can hardly be good news when more than two-thirds of the students at a faith-based college, presented with the opportunity, cheat. But exactly what kind of bad news is it? Suppose the sociologist who conducted the experiment followed it up with a seminar in which the students discussed the meaning of what they did. Because right and wrong apply to particular acts, and not just to the individuals who carry them out, many students, upon reflection, might allow that they were engaged in wrongdoing, for doing so would not necessarily imply that they themselves were at fault. ("What I did was wrong," I can imagine someone saying, "but everyone else did it, and in any case I promise to do the right thing next time.") Fewer students, most likely a very small minority, might go further and concede that what they did was immoral. Morality establishes a more demanding standard than right and wrong; immorality suggests a lack of good character, and not all that many students would want to acknowledge that they had been badly brought up or that they suffered from a serious character flaw. ("Yes, I cheated on the exam," this individual might acknowledge. "The problem is that I also stole a car in order to get to the exam on time.")

The most interesting question, though, is whether, by their decision to cheat, these students had sinned. People sin, not because they have made a mistake or because something has gone wrong during their upbringing, but because human beings are by their very nature stained creatures; their sin is universal and reflects man's original sin. To acknowledge that we have sinned is to make a promise that, from the suffering we experience as a result of our actions, we will try, with God's help, to rethink how we live and what we live for. (I imagine this person saying something like this: "From the mistakes I have made, I have learned the need to be born again in Christ in order to seek his forgiveness.") Sin, in short, implies not only a higher but also a different standard. Some sins, such as dancing or drinking, are not, on a hierarchy of wrongdoing, all that serious; what makes them serious is whom they offend. As the theologian Cornelius Plantinga has written, believers commit themselves to the truth that God designed a universe in which everything has its place; to disturb that sense of order "is not only the breaking of law but also the breaking of covenant with one's savior." If Plantinga is right, then a seemingly trivial act such as accepting a one-point advantage in a grade, because it breaks widely accepted rules about the way things are supposed to be, might well be considered sinful.

We do not know, because they were not asked, whether those students, when presented with evidence of their behavior, confessed to sinful conduct. But it is easy to imagine that they did not. As Plantinga puts it, "where sin is concerned, people mumble now." A religion as practical, optimistic, and purposeful as American faith is unlikely to dwell for too long on such unpleasant subjects as the inherent corruption of human nature. Religions differ in the way they approach sin, but all of them find themselves dealing with believers who do not necessarily think of their God as stern and unforgiving, waiting for the next chance to punish the unpenetent for their wayward behavior.

GOD LITE

Conservative Protestantism is literally built upon the idea that people seek, through a rebirth in Jesus, redemption for the severity of the sins inherent in the human condition. It stands to reason, then, that its history is replete with strong statements on the subject. When E. N. Bell, an official in the Pentecostal Assemblies of God, was asked in 1922 about his views on how women should arrange their hair, he answered that Christians should not be engaged in frivolous pursuits such as improving their looks or making themselves attractive to members of the opposite sex. In their relentless crusade against sin, Pentecostals sought to forbid many of the routine activities of daily life that even other conservative Christians allowed. "The standard evangelical sins of smoking, drinking, dancing, and gambling were too obviously heinous to require much denunciation," as the leading historian of American Pentecostalism has written. More impressive were the new sins that Pentecostal enthusiasts—usually called saints—added to the list of prohibitions. "At one time or another saints forbade or strongly discouraged (in alphabetical order), bands, baseball, boating, bowling, circuses, fireworks, football, loitering, parades, skating, valentines, and zoos. They also denounced amusement parks, beach parties, big dinners, chatting on the telephone, Christmas trees, crossword puzzles, home movies, ice cream socials, kissing bees, scenic railroad trips, and visiting relatives and going on automobile joyrides on Sundays." Speaking in tongues and ecstatic with enthusiasm, Pentecostals may have been radical in their religious practices, but socially they were as conservative as seventeenth-century Puritans—or twenty-first-century Orthodox Jews.

One can find Pentecostals today who view alcohol consumption, premarital sex, abortion, or homosexuality as a violation of God's covenant with the human race. Among them would surely be John Ashcroft, the attorney general of the United States in the administration of George W. Bush, who, in his first year in office, covered a partially nude statue in the Great Hall of the Department of Justice and spent considerable energy trying to close a house of ill repute in New Orleans. But because it is such a popular and capacious form of religious expression, Pentecostalism also includes adherents who have moved fairly far down the road away from traditional understandings of sin. The best illustration is offered by those attracted to Aglow International Fellowship, a Pentecostally inspired parachurch movement that reaches out to primarily middle-age women, offering them salvation through faith in Jesus. The women attracted to this organization have addressed themselves to precisely the same question as

E. N. Bell—how should women present themselves?—and have come up with a radically different answer.

To demonstrate the power of God in their lives, adherents to Aglow are encouraged to make themselves as presentable as they can. Manicures, neatly arranged hairstyling, broad smiles, and bright and attractive clothing are the order of the day. These women both feel pampered and pamper themselves; one Aglow official in 1992 came up with the idea of an outreach program called "Ladies, It's Your Day," designed to reach out and attract new members by working to enhance their self-esteem. Before meeting with a prayer counselor to talk about Jesus, they were provided not only day care for their children but also a free appointment in a beauty parlor. "We wanted to encourage the women in their womanhood, and let them know that they are special, they are beautiful," says one of the directors of a similar outreach program designed for inner-city women in Detroit. Of course these women know that such changes are only skin deep. But they also understand that the process of becoming a new creature in Christ requires active (and outward) signs of conversion, and what better way to demonstrate their newfound faith than to let the world take notice of them?

There are good reasons why Aglow takes questions of personal appearance so seriously; many of the women attracted to its version of Christian faith were, at earlier points in their lives, deeply troubled. Margit had suffered numerous breakdowns throughout her life. But, she says, "as I continued in my walk with the Lord, praying in the Spirit, worshipping Him, and confessing the Word, I started to feel like a new person." Now that she feels she is "worth something," Margit is better able to face the world; her faith and her sense of self-worth work hand in hand, one influencing the other. The importance that believers like Margit attach to personal transformation would have struck the founders of Pentecostalism as far too worldly for a good Christian, but these women, in turn, understand something the founding saints of their faith may have missed, which is that Jesus loves them and they love Jesus, not just in an abstract sense, but in deeply emotional and personal ways that, in their view, require evidence of their devotion. Self-hatred, feelings of personal inadequacy, codependency, alcoholism—whatever devotion that might come from tainted sources such as these, they believe, can never be genuine. Once, believers were expected to prove their faith through ascetic withdrawal from the world. These days, it makes more sense to these women to pursue the goal through personal recovery.

Although there is a strongly therapeutic cast to their religious practice, it would be wrong to conclude that the preoccupation with clothes and hair shown by these women—or the comparable attention paid to fine (and quite expensive) hats by members of the primarily African American Church of God in Christ—should be taken as proof of self-indulgence. In fact, both kinds of women believe in the power of sin and often see Satan lying behind its temptations. One of the most tempting of the sins, moreover, is gluttony, which should not be all that surprising. "Food has long been viewed as a source of temptation," writes a prominent student of American religion, "indeed, in post-Augustinian Christianity, as a distorted desire. The fact of so many overweight Americans as well as the prevalence of eating disorders both signal serious spiritual struggles with food and account for why, within Evangelical Christianity especially, so many special-purpose groups now address these concerns."

Address them they certainly do. "Did you ever hide that last piece of cake so you could have it later?," asks Patricia B. Kreml, author of *Slim for Him*, a popular seller in evangelical bookstores. "Do you ever find yourself hoping there will be leftovers from your favorite dish so you can eat it all by yourself the next day? . . . All these are . . . breaches of trust in God." Conservative Christian women try hard to lose weight, not only to make themselves attractive but also to please the Lord. For that purpose, Kreml's book is just one of many; the past few years have seen the appearance of *What Would Jesus Eat? The Ultimate Program for Eating Well, Feeling Great, and Living Longer,* by Don Colbert; *Daily Word for Weight Loss: Spiritual Guidance to Give You Courage on Your Journey,* by Colleen Zuck and Elaine Meyer; *The Prayer Diet: The Unique Physical, Mental, and Spiritual Approach to Healthy Weight Loss,* by Matthew Anderson; and *More of Him Less of Me: My Personal Thoughts, Inspirations, and Meditations on the Weigh Down Diet,* by Jan Christiansen. This last refers to the stupendously popular *Weigh Down Diet* of Gwen Shamblin, which has become such an integral part of congregational life in evangelical circles that by one estimate ten thousand churches feature it. ("When you give your heart to God," Shamblin holds, "the body will follow.") Even while recognizing that obsessions over food may have more to do with anorexia and bulimia than sin and salvation, evangelical writers often equate the joy one feels by looking good with the radiance one feels by giving oneself up to God's power.

Not only do religious women turn to diet in order to demonstrate their faith, secular women turn to religion to help them with their weight loss. "The diet is within me I shall not cheat," runs the mantra at one weight-loss program:

> It leadeth me to choose the legal food whenever I have the urge to eat
> Yea though I may wish to eat sweets or cake
> I shall eat them never
> For the diet is with me
> And I shall reach my goal
> And remain slim forever. Amen.

If one were looking for examples of the ways in which the secular and the sacred meet in American culture, no other area would be more representative than this simultaneous desire to please God and to make oneself fit and attractive.

Women who want to feel better about themselves in order to demonstrate their faith commitments are not, in their own view of the matter, sinning; on the contrary, out-of-shape bodies and unkempt hair would constitute the real sin, since God could hardly be pleased with human beings who cared so little about how they appear to him. There may well be some justification to their claim, for if God is inscrutable, who can really say that he would prefer human beings to honor him by denying all earthly pleasures rather than by working strenuously to improve themselves? If one believes that those attracted to organizations like Aglow are sincere in their faith—there is no reason whatsoever to believe that they are not—their desire for self-improvement is worthy of comment, not because it means that they are unwilling to sacrifice for the sake of a distant and remote God but because their religious practice testifies to the emergence of a new conception of who God is and what he requires. The meaning of sin has changed because the meaning of God has changed—and not just for evangelicals but for Americans from a wide variety of religious traditions.

Mainline Protestants are among the leaders in searching for less commanding concepts of God and what he demands of us. One can see this in the leader of a Bible-study group in a Philadelphia Presbyterian church who tells those who meet with him "to stop perceiving the Bible in the terms and images they acquired in Sunday school and instead to view it through the lens of their own experience, emotions, and creativity, and through available historical information." One of the images that many members of his group are prepared to jettison is an image of God as "unknowable but powerful and authoritative," as one of them, who is actually an exception to the rule, expresses herself. More common is a conception of God that allows considerable autonomy to the individuals who believe in him. "God hung onto me until I was ready to let my Self develop," one says, while another adds that "God created the world and me." God has many capacious qualities for these women; among them are having a feminine side, being a friend, and (in the case of Jesus) possessing authenticity. "I think God honors the fact that I *want* to believe in Him, whether I feel sure or not," as one of them asserts. "I believe He honors my *desire* even if I feel mad at Him."

Strong conceptions of sin require not only a conception of a demanding God but also the idea of a powerful, and tempting, Satan. Yet polls routinely show that while Americans frequently believe in the existence of heaven, they are not that sure about the reality of hell. This is certainly true of these mainline Presbyterians. Many of them possess an active spiritual life; they believe that supernatural things happen in the world and even, on occasion, happen to them. Often reluctant to share their supernatural experiences publicly, for fear that this will set them apart as strange or unconventional, they talked about such events with the ethnographer who listened to them, and she was struck by the fact that "their spiritual histories were *all* positive, and were notable for their complete omission of any material concerning punishment or evil." "Americans may be drawn to the miraculous because it makes them feel good rather than filling them with awe or fear," writes a leading sociologist of religion. "Although many popular treatments of angels and of warm, enveloping visions of light also mention dark spirits, ghosts, and demonic beings, the malevolent forces receive far less attention." The thing about angels is that they "never scold. They give unconditional love. They have a good sense of humor. They also protect people, giving something to hope for or depend on when life seems like too much to handle on one's own." In American religion, God conveys the power of positive thinking because he thinks positively himself.

Catholicism features its own particular versions of "God Lite." Catholics once possessed what historian Robert Orsi has called a "culture of suffering," in which pain and disease could be interpreted as a doorway to God's grace. (As Thomas Dooley once memorably expressed the point, "God has been good to me. He has given me the most hideous, painful cancer at an extremely young age.") Such a culture was especially compatible with strong conceptions of sin, for believers did not regularly attend mass or perform the sacraments in order to feel good about themselves; at a Polish parish in Detroit in the 1970s, fears of eternal damnation motivated many of the faithful. "Hell, when we were kids they told us our fingers would fall off if we touched the host; and that we were committing a sin if we tried to chew it," as a forty-something tool and die worker named John Krajewski says. Krajewski, like many of those traditional Catholics who feel that something is amiss in the reformed liturgy associated with Vatican II, is not happy that the language of sin is disappearing from his parish. "Now everything is different. . . . We don't feel holy when we go to church, anymore." His fellow parishioners were told by their priests that, according to newly developed theological positions, children under the age of seven could not commit a mortal sin and therefore did not need to confess before receiving First Holy Communion. This did not go over well with many members of his generation. "How can you go to communion without going to confession?" one woman asks, "even if you are only seven years old."

The more authoritative forms of Catholicism admired by these believers are hard to find in America these days. "In the first half of the twentieth century," as the authors of one study of Catholic attitudes write, "the Church promulgated a punitive image of God. It enforced strict rules that applied to nearly all areas of social, spiritual, and moral life. . . . Sins varied in magnitude from venial (relatively minor) to mortal (the most serious)." Today, by contrast, "the Church hierarchy has emphasized a loving God, one characterized by unconditional love, compassion, and kindness. . . . According to this view, God knows people will treat one another unjustly now and then, but God also understands their human frailties. God does not punish them; God loves and forgives them." With these changes in theology, American Catholicism transformed its culture from one of suffering to one of warm acceptance, a transition that surely made it possible for the Church to retain the allegiance of ever more modern Catholics who no longer lived in the parish-bound, priest-dominated parishes of American cities. But it also made it harder for the Church to maintain even its belief in venial sins, let alone mortal ones. Catholics once held on to such rites as eating fish on Fridays, but that requirement no longer exists and, because it does not, neither does the conception of sin that once provided its justification. Those are distant memories for many contemporary Catholics. "Do they really know what is a sin?" asks one (older) parishioner in exasperation about the disappearance of the Friday rite. "Who knows what's a sin?"

In part because of questions like the one asked by this parishioner, the Vatican has in recent years reiterated traditional conceptions of sin, as, for example, in its 1992 edition of the catechism. Still, younger American Catholics are by no means sure that such traditional teachings are relevant to them. Their forms of religious practice have by and large abandoned what one study calls a "quasi-scientific character" in which "virtues and vices were broken down into various subcategories" and "sins were catalogued and classified in step-by-step procedures known to generations of Catholics standing in Saturday afternoon confessional lines." It is as if an entire generation of believers has come to realize that being a good Catholic can be uplifting, even enjoyable, although the price paid can be significant movement away from Catholicism as it used to be understood.

Unlike Christians, Jews do not believe that Jesus had to die to redeem humanity for its frailty, or that grace can be achieved either by good works or by faith alone. Nonetheless, religious Jews do atone for the sins they have committed, especially during Yom Kippur, the holiest of Jewish days. Of all such sins, the most serious is disobedience of the law, since the law is divine in its origin. The God of the Old Testament was not hesitant about confronting human beings with their failures, including their failure to honor him; disloyalty, in fact, comes as close to an original sin as one finds in the Jewish tradition. Whatever their differences with Christianity, Jews require the presence of a commanding, forceful, and authoritative God in order to know how and why they have gone wrong. Still, many contemporary American Jews, however much they understand and appreciate such an Old Testament conception of God, find themselves reluctant to cede so much authority to him.

Thus it comes as little surprise that only seven of the fifty moderately affiliated Jews interviewed in one study believe in a "God who hears prayer, intervenes directly in history or in the lives of individuals, or rewards human beings after death in accordance with their deeds in this life." These are people who observe Jewish law, but they do not do so because God demands it or out of fidelity to, as Jewish prayer calls him, "the Lord of all creation" or "the Lord whose word brought the world into being." One of these observers, Gil by name, says that "There are times when I think of God as being the best that all of us can be—in a humanistic, secular sense. In a sense I believe in a primal force—a spirit that causes things to happen, that set the world in motion." Such a view is not especially Jewish; indeed, it seems indistinguishable from many of the comments of mainline Presbyterians. Assimilated Jews have made their peace not only with the American melting pot but also with a general American tendency to find a comforting and rewarding God.

Even Orthodox Jews have been influenced by these trends. In theory, one should obey God for no other reason than that God commands obedience. But in reality, the reasons for observance have as much to do with the needs of the person as with the commands of an authoritative deity. At Lincoln Square Synagogue in Manhattan, rabbis, in the words of one sociologist, "marketed the religious worldview by attempting to convince recruits that it represented the *best* choice for them. . . . They called it the most ethical, the sanest, and the most psychologically sound way to live." The laws of kashrut, or keeping kosher, these rabbis insist, should be obeyed for "rational, ethical, and social reasons." This sociologist attended a koshering party for new recruits to the synagogue, only to discover that the rabbi did not offer "a single theological rationale for kashrut." (The convenience of inviting other observant Jews to your home as well as respecting the sanctity of life were emphasized.) Along similar lines, the rabbis also emphasize that Sabbath observance is a blessing for people who need to spend more time with their children or who are stressed out from hectic workaholic lives. Most American Jews, and certainly most Orthodox Jews, understand full well that breaking Jewish law is an offense against God, which makes it all that more significant that so much of the everyday conversation about observance, including formally religious conversation, becomes focused on the advantages to human beings of leading a life without sin.

It is clear from these accounts, stemming from many religious traditions, that the God in which large numbers of Americans believe, in the words of Robert Wuthnow, "is a God of love, comfort, order, and security. Gone is the God of judgment, wrath, justice, mystery, and punishment. Gone are concerns about the forces of evil." America's God has been domesticated, there to offer solace and to engage in dialogue with the understanding that, except under the most unusual circumstances, he will listen and commiserate. In a world governed by this more accessible God, sin still exists and atonement is still possible. But the sins are less numerous, less serious, and more forgivable. The wrongs that people do are the sorts of things that can be set right by pleading to God's good side, not his commanding presence. The light that God holds in his hands is not the searchlight of a security guard surveying the landscape in the hopes of exposing people who have done wrong; it is the flashlight of a guide trying his best to help people find their proper destination.

THE RELIGIOUS ORIGINS OF NON-JUDGMENTALISM

"I was more of a judgmental person even though I didn't want to be," says one believer from Muncie, Indiana—Teri, the woman who felt rejected by her Southern Baptist Church because of her divorce. So long as she found herself in a judgmental church, however, she felt that she had no choice. It was "because I was judged so much that I just turned it around and judged you," she continues, "because you're going to judge me first so I might as well get you first." But now that she has joined a rapidly growing Pentecostally inclined church, Teri feels that she has grown up and can leave all this business of disapproval behind her.

In their never-ending quest to reach out to new members, growth-oriented and spirit-filled churches like the one Teri has joined not only dispense with doctrine, denomination, and theology, they also want to avoid any actions that will make people feel that their faults have taken on cosmic significance. This does not mean that they throw out conceptions of sin; preachers in megachurches in the United States will still talk of human misbehavior and God's insistence on judging it. But they generally do so in a language that, as one expert on megachurches puts it, frames the "discussion in terms of how sin harms the individual, rather than how it is offensive to a holy God." Their pastors "believe that if they can successfully portray God as reasonable rather than mystical they will be able to attract more seekers." To accomplish this, they appeal to a "nurturing" rather than to an "authoritative" version of Christianity, one that, instead of condemning people for their shortcomings, seeks to build up their confidence. With so much attention dedicated to helping individuals find their way to personal and spiritual health, today's all-embracing congregations are not about to remind them of the prospect that they are likely to burn in hell.

Rick Warren, the senior pastor of Saddleback Church in Orange County, California, the most famous megachurch in the United States after Willow Creek, does not come close to even mentioning hell. On the day I heard him in the summer of 2002, Warren was in top form; he is without doubt one of the most captivating public speakers to whom I have ever listened. Addressing himself directly to the question of sin, which he prefers to call temptation, Pastor Rick begins by pointing out that, puritanism to the contrary, "too much self-discipline can be a bad thing." Rather than confronting temptation directly, he offers a one-word alternative: flee, or, as he also puts it, "get out of Dodge." Avoid a John Wayne complex is his advice.

"Don't stand there and fight the temptation, you idiot," he jokingly admonishes his audience. Instead, you should work on restoring your soul by putting yourself in touch with God. Temptation, he goes on, is diagnostic; it tells us what our vulnerabilities and weaknesses are. Once we know them, we can turn to others for support, such as the small groups that flourish at Saddleback. "If you have a sin we never heard of," he tells them (in one of the few times he actually uses the word), "we will find a group for you." Mixing put-downs of therapy with his own quasi-therapeutic message, as if he had measured exactly the degree to which his audience both wanted help and wanted to avoid the appearance of wanting help, Rick Warren manages to talk about sin while rarely using the word—all the while suggesting through his warm and self-deprecating manner that he is simply not the kind of guy who is going to preach, even while preaching with considerable brilliance.

Not all of America's churches avoid passing judgment the way Saddleback does; the Southern Baptist one that condemned Teri from Muncie for her divorced status did not, a significant fact in itself since Southern Baptists are the largest conservative Christian denomination in the United States. Widely known for their adherence to old-fashioned fire-and-brimstone preaching, Southern Baptist churches tend to be places that have not yet caught up with the therapeutic individualism and egalitarian inclusion so prevalent in the rest of American religion. (There are exceptions; Saddleback, for one, retains its affiliation with the Southern Baptist Convention.) A 1986 survey of Southern Baptist preachers and lay activists found that self-identified moderates and fundamentalists differed on whether Christians should smoke, play cards, or engage in social dancing, but it also discovered that 94 percent of all Baptists agreed that they should not swear and 91 percent said that they should refrain from drinking alcohol. Even in contemporary American society, there exist denominations and individual believers who appear to be not all that different, in their approach to sin, from conservative Christians of the early twentieth century. Speak to a Southern Baptist about sin, and you are likely to be told that it is the need for human beings to be born again in Jesus in order to seek salvation from their sins that constitutes the heart of this particular church's outlook on the world.

Appearances, however, can be deceiving. Many American Christians are familiar with the parable of the prodigal son from Luke (15:11–32), in which Jesus speaks of a man whose younger son left home and led a dissolute life, only to return and ask for forgiveness, which his father then gave, even though his generous act offended his loyal and devoted elder son. One student of American religion studied forty-seven sermons addressing themselves to this parable from both Presbyterian and Southern Baptist ministers. Of all the sermons, the only ones that spoke in classic Christian terms about judgment and sin were Southern Baptist. "The wages of sin is still death," as one such sermon expresses it. "And God hasn't changed at all his attitude toward sin. You may change your attitude about sin, but God still cries out with a voice of judgment against our sin." Some of the Southern Baptist preachers who spoke to the story in traditional ways emphasize the sins of the younger son who had led the dissolute life. "The younger son [sinned] because he didn't want to do what was expected of him—he wanted to be free and independent. Doesn't this sound familiar?" one of them asks, making it obvious that those who suffer from excessive concern with the self share the same sin. "He became involved in wickedness," says another preacher, referring to the younger son's previous life among harlots. This preacher's message is clear: Rebel against authority and you too may "find yourself down in the pigpen, down in the far country, down in the place where the world lives in all filthiness." The older brother's resentful jealousy can be considered sinful as well. "[He] pretended to worship God," one of the sermons points out. "In actuality, he is his own god worshipping himself."

Still, even Southern Baptist churches have been influenced by the transformation of American religion, for only 16 percent of the sermons examined in this study conformed to the classic image of fire-and-damnation preaching. Southern Baptists are much like other American religious believers in their desire to hear messages of hopeful uplift. That is why so many build small groups into their religious practices, and one of the consequences of such groups is to encourage a feeling of belonging that is not always compatible with strong judgmentalism. "I think I've learned a lot about being myself and not putting on the holy little front that I used to put on a lot," as one member of a small group in a New Jersey Southern Baptist congregation puts it. "I think I'm a different person now than when I started house fellowship. It's a place for learning how to live with other people during the times they're struggling with something and being able to love them even when you don't like what they're saying or doing."

The energy and commitment that made possible the group to which this person belongs is provided by a man named Allen Scott, one of the many former Catholics who have found a home in a conservative Protestant church. One day in 1992, Scott dropped a bombshell; despite frequent meetings with a Christian therapist, he and his wife could no longer live together and were seeking a divorce. Scott resigned from the group's leadership, but after he did, the group began to flounder. Despite strong opposition to divorce in the Southern Baptist Convention—fundamentalist leaders in the 1980s stressed their opposition to divorce in their efforts to wrestle control of the SBC away from moderates—the group knew that it needed Scott's leadership. In addition, other church leaders had been through difficult marital breakups. After extensive discussion, the group decided to invite Scott back. As the sociologist who observed these events notes, the whole episode demonstrates that "the group made judgments about religious character based less on abstract standards of appropriate 'Christian' behavior than on the subjective experiences related in their personal narratives."

Because there are so many ordinary Baptists like Allen Scott and his group, most preachers in the tradition know the importance of avoiding words like "pigpen" and "filthiness" to describe the human condition. Far more common are messages of the glory that salvation can offer. Their sermons, including those dealing with the story of the prodigal son, tend to emphasize the rewards that God offers to those who atone for their sins instead of stressing God's fearsome power to punish wrongdoers or the unsaved. Atonement is to be achieved, moreover, not to win God's grace in the next world but to help the individual cope better with this one. In fact, only two of the forty-seven sermons addressing themselves to this parable depict a world in which people ought to fear God's judgment, and even those two do so indirectly, as if the preachers know that an explicit defense of God's capacity to judge would be taken by their listeners as evidence that he disapproves of them and the choices they make.

Reluctant to judge, conservative Baptist preachers often deflect sinful acts away from churchgoers by attributing them to those who do not know better, such as children or, in one not very Christian-sounding sermon, "criminals, prostitutes, addicts, homosexuals, the obese, the ugly, and the different." Others emphasize the universality of sin but in ways that leave listeners with the hope that since everyone is a sinner, they are not especially blameworthy or at fault. On one occasion, sinful acts are explained away when the preacher invokes the classification of diagnostic disorders assembled by the American Psychological Association to describe the elder brother's narcissism. Rare is the sermon that dwells on sin if doing so leaves a gloomy message that leaves little reason to feel joy in the presence of the Lord. Indeed, for one preacher, the lesson of the story lies in the fact that what should have been a joyous event—a family reunion—was dampened by the behavior of the two sons: "It's a tragic thing to be at a celebration and not be able to celebrate. To be a wallower at God's party and not be able to dance and sing. To miss the joy: that's to miss everything!"

Interestingly enough, this disinclination to pass judgment that one finds in evangelical circles can end up modifying one of the central aspects of evangelical religion. Conservative Protestants have a history not only of condemning behavior such as alcoholism or premarital sex as sinful but also of concluding that anyone who is not a "Christian"—by which is meant anyone who is not specifically an evangelical—is living the wrong kind of life. Yet confronting others, even mainline Protestants and Catholics, with the news that their faith is forcing them to live in sin represents an in-your-face kind of judgmentalism that makes many conservative Protestants uncomfortable. College students at McMaster University in Ontario, who belong to the evangelically oriented InterVarsity Christian Fellowship, have developed interesting ways of responding to this dilemma. Among themselves, where they speak in a language they call "Christianese," they will make sharp distinctions between Christians—by which they mean themselves—and others. But outside their own circles, other rules apply. "I try to avoid using that word," says one student named Martina about the term "Christian." Her preference is for "not-yet-Christians," a term developed by one of her religious mentors. Another student takes a "hard line" on the issue. Her father, she says, calls himself a Christian on the census form, but "I really don't think he is," she continues, since her father does not have a personal relationship with Jesus. Still, although she wants to call people like her father non-Christians, "I don't necessarily call them this to their faces," for, as she knows quite well, "it's not that he's a bad person or anything." Her solution—to pray for him—is a form of judgmentalism, to be sure, but not among the stronger forms one can imagine.

Mainline Protestants are even more unwilling than these conservative Protestants to pass judgment on the religious choices of others. As if he were an academic under the influence of Michel Foucault, one of the Presbyterian preachers interpreting the parable of the prodigal son tells his flock this: "I discovered that by trying to name the two young men, I was passing judgment on them . . . especially the elder brother. . . . My names for them were really labels and to label a person is sometimes to be done with that person." Mainline churches, especially the more liberal ones, have been predisposed to do away with strongly judgmental attitudes since the 1960s, when so many of them either were sympathetic to, or actively joined, leftist protest movements. These liberal voices shy away from any discussion of sin, finding in the Christian preoccupation with individual wrongdoing a doctrine that, in the words of one liberal Protestant theologian, "has all too often been placed in the service of social control and the preservation of basic social arrangements." As another theologian wrote in his 1993 book dealing with the subject, "the very idea of a book on sin . . . is likely to raise many red flags, especially the fear that even broaching the subject may be a small but fatal step backward into the dark ages from which our predecessors worked so hard and tirelessly to free us." His tone suggests irony, yet "dark ages" is not an inappropriate description of the attitude that many liberal preachers took toward an era in which some people routinely judged the conduct of others as sinful. Relying on one of their favorite passages in Scripture, they are not going to cast the first stone.

In the absence of a clear and commanding God who passes judgment on people, are people less likely to pass judgment on each other? The ubiquity of small groups throughout mainline religion suggests that they are. After spending considerable time with a small group in a mainline Methodist congregation, a sociologist wrote that "Many participants told me that their experience with the group had changed their relationships with other people, helping them to be more accepting, forgiving, and willing to reach out." Even more so than Southern Baptists and other forms of conservative religious practice, mainline believers seek through their small-group experience something resembling the support groups that emerged out of the feminist movement of the 1970s: a safe haven in which to confess to one's problems without being lectured on one's failings. As one small-group member says of her experience, "This is for me. These are women who are vital, nobody's putting anybody down, nobody had it all solved." Building trust is the key to the ways these groups work, and members know that trust will inevitably be broken if members sit in strong judgment of each other.

Because Jews and Catholics have become part of mainline American religion, they, too, find themselves fairly active participants in the world of religious nonjudgmentalism. This is particularly true of those liberal believers whose religious practices were shaped and reshaped by the cultural upheavals of the 1960s. In the aftermath of Vatican II, some left-wing Catholics experimented with "folk masses," which featured priests out of uniform and folk music such as "Kumbaya" and "Michael, Row Your Boat Ashore." The God these worshipers celebrated was not, in the words of one observer, "a judgmental overlord" but instead, as one believer put it, a "facilitator" who "ask[s] us to care for each other." But it is no longer just liberal Catholics who have moved away from traditional judgmentalism. Most American Catholics indicate by their disagreement with the Vatican that they would never judge as sinful someone who used birth control or had an abortion—because there is a chance that they would likely be including themselves. Their disinclination to engage in the sacrament of confession, moreover, suggests not only discomfort with the mechanics of the process, but the fact that, as one study puts it, "they are not as inclined to think of themselves as sinners in the first place." Increasingly, it seems as if there will be two versions of Catholicism in the future: a third-world church at home in Africa and Latin America in which sin will be featured in homilies and other church practices and a North American (and European) one that will resemble the turn away from the judgmentalism characteristic of other religions.

Similar, if less visible and dramatic, developments have been taking place among American Jews. The 1960s' fascination with *havurah* resulted in the emergence of what one member of an Oregon home-fellowship group called "non-judgmental Judaism"—more concerned with creating community than assigning blame. And while such experiments were limited to a minority of Jewish worshipers, the non-judgmentalism they featured has spread out to the rest of the Jewish community in the United States. This is reflected in the comments of a teacher in Queens, New York, who believes that "My way is not right or wrong, it's just my way" or a Queens salesman who, when speaking of Jewish observance, says that "I don't have any problem with what anybody does, as long as they don't tell me what I have to do. So, if you want to be involved in something that's very dear to your heart that's fine, but don't sit there and tell me about something that is clearly an option in life, that I have to be doing it, and I should be doing it because I am [Jewish]." Strong strains of judgmentalism remain among some American Jews, especially Orthodox Jews who have little trouble declaring their more liberal coreligionists insufficiently faithful. But the overwhelming majority of Old Testament believers in the United States have problems with the judgmental aspects of the testament in which they believe.

One arena in which religious nonjudgmentalism has particularly important consequences is in the inner city. On the face of it, sin would seem to surround inner-city churches, and not just any sins but ones, such as adultery, fornication, violence, and addiction, that have generally been at the center of conservative religious attention. Not only that, but many inner-city churches have roots in conservative traditions such as Pentecostalism or ethnic Catholicism that have taken strong positions on the ubiquity of sin and the absolute requirement of salvation. When, as president of the United States, Bill Clinton spoke at a black church in Memphis and called for strong religious discipline in the face of temptation, he was very much in the tradition of African American faith. African Americans may lean toward the left in politics, but in matters of religious authority, they have traditionally leaned toward the right.

Yet these days, even African American churches find themselves anxious to avoid passing too firm a judgment on the people who attend them. To take one example, the Ten Point Coalition ministers in Boston, committed to a "tough love" approach in working with young people in their area who have been led astray, are also realists who understand that if their message is too tough, no one will listen to it. They are aware of the case of an old-fashioned fire-and-brimstone preacher in their midst who likes to speak about what he calls "sinning and going to hell." He does so, however, to very small audiences; when an ethnographer attended his service, which took place not in a church but in a two-family flat, only eight people were in attendance, and four of them were the sociologist, the pastor, and his two children. This preacher attributes the low turnout to the sternness of his message. A true holiness church like his own will always be poor, especially in comparison to churches that "only preach things that people like to hear," which he calls "sweetwater." He will stick to the old ways of his Southern past, whether or not the message is popular. "Something is *wrong* if a holiness church is too large on an ordinary Sunday," he concludes.

Activist preachers like Eugene Rivers and others associated with the Ten Point Coalition want a larger audience than eight people. To get it, however, they have to modify, even if in subtle ways, the toughness of the love they offer. Reflecting the sterner side of their faith, Boston's activist ministers will contact the police and point out dangerous young men who need to be taken into custody, and this despite years of historic distrust between the black community and the Boston Police Department. But at other times, they will plead with judges for alternatives to jail time, convinced that many young people need a second chance. "It's so easy to condemn—it doesn't mean anything to be a crook, a crackhead, a prostitute," says the preacher who fashioned the "whole person" approach to salvation. "Our job is to lead them to the Lord. And all this beating people over the head and saying people are going to hell is not the way." The message of tough love remains, but it is surrounded by talk of compassion and hope, and it is not clear which message comes across loudest among those to whom the messages are addressed.

Even more than African American churches, those that attract Latino worshipers have a particular reason to avoid sounding too judgmental: many of their members are, technically speaking, committing a sinful act by living in the United States illegally, which means that they would face deportation if they decided to put the Ten Commandments into practice. Thus, when an East Los Angeles Pentecostal named Catalina talks about her status, she acknowledges that living in the United States without papers is "lying," but, in her view, it is "not really a sin." What matters, she believes, is the individual's intentions, and since hers are good, her sins can, and should, be overlooked. Evangelical Protestant churches in Latino neighborhoods encourage strict standards of personal conduct, but, as is often true of African American congregations as well, they also know how often individuals can backslide, and rare is the person who will be turned away for doing so, as long as one promises to seek Jesus's help.

The conclusion that emerges from these examples of religious nonjudgmentalism from so many different walks of American life is clear: Any religion that insists on the stain of human depravity, upholds a commanding and authoritative God as an alternative, and demands of ordinary believers that they look into their hearts in order to correct their sinful ways is not going to win too great a following in contemporary American culture. Americans have nothing against holiness; as the growth of Pentecostalism illustrates, large numbers of them seek it avidly. But they do have a problem with people who strike them as "holier than thou," so insistent on judging others that they fail to look at their own flaws and foibles.

The widespread fear of judging others that runs throughout contemporary religious practice suggests how deeply sunk the roots of nonjudgmentalism have become. Critics of the phenomenon tend to blame secular humanism for it, as if the left is at fault because criminals are given a second chance, students at prestigious universities are handed a disproportionate number of high grades, or psychologists dismiss bad conduct as an addiction or disease rather than as an immoral act. But there are religious origins to the culture of non-judgmentalism in the United States as well as secular ones, as anyone who recalls Jesus's admonition to "judge not" will understand. Believers who have a warm and personal relationship with the deity will probably want to have a warm and personal relationship with everyone else, and this precludes them from being ever on the lookout for behavior to condemn. Once specific behaviors have been removed from a category called sin, there is no place for them to go other than to a category called understanding—and understanding, along with empathy, warmth, and friendship, is what a large number of faithful Americans seek.

TAKING CHARGE

Sin existed long before psychology. When God called down his wrath on those who had been led astray, or when preachers, speaking in the name of God, singled out sinners for special treatment in hell, no one thought that a better way of framing the problem was to explore whether conduct deemed sinful from a religious perspective could more appropriately be labeled dysfunctional from a psychological one. Now nearly everybody does, none more so than religious believers themselves. It has been a full century since liberal theological seminaries, such as those at Hartford Seminary, the University of Chicago, and Boston University, began offering psychology of religion courses, and almost as long (1916) since they began to introduce courses on psychotherapy. These days psychological language routinely permeates the sermons, publications, appeals, and small-group efforts of mainline American religion. "Low self-esteem can keep us from achieving our goals, forming solid friendships, and seeing the good in others," suggests an article in a Methodist magazine aimed at teenage readers, before going on to add that "it can even hinder our relationship with God."

When psychology reigns, sin is driven out. "Sin isn't one of our issues," says a New York rabbi in charge of religious education at a reform synagogue. "My guess is that in twelve years of religious school our kids will never hear the word." This rabbi could argue, correctly, that sin is not as important a concept in Judaism as it is in Christianity, but the same could not be said for the principal of a Catholic school in San Antonio, Texas. How would you deal with a student who stole something from another student, she was asked? "First," she responds, "I'd ask them why they did it. I'd ask them about how it makes them feel, and how would they like it if somebody did that to them." The follow-up question was obvious: Suppose that they did it because they just wanted to? "I'd say," she answers, "you know, you can't get away with it all of your life. It just doesn't work that way." Finally asked if she would ever use specifically Catholic language in such a case, her reply is unequivocal: "Oh, no, that kind of language would probably not relate to them anyway. When I was growing up I personally might have responded to someone if they said, 'hey, this is a sin.' Today, though, I don't think that young people would respond to that." This principal's views are perhaps more liberal than those of ordinary Catholic believers, but her reluctance to rely on language filled with images of sin is fairly common.

Given their history, one might expect that conservative Protestants would be resistant to the incursion of psychology into what were once considered matters of doctrine and devotion. Certainly some conservative fundamentalists once were. Freud was never quite the enemy of the faith as Darwin in the eyes of fundamentalists, but he certainly came close, for the entire Freudian method—not only its emphasis on sexuality but also its insistence that there is another story behind the ostensible story being told—was completely incompatible with both an emphasis on biblical inerrancy and a preference for sinless personal conduct. To this day, psychology is looked upon as a dubious, if not diabolical, enterprise in some quarters of conservative Christianity. The Psychoheresy Awareness Ministries of Santa Barbara, California, to take one example, is, according to its website, "a non-profit religious corporation for the purpose of informing and educating Christians about psychoheresy. Psychoheresy is the integration of secular psychological counseling theories and therapies with the Bible. Psychoheresy is also the intrusion of such theories into the preaching and practice of Christianity, especially when they contradict or compromise biblical Christianity in

terms of the nature of man, how he is to live, and how he changes."
Groups like this know the appeal of psychology and have made it
clear that they want nothing to do with it.

Evangelicals, however, have proven themselves far more responsive to psychology than fundamentalists. To understand how far
evangelicals have moved toward full acceptance of psychology as an
academic discipline, it is helpful to visit the Fuller Theological Seminary, founded in 1948 to give intellectual strength to fundamentalism but which is now the leading supplier of evangelicals to the
ministry in the United States. (My visits took place in the spring of
2000 and the fall of 2002.) In the 1960s, Fuller created a school of
psychology that was accredited by the American Psychological Association a few years later and began to offer doctoral degrees in clinical psychology, thereby embarking on a course that would bring it
closer to Freud and Jung than to Jonathan Edwards. All students in
the Fuller School of Psychology are required to take theology
courses, because the mission of the program is to integrate faith and
mental-health practice. At the same time, Fuller's psychology program covers subjects one would expect to find in any clinical psychology program, such as human sexuality and child abuse. God only
knows what Charles Fuller, the seminary's originator, would have
made of his institution's turn toward psychology; introspection was
never one of fundamentalism's noteworthy features. But acceptance
of American culture has been a noteworthy characteristic of evangelicalism, and to reach American culture, the most direct road lies
through psychology. Hard-science topics such as psychometrics and
psychopharmacology are taught at Fuller, but the program does not
emphasize them. Fuller's psychology is meant not to divide and classify but to unite and heal, and for that purpose, clinical approaches,
and especially ones that resonate with popular therapeutic methods,
find a central place in Fuller's curriculum.

Enter the School of Psychology at Fuller, turn right, and look immediately to your left; you will see a bookcase devoted to the writings of M. Scott Peck, one of America's best-known New Age
psychologists. That exhibit, I later learned, is only a small part of
Peck's relationship with Fuller. Peck has donated his personal papers
to the seminary's library, and during my visit, I attended one class in

a semester-long course devoted to his writing. Leading the class was James D. Guy, the product of as pure an evangelical background as one could find. Guy is a Wheaton graduate with a doctorate from Fuller, who spent most of his career at Biola University (formerly the Bible Institute of Los Angeles). The dean of Fuller's School of Psychology when I visited, Guy, like just about everyone else I met at Fuller, was gracious and welcoming. (He has since left the school.) He and the class were discussing Peck's most famous book, *The Road Less Traveled*. This is not a book that would seem at first glance to appeal to the evangelical mind. Peck, a psychiatrist, grew up in a "high church" Episcopalian environment; his book, reflecting his sympathy for a wide variety of Eastern religions, argues for a capacious understanding of religion that need not even include belief in God, exactly the kind of thing that would displease the Psychoheresy Awareness Ministries, which in fact warns readers on its website that Peck's theology "clashes with Christianity at every crucial point."

But Peck's writings do not clash with Christianity in Jim Guy's class. Guy resonates with Peck's criticism of science, his belief in miracles, and his flirtation with mysticism. Twenty-five years ago, Guy explains to his class, we were convinced that science could allow us to know everything. Now, attracted to postmodernism, we think we cannot know anything. Peck stands right in the middle, the proper place to be. Guy proudly informs his students that they will have a chance to talk to Peck themselves—for although Peck's retirement and declining health prevent him from giving lectures, Guy has arranged for him to place a conference call to the class the week after my visit. "This is one powerful guy," he says. "Throw him anything." In anticipation of the event, the rest of the class time is devoted to a discussion of what questions the students ought to pose.

To a certain kind of skeptical liberal, M. Scott Peck is the very embodiment of mindless twelve-step recovery. "Even Peck's most avid readers," Wendy Kaminer wrote in *I'm Dysfunctional, You're Dysfunctional*, "would probably have trouble explaining his ideas." If Guy's class is any indication, Kaminer is right; the discussion rarely moves beyond an exchange of clichés. But the class environment was as warm and caring as Peck's reassuring text. Every student's comment, no matter how trivial, is taken as a serious reflection on the human condition. (My impression, based on what I admit is an unrepresentative sample of classes, is that the ethos of Fuller makes it inconceivable that any professor would ever say that a student's comment was simply wrong.) No one wants to reject any of the students' suggestions for questions to ask Peck during the conference call, and when one suggestion is received lukewarmly ("Would Peck be as sympathetic today to sometimes breaking the rules of therapeutic treatment as he was in *The Road Less Traveled?*"), considerable time is spent revising the wording to make it acceptable. The students I spoke to after class, all of whom planned to become either ministers or mental-health professionals, loved the class and loved Guy. Their jobs will require them to maintain an optimistic outlook on the world, and Peck's spiritualism will come in handy when they are plagued by doubts.

Looking back, it makes perfect sense that a seminary with fundamentalist origins would turn to psychology if its mission is, as Fuller's president, Richard Mouw, told me, "to reach people where they are." But such a move can also play havoc with strict conceptions of sin. Before he became president of Fuller, Mouw, then a professor of theology and philosophy at Michigan's Calvin College, wrote about sin in searing terms. "Jesus Christ did not come into the world merely to give men 'peace of mind' or to make them 'happier' or to help them to be less selfish," as he put it. "He came to rescue the entire created order from the pervasive power of sin." Inspired by the strictness of the Christian Reformed Church to which he belongs, Mouw's understanding of salvation is old-fashioned in its prophetic sensibility: "The primary aim of Christ's atoning work among men is . . . to create a new quality of human life." At the same time, Mouw is an evangelical as well as a Calvinist, and as an evangelical he understands that although "sin does afflict our lives on all levels . . . , sin also has its beginning in the rebellion of individual hearts," which means that if we are to transform those hearts, our best method is to proceed "softly and tenderly." Mouw's choice of terms is a far cry from the day when Solomon Stoddard, Jonathan Edwards's grandfather, claimed that "The word is a hammer, and we should use it to break the rocky hearts of men." However much and in however many ways contemporary Americans sin, Mouw is correct that, in a psychological age, the best way to get them to have a closer relationship with God is not with a hammer but with words of compassion and concern.

Calvinists like Mouw hold to the doctrine that because God's grace is inscrutably given, there is not much that individuals can do to overcome the inherently sinful nature of their condition. But not all conservative Christians agree with that position. Take, for example, those churches that have grown out of the holiness tradition, which originated in Methodism but which now can be found in denominations such as the Church of the Nazarene, the Wesleyan Church, or the Church of God (Anderson, Indiana). For these believers, individuals can take responsibility for their own salvation in at least one respect: They must rededicate themselves to Christ through a "second blessing" of the Holy Spirit. If they do that, they could, unlike more traditional evangelicals, find themselves living in such perfection with the Holy Spirit that their struggle against sin can come to an end.

Because holiness churches assign such importance to the individual's own responsibility for his or her condition, they hold little back when it comes to sin. Among other things, holiness churches are responsible for the persistence of revivalist camp meetings in the United States. At one held in St. Petersburg, Florida, in 1987, Brother H. E. Schmul, of Salem, Ohio, told the assembled crowd that sin "is a moral corruption that will result in final separation from God." Sinful behavior, he went on, is "a madness." When people say that "regardless of the consequences I have to do it. I have to shoot it. I have to drink it. I have to smoke it," Schmul believes that they are revealing how out of control they really are. In condemning them, he makes perfectly clear his disdain for the view that some forms of behavior, like homosexuality, are genetic in origin. That is why he believes that the AIDS epidemic is not all bad. "Some people are backing up on this homosexual thing. Some of the gays that had to have sex the homosexual way are changing their minds after seeing their buddies drop off or fall over like flies."

However much I may disagree with Brother Schmul's view of AIDS, he does make clear that strong conceptions of sin and strong conceptions of individual responsibility are linked. The same is not

necessarily true of those evangelicals who believe, in the words of sociologist James Davison Hunter, that psychology is "theologically
and morally neutral" and can be co-opted to serve Christian goals.
Large numbers of them apparently do; a brief look at Recovery-
Books.com on the web showed forty-seven Christian titles on self-
esteem, including Charles Gerber's *Christ-Centered Self-Esteem: Seeing
Ourselves Through God's Eyes* and Tamyra Horst's *A Woman of Worth:
Living as a Daughter of the King*. The message of these books has almost nothing in common with the message of Brother Schmul. In
Gerber's book, for example, low self-esteem is attributed to such
mistaken behavior as comparing yourself to others or valuing the
wrong things, concepts that, indistinguishable as they are from secular treatments of the same problem, need not be accompanied by any
talk of sin. One reader, D. L. Moore, clearly a conservative Christian,
responds to this point by saying that "almost every one of Dr. Gerber's listed 'behaviors' could potentially allow people to blame
someone else for their 'low self-esteem.' By not calling these sins
'sin,' one could potentially take almost all of these 'behaviors' and
play the Blame Game, explaining them away one by one, justifying
them with any number of excuses . . . without ever acknowledging
and repenting of the root sin itself. This, despite Jesus' warning to
repent or perish (Luke 13:3) because no one who refuses to repent of
such "behaviors" will enter the Kingdom of God (1 Cor. 6:9; Gal.
5:21; Eph. 5:5)."

Few people are going to listen to Mr. Moore, however, especially
when compared to the widespread popularity of self-help movements in so many quarters of conservative Christianity in the United
States. And evangelicals are just the tip of the iceberg when it comes
to blending themes of personal recovery and spiritual regeneration.
It is not just the popularity of small groups and the proliferation of
therapeutic language that can be found everywhere in American religion, nor even the cornucopia of diet books and self-help manuals.
Many Americans consider themselves spiritual more than they do religious, and they often turn for inspiration to writers such as M.
Scott Peck and Thomas More, who, while not identified with any particular religious tradition, incorporate into their explorations of self-
hood spiritual themes from many different faiths ranging from

traditional religions to New Age consciousness and ecological wholeness. Some writers believe the "spiritual but not religious" category is in fact America's largest religion, claiming more adherents than Catholics or Baptists, usually thought of as the most popular religious denominations in the United States. Somebody, it is clear, is buying all those self-help guides, and whether or not those who do formally share a religious designation matters less than the fact that few if any of them contain much language about sin and the damage it can do to people, God, and society.

Popular psychology is bound to influence churches more than the other way around, if for no other reason that, in their attempts to reach the "unchurched," religious leaders have to pay attention to what Americans are buying and reading in such copious amounts. Tom Rivers, for example, has changed his faith as many times as he has changed jobs; he calls himself a "spiritual junkie" who is "all over the place." Whether flirting with Buddhist beliefs, listening to self-help tapes, or channeling, his eclectic approach to faith, as for more conventional religious believers, gives him a sense of place: "When you feel connected, then you feel at home. When you're in touch and you're feeling that spirit, then the respect you're giving is coming back to you." If his views express what it means to be unchurched in America today, it is no wonder that churches intent on reaching out to people like him will take such giant steps away from their historic beliefs and practices in an effort to bring him in.

This blending of psychology and religion has its positive side, for there is no necessary reason to conclude that those who focus on their own needs will automatically neglect the needs of others. Still, the psychologizing of American religion makes it difficult for the faithful to emphasize classic religious themes such as duty and responsibility. One example is provided by a Bible-study group led by a woman named Karen. Leading a discussion of 1 Timothy, Karen refers to certain religious injunctions such as "Avoid arrogance" or "Don't put your hope in wealth." Her point is this: "You may not consider yourself rich, but relative to the rest of the world, you have quite an abundance of things!" Members of the group might respond by concluding that she is correct and that they are therefore obligated to take some responsibility for the world's poor. But most do not. "Boy, you wouldn't believe how much I'm paying to send my kids to camp," one claims, while another says that her husband felt she spent too much on her clothes.

We should not conclude from Karen's experience that the United States would be better off if more people pointed the finger of sin at others, for example by blaming homosexuals with AIDS for their own illness. But there is something to be said for belief in sin if it is accompanied by the ability to focus on matters outside the self. In the ways in which they dispense with doctrine, reinterpret tradition, and transform worship, Americans have long ago left behind ways of practicing religion that would satisfy the prophets and martyrs who shaped their faiths, yet in no other area of religious practice, especially for evangelicals, is the gap between the religion as it is supposed to be and religion as it actually is as great as it is in the area of sin. As a nonbeliever, I ought to be encouraged by this development, for it suggests that we will be less likely to point invidious fingers of shame at those who do not happen to agree with the majority's determination of what is acceptable morality and what is not.

But somehow I am not pleased with this retreat from sin, for the ease with which American religious believers adopt nonjudgmental language and a psychological understanding of wrongdoing is detrimental to anyone, religious or not, who believes that individuals should judge their actions against the highest possible ideals of human conduct, however those ideals are established. One need not be a Calvinist preoccupied with the dark side of human nature to recognize that covenants exist and that we break them only at great cost to ourselves and to others with whom we share our society.

CHAPTER 7

WITNESS

THE RELIGION THAT CAME TO DINNER

America's religions take widely different attitudes toward the process of reaching out and embracing others. Jews tend not to be evangelical at all, at times going so far as to set high barriers before potential converts, although Ultra-Orthodox Jews like the Lubavitchers do try to convert others, even if their efforts are directed at their own coreligionists and not members of other faiths. Nor is the term *evangelical* generally used to describe Catholics and mainline Protestants, despite the fact that the former has had an on-again, off-again history of missionary activity and that one mainline denomination, Lutheranism, includes the word *evangelical* in its official name. Evangelization in the United States has become controversial because of the growth of conservative Protestantism. When conservative Protestants are compared with each other, real differences emerge that make it valuable to distinguish between fundamentalists, evangelicals, and Pentecostals. But when conservative Christianity is compared with other religious persuasions, all of its forms are committed to witnessing and for that reason can be grouped together.

Because conservative Christianity has been growing, Jesus has been making more of an appearance in American life over the past few decades; rare is the American who has not been exposed to individuals anxious to witness, with little or no provocation, their faith in the Lord. And because the name of the Lord is so frequently invoked, the question of where to draw the line between freedom of public religion and freedom from public religion has become as contested as the legal controversy in the 1940s over whether Jehovah's Witnesses could be compelled to salute the flag. Evangelicals lack the authority of government to enforce their practices. And they insist that they treat other religions with respect. Still, they believe that those who do not share their faith are missing something in their lives, an attitude that gives energy to their religious enthusiasm but that can easily translate into intolerance toward the ideas and practices of faiths different from their own. Many Americans are thus made uncomfortable by the proselytizing character of evangelical faith; some mainline denominations worry that it will give all religion a bad name, while others—believers and nonbelievers alike—object to what they consider to be the inevitably coercive effects of even nongovernmental efforts to inculcate one religion's, especially the majority religion's, truths. Invite a member of an evangelical faith into your house, and the fear is that, like the hanger-on in the Broadway play, he will stay for dinner.

Evangelicals do evangelize; one survey found that 91 percent of evangelicals and fundamentalists said that "converting people to Jesus Christ" was very important to them compared with 76 percent of mainline or liberal Protestants. Other religions such as the Mormons, moreover, make missionary activity, both inside and outside the United States, central to their faith. The interesting question, however, is not whether evangelicals engage in spreading the word, but how they do so in a society in which religious belief so often serves private needs, few opportunities for genuinely public interaction exist, and culture is shaped by many institutions, not just those that have a religious character.

SALVATION INFLATION

"I love Christ so much and He's done so much for me I can't shut up about it," a thirty-three year old evangelical recounts. "So I've got to let people know." (This woman is Canadian, not American, a difference that in this context means little because North American evangelicals share common traditions and approaches to religious practice.) For her, as for her coreligionists, witnessing the faith is as natural as drinking water. "Christ has affected my life, and decisions that I've made, the roads that my husband and I have taken, and I've seen peace, and a conviction that that is not out of my own strength . . . and I think that everybody is searching these days, um, why would I not want to share that?" as another believer puts it. Neither of these women would ever think of themselves as intruding on others. Knowing that Jesus saves, it seems obvious to them that others ought to know as well.

As they go out into the world, however, evangelicals often discover that their attempts to share their joy turn out to be more complicated than they may at first have realized. Some of them, for one thing, are not confident of their intellectual abilities. "What am I going to say if someone asks me about fossils or Hinduism?" as one evangelical student (also Canadian) asks rhetorically. "Look, I just don't feel comfortable trying to answer all those questions," another responds. "That's not really my thing, you know? Why don't we just talk about God's grace in the world instead." A third expresses the point this way: "I'm willing yes, I guess, I think I'm willing, but I don't think I'm that able. I know someone would have to confront me and ask me questions about it." While one can easily find religious believers brimming with self-confidence, there are also large numbers of evangelicals so marked by nonjudgmentalism, so new to their congregation because they were so recently members of another one, and so in need of religion for intensely personal reasons that the thought of talking to strangers, let alone trying to persuade them to change their ways, is capable of inducing a cold sweat.

Like most people, moreover, conservative Christians do not want to stand out as unpleasant and ill-mannered, and hence they often tailor their efforts at proselytism to account for the conventions of daily life. In some cases, this may mean taking steps to avoid appearing overly aggressive. "It's our duty to promote the gospel," says an evangelical of her outreach to others but only "if they're willing to receive it." This individual would talk about her faith if an opportunity arose, but "if somebody is not interested then I'm not somebody that would push it on anybody in any respect." As much as Christians may be obliged to spread the news, they are also commanded to practice virtues such as humility, and when one conflicts with the other, the best course may well be to abstain from potentially unpleasant encounters. A determination to be nice can constitute as much of an obstacle to aggressive proselytizing as a lack of intellectual self-confidence.

In part, the reluctance of believers to impose their views on strangers simply reflects reality, for cold calling is not a very effective recruitment technique; efforts by Mormon missionaries to knock on doors produces a success rate of one in a thousand, compared with a rate of one in fifty for conversions begun in the home of a potential convert's friend or relative. But the reluctance of believers reflects something else as well; as women in particular talk about their unwillingness to impose their views on total strangers, one hears echoes of the particular kind of gender politics characteristic of evangelical faith. To a considerable degree, the rise in evangelical religion can be directly attributed to an increase in religious feeling and religious participation among women. Yet because so many conservative Christian women seek forms of faith that emphasize a warm and personal relationship with the deity, they are also likely to reject forms of witnessing that resemble the impersonal tactics of telephone solicitation.

In one study of women attracted to conservative Christianity, conversion stories invariably emphasize how, over a long period of time, these women searched for answers to the personal difficulties they were having with their lives, only to discover, often through a chance encounter, the reality of Jesus. "I went to the beach with a friend of mine," one remembers, "and they were having a baptism down there. . . . I knew at that moment, I'd found a strong calling, that the Lord wanted me to be baptized." For a woman like this, self-discovery is the dominant theme in how she came to be born again, while the organized efforts of the congregation she joined are barely mentioned. Women whose conversion is so personal are bound to have mixed feelings about undertaking highly public efforts to convert others. Of course, they pray for the souls of the unsaved and gladly welcome them into their midst. But they also recognize, from their own experiences, that there is only so much they can do to help others; when those others find the right moment in their lives, they will find their own path to salvation.

Evangelical women often lack the zealotry of far stricter believers who consider proselytizing, however uncomfortable or time-consuming it may be, a duty they cannot easily shirk. Fully aware of this, some go out of their way to insist that they are evangelicals, not fundamentalists; the difference between the two, in their minds, lies in the fact that the latter too often become involved, as one of them points out, in "shoving the Bible down people's throats." These evangelicals, however, may have a distorted view of what fundamentalists are really like, for in real life even the most zealous believers quickly confront the limits of strong evangelization.

At Southside Gospel, a fundamentalist church in the Northeast, classes are regularly conducted in witnessing; members are taught to recognize evangelistic opportunities, are offered the right language to use when they arise, and, through role-playing exercises, are instructed what to do when they step outside the shelter their church provides. True to their mission, some Southside members engage in what one of them calls "really witnessing." Ever on the lookout for vulnerable people, like those who face health and personal problems, they start conversations about the Lord's miraculous works even when doing so could easily be viewed by their targets as invasive. Persistent to the point of being aggressive, they can and do cross the border into rudeness. Some use every holiday to get in a word about Jesus. Others keep their radios set to Christian stations in the hopes that other people will take notice and ask them about it. Since their faith is defined by the depth of their evangelical commitments, they have, in their own view, no choice but to turn every encounter into a conversion opportunity.

Still, they have their fears and doubts. One declares certain environments, such as the workplace, off-limits. "I make it clear that my life is the Lord's," she explains, "but I try not to choke it down anybody because I'm there to work." Others, even as they engage with strangers, tend to stick to the script and try to end the encounter quickly. Some even shy away from any direct involvement with other people. Southside keeps on hand a number of tracts—small pamphlets that spell out, often in question-and-answer form, the need for salvation (and the awful consequences that can follow from its absence). The idea is to hand them out in order to start a conversation. While some Southside members do that, others "place tracts where they are sure to be found by someone who has been otherwise unreceptive," writes the sociologist who studied them. "Southside members know they have been commissioned to tell everyone about being saved, but not every social encounter is conducive to religious persuasion. When the encounter is too brief and impersonal, or when personal conversations seem fruitless, written words from some other Christian provide a useful way to introduce the subject of salvation."

Studies of converts to conservative religions such as Orthodox Jewry find that at least for some believers, withdrawal from the secular world involves a withdrawal from one's own parents. However painful this process may be, it is mild compared to converts to fundamentalist Protestantism, for these believers not only leave their family behind but also find themselves, unlike nonevangelistically inclined Jews, obligated to then save the souls of those they have just rejected. Facing the daunting prospect of spoiling every wedding or family function to which they are invited by calling attention to the smoking, drinking, and dancing of their relatives, it is not long before many of them decide that their own family members are either hopelessly lost or not proper candidates for conversion. "When people become committed members of Southside Gospel Church, they often exchange one family for another. They begin to understand what the Apostle Paul meant about having brothers and sisters in Christ and what Jesus meant about leaving father and mother to follow him."

Now members of a new family united by faith rather than by blood, not many of the believers at Southside report having close relationships with people outside the church. "It is going to be sad to lose all of our friends," a member named Mary Danner recalls feeling. "But to tell the truth, as time went on the new friends that we got were really wonderful. There were so many, and they thought the way we did." It is typically with their new friends that many evangelicals witness, for at least there, among the like-minded, one finds people with whom one can share the thoughts that really matter and receive a respectful hearing, one reason why evangelicals in groups ranging from Promise Keepers to students at universities tend, their obligations to witness to the contrary, to restrict their efforts to the already converted. Like those attracted to a political cause, fundamentalists are characterized by closeness within the group and suspicion of those outside it. Witnessing among the like-minded becomes a way of fulfilling evangelistic obligations for those wary of the larger world.

Because they form subcommunities of the like-minded, fundamentalist believers, presumably given to sticking their noses into the affairs of strangers, actually tend to avoid encounters that would bring them into contact with people they do not know. Their way of witnessing tends to a reinforcing conversation among the already committed, a way of finding a congregation, choosing a neighborhood, selecting schools for the children, deciding what books to read and what television stations are trustworthy, and even picking where to be buried—all with minimal contact with the outside world. Of course, some such contact is unavoidable; Christian academies, which conservative Protestants establish to reinforce their own way of life among their children, cannot avoid making compromises with the culture around them. But the point is that they try; at the Bethany Baptist Academy in Illinois, a fundamentalist school, the ideal is "limited contact with non-Christians and . . . enduring bonds with Christians." Withdrawn into their subcommunity, fundamentalists sometimes feel that they are on the outside of society looking in. "It's . . . like when you've gone to the aquarium and you're watching through the window everything that's going on inside, and you're protected from what's in there," as one Southside member observes. When the obligation to witness conflicts with the need for solidarity and identity, the obligation to witness is likely to be sacrificed.

This kind of dramatic withdrawal from the world is not the only alternative facing conservative Christians as they try to witness to people who are too busy or too engaged with their own families and friends to spend much time listening to them. Fortunately for them, there is a way to witness without embarrassing oneself in front of strangers; one can try to live a model life such that others will notice the glow of happiness and turn to God as a result. "Whenever I hear 'evangelical' I think of someone up front, talking, preaching," as a believer expresses the point. "I guess I'm not a preacher in that sense, but I . . . do feel that my life and the way I conduct it is . . . a testimony."

One sociologist calls this idea that one can witness well by living right "lifestyle evangelism." Muncie's Spirited Church offers an example. Spirited Church informs potential members that "it is the responsibility of every believer to carry the message of the gospel to others," and, true to its word, it engages in some form of old-fashioned evangelism such as missionary work abroad. But the leadership of Spirited Church also recognizes that a one-size-fits-all approach to evangelism, and especially one that insists on confrontational practices that might make its members uncomfortable, would be counterproductive. The church therefore attempts to balance its commitments to proselytizing with the idea that "individuals can choose a way to evangelize that suits them." Not surprisingly, the soft-edged religious switchers and doctrinally indifferent believers attracted to the church will choose ways to evangelize that make relatively few demands upon them. Whether they recognize the parallels or not, believers who practice lifestyle evangelism are copying the countercultural enthusiasts of the 1960s and 1970s, who were sure that eating organic foods or recycling one's trash would do more to undermine the capitalist system than conscious attempts to organize politically.

Lifestyle evangelism, in this sense, is a good fit for religions that seek to maintain historic commitments to spreading the word but to do so in ways that avoid any direct confrontation with the built-in individualism of contemporary American culture. So good is the fit, in fact, that forms of lifestyle evangelism influence even strict religious fundamentalists. In contrast to Muncie's Spirited Church, members of Southside Gospel Church would surely shy away from any talk about individuals finding their own way to witness, just as its members would be suspicious of any term linking a sacred word such as *evangelism* with a profane one like *lifestyle*. Yet because the work of spreading the gospel to others is so difficult, these believers also find themselves falling back on the notion that, as the sociologist who studied them puts it, "living . . . an exemplary Christian life is sometimes the only means for witnessing that believers feel they have at their disposal." For conservative Christians of all stripes, witnessing means putting one's own house in order before telling others how to redecorate their own.

Although it may not involve direct interaction with others, lifestyle evangelism is, in its own fashion, demanding, for the believer is commanded by God to live an exemplary life so that others may have a model to follow. But some church leaders worry about approaches that "ask people to do more in evangelism than they are capable of doing," as Steve Sjogren, senior pastor of the Cincinnati Vineyard Fellowship, puts it. Even supplementing traditional efforts to get out the word through reliance on videos and seminars, he believes, does not get at the heart of the matter, which is that most contemporary believers find the task of talking with others about their faith about as pleasurable as going to the dentist. Sjogren, like many evangelical pastors throughout the country, wants to bring people into his church who have long been uncomfortable with religion, and to do so, he makes his services as nonthreatening as possible. His particular contribution to evangelical practice has been to apply the same kind of comfort level to his church's outreach to the wider community. "You can't be an evangelist because you don't make people feel bad," is the way he describes the reaction of more old-fashioned Christians to his approach. His response has been to develop a form of witnessing that makes people feel good, a "low risk" strategy that removes the guilt and fear built into traditional evangelical encounters.

Sjogren calls this low-risk approach "servant evangelism." Believers should simply commit random acts of kindness, explaining to others along the way that this is how they best serve God. Giving out popsicles to joggers or washing the windshields of the cars of strangers are Sjogren's favorite examples. One day when they were out windshield washing, he recalls, two Mormon missionaries stopped at a red light, and Sjogren and his church members immediately began scrubbing away. "Just to show you God's love in a practical way," they answered when the Mormons asked them what they were doing. The Mormons, Sjogren writes, were "dumbfounded" into unaccustomed silence. "They had nothing to say because we had beaten them to the punch with a demonstration of the reality of God that no verbal comeback could match." Indeed, Sjogren goes out of his way to practice servant evangelism in unexpected places; once, he told me, he and some of his flock went into a local mosque and began cleaning the toilets in order to demonstrate, not the power of Jesus— for Sjogren knows how politically incorrect that would be to Muslim believers—but the power of a lord in which both Christians and Muslims can believe. Evangelization, the lesson is clear, need not be didactic and preachy. Reinterpreting the Bible with the same inventiveness he applies to Christian practice, Sjogren developed a slogan that, in his words, comes *"almost* straight" from Scripture: "Where the Spirit of the Lord is, there is fun!"

Committed to reaching out to the unchurched with innovative methods, however turned off from religion the unchurched may be, evangelicals like Sjogren assign considerable importance to church growth; the cover of Sjogren's book *Conspiracy of Kindness* points out that his own church is one of the twenty-five fastest-growing churches in the United States. Church growth tends to be a hot topic wherever evangelical leaders gather: They judge their movement successful if it registers ever-increasing numbers of new members; churches that grow are invariably celebrated, whereas those that do not are judged to have gotten God's message wrong; and methods that work are copied and those that fail avoided. As their ranks expand, evangelicals can perhaps be forgiven for concluding that the people who join them testify to a deep desire for spiritual connection that only religion can offer. Yet the rapid growth of evangelical religion in the United States can just as easily be cited as evidence of secularism's powerful appeal. Indeed, the very notion of church growth—which, in evangelical circles these days, comes complete with case studies borrowed from business schools and analyses of the success or failure of various marketing plans—suggests that there is much more than a purely religious dimension to the story of evangelical Protestantism's popularity. "The church as a whole often loses sight of the modern world," Sjogren writes, but he himself, he makes clear, will not. Refusing to bend to convention and dogma, his desire "isn't to imitate someone else's Christian life, but to be the unique child of God he has created me to be." For Sjogren, religion is not the alternative to such modern ideals as individualism but a more effective way to realize them. "You know," he told me, "Jesus was an existentialist," since he spent so much of his time daring to act.

As is the case with so many of the other activities in which they engage, churches that take on an evangelical mission can be of two minds as they confront the realities of living in a culture that goes out of its way to tame strong forms of faith. On the one hand, they appreciate the seriousness of an evangelical undertaking. Unlike salespeople concerned only with getting customers to buy their product, they recognize that what they are offering—salvation—is not something to be taken lightly, either by those who offer it or by those chosen to receive it. At the same time, evangelicals know that they were once sinners and are constantly in danger of lapsing back into sin themselves. Not only that, they understand that bringing others into their faith invariably means reaching out to people whose sexual promiscuity, drinking problems, criminal proclivities, or mocking skepticism serve as markers of their need for salvation. To be effective recruiters for Christ's message in a less than perfect world requires that they be open to opportunity and eclectic in method. And so, while the product—the soul—is not equivalent to a vacuum cleaner or a mutual fund, the techniques by which salvation is offered inevitably come to resemble the latest fashions in marketing and advertising.

Precisely because efforts at witnessing are so important to them, evangelicals feel that there would be something amiss if they did not explore any and every method that is likely to work in bringing the largest number of people to Jesus in the shortest period of time. "I take what is worldly, and baptize it," says H. Edwin Young, pastor of the Second Baptist Church of Houston, Texas. And among the worldly things sponsored by his church are sixty-four softball teams, forty-eight basketball teams, six bowling lanes, an indoor jogging track, weight and aerobics rooms, and an orchestra and chorus. Religion, it seems, offers an alternative to the much-discussed tendency of Americans to bowl alone, not only by offering them a place to worship together but also by putting more bowling alleys at their disposal. "People think because we're a church, maybe we shouldn't market," adds Second Baptist's music minister. "But any organization, secular or otherwise, if [it's] going to grow, [it's] got to get people to buy into the product."

If all evangelicals evangelize, not all who evangelize are evangelical. Anyone who loves something that can transform another person's life will feel a duty to share it, surely one reason why, as a child of parents who never attended college, I approach my own college teaching with something of a missionary zeal. Yet I know that as important as Lincoln's Second Inaugural Address or de Tocqueville's *Democracy in America* may be to me, my students, who face competing demands not only from other teachers but also from the entire American culture, may well resist even my most enthusiastic sermons. There is no reason to believe that just because large numbers of Americans say they believe in God, the situation involving religion will be any different; after all, large numbers of Americans, no doubt including many of my students, also consider Lincoln one of our greatest presidents. Every college teacher knows about both grade inflation and assignment deflation; as the amount of assigned work has decreased over the past two or three decades, the rewards students have received have increased. Much the same phenomenon—call it salvation inflation—has taken place as evangelical Christians carry out their duty to witness; as less becomes expected in order to achieve salvation, the blessings of salvation are offered with fewer strings attached.

WITNESSING IN CITY AND SUBURB

Already dealt serious blows by their own personal insecurities and by the resistance of their targets, evangelical Christians are dealt a further blow by such mundane sociological realities as unsafe streets, the decline of downtown areas, suburban migration, and the rise of exurban sprawl. There are many reasons why the United States has relatively little public space compared to other societies, and religion probably has little to do with them, but it remains the case that if one were looking for ways to limit the activities of evangelical believers, reducing the number of places in which strangers can encounter each other would be one of the most effective.

One reason why evangelical Christians are not likely to be found walking the streets of the United States looking for converts is because not all the streets in the United States are safe places to walk. Like evangelicals from middle-class neighborhoods, inner-city Christians constantly worry about the fear of rejection. But they also have to confront fears of violence in the areas surrounding them. This is particularly true of the most determined evangelists in inner-city communities, the Jehovah's Witnesses. To prepare for their street encounters, "publishers," as the movement calls those who walk door-to-door, spend considerable time in training classes, part of which are devoted to biblical knowledge and part to developing self-confidence. But in an inner-city Philadelphia neighborhood, publishers are allowed to depart from the script written by the Watch Tower Society's national headquarters to engage in role-playing exercises that take account of the realities of the neighborhood in which they witness. They are taught not to give in to the ever-present temptations of dishonesty or high living. They are encouraged to dress well and to avoid slang in their speech. Male publishers are trained, in particular, to respond to threatening situations, not by threatening violence in return but by demonstrating persistence in the face of abuse. The Witnesses recognize that just because publishers are religious and are residents of the neighborhoods in which they evangelize, they have no special protections if that neighborhood is a dangerous place.

In most American cities, urban ministries located in the most poverty-stricken areas are affected, in one way or another, by unsafe streets. One of the ministers in Boston's Four Corners neighborhood has had little success encouraging his basically middle-class membership to go out and bring in local residents. "Once you understand what Jesus has given to you and what he wants you to do with it," he says, "you have a responsibility to make sure other people know about it." Yet he recognizes that his efforts at outreach are limited by the fear that he and his members have because "you can't turn on the television at night and not hear about somebody getting killed—in this area! There are some rough people that walk up and down the street," he continues, "and there are some people that come in the church building demanding certain things." At least this minister tried. Another speaks of the time he saw two young men standing on the corner, and to avoid them, he went into the church and locked the door behind him. Later a member came and asked him why the door was locked. "I'm being wise as a serpent and humble as a dove," he answers. "I don't know who's gonna walk up in there."

The streets of Four Corners are unsafe because so many Americans, including in recent years African Americans, have moved to the suburbs. While sociologists such as William Julius Wilson have traced the effects of this kind of mobility on the economy, particularly on the distribution of jobs, less has been written about the effects of downtown depletion on religion. Critics of religion often treat faith as if it flourishes best in the rural byways of society, with the consequence that, to the degree cities grow and prosper, religion will inevitably decline. But there has always been an urban side to American religion. No nineteenth-century American city could consider itself founded until a substantial Protestant church planted itself there, and even when fundamentalists began to challenge mainline religion in the early twentieth century, their centers of activity were as likely to be Los Angeles or Chicago as rural Tennessee. If anything, the arrival of non-Protestants in the United States strengthened the urban character of religion; Jews and Catholics were especially attracted to city life and built imposing synagogues and churches designed to make a statement about their importance to the community. And while one can find a few new immigrants from Asia or Latin America in rural states like Iowa, most of them have settled in urban areas, revitalizing them as the children and grandchildren of previous generations of immigrants leave.

Despite its historically urban character, however, American religion has been dramatically transformed by the shift toward suburban life that took place in the years after World War II. Established denominations began the process. "Those who bought a station wagon and a house with a picture window," writes one historian, "were, initially, overwhelmingly middle to upper-middle class, concentrated in the Northeast, Far West, and industrial Midwest, white, of British or German ancestry, and college educated. These were precisely the same demographic characteristics associated with liberal or mainline Protestantism." The effects of suburbanization on their religious practice could be immediately detected, for, as a number of 1950s' social critics pointed out, suburbia was as incompatible with spiritual seriousness as it was with the promotion of social justice. For these new suburbanites, as for those Jews who moved out to what was once called "the suburban frontier," fund-raising, membership drives, and construction projects, rather than a concern with God's word, seemed to be the major focus of their religious lives. Even Catholics, the most reluctant of all religions in the United States to leave the city behind, eventually began to do so, especially after the reforms of Vatican II gave them the right to attend parishes of their own choice—and their rapidly rising annual incomes gave them the means. And as they did, they, too, became more involved with adjusting to suburban life than to maintaining the dense network of Catholic schools and social clubs encouraged by ethnic urban concentration.

While all such churches face problems and pressures as the changing demographics of American society weaken towns and cities, those with a strong commitment to evangelization are put in an especially vulnerable position. This did not matter so long as evangelicals lived disproportionately in rural areas or in urban downtowns. But the same forces of suburbanization that have affected other faiths have begun to have a significant impact on evangelicals. In the mid-1990s, 11 percent of the evangelicals in one survey had a master's degree or beyond and 6 percent earned more than one hundred thousand dollars annually. (Their educational levels were comparable to members of other traditions, although the percentage of high-income earners was lower than among mainline Protestants and Catholics.) Even more important, evangelicals have the highest rates of upward mobility of all religious believers in the United States; on average, they spent three more years in school than had their parents and were more likely to believe that their economic situation had improved over the past decade. As their members prospered, evangelical congregations began to follow them to the suburbs, not quite certain, as they did so, what this would mean for their obligations to witness.

One city that offers an especially interesting take on the effects of suburbanization on evangelical religion is Memphis, Tennessee. As one of the most "churched" cities in the United States—there really does seem to be, as residents insist, at least one church on every corner—Memphis is home to the rapidly growing Church of God in Christ. It is proud of its recent record on race—it was in this city in 1994 that blacks and whites came together to form the racially integrated Pentecostal/Charismatic Churches of North America—yet it's also the place where Martin Luther King Jr. was assassinated. Given its sizable African American population, its history of racial tension, and its relative lateness to downtown revitalization, one finds many examples in Memphis of "white church flight," in which evangelical congregations leave the city for the surrounding suburbs.

When *Christian Century* selected its great churches in 1950, one of them, Bellevue Baptist, was located in the heart of Memphis. Now, as evangelical as ever, it offers its members old-time religion thoroughly colored by what local residents call the "creek bank" theology of biblical inerrancy, conservative politics, and commitment to witnessing the faith. But it does this from a 376-acre campus in Cordova, eight miles from the city, complete with athletic fields, cavernous worship spaces, at least three grand foyers closely resembling those found in upscale hotels, a bookstore featuring CDs and tapes mixing religious and financial advice prepared by the church's preacher, Adrian Rogers, and a parking lot that rivals in size the one in the supermall built right across Interstate 40. Bellevue Baptist is not identical to Willow Creek; it does display a cross—three of them, actually, towering into the sky—and it retains a distinctly denominational—in this case, Southern Baptist—approach to faith. Yet Bellevue Baptist has a strong megachurch character nonetheless: "Six Flags over Jesus" was how it was described to me by another Memphis Baptist pastor with whom I spoke on a visit to the city. "You have to go where God calls you," he continued with heavy irony, "but God always seems to be calling you east," the direction middle-class Memphians generally take when they leave the city for the rewards of suburbia.

Because it remains a church very much in the Southern Baptist tradition, Bellevue Baptist, for all its modernistic touches, remains a revivalist church at heart. "Lots of people came to this town with mud on their shoes and became reasonably prosperous," one of its members points out, and, despite having a college education or a career as a professional, "they've brought their theology with them from the creek bank." Yet the growth and prosperity of Bellevue Baptist and other similar suburban evangelical churches are seen by many others in Memphis as a distraction from any serious commitment to religious purpose. Both evangelical and mainline churches have an obligation to promote Christian charity and social justice as part of their outreach efforts, yet a number of more liberal Memphis pastors, especially those who chose to remain in the city, wonder if this can be done from the outskirts. The newly suburban churches, which rely on modern technology to streamline their message, do not want their members to feel bad because they do not know much about their faith, one of them told me. But, he asks, isn't it the purpose of religion to raise uncomfortable questions for the complacent and the satisfied? The Reverend Billy Vaughn, who is affiliated with mainline Idlewild Presbyterian, is proud that his church has not decamped for the suburbs, for he is not sure that thriving churches recognize "the power of God to transform the city." As he and some of his colleagues see it, suburban evangelism is not really evangelism at all. "Megachurches say that they are practicing the faith," Rev. Jeff Irwin, director of urban ministries for the United Methodist Church of Memphis adds, "but what they are really doing is practicing the culture." Pastor Irwin thinks that what he calls "the full service church" is a church that has forgotten that its primary obligation is service to God. For these ministers, nothing in the tradition of evangelical religion is more important than reaching out to the poor and oppressed, and newly prosperous evangelical churches, like the mainline ones that preceded them to the suburbs a generation ago, are not well positioned for the task.

Bellevue Baptist is lucky; it managed to find good land only a few miles from the city. As other evangelical congregations follow their members out of the city, they often discover that the closer suburbs are already filled. (Still others, moreover, have prospered in portions of the South and the West that have no real central cities and suburbs at all but are instead characterized by extensive sprawl.) This helps explain why megachurches, a relatively recent phenomenon in American religion, tend to locate themselves well beyond the suburbs, where land is cheap. The former farmland that can be transformed into housing developments and shopping malls offers them a number of advantages, like safe streets, low taxes, and affordable homes. But for exactly the same reasons that make it affordable, the "exurban frontier" does not offer many accessible public spaces in which evangelists can evangelize.

Nevertheless under an obligation to witness their faith, evangelicals respond to their somewhat isolated surroundings in various ways. One way is to use already existing public facilities like the schools (if after hours) for evangelical purposes, with the hope that the Supreme Court, as it recently has done, will allow them to continue to do so. Another is to rent purely private spaces—hence the attraction of athletic stadiums for Promise Keepers and hotels for Aglow. A third is to try to proselytize in quasi-public places, such as on fairgrounds or in airports, thereby forcing the courts to choose between their rights of religious practice and the rights of property owners to keep them away. With similarly mixed results, the courts have also tried to establish guidelines that would enable individuals to exercise their right of free speech in shopping malls, which seems only appropriate now that churches like Hope Evangelical Covenant Church of Grand Forks, North Dakota, have begun to relocate directly into shopping malls themselves. Whatever the tactic used, the burden is generally upon evangelicals to find public places to witness that, except for their determined efforts, would not exist.

Given the problems they face in getting out the word, megachurches are often very successful in doing so, if success is defined by their ability to recruit new members. Hebron Baptist, founded in 1842, is one of the oldest churches in Gwinnett County, Georgia. Once a small-town church, Hebron Baptist expanded along with the county in which it was located, eventually transforming itself into a megachurch. Its growth has been fueled by tactics such as age-specific evangelism which uses young people to talk to other young people, singles to singles, and so on, as well as by a dynamic minister willing to innovate. So successful has the church been in attracting believers that members of older congregations in the area speak of being "hebroned." As the minister of the competing First Baptist Church puts it, "Hebron has sucked teenagers out of here like a vacuum cleaner," a sentiment which the urban pastors to whom I spoke in Memphis, who also find younger people looking for more popular forms of religious participation, would understand.

One reason why megachurches thrive is because of the atmosphere they create. Compared to the often depressing exurban locations in which they place themselves—often, as is the case with Steve Sjogren's Cincinnati Vineyard Church, where two sections of a ring road surrounding a city meet and are bordered by warehouses, self-storage facilities, and discount shopping outlets—megachurches offer an atmosphere of warmth and hospitality. At Hebron Baptist, the congregation goes out of its way to make people feel welcome rather than to make them feel bad. "Hebron," writes one sociologist, "like most megachurches, provides high-intensity experiences of communality with relatively weak systems for insuring individual religious accountability—the assurance of right without the punishment of wrong." The church does this by toning down its hellfire preaching in favor of more contemporary sensibilities. Leonard Boswell, a former Episcopalian who recently switched to Hebron Baptist, loves the new environment. "When they introduced the visitors, everybody shook our hand—they'd come from other pews. It was a real friendly place. But the thing that was really good was the preaching. And the singing, too. It is conservative fire and brimstone, but with everything all together it isn't scary. It is just the truth." Hebron Baptist is an example of what has been called a "family congregation," one that aims to provide for its members "a general sense of well being, acceptance, and belonging." These are churches that recognize the paucity of places in the United States where one can feel welcome, and they respond by opening their doors to all those willing to proclaim their faith in Jesus.

There is much to be said in favor of family-style congregations, which tend to work hard at meeting the needs of those who join them. And it is also the case, as Bob Hansel of Memphis's Calvary Church told me, that more mainline churches have not done a good job of making their members feel wanted. But new forms of exurban worship that bring otherwise isolated individuals and families into warm and caring church environments do so by transforming the dynamics by which evangelization has traditionally taken place. In traditional evangelism, the church, standing in for God, is the savior and the sinner is the penitent; believing themselves to be in possession of a truth that will set others free, evangelicals seek to bring the power they possess to those whose empty spiritual lives render them weak. Lacking either downtown locations that bring them in contact with strangers or public spaces in which they can reach out to passersby, evangelical megachurches, by contrast, have little choice but to offer incentives that will bring people to their doors. That process inevitably transforms the balance of power between institution and individual. The unchurched and the newly churched know that they have something the megachurches want—their potential or continuing membership—and they are willing to drive a hard bargain before they offer it up. Savvy church officials search out savvy consumers (and vice versa), and the result is a form of religious practice capable of pleasing both parties.

Because the evangelical efforts of megachurches attract people without much regard for doctrine, and because the people who are attracted to them are so often religious switchers perhaps on the way to yet another congregation or denomination, the commitments new members make are often as transitory as exurbia's rates of residential-home ownership. Megachurch evangelism aims for quantity rather than quality, as if an alternative conception of witnessing that pronounced itself satisfied with fewer, but more committed, converts is simply out of the question. The security such churches offer, while undeniably real, is also somewhat superficial and shallow, masking, as it does, the fact that membership so easily gained can also be easily lost. And when conflicts arise, which invariably happens at even the most family-oriented congregations, members, who tend to shy away from conflicts of any sort, are often poorly prepared to stick with the congregation in order to work out their difficulties. Megachurches are often treated as a revolutionary new stage in the ways in which people worship, but they may also turn out to be a passing fad, their success anything but guaranteed.

No longer residing in close proximity with others, dependent on cars to get them where they want to go, time-starved and consumer conscious, impatient with complexity and ambiguity, American evangelicals live in a society that makes serious conversation about any topic, especially one as important to individuals themselves as their faith, difficult. For all the commitments to witnessing they make, therefore, evangelicals are no longer certain why they make them. The charge to win people to faith is treated by evangelical theologians as having originated in the Great Commission: "Therefore go and make disciples of all nations, baptizing them in the name of the Father and of the Son and of the Holy Spirit, and teaching them to obey everything I have commanded you" (Matt. 28:19–20). Yet in a 1994 survey, only 9 percent of Americans in general and 25 percent of self-described evangelicals could say what the Great Commission is. (More, but still not a majority, could place John 3:1—"For God so loved the world, that he gave his only begotten Son, that whosoever believeth in him should not perish, but have everlasting life"—another important text for evangelicals, but one whose promise of life after death is less demanding than the command to evangelize.) Even when evangelicals overcome all the obstacles put in their path in order to bring people to Jesus, the majority of them, it would seem, have lost touch with the theological reasons for doing so.

The phenomenal growth of megachurches and similar forms of evangelical Protestantism in the United States leaves the impression that more and more Americans are using every opportunity at their disposal to poke their noses into other people's hearts (if you are critical of evangelicalism) or to bring much needed aid and assistance to people in desperation (if you are a practitioner). Yet neither the negative nor the positive is much in evidence when we consider what these churches have to do to gain and keep members in the outer corners of exurbia in which they have located themselves. "If you put on a three-ring circus to get them in," one of the urban pastors with whom I spoke in Memphis put it, "you have to keep putting on three-ring circuses to keep them in."

THE FAUSTIAN PACT
OF THE EVANGELICALS

If the United States, as it is so often said, is a country that takes its religion seriously, evangelical Christians ought to have a relatively easy time witnessing. True, overt appeals to Jesus may rub some the wrong way, but at least the use of terms such as God, faith, piety, and tradition ought to be well received by others, whatever their particular beliefs. Not only that, there is a venue readily at hand available to evangelicals for conveying their views. Although there are comparatively few public spaces available to anyone with strong views and a desire to reach out to others in a face-to-face manner, there is, as if to substitute for that absence, a ubiquitous American popular culture that one way or another seems to touch just about everyone. For every suburban and exurban housing development that removes people ever farther from the buzz of the city, innumerable numbers of radios, televisions, and computers with Internet access have been purchased. Witnessing to others need no longer be done through random street encounters when millions of the unchurched can be reached as they drive to work, watch television in the evening, log on, or listen to music.

For evangelicals to witness their faith using popular culture, however, they first have to overcome a history of opposition to it. "Sometimes people ask what are the objections to dancing and theatres and card playing and such things," wrote a Michigan fundamentalist, the Reverend Oliver W. Van Osdel, in 1919. "You will notice," he continued, "that the people who indulge in these worldly things are always loose in doctrine . . . and when you find people indulging in worldliness . . . apostasy easily creeps in, the union of Christendom becomes possible and probably will be united through corrupt doctrine under one head, the Pope of Rome." For a significant number of conservative Christian spokesmen in nineteenth-and early twentieth-century America, indulgence in popular entertainment was the first step down a slippery slope toward Catholicism, or perhaps even worse. (And this is not limited to just popular culture; the great revivalist Charles Grandison Finney once said that he "cannot believe that a person who has ever known the love of God can relish a secular novel . . . Let me visit your chamber, your parlor, or wherever you keep your books. What is here? Byron, Scott, Shakespeare and a host of triflers and blasphemers of God.") To this day, such views continue to echo in some corners of the conservative Christian world. At institutions like Bob Jones University—and among individuals such as John H. Evans, a former petroleum executive who founded the Movie Morality Ministries in 1996, or the Reverend Donald Wildmon and his American Family Association—fundamentalists approach American popular culture as if they are dealing with the Antichrist himself.

Yet almost from the start, other evangelicals recognized that such puritanical stringency would cut them off from the people they were obligated to reach, for the people themselves, often located in remote parts of the United States and, compared to others, lacking in education and cosmopolitan sophistication, were easily seduced by such forms of popular entertainment as vaudeville, magic shows, the circus, and traveling theatrical companies. As the nineteenth century turned into the twentieth, at least some evangelicals responded by trying to adopt the forms by which popular culture was conveyed while rejecting the messages associated with them; hence the proliferation of Christian publishing houses, magazines, book-reading groups, and radio stations. But even these were not sufficient for evangelical purposes, for by creating a Christian subculture in an otherwise secular society, they threatened to leave the rest of the culture alone. Throughout the twentieth century, then, even when conservative Protestantism was deeply sunk into its most antimodernistic phase, it persisted in manifesting more of an ambivalent than a hostile relationship with the popular culture surrounding it: Charles Fuller, founder of the Fuller Theological Seminary, hosted the most popular radio program in the United States, outdistancing Bing Crosby and Bob Hope; Bob Jones Sr., despite the strictness of the college that bears his name, loved the movies, used them to evangelize, and called the moving-picture machine the "most thrilling invention in the world"; Bob Jones Jr., unlike Finney, possessed a taste for Shakespeare; Paul Rader of the Chicago Gospel Tabernacle borrowed his promotional techniques directly from Hollywood; and Homer Rodeheaver, the trombonist for Billy Sunday and the Winona Lake Bible Conference, played with enough spirit to be attacked as too "jazzy." The point was to get the message across any way one could. "The business of the church is to take the message to the people," as Bob Jones Sr. put it during the roaring twenties. "The day has passed when you can ring a church bell and expect a crowd."

Whatever the history, the sheer ubiquity of the media in contemporary American life leaves evangelicals no choice but to rely
upon them. "Born again adults spend an average of seven times
more hours each week watching television than they do participat-
ing in spiritual pursuits such as Bible reading, prayer, and worship,"
says a report prepared by a survey research firm that works with
evangelicals. If those are the viewing habits of the churched, one can
only imagine how the unchurched spend their leisure time. Given
the hand conservative Christians have been dealt, little is gained by
efforts to ban textbooks or to rate television programs on the basis
of their profanity. Realists in the world of Christian evangelicalism
recognize that conservative churches are better off trying to influence the popular culture than they are trying to shun it. "Reaching
Hollywood, you reach the world," is the way one member of Mosaic,
the multiethnic church in Los Angeles with strong Hollywood ties,
puts it. That may represent something of an extreme approach for
conservative Christians, but nearly all American evangelicals are
widely attuned to what is happening in the popular culture surrounding them.

No other example of the evangelical receptivity to modern means
of communication has received as much publicity as "televangelism,"
the effort on the part of figures such as Robert Schuller, Jimmy Swaggert, Jim Bakker, and others to reach a mass audience for their message through television programming. The fact that some of these
efforts ended in scandal, financial or otherwise, neglects what might
have happened had more of them actually succeeded. For any success
surely would have come at the expense of the religious messages being delivered. "The subtleties of theology do not carry well over television," write the sociologists who studied the phenomenon. "The
medium is fundamentally visual, not cerebral." In theory, televangelists, like all evangelists, are committed to the Great Commission.
But in practice, theological considerations inevitably give way to financial ones. Like exurban churches that must supply inducements
to bring people to their doors, televangelists, intent on gaining and
keeping their audience, preach a kind of prosperity theology on the
one hand and fund-raise from their viewers on the other. As this
study concludes, "fund-raising has virtually become the tail that

wags the dog, even to the point of dominating, in some instances, the theologies of some of the televangelists."

A less-well-known, but in many ways more interesting, example of the uneasy mix of religious witnessing and commercial temptation is provided by the ways in which contemporary Christian music has spilled out of the churches into the culture that surrounds them. There are, needless to say, some lingering fundamentalist sentiments in conservative Christian quarters that warn against any involvement with so decadent a phenomenon as popular music in any form. "What are the Backstreet Boys, 'N Sync, and Britney Spears *really* saying?" asks Dial-the-Truth Ministries. The answer is that they are selling sex, as the French would say, pure and simple. Richard Wagner believed that opera united all the arts. For strict fundamentalist Christians, rock music—its rhythms suggestive, its lyrics satanic, its performers decadent—rolls all the sins into one.

While some conservative Christians shun rock, however, others just as surely adopt it for their own purposes. Popular within churches, many evangelicals assumed that their Christian rock music could have broad public appeal, thereby introducing unchurched individuals to Christian messages. An opportunity to do so certainly existed. In a 1983 survey, the National Association of Religious Broadcasters discovered that religious radio stations had an audience share of 1.6 percent, about the same as Spanish language, jazz, and classical-music stations. That hardly constituted effective witnessing. And so evangelical Christians began a determined effort to create their own commercial rock as a way of increasing their audience share. Those efforts were remarkably successful. Drawing on country and western and gospel traditions, contemporary Christian music attracted such artists as Michael W. Smith, BeBe, and Amy Grant, whose 1982 album *Age to Age* sold over one million copies. The idea that a singer of such gospel favorites as "My Father's Eyes" and "Sing Your Praise to the Lord" was also capable of making real money brought Grant's Word record company to the attention of CBS, just as it held out the promise to evangelicals of reaching unchurched young people with messages of religious devotion. Nine years later, Grant's *Heart in Motion* album sold five million copies and produced a number of Top 40 singles. The result was that the stars of Christian rock were invited to the White House and featured in *People*. For artists like Grant, all this was proof that one could reach a large audience without pandering to vulgarity and blatant sexuality.

As it turns out, however, the marriage between evangelicals and commerce was not made in heaven. Like the attempts by popular-front screenwriters to slip in positive references to the Communist Party in Hollywood movies, one has to pay careful attention before the coded religious messages of *Heart in Motion* can be detected. Grant herself said that she wanted to produce songs "about life experience without any hidden spiritual agenda," and with her 1997 release of *Behind the Eyes* she achieved her goal, for this album, in the words of one communications scholar, "contained no explicit references to God or Jesus." There is always a price to be paid by those who cross over into the mainstream, and for evangelicals, the price is self-effacement. To meet the standards of commerce, Grant had to tone down her evangelism, and while the result was profitable, it left more conservative Christians wondering what the fuss was all about. Grant may have reached the top of the Billboard charts with "Baby, Baby," but religious radio stations, appalled by its soft-edged sexuality, refused to play the song, and before long, conservative Christian watchdogs were just as likely to denounce Christian rock for its satanic content as they were any other kind of rock. (Nor, by the way, were they off base in doing so; Christian rock groups such as Stryper and singers like Steve Taylor really are often indistinguishable from heavy-metal bands and sometimes go out of their way to mock right-wing fundamentalism.) Eventually, the Amy Grant story ended badly. After Grant received a 1999 divorce and remarried a year later, she found herself even more estranged from American evangelical subculture, her albums no longer available at many Christian bookstores, her songs no longer played on Christian radio, and her invitations to appear at evangelical crusades all but disappeared.

What did evangelicals gain by overcoming their suspicion of popular entertainment in favor of contemporary rock? The answer seems to be very little. For one thing, the notion that young people were going to be lured into stronger faith commitments after listening to watered-down gospel music seems rather naïve. And just to set the record clear, the firm that conducts survey research for evangelicals asked those who considered Jesus their savior and found that none of them mentioned Christian music as responsible for their conversion. (Thirty-eight percent cited families and upbringing, 14 percent cited a sermon, and 10 percent a conversation with a friend about Jesus.) There is no way to know for certain, but Amy Grant is probably responsible for saving as many souls as athletes who use their talents on the field to make a statement about their God.

Perhaps because they were once so hostile to it, evangelicals have been late to learn about how difficult it can be to move the popular culture one way or another. It is true that evangelicals constitute a large enough market to be noticed, which in turn translates into enough clout to sustain Christian radio and television and even an occasional Hollywood film. But, then again, the mass media in the United States have become niche media, as any group with a well-defined interest, including those preoccupied by cooking or travel, can get their own cable-television station. (And, of course, no industry flourishes as much in the highly fractured media environment in the United States as the pornography industry, as if sin has one channel and the combatants of sin have another.) In a way no one could have intended, the conservative Christian decision to make peace with popular culture in order to avoid ghettoization produced a certain amount of ghettoization. Just as evangelicals have their own colleges and publishing houses, they now have their own favorite travel destinations and pop-music stars. For every evangelical who makes the big time, the more common effects of evangelicals to spread the word through the media work to persuade the already committed to keep their commitments.

Conservative Christians also find their own religious practices being transformed by the very popular entertainment they were seeking to emulate. As he concluded his travels throughout evangelical America, historian Randall Balmer was "astounded at how the media, especially television, have permeated evangelical worship. Soloists and musical ensembles gyrate to 'canned' orchestra music from cassette tapes played over elaborate sound systems. Applause regularly punctuated Sunday morning services almost everywhere I went, as though each congregation was a studio audience. God apparently likes applause, a fact that had eluded me as I grew up within the evangelical subculture." When evangelicals search for God in popular culture, not only does faith give way before commerce but also commerce, in the form of popular entertainment, reaches down into the inner sanctums of faith. "Turning mass recordings and rock tours into a form of 'ministry' took church pastoring from the world of local, personal relationships, premised on trust and familiarity, into the impersonal world of entertainment, characterized by the market-driven terms of production and consumer choice," as one professor at Calvin College, an evangelical institution, puts it.

Pleased by their success at bringing in new members, the leadership of fast-growing evangelical churches is busy counting filled pews, tabulating the sales of their CDs, and raising funds for the next church construction on the new ring road being completed as part of the interstate highway program. Yet one has to wonder whether their efforts are worth it. As conservative Christians change their attitudes toward popular culture away from ambivalence to active involvement, the results seem suspiciously like the kinds of Faustian pacts against which Christians often warn. For the truth is that there is increasingly little difference between an essentially secular activity like the popular entertainment industry and the bring-'em-in-at-any-cost efforts of evangelical megachurches. As evangelicals since the days of popular revivalist George Whitefield learn over and over again, the spirit of Jesus has existed for two thousand years and the United States for just a little more than two hundred, but whenever American popular culture clashes with that of time-tested religion, it is usually the latter that finds itself giving way.

As is true of so much else of their approach to modernity, evangelicals swing back and forth from rejecting popular culture to embracing it. The bitter truth seems to be that neither makes much of a difference. American popular culture is both amazingly indifferent to those seeking to shape its direction and astonishingly competent at absorbing and transforming anyone who tries. There is, contrary to what evangelicals sometimes think, no systematic bias against religious believers in the media because they are run by liberal elites ensconced in Manhattan; nor is there a rush on the part of the media to embrace Christian themes as a way of tapping into new sources of advertising revenue. Popular culture is instead about itself; it has its own imperatives, its own forms, and its own priorities. As willing to feature Jesus as it is Satan, it will reduce both to the lowest common denominator of its deeply entrenched conception of popular taste. Evangelicals are free to use the media to gain adherents, but in the process, they are likely to be used by media outlets desperate to fill twenty-four-hour programming. The whole unseemly process makes one think that perhaps those fundamentalists who warned against the temptations of popular culture may have known a thing or two. At least Faust was aware of the consequences of the pact he signed.

COMMITTED TO CONVERSION

One religion scholar describes what happened to him when he accompanied members of an evangelical student group on a worship retreat. After asking him about his research, a student changed the topic to his faith and learned along the way that he was a Unitarian. "Well," she responded, "it says in the Bible that only Christians will go to heaven. What do you say to that?" In this interaction, the ethnographer discovered what many nonevangelicals fear: triumphal rudeness creating a most unpleasant encounter. Yet in the three years of research he carried out with this group, he reports, this was the only time such an incident took place. Moreover, the student who accosted him had only been in the group for two weeks when the incident took place and had yet to learn the degree to which her evangelical colleagues try to be a bit more subtle in their approach. Conservative Christians talk a lot about "spiritual warfare," treating nonbelievers or those who believe the wrong things as enemies against whom one must be on constant guard. But a good deal of the actual spiritual warfare in the conservative Protestant world takes place as one conservative tendency attacks another; when it comes to the larger world outside of evangelical circles, fear combined with suspicion produces something more akin to spiritual avoidance.

This is not to suggest that evangelicals have become so tame that they have given up any obligation to spread the word. Evangelicals remain committed to conversion, and in their efforts to do so, they can indeed be intrusive, or even offensive, especially when they set their sights on non-Christians in the firm conviction that they can save them from an awful fate. This will especially be the case in regions in the United States where evangelicals constitute the dominant majority, such as small towns in Texas or South Carolina. Members of non-Christian faiths, let alone atheists, have considerable justification for believing that when Christians in those circumstances pray to Jesus in highly public places such as high-school football games, they lack sufficient appreciation for the rights of others not to hear their message.

Still, the fact that some religious believers witness their faith in ways that are invasive can obscure the fact that the overwhelming majority of those seeking to share their religious truths find so many obstacles in their path. When we think of evangelization, we often call to mind a Jehovah's Witness knocking unwanted at the door, eccentric characters holding up signs that say "Jesus Saves" at parades or demonstrations, Salvation Army enthusiasts braving cold winters to ring bells and collect funds, Scientologists claiming to belong to a genuine religious faith, Hare Krishnas trying to put flowers in people's lapels, and Jews for Jesus asking strangers whether they are Jewish. What we often fail to consider is that evangelicals obligated to witness live with the same unsafe streets, suburban and exurban anomie, long commutes, scarce public spaces, and homogenizing electronic media that all Americans confront in their daily lives. Given that, it is surprising that they get their message across to anyone at all.

CHAPTER 8

IDENTITY

THE NEW IMMIGRATION

Since 1965, when Congress liberalized once-restrictive quotas, waves of new immigrants have transformed the United States. Their experience raises the possibility that the transformation of American religion could come to an end. Arriving from societies that honor tradition, committed to ritual and observance, sincere in their devotion, immigrants, it is widely believed, practice their faith in ways that allow little room for gender equality, freedom of choice, the satisfaction of individual needs, and populistic suspicion of authority. Here seems to lie a built-in source of resistance to all the forces working to transform American religious practice.

Such expectations, for better or worse, may, however, never be realized. Religious identity, as the anthropologist Clifford Geertz has pointed out, can be difficult to preserve unchanged even for those who live in the most traditional of societies. But it can be especially difficult to maintain when faced with the individualism and mobility of American life. Christians and Jews who have long lived in the United States, after all, have ignored doctrines, reinvented traditions, switched denominations, redefined morality, and translated their obligation to witness into a lifestyle. Having met and conquered those religions, it is perhaps unrealistic to expect that American culture will stop exercising its imperatives just because it confronts religions that lie outside the Judeo-Christian heritage.

SWITCHING BEFORE ARRIVING

One phenomenon that complicates the story of immigrants struggling to protect their religious identity against the seduction of American culture is that some groups have relatively little indigenous religious identity to protect. Like immigrants of old, they see in the United States neither a colonial power nor the embodiment of Satan but a society in which individuals constantly make themselves over, and they are determined to make themselves over as well. One of the ways they can do so is by switching their faith—in some cases, even before they arrive—to ones that they believe will help them and their children in this process of adjustment. Koreans offer a striking example.

Christians compose 25 percent of the population of South Korea, making them the second largest religious community in that country. (Twenty-nine percent of South Koreans are Buddhists.) Yet in the United States, three-quarters of Korean Americans are Christian. One reason for the discrepancy is that Koreans do not emigrate randomly to the United States; the bulk of Korean immigrants are middle class, and more middle-class Koreans are Christian. But even selective immigration cannot fully explain why, of all the recent immigrants to the United States from historically non-Christian lands, Koreans are the most attracted to Christianity. For while half of all Korean immigrants to the United States were Christians when they left Korea, another half of the total switch to Christianity upon or shortly after arrival. "I never went to church back in Korea, nor was I a believer," says one Korean immigrant. "But I began to attend the [Houston Korean Ethnic Church] shortly after my arrival here. Yes, I admit, I went to church to see other Koreans, . . . to talk to them, to hang around with them."

Korean American congregations that appeal to first-generation immigrants generally have little in common either with liberal Protestantism or with the more therapeutically inclined practices of evangelical megachurches. According to a study conducted by the Research Center of the Presbyterian Church (USA)—half of Korean Americans are Presbyterians, mostly of the deeply conservative variety—Koreans are committed to intense Bible study, are supportive of the idea of biblical inerrancy, strongly distrust heterosexual cohabitation and homosexuality, and agree on the obligation of Christians to spread the word of salvation through faith in Jesus. As befits strong religious believers, moreover, their participation in congregational life is unusually active: 78 percent of Koreans reported attending weekly services, rates significantly higher than those found among white (28 percent), Latino (49 percent), or African American (34 percent) Presbyterians. When they pick a form of Christianity as their worship, in other words, first-generation Korean Americans tend to pick a demanding one.

It would be wrong, however, to conclude that Korean Americans are attracted to strict forms of worship solely for religious or theological reasons. Nearly all Korean Americans, like the one from Houston, join congregations that are themselves overwhelmingly Korean in their membership. Evangelical efforts on the part of Korean Americans, moreover, are typically directed to other Korean Americans, and Korean American congregations rarely participate in charitable or social-justice efforts that reach out to non-Koreans. For these reasons, there is a strong "ethnic" factor in the Korean American attraction to conservative Protestantism. Sociologists suggest that it is impossible to make sharp distinctions between religious and ethnic motivations among Korean immigrants, since both their identity as Christians and their identity as Korean Americans reinforce each other. Still, at least for the first generation of immigrants, there is no doubting that, from the language being spoken to the sermons being preached, Korean Christian churches are as Korean as they are Christian.

Adherence to an old-time religion, with its belief in absolutes and its insistence on strict moral teachings, clearly helps immigrants through the difficult transitions they experience. "Many contemporary immigrants," writes one sociologist, "moved first from the village to the city before immigration, then plunged into a highly developed modern or postmodern American metropolis. Living in this fast-changing, pluralistic, relativistic, and chaotic world, conservative Christians are assertive in proclaiming that the sole and absolute truth can only be found in an inerrant Bible." Yet this need for certainty hinders their effort to pass their faith on to their children.

Born in the United States, raised in neighborhoods that are ethnically mixed, and fluent in English, second-generation Koreans often
manifest a desire to strike out on their own in matters of faith. "I felt
like I had a grasp of what the Korean church had to offer," as one college student comments. "I just wanted a new direction, wanted to
see what else was available." This student's views are not atypical;
more than half of second-generation Korean Americans have engaged in what has been called a "silent exodus" from the church of
their parents. Characterized by relatively high rates of upward mobility and intermarriage compared to other immigrant groups, second-
generation Korean Americans seek an approach to religion that, in
the words of the founding pastor of the Parkwood Community
Church of Glen Ellyn, Illinois, "might be more appealing than one
that demands a blind loyalty to the Korean culture and its value system."

To some degree, this need is being fulfilled by efforts on the part
of Korean churches to recast themselves in ways that directly appeal
to second-generation believers. At one such church in suburban
Boston, leaders recognize that too strict a form of conservative
Christianity is likely to deplete their pews of young people, and they
have responded by creating an English-language ministry—a church
within a church—that modifies both the Korean and the conservative
character of first-generation forms of worship. Candle-lighting rituals and hymnals are out; hand clapping and enthusiasm are in. A
small but still significant number of non-Koreans now come to the
church. Small-group activities, including dinners, picnics, prayer
meetings, and Bible study, are encouraged. This church is still very
much evangelical in the tradition of conservative Christianity; its
English-language leaders are, if anything, more likely to be graduates
of conservative Christian seminaries than the Korean-born leadership, which, for reasons of missionary legacy more than ideological
sympathy, had formal ties with liberal Protestant institutions. Yet its
second-generation appeal is also very much in the style of new-paradigm Pentecostal churches, which helps explain why, in the name of
growth, it downplays Koreanness in the same way megachurches de-
emphasize denominations. No mention of the word *Korea* appears on
the bulletins of the English-language worship service or the English-

speaking pastor's voice-mail message. The worship style at second-generation Korean American churches is usually designed to appeal, as one pastor puts it, to "American-born, English-speaking Asian Americans who liked contemporary music and weren't interested in a very liturgical, high church kind of experience."

"I am Christian first . . . Korean American second," says a woman named Grace, who is a student at a large urban university in the Northeast. Among those second-generation Korean Americans who do not join the silent exodus and leave the church altogether, her attitude is widely shared. Believers like Grace have had a born-again experience that gives them a personal relationship with Jesus. They are less likely to identify with specific denominations, like the Presbyterianism of their parents, and more likely to be attracted to parachurch movements, such as the Korean Christian Fellowship or the Korean Campus Crusade for Christ. Although unwilling to proclaim themselves feminist, they are not completely comfortable with an all-male church leadership. In similar fashion, they are, as a sociologist writes of one believer, "troubled by the Korean tendency to give uncritical respect to people in positions of authority." Like their elders, they believe in the authority of the Bible, but they also focus less on the written word in favor of engagement with upbeat religious enthusiasm. They are still Korean in the sense that much of their religious practice is carried out in the company of other young Korean Americans, but the religion that inspires them is American to its core.

Koreans are not the only Asian immigrants who adapt—or even change—their faith to take account of American realities. Although only 2 percent of the population of Taiwan, Christians constitute from one-quarter to one-third of Taiwanese immigrants to the United States, and in numerous Taiwanese Christian congregations in America as many as two-thirds of the members are converts. Like Koreans, immigrants from Taiwan and China become American, as one sociologist puts it, by becoming Christian. Religion, for them, is an empowering force, giving them the confidence to adjust to a whole new world. "Right after I became a Christian," says one deacon in a San Francisco Bay area congregation, "I started seeing things differently" because "there was a lot of confidence in me." But-

tressed by that confidence, he goes on, "I participated in choirs, fellowships, activities, leadership training, leading Bible studies." The
emphasis that Alexis de Tocqueville placed on voluntary associations
in mid-nineteenth-century America continues to be applicable to the
conditions of immigrants at the start of the twenty-first century. Active participation in an individualistic faith such as Protestantism
smoothes the transition to a new society.

The effects of this adoption of a new faith can be viewed at the
nondenominational Chinese Christian Church (CCC) of Washington, D.C. There is no doubting that CCC is a *Chinese* Christian
church. Nearly half a century after its founding, Mandarin remains
its official language. A Chinese-language school teaches Chinese to
the second generation. Chinese New Year is enthusiastically celebrated. And Confucian values, such as filial piety and harmonious relations among loved ones, shape the moral worldview of many
church members. "These immigrants did not come to America to
give up their Chinese identity," says the sociologist who studied
them. "On the contrary, many came to America with the explicit intention of better preserving their Chinese identity."

Yet losing it they are. As one might expect, English-language services are increasingly popular among the young; in fact, reliance on
English can be considered an obligation if one is to evangelize effectively among the second generation. An English-speaking pastor was
hired for this purpose, and in his sermons, "he cites no Chinese
stories [and] refers to no Chinese cultural values or customs." The
minutes of church meetings are now recorded in English. The nondenominational nature of the church and its congregational governance structure owe much to American democratic practices. And
even the Confucian values so essential to Chinese identity are di-
luted in the course of adjustment to American ways of life, including
religious ways of life. "Many Confucian ideals are similar to Christian ideals—like honoring your parents, living a moral, virtuous life,
and working hard," as one student at CCC comments. "My parents
used to say bow to your grandmother when she comes. I might have
just done it but I tended to be rebellious. But now I know from the
Bible that that's a very Biblical thing."

As much as believers would like them to blend, Christian values and Chinese values cannot always be mixed together. When faced with potential conflicts between these worldviews, CCC members develop ingenious arguments for reconciling them. Confucianism, they argue, required the traditionalism of feudal China to be realized, and now that feudal authority has been broken, God's authority is the next best substitute. Or they maintain, correctly, that Christianity was once able to absorb Greek and Roman philosophies and thus may be able to do the same with Chinese ones. One minister from Taiwan even argues that there is no conflict between the dragon of the Orient, whom the Chinese celebrate during their year, and the beast of the Bible, whom Christians fear as a harbinger of the Apocalypse. Yet despite their efforts to breathe new life into Confucianism through Christianity, members of CCC recognize the dangers of "syncretism," a blending of faiths so thorough that nothing distinctive about either one is left. In matters of doctrine and practice, American evangelical Protestantism has proven flexible, but it may not be flexible enough to allow adherents to incorporate all, or even most, of the elements of indigenous beliefs from all over the world.

Given the sheer numbers involved, one final example of immigrants who switch their faith before they even arrive in the United States may prove to have especially important consequences for the future of American society: Hispanic Americans. While there is some evidence that the attraction of evangelical Protestantism among Latinos has tapered off in recent years, the phenomenon is widespread enough to raise the question of whether such conversions are a mechanism through which immigrants from relatively poor backgrounds assimilate into American society, which remains overwhelmingly Protestant in its religious identity, and more specifically into its middle-class culture.

Some evidence that they do is provided by Los Angeles's impressively growing network of Latino Pentecostal churches, Alcance Victoria. Among the methods used to recruit new members is the staging of dramatic presentations illustrating the power of religious conversion. One such play, written and produced by members of the East Los Angeles congregation in Boyle Heights, is called *Sueño Américano* (American Dream). In the play, a Catholic family emigrates (illegally) to the United States. They ignore warnings from

neighbors back home that Los Angeles is a city of sin and degrada-
tion, and, upon arrival, the father becomes an alcoholic and the children get involved with drugs. Predictably, they meet an evangelical
missionary and discover Jesus, learning along the way that salvation
in the religious sense can translate into salvation in the social sense.

The story told in *Sueño Américano* may be trite, but it has real
meaning for those who hear it; conversion, because it represents an
active choice on the part of the person who makes it, is a form of empowerment, an especially important attribute when individuals live
in poverty and face the lures of street life. "The change, the change is
the most important thing," one member, Manny Martinez, explains.
"I was a drug addict before. I went to jail and everything, but now
God has changed my life." The Pentecostal congregations so frequently joined by converts are rarely activist churches in the political
sense; the religion is not only conservative but also preaches a message stressing the limits of individual choice in the face of God's om-
nipotence. But for many believers, the engagement and enthusiasm
of their new religion stands in sharp contrast to what they consider a
sense of resignation associated with the Catholicism they left behind. "My relatives who are still Catholic are always waiting for the
priest to tell them what to do," says a deacon in a Protestant storefront church, the *Iglésia de Dios,* in Houston, Texas. "Here we are each
responsible for ourselves and for each other. The entire burden of the
community does not rest upon the shoulders of a pastor who will
only be moved within a few years anyway."

It is a giant step from being a peasant in Mexico to living in a
middle-class suburb of Los Angeles or Houston, and few immigrants
can ever expect to take it. But they can take the smaller step of holding a regular job and earning a decent, if never high enough, income.
Toward that objective, Protestant churches offer advantages that
Catholic parishes typically lack. Among the most important are the
opportunities offered by participation in the clergy. Serving as a pastor to a storefront church or establishing a new congregation in one's
own home does not require advanced training in theology; among a
sample of twenty-eight primarily Puerto Rican Protestant ministers
in Philadelphia, for example, only two attended graduate school, the
same number as those whose highest educational achievement was a

grade-school education. A relative lack of formal barriers to clergy status is enormously important to Latinos because taking a position in a church allows them to legalize their immigrant status. Because married men can become clergy, moreover, they can reunite their families in the United States. Even though most conservative Protestant churches frown on the idea of female clergy, not all do—and even in those that permit only men to occupy leadership positions, the role of *la pastora*, or minister's wife, is often an important source of personal empowerment. Religion can be a source of upward mobility, not only because it teaches middle-class values but also because, through its clergy, it offers something resembling middle-class jobs.

Pentecostal and evangelical religions provide other important benefits to immigrants. Single mothers typically face no restrictions on membership because they live in nonconventional families. An emphasis on the literal truths contained in the Bible can be an important stimulus to literacy for those who lack such basic skills. One need not accept Pentecostalism's belief in spiritual gifts and miracles to recognize that the laying on of hands and other forms of faith healing can serve as a religious person's equivalent of assertiveness-training or confidence-building techniques. Personal storytelling and dramatic presentations improve an individual's capacity for self-expression. Compared to Catholicism, with its insistence on a male-only priesthood and its hierarchical structure, evangelicalism offers to immigrants a faith that seems to resonate with the emphasis on choice and participation they view as characteristic of the North American way of life.

Churches like Alcance Victoria have been successful recruiting inner-city youth because of their emphasis on stern moral teachings and the need for strict self-discipline. Sonny Arguinzoni, the former drug addict who founded the church, takes something of an "old world" approach to his religion that stands in sharp contrast to the inclusive leadership style and denominational indifference that characterizes suburban middle-class evangelicalism. He is hands-on, if not authoritarian, in his leadership style. He has little tolerance for New Age beliefs and other versions of what he calls "weird doctrines." He is not even sure that church growth ought to be his main objective, especially if it comes at the cost of relaxing approaches that work so well in turning people's lives around. It is as if his version of conservative Protestantism, although flourishing at the end of the twentieth century, constitutes a throwback to the way conservative Christianity used to be as the century began.

Yet as Alcance Victoria faces the problem of holding on to its members—as well as appealing to the next generation—it inevitably finds itself facing all those pressures that encourage conservative Protestantism to adapt itself to American culture. At one point, Sonny Arguinzoni Jr., the founder's son, traveled to Willow Creek, the most famous megachurch in the United States, and returned impressed by the ways in which reliance on small groups can help expand church membership; now *grupos familiares* meet on Wednesday nights. Along similar lines, Latino Protestantism borrows more generally from American Protestantism the idea of a personal relationship with God that does not necessarily require an institutional outlet. One of the members of Alcance Victoria's mariachi band speaks like a Willow Creeker when he insists that the evangelism in his church is not a "religion." Catholicism, in his view, is a religion because it is institutional and hierarchical. Evangelicalism, by contrast, "is a relationship with God—this must be the most important thing in your life." Protestant churches that attract Latino members may be located in neighborhoods that suburban Anglos prefer to avoid, but that has not prevented them from developing styles of religious worship that share much in common with the membership-pleasing activities of Anglo churches. Latinos, as writes a Jesuit who studies them, "are at various stages of modernization. They sense that their communal orientation to religion is inadequate. They seek a more self-conscious, individualized faith." And various forms of evangelical Protestantism constitute the faiths that substantial numbers of them choose.

Alcance Victoria borrows from the witnessing strategies of middle-class Pentecostalism, but the same thing also happens in reverse; churches that appeal primarily to middle-class whites see a need to evangelize among Latinos and adapt their own practices accordingly. Latino versions of Calvary and Harvest Chapels and the Vineyard Fellowship churches have sprouted throughout the greater Los Angeles region. Ryan DeLaTorre, the youth pastor of the Vineyard Church in Monrovia, California, with his dyed-blond hair, earrings, and body tattoos, seems like a first cousin of the Jesus freaks who were first attracted to the movement in the 1970s. And even when these new-paradigm churches are more mainstream in their appeals, they still stand in sharp contrast to the more old-fashioned conceptions of religion that motivated Sonny Arguinzoni Sr. In what amounts to a brilliant recruiting strategy, Vineyard churches reject even the necessity of conversion in order to appeal to Latino Catholics; Catholics can remain Catholic even as they join Pentecostal churches because it is "faith" and not "religion" that counts. Nor do they ask Latinos to drop their identity as Latinos in order to be welcomed into the church. Conservative Christians are usually viewed as opponents of multiculturalism, but one would never know this from the mission of Harvest Bible College, founded in the early 1990s by the Vineyard Fellowship to train ministers, many of them Latinos. "Harvest leaves people's 'ethnicity' and socioeconomic identity intact," reads one of its statements. "It is a multiethnic school that helps each group develop its own approach to reaching its people for Christ. Harvest is designed . . . for people who come from oral tradition cultures and therefore do not fit well with the white academic establishment; and for people who have been marginalized by the system for any number of reasons."

Because of its immigrant history, the United States is, in a very basic sense, a nation of switchers, and it therefore makes sense that some people will want to change their faith as they change their country. And when they change their faith, it follows that evangelical Protestantism is, of all the religions in the United States, the one to which they are predominantly attracted, for the experience of immigration is, like the experience of religious conversion, a process of being born again. Latinos who were once Catholic—like the immigrants from Korea or China who are more Christian in the United States than they were at home—serve to remind us that it need not take two or three generations before religion's collective identity gives way to an individual need to belong in an often strange new land. Sometimes the process happens in the very act of movement itself.

THE AMERICANIZATION OF ISLAM

Immigrants from Muslim lands face a situation exactly opposite to those who are attracted to a new country because it offers the prospect of a new religion. Of all the recent immigrants to the United States, those who arrive from Islamic countries in the Middle East, Africa, Asia, and even Europe—more than sixty different countries in all—are among the most determined of America's recent immigrants to maintain the faith that has guided them and their families for centuries. Yet Islam in the United States is finding a variety of ways to transform itself in its North American environment.

One somewhat typical tradition-minded believer is Latifa Ahmad, an Indian-born Muslim who lives in the Raleigh-Durham area. Back home, she did not socialize with the opposite sex and married a Pakistani man based on a family recommendation because, as she puts it, "[Our] common tie is the religion. In Islam you marry and begin to love that person." After she and her husband moved to the United States in 1979, they were determined to raise their children as strict Muslims. Only *halal* meat is allowed in their kitchen. They are thinking of building a swimming pool so that no one in the family need ever swim in mixed-sex groups. They live in a three-generation household dedicated to performing their prayers together as a family. Her husband takes his vacations during Ramadan so that he can better observe the requirements for fasting and prayer. Their five-year-old son and four-year-old daughter are mastering Arabic. "The children," writes the observer who studied them, "have an awareness and knowledge of their ethnic and religious heritage and ritual practices that is rare for such young children."

Although the Ahmad family's experience shows that it is possible for Muslims to maintain their faith in their new land, it also demonstrates how radically different their way of life is from the lands they left. Latifa Ahmad and her husband are both physicians; he is an anesthesiologist, and she is a psychiatrist. As dedicated as they are to keeping Islamic customs inside their home, they cannot, as upper-middle-class professionals, maintain them in the same way outside their doors. Mrs. Ahmad does not attend prayers at the mosque on Friday, since she has to work. (This is not in violation of

Islamic law; Friday prayers are required only for men.) She wears Western clothes in the hospital. And she not only meets one-on-one with men, she also, as a psychiatrist, has to interview them about their sex lives, a job requirement no tenet of Islamic law could possibly cover. Even her reasons for raising her children as Muslims are based as much on mental-health reasons as religious reasons; "I want my children to be Muslims for their emotional wellbeing," as she puts it. As she discusses the inevitable compromises she has to make to practice her profession in the United States, one begins to realize that it is indeed difficult, if not impossible, to be a Muslim in Durham the way one can be a Muslim in Karachi, no matter how hard one tries.

There is, in fact, no aspect of Islam that can be maintained in the United States in the same manner it is maintained in Muslim-majority societies. Consider the mosque. Rare is the mosque in America that devotes itself solely to prayer. At the Islamic Center of Orange County, in Garden Grove, California, one finds a Montessori school serving about four hundred children, a counseling service designed to resolve familial or business disputes, a wedding chapel, and a mortuary. Such community-outreach services are enormously important to Muslims, especially to immigrants and their children. One study interviewed 347 frequent mosque attenders in Muslim communities throughout the United States and found that 67 percent believed that "special educational and recreational programs for teenagers" ought to be an important function mosques perform. Like other religious believers in the United States, they want institutions that serve their needs. "The prevalence of mosques not far from each other creates a situation in which Muslims can 'mosque shop,'" write this study's authors, "selecting the institution that seems most congenial to them for any of a variety of reasons."

Even the more narrowly defined religious practices that take place inside American mosques differ significantly from those found in the Muslim countries of origin. Without intermediaries that stand between the believer and God, Islam has not traditionally had churches in the way Christians understand that term. Rather than a congregation with a fixed membership, mosques in Muslim societies were—and continue to be—convenient places into which one steps in order to pray, depending on where one is in the course of the day. Only on Friday, the day designated for special prayers, does anything like the Western experience of church take place, and even then, it is traditionally only for men and follows few of the organized procedures identified by Christians and Jews as a service. (Friday worship, however, does usually include a talk on a topic involving Islam.)

But in the United States, mosques inevitably come to resemble churches. When I interviewed the director of the Islamic Society of Orange County in California, he spoke of his "congregation" as if it were perfectly normal, as indeed it was in his mosque, for people to become members. Back home, where there is no separation of church and state, mosques are supported with public funds, he pointed out, but in the United States, mosques support themselves through the voluntary contributions of members. In return for the financial support they offer, members have a voice in how the mosque is run. They elect a seventeen-member governing council, composed of both men and women, who in turn select the committees that choose the officers of the congregation and its many associated activities. In American society, religions do as Americans do.

Like other mosques in America, the Islamic Society of Orange County is an extremely busy place on Sunday. Although Friday services are extremely well attended, not all members can take time off on Friday in order to worship, which makes the Sunday option attractive to them. Open to women and children, Sunday activities typically include not just sermons but instruction in the tenets of Islam. Throughout North America, Sunday worship has proven extremely popular. Religious reasons predominate but so do opportunities to socialize similar to the mingling that takes place in Christian churches on Sunday. In East Dearborn, Michigan, the largest Muslim community in the United States, "the Sunday service—or any service, for that matter—is a time to meet with friends," writes an anthropologist who lived in and studied the community. "This is very much the case for young unmarried men, who cluster in corners of the building. Not always welcome in the homes of one another's parents because of the unmarried sisters who may be present and because they are often perceived as a general nuisance, the mosque is a safe haven for them. Unless they have pretensions to religious sophistication . . . enlightenment by the sheiks is probably not their primary concern."

An even more striking adaptation to American religious practices involves the role of the clerics. In Islam, religious authorities are interpreters of Islamic law; their main task is to offer guidance to believers perplexed by what their tradition requires of them. This function is extremely important when Muslims move to non-Muslim lands—one reason why, especially in the early years of recent immigration, a large number of clerics were brought over from Middle Eastern countries to work in the United States. Yet when they arrive here, they often find that, contrary to Islamic tradition, they are expected to act as professional clergy. America—if for no other reasons than legal ones—wants its religious meetings run by people who are responsible for their congregations, and that is increasingly the way Islamic religious gatherings in the United States are run.

The role of a professional clergyman is unusual but so are the duties. Newly designated clergy are often bewildered by what is expected of them. Instruction in Islam, with which they are familiar, turns into something resembling a church service, which to them is strange. Prayers continue to be offered in Arabic, the holy language of the Koran, but other activities, including the sermons, often must be conducted in English if they are to be understood, not only by second-generation immigrants but by converts as well as by Muslims from non-Arabic societies such as Pakistan and Malaysia. Muslim clergymen are frequently invited to participate in interfaith dialogue with Christians and Jews, not an activity for which their training in Muslim-majority societies has prepared them. In the most significant departure from religious practice back home, clerics are called upon to answer questions and offer advice to people about their personal problems. "The role of the imam in the United States is completely different from the role of the imam in the Muslim world," as one of them puts it.

> In the Muslim world the imam's job is just to lead the prayer, but when you come to the United States, the role of imam is several roles. For example, here the imam conducts the funerals, a job which the imam back home would not do. . . . Here

too the imam practices the job of marriage counselor, or an arbitrator between husband and wife, parents and children. This role of course is not practiced by the imam in the Muslim world. The mosque in America serves the Muslim affairs from cradle to death.

The famous five pillars of Islam—faith in God alone, daily prayer, charity, the fast of Ramadan, and the pilgrimage to Mecca—define the religious practices in which Muslims are expected to engage. To do so in the United States requires considerable flexibility. *Salat,* (or *Salah*) for example, the second of Islam's five pillars, does not just require frequent prayer, it also demands ablution, or cleansing, before each one. In a city like Houston, Al-Noor, which is the largest mosque in Texas, contains a special *Wudu,* or ablution, area, but Houston is notorious for its urban and suburban sprawl, which makes it nearly impossible for most of its Muslim residents to get to Al-Noor more than once a day, and even the building of new mosques throughout the metropolitan region has not solved the problem. Sometimes a Muslim may find himself working for a sympathetic employer willing to allow frequent prayer, but rarely is there a shower nearby that serves as adequate preparation, let alone a room without pictures on the wall, as required by Muslim law; as one Pakistani believer says, "It is hard to pray five times on the job, when you need to wash more often." Schools in an area like East Dearborn are overwhelmingly attended by Muslim children, but, unable under American law to conduct Christian or Jewish prayers, they are hardly likely to accommodate *salat.* Even under the most favorable of conditions, in short, it is impossible to perform *salat* the way it is practiced back home.

Many immigrants insist that prayer is even more important to them in the United States than it was back home. And indeed it is; anyone who has observed Muslims pray must be impressed with their devotion. Still, the way they pray can be changed to meet the environment in which they are performed. Practicing *salat* is no easy task; people who do not learn the right way to do it as children will probably never learn it completely. Anxious to pray, but unsure of how to do so in traditional ways, second-generation Muslims find themselves not always able to carry out the duties their faith demands. Wafa, who lives in East Dearborn, confesses to approaching *salat* the way many women approach their diet. Constantly urging herself to do what is right, she also finds herself frequently failing, and as a result, she is in the process of making an appointment with the sheik to discuss what she called her "prayer problem." Other believers adopt Christian ways of expressing their devotion; "I pray in my heart" or "I pray in my own way" are among the ways they describe their worship. Another simply makes up her prayers as she goes along, certain that God will reward her for communicating directly with him. Yet another believes that her God is a forgiving God. There are many inventive ways indeed to modify the requirements of *salat* to accommodate American realities.

Similar modifications of dietary practices take place alongside changes in the practice of prayer. Strictly speaking, Muslims in the United States ought to eat meat exclusively prepared by *halal* butchers. Some, of course, do. But this is not always possible, either because there are too few Muslims in a particular community or because Muslims must interact with institutions such as schools and hospitals that have their own dietary rules. As befits a religion that has spread to all corners of the world, Islam can be flexible in responding to Muslims' needs; in Raleigh, to take one example, an Indonesian believer asked the legal authorities back in Jakarta what to do in the absence of *halal* butchers and was told that supermarket meat was acceptable because the United States was a Christian country and therefore its business firms could be considered Christian as well. Throughout North America, a series of informal laws have evolved to govern the consumption of meat. Here are some of them:

- If *halal* butchers are available, they should be used.
- If they are not, kosher butchers are acceptable.
- If there are no kosher butchers, one must at least refrain from eating pork.

When American Muslims say that they eat *halal*, in other words, they do not necessarily mean that everything they eat is *halal*. One anthropologist estimates that "perhaps more than half" of the Muslims in East Dearborn restrict themselves to *halal,* and this is a community filled with appropriate butcher shops.

The most well-known Muslim holiday is Ramadan, which requires fasting for eighteen hours a day throughout the ninth month of the Islamic calendar. As with other aspects of religious practice, observance ratios can vary widely; one study reported that Pakistanis were the most observant (three-quarters said they fasted) and second-generation Muslims, not unexpectedly, the least (one-third). But the more appropriate way to approach the subject is not to contrast those who are strict in their observance with those who are not; it is to recognize that most Muslims in North America try to obey the rules even as they change them at the margins. Ramadan tends to be taken with great seriousness by Muslims in the United States; the occasion is holy enough, and the practice sufficiently different from what non-Muslims are doing during the same period, to reinforce a strong sense of religious identity. At the same time, the holiday is so long that not all of its strict requirements can be met. Reflecting both aspects of the practice of Ramadan, fasting in Dearborn tends to be more common when the holiday begins and when it ends compared to the days in the middle.

Perhaps the most difficult injunction of Koranic law to fulfill in the United States is the one that treats usury as *haram* (forbidden). Many Muslims nevertheless try to honor it. As anxious as immigrants are to build mosques in their new environment so that they can fulfill their obligations to pray, laws against profiting from or paying interest generally lead to decisions not to seek mortgages that would expedite the building process. Some individuals apply the same principle to their own real-estate needs. Farrukh Siddiqui, a Pakistani-born website engineer from Levittown, Pennsylvania, is one; he will not apply for a mortgage to build a house. It is not clear that he needs to be so scrupulous, for the theological points involved are actually murky, and there is enough room for compromise to allow banks in areas like the one in which Mr. Siddiqui lives to tailor special mortgage loans for Muslim customers. Still, like those Ultra-Orthodox Jews who overexaggerate their performance of rituals as a way of reinforcing their religious identity, he prefers to err on the side of caution. If his example is at all representative, there may be a significant number of Muslims in the United States who are even stricter in their interpretation of Islamic law than they would be if they had remained in their countries of origin.

Not all American Muslims are quite as zealous as Mr. Siddiqui. As is the case with *halal* meat, informal rules tend to develop around the question of usury, including these:

- It may be permissible to obtain a mortgage so long as it is for one's own personal house.
- Mortgages can be acceptable if the house is not too large.
- Making a profit off a loan can be considered wrong, but paying interest to another is not necessarily wrong.

"So many times we have Muslims who are trying to buy a home, trying to get into business, trying to compete with the business man in this country," says one believer. "Often times we do have to take loans and we do have to pay interest on them. I don't believe Allah will hold that against us." And when it comes to receiving interest rather than paying it, the rules are relaxed even more. Nearly all Muslims in the United States deposit their money in banks. Since the bank is going to make money on your deposits in any case, they argue, it makes little sense to refuse to collect the interest, thereby allowing the bank's profits to increase that much more. And who knows what the banks would do with the money that does not go to you? "You deposit your money in the bank, and if you don't collect interest from the bank, the bank takes it and gives it to the National Council of Churches in New York," as one of them puts it.

Islamic law hardly stops with rules about prayer, diet, and interest; in 1984, for example, the Ayatollah Khomeini issued his *Clarification of Questions,* which offered 2,897 opinions on matters ranging from the bathing of the dead to the menstrual cycle. These opinions apply only to Shiites, and not the more numerous Sunnis, but all Muslims are guided by the *hadith,* the sayings of the Prophet Muhammad, which, as interpreted through the ages, amount to a veritable catalog of dos and don'ts, including restrictions on the consumption of alcohol or physical contact between the sexes. As fundamentalist Christians frequently discover, religions that seek to govern every as-

pect of human life invariably have to expect less than 100 percent
compliance, encouraging some to scoff at the whole idea. "The
Prophet cursed the one who is selling the wine and drinking the
wine and sitting where the wine is distributed," as one Muslim man
recounts. "But, how can I apply that hadith while I am on a TWA air-
craft and all the people on the plane are drinking? Should I throw
myself out of the window because I am sitting with the drinkers?"
The correct answer, of course, is that one can remain true to this *hadith* by not flying at all, but if that is the price that must be paid, few
immigrants—nearly all of whom arrived in the United States by air—
will pay it.

There is one area of human life in which the contrast between the
demands of religious fidelity in the Muslim world and the actual
practices of everyday life in the United States is so significant that no
discussion can ignore it: the relations between men and women. Although Muslim women will frequently talk about the respect they
feel they are given by Islamic customs, there can be little doubt that
traditional Islam, like Orthodox Judaism, gives certain privileges to
men that are unavailable to women. The professional clergy that has
emerged is a male-only clergy. Friday prayers in the mosque are still
primarily for men. Some women continue, in the name of modesty,
to wear traditional dress that entirely covers their bodies. Yet because so many Muslims now practice their faith within a society that
contains legal and cultural guarantees of women's equality, Muslim
religious practices in the United States are clearly shifting in the direction of greater gender equality. Sunday religious activities fill up
with women, even as Friday activities exclude them from the main
prayer room. Some mosques even have done away with the curtain
that once stood between the men and the women, and others seat
both sexes together. Whether or not a woman wears the *hijab*, the
decision tends to be hers to make. And further changes seem inevitable. At the Al-Noor mosque in Houston, not all the women are
satisfied with being relegated to subordinate positions. "Actually,"
one insists, "I am against the Women's Committee. Yes, there are
some things that women or men can do better, but there are areas
where women can share too." This mosque, like all those in the
United States, will discover that any efforts to keep women in second-

class positions are likely to clash with the lessons taught by the society to which they have relocated.

Greater sexual equality in religious practice often translates into greater sexual equality in most aspects of life; it is difficult to imagine any woman in the United States, even one from the most conservative Middle Eastern background, being quite as subservient to her husband as Amina Abd al-Jawad, one of the main characters in *Palace Walk*, a novel by Egyptian Naguib Mahfouz. Arranged marriages are far less common in North America than in the Middle East. The longer Muslims reside in the United States, the more accustomed they become to such practices as dating or women entering the labor force. One survey of American Muslims found surprisingly liberal views on abortion, even as most respondents agreed that abortion is impermissible under Islamic law. Muslims of both sexes tend to view the political movement known as feminism as alien to their values, but this has not prevented both men and women from creating a way of life within their communities that bears no relationship to Afghanistan under the Taliban.

Just because Muslims accommodate their religious practices to modernity does not mean that they fail to take their faith seriously. But it does mean that they take other things seriously beside their faith, including their careers and material well-being. Instead of Islamic spiritual standards, a Pakistani research scientist living in the Raleigh-Durham area finds in the United States that "the standard of success in this culture is based on material accumulation." Yet this scientist, like many better-off Muslim immigrants, came to the United States in search of professional success unavailable to him in Pakistan. His comment teaches us to reject the view that immigrants in the United States hold on to their religion as a way of palliating their misery or making sense of forces outside their control. On the contrary, devotion to traditional creeds requires sufficient financial means to live as best as one can by the rules of one society while residing in another. It is, for example, because Latifa Ahmad and her husband are well off that they can even consider building their own swimming pool to protect women against the evil eyes of men or affording Sunday-school lessons for their children. Money is not always alien to faith; in some cases, it makes possible its exercise.

The fact that Muslim immigrants who have the means want to

pursue both career goals and religious objectives, and to do so in a place that makes it possible, is testimony to the transformations that have taken place, not only in the United States in the past half century but also in the Islamic world. Indeed, it is difficult to know which is more remarkable: the fact that a once-Christian country like the United States is willing to accept so many Muslim immigrants or the fact that countries that once considered it undesirable for Muslims to live under non-Muslim rule now allow so many of their citizens to migrate and to do so voluntarily. No matter how traditional the faith of a recent Muslim immigrant may be, the very act of becoming an immigrant, for a Muslim, to some degree defies tradition.

Muslims make a distinction between Dar al-Islam, the "house of Islam," and Dar al-Kufr, the "house of unbelief," and the obligation of the believer is to strengthen the former and to avoid the latter. Because the lure of the United States is so powerful, one can understand why Islam resists close contact with ways of life it considers heretical; for all the talk of *da'wa,* or the duty to be a missionary, American values influence Muslim religious practice far more than Muslims reach out and convert Americans to their way of life. It is therefore encouraging that some American Muslims are beginning to recognize that the United States may not be, as many originally thought it was, a house of unbelief after all. At an interfaith dialogue I attended in Pasadena while leading a seminar for scholars from the Islamic world, Hassan Hathout, director of outreach for the Islamic Center of Southern California, told the group that one is freer to be a Muslim in the United States than in many Muslim-majority countries. Simply by acknowledging that fact with their presence, immigrants to North America have transformed their faith into something for which there is little or no historical precedent. Their attempts to preserve their religious identity have given rise to a new religious identity all it own.

THE LIMITS TO BLENDED IDENTITY

Unlike immigrants who convert to Christianity upon arriving in the United States, there are numerous Americans who convert to religions that immigrants bring with them to the United States. The

most popular among them is Buddhism. Both the immigration reforms of 1965 and the end of the Vietnam War brought significant
numbers of Asian Buddhists to the United States. Here, they have
been met by American-born intellectuals, poets, 1960s-style counterculture enthusiasts, therapists, and Hollywood movie stars who
have found in Buddhism a religion that strikes them as less violent
and sectarian than either Christianity or Judaism. The result is a fas-
cinating experiment in religious blending. What the intermingling of
these two groups produces is not a new faith—Buddhist immigrants
and American converts frequently talk past each other—so much as
two distinct faiths, each of which is shaped by American culture in
its own way.

Immigrants from historically Buddhist societies, like other immigrants in the United States, retain both the ethnic and the religious
character of their faith in order to make sense of the difficult passage
they have undergone. "I've lived in this country for thirty-seven years
and I still get so cold," says a Thai immigrant from Philadelphia. For
many Asians who have made the United States their home but who
still feel less than comfortable living here, Buddhism offers a warm
and accepting environment to which they can retreat. In some cases,
their relative indifference to Buddhism in Asia is replaced by active
involvement in America for no other reason than the fact that they
do *not* want to convert to Christianity. "Becoming Christian is like
giving up your parents," as one California woman puts it. Wanting to
be religious, but not wanting to break with the world from which she
arrived, she has become a more committed Buddhist here than in
Taiwan.

Her experience is fairly typical. In their countries of origin, many
Asians do not approach Buddhism as a religion in the Western sense;
it is more simply a taken-for-granted part of their culture. But on arrival in the United States, a significant number either convert to
Buddhism (as they also do to Christianity) or begin to practice their
Buddhist faith in ways that resemble Western religious practices.
They often treat Buddhism as a ritualistic faith, and rituals usually
take place at specific times in specific places. Precepts are treated
more like commands than suggestions. Practitioners are often attracted to chanting (rather than meditation), an activity practiced to-

gether with others in congregational style and not in forms of solitary retreat. Monks are usually poor, supported by the contributions of worshipers. Asians generally treat dharma, or Buddhist teachings, cosmologically, as reflecting an entire explanation of how the world came to be the way it is.

Immigrant Buddhist temples found in American cities are therefore decidedly religious buildings. There are, for one thing, numerous shrines and statues before which most immigrants will bow. (Although Buddhism is not God centered, it is a religion with many gods.) To be sure, immigrant temples have their ethnic as well as their religious symbols; at Wat Dhammaran in Chicago, for example, Thai culture is everywhere on display, including pictures of the Thai king and queen as well as a "culture room" that keeps members in touch with their ethnic roots. But even such ethnic elements resemble some traditional Christian practices, especially the Italian saints worshiped by immigrants in ethnic Catholic churches at the end of the nineteenth century—or the shrines of Latino Catholicism at the present time.

Despite their best efforts to retain their religious and ethnic identities, however, immigrants from Asia experience the same kind of Americanization as those from Muslim countries. For obvious reasons, monks at Wat Dhammaran are not expected to adhere to the traditional dress code—three cotton robes—found in Thailand. Although the traditional texts of Theravada Buddhism in Asia frown on monks even riding in vehicles, in North America they are usually allowed to drive, although not without provoking considerable controversy. Strictures against monks touching women, in the words of the Venerable Dr. Ratanasara of Los Angeles's Dharma Vijaya Buddhist Vihara, which has its ethnic roots in Sri Lanka, seem "rather silly" in the American context. And so it goes throughout the rest of North America. Three-day rituals back in Laos are condensed into one day among Laotian immigrants in Toronto. Weekends, especially Sunday, have become popular worship days, as they are among other immigrant groups. Japanese Buddhists in Toronto, many of whom are anxious to assimilate, opt for Sunday-school classes, pews, organs, hymns, and sermons, and, in what might hold the all-time record for religious blending, play Mendelssohn's "Wedding March" during nuptials, thereby introducing to Buddhism in Canada music written by a German composer whose father converted from Judaism to Christianity. As Muslim immigrants could remind them, no religion can be the same in a society in which its members are a minority as it can be when it defines the collective identity of an entire people.

In contrast to immigrants, Americans who convert to Buddhism are often motivated by a desire to escape from "religion"—which they associate with the Judaism or Christianity of their upbringing—in favor of a more spiritual approach to faith. At the Cambridge Insight Meditation Center (CIMC) in Massachusetts, many practitioners do not even identify themselves as Buddhists because that would mean promoting a particular belief system; indeed the CIMC itself made a deliberate decision not to include the word Buddhist in its title. A practitioner named Kevin, born a Mormon, rejects the whole question of whether he is or is not a Buddhist. "I do not see the purpose of calling myself a Buddhist because it feels like another layer. I'm not putting on layers, I'm taking them off." Others described themselves as Jewish because of their looks, heritage, or name, making it clear that such a label describes them ethnically, not spiritually.

Because American converts so often seek to escape from religion through Buddhism, they differ significantly from immigrants for whom Buddhism remains very much a religion in traditional terms. One of the most popular choices among converts, for example, is Vipassana Buddhism. At one level this is an odd selection, because Vipassana, or insight, Buddhism originates in the most conservative of all the Asian varieties. The reason for its attraction is not to hard to find, however. Vipassana Buddhism, like Zen Buddhism from Japan, is committed to meditation, and meditation is what most counterculture converts find attractive in the religion as a whole. One survey of "new Buddhists," native-born Americans who converted to the religion, showed that 92.4 percent of them identified meditation as the most important aspect of their religious practice. By contrast, a survey taken of Asian immigrants revealed that only 11.5 percent said that meditation was so central. To facilitate meditation practices, American-born adherents can buy CD-ROMs that will put them in touch with distant instructors and can join online e-mail groups that enable them to talk with "Cybermonk." Meditation retreats are also enormously popular among the new Buddhists; 93 percent of the converts surveyed have attended a retreat, usually at a rate of one per year. Zen retreats typically last a week, Vipassana retreats for ten days. The kind of Buddhism practiced by American converts may not be a religion in the traditional sense, but it can be as demanding as any other form of faith.

There are many ways in which American converts to Buddhism practice their faith differently from immigrants. Reverence for authority, especially male authority, runs counter to the democratic and egalitarian proclivities of most American practitioners. Veneration of symbols can strike some as too close to the forms of superstition they find in Western religion. Chanting and singing are less common than silent and walking meditation. No special clothing is required. Practitioners will use any and every opportunity to meditate, for example by driving, washing dishes, or cooking mindfully. As opposed to a cosmological approach to dharma, beliefs can be extremely eclectic, blending Asian doctrine with New Age religion, psychotherapy, and self-awareness. Although it would be incorrect to describe American Buddhism as doctrinal—one popular book in these circles is called *Buddhism without Beliefs*—it is also true that American Buddhists typically take an intellectual approach to their religious practice, compared to an Asian emphasis on ritual, even if American converts are not always familiar with the intellectual traditions from which they are borrowing.

Worlds apart in their approach to religion, Asian-born and American-born Buddhists rarely meet. At Wat Phila, an immigrant temple in Philadelphia, most of the American-born people in attendance are married to Asians and are not necessarily Buddhists themselves. And even when Asian-born and American-born Buddhists do interact, they cannot always understand what the other is doing. "It seems pretty much lately that more and more people are interested in Buddhism," as a Thai immigrant named Noo puts it. "But most of the time I can see that they are modifying it more than the real Buddhism." Asians typically tend to be puzzled by the therapeutic uses of American Buddhism, which strike them as reflecting a preoccupation with the self, and this in a religion that denies the reality of the self. They are also unlikely to identify with the American tendency to link Buddhism with political and social causes; when I attended a lecture by Thich Nhat Hanh—the Vietnamese-born practitioner of an "engaged Buddhism" that speaks to issues such as world peace—in a cavernous Boston convention center room holding two thousand people, I expected to see a significant minority of Asians but was surprised to discover only a handful. And when American-born Buddhists turn from world peace to such forms of identity politics as gay rights—a significant number of American practitioners are gay—Asians tend to be even more put off. Not only are they unlikely to share the objectives of Dharma Sisters, a support group for lesbian Buddhists, but also the whole of forming parachurch interest groups to advance particular identities would strike them as standing in sharp conflict with Buddhism's otherworldliness, let alone its suspicion toward any dualities such as gay and straight or male and female. It is not that Asian Buddhists are hostile to Americans or fear an invasion from them; some, no doubt, are glad to see that their culture can be so appealing to others. But as much as Asian immigrants accommodate their religion to a new environment, they are not going to watch their religion transform itself into something resembling secular psychotherapy.

Americans, in turn, however much they may find ethnic Buddhist rituals too confining and old-fashioned for their religious sensibilities, are unlikely to condemn Asians for their backward ways; they are too liberal and politically correct for that. Two members of Wat Dhammaran, John Knox and Robert Ryan, are fascinated by the relative lack of attention to meditation or to the prevalence of Thai rituals in the religious practices of their Asian counterparts, even if their fascination does not result in a rejection of their own forms of Buddhist practice. Still, the differences stick out. American converts, as one sociologist writes, seek in Buddhism an "expressive" ethic of self-realization in contrast to the "authoritative" ethic they associate with traditional religions. At its worst, this approach can take the form of believing that there is something wrong with those who find in a religion like Buddhism the strong moral prohibitions they associate with Christianity and Judaism. "If Buddhists propagate cultural Buddhism, they may do so to the detriment of Buddha's teachings," as one prominent practitioner of American Buddhism once put it, as if he knew better than the ethnic practitioners of cultural Buddhism what Buddha's teachings really are.

Buddhism began in one country, India, before spreading rapidly throughout Asia. The popularity of Buddhism among American-born converts ought to be one more step in the worldwide evolution of this remarkably flexible faith, for, as one religious studies scholar puts it, "Our era marks the first time in the history of Buddhism that all its forms, from all the various Buddhist traditions, have been present in one place at one time." Yet little blending has yet to take place on American shores. Instead, the forces that have so transformed other American religions are busy at work transforming this one. On the one hand, democratic sensibilities and individualistic inclinations have seeped into ethnic Buddhist temples in the United States, making them more like Christian churches than similar temples in Asia. On the other hand, converts, already drawn from those segments of the American population most attracted to the cultural forces that swept over their country in the 1960s, find in Buddhism a faith that can enable them to express their spirituality without the trappings of doctrine and ritual they associate with the historically influential religions of the West. Immigrants and converts may have not yet come together to practice one faith in common, but they do share a common culture that shapes them both.

THE NECESSITY FOR CHOICE

Only forty years have passed since the United States revised its immigration laws in 1965, but one conclusion has already been established. Once immigration takes place, religion can no longer serve as a source of identity the way it did in one's country of origin. To move is to choose; once a person opts to live in a society in which his or her faith is a minority faith, no amount of religious observance, no return to traditional practices, and no strict adherence to the letter of the law can ever equate one's faith in the new land with the way it was in the old country. Some immigrants recognize this by switching their faith when they switch their residence. Others try as hard as they can to hold on to the ways of their ancestors. But no one escapes the necessity for choice. Indeed, the reality of choice is even more true of the nonswitchers than the switchers. A Buddhist from China or a Catholic from Mexico who becomes Protestant upon arrival in the United States has made one giant step, and after it is made, follow-up choices are never quite as momentous. But the Muslim believer eating *halal* and worshiping on Fridays, never having made the big switch to a new faith, faces numerous choices with every passing day about what ought to be appropriate in the new environment and what ought to be forbidden. Defining who one is (and who one is not) through one's faith can be a never-ending process for a person used to thinking of faith as timeless and eternal.

The presence of so many religions in the United States, including so many that lie outside the Judeo-Christian tradition, poses enormous challenges for American pluralism. Some have questioned whether the United States is sufficiently tolerant to accept within its borders people of faith whose practices and beliefs stand in such sharp contrast to the Christianity that has so long defined the American nation. Time will tell whether the United States will ever achieve the kinds of interfaith dialogue that advocates of strong forms of pluralism encourage, even if it is already clear that, simply by welcoming new immigrants to its shores, the United States has already taken giant steps away from its once predominantly Christian—and later Judeo-Christian—self-understanding.

A less-appreciated aspect of the new immigration to the United States is the challenge posed to religious believers themselves. Somehow, in some way—the choice, after all, is up to them—new arrivals will have to take individual responsibility for the way their faith is practiced in their new land. In doing so, they will also have to recognize that they are shaping their religious traditions as much as their ancestors were shaped by them. By blending ethnic and religious themes in their church membership, holding on to some sacred teachings while modifying others, and joining American-born converts in some ways while keeping their distance in others, most American immigrants have already begun to transform the religious identities with which they will live. Having undergone the enormous transformation required in moving from one society to another, we should not be surprised that they change either their faith or the way it is practiced—or both.

IS DEMOCRACY SAFE
FROM RELIGION?

RELIGION AND EVERYTHING ELSE

Of all the activities in which human beings engage, religion is generally presumed to have special status. It involves people with a world they cannot see and can only barely know. It asks them to consider how the reality around them came to be created and what purpose they serve by being a part of it. It defines for many an individual who she is, and just as importantly, who she is not. It offers moments of eternal peace to some and glimpses of immortality to others. No matter the God in which they believe, nor how much they believe in him, human beings are expected to treat their faith as distinct from those other activities—such as earning enough money on which to live, consuming sufficient goods to enjoy their lives, and deciding with others the form and functions of their society—that do not involve a relationship with the divine. Religion, in short, is valued because it opens a window on the sacred, a realm of life that we treat, in the words of sociologist Peter L. Berger, "as 'sticking out' from the normal routines of everyday life, as something extraordinary and potentially dangerous." Whatever else religion is, it cannot be like everything else.

Yet in America, religion *is* like everything else. Americans are remarkable for the ways they link their religion to their secular world. Religion moves people because its ideas are powerful, yet

Americans, who shun overly intellectual ideas on radio and television, are also likely to avoid faiths that ask them to take doctrine seriously. They define themselves and each other by their religion, yet they are willing to shape and reshape the traditions that offer religions their distinctive identities. They pay homage to a force larger than themselves, even while asking for things for themselves. Americans know that faith offers fellowship, but then they treat the institutions capable of offering fellowship with a decided suspicion. They believe that religion is a precondition for morality but are not at all surprised when religious figures prove themselves immoral. They understand that God judges some of what they do as sinful, but they do not believe him to be too demanding and they avoid trying to judge each other. And those who feel a special obligation to spread their faith acknowledge that, for the sake of neighborliness, they are reluctant to shove anything down anyone else's throat.

Although they represent two different realms of being, the sacred and the profane can never be separated completely. Social scientists have begun to explain religious activity as a product of individual choices made by rational people, an approach upsetting to those who believe that religion has an especially sacred character. Despite the fact that faith touches on the ineffable, however, there is no reason why it should not be treated by people with the concern for utility they bring to the economy; the only issue worth discussing with respect to rational-choice theory is not whether it ought to be utilized but how much it actually explains. (In my view, it does a fairly good job of explaining why religions intent on recruiting new members come to resemble each other—since each one has to attract people who might be attracted to others—but it does not do as well explaining why people shift from one religion to another, for their reasons often have as much to do with emotional resonance as with a series of utilitarian calculations.) It may seem sacrilegious even to suggest that the process of choosing a good make of car or finding decent child care can have anything in common with the process of discovering why God's commands ought to be obligatory. Yet religions themselves, however much they appeal to the sacred, have been too active participants in such profane activities as developing their own rock music or offering liturgies for dummies to claim any special innocence from the market.

If the choices made by believers are like those they make in the marketplace, the way they believe resembles their approach to politics. In politics, Americans generally lack familiarity with the details of legislation and policy upon which they are presumably voting. And in religion, whatever the Lord requires, knowledge of his teachings is not among them; 58 percent of Americans cannot name five of the ten commandments, just under half know that Genesis is the first book of the Bible, fewer than that can tell interviewers about the meaning of the Holy Trinity, and 10 percent of them believe that Joan of Arc was Noah's wife. Americans care about both religion and politics in the sense that they can as little imagine their country not being a democracy as they can imagine it stripped of its faith. But both commitments come, in a sense, tax free; citizenship and salvation go to those pure in spirit, not necessarily to those who can cite either the constitution or the Bible chapter and verse.

None of this means that Americans lack sincerity of belief. I am not able to enter into the heads of other people, but neither the observations I have undertaken nor the sociological literature I have consulted gives me any reason to believe that those who join small groups or transform the liturgy to suit their own needs or alter their faiths to American realities are being hypocritical. Faith means as much as ever to the faithful, even if the forms it takes can be inventive and unexpected. Religion matters, which is why individuals take so many steps to make it part of their lives and to bring it in line with the ways in which they live.

Nor should any of what I have described be taken to mean that, in its public life, the United States has lost is religious character. This is, after all, the only modern society in the world in which it is possible for a presidential candidate, when asked to cite the philosopher whose ideas had the greatest impact upon him, to respond by naming Jesus Christ. Let a court try to decide, as one did in San Francisco, that the words "under God" should not be in the Pledge of Allegiance, and the reaction will be both swift and furious. When Americans need to come together, as they did in the aftermath of the attack of September 11, it is to religious buildings that they will turn.

It is true that, in the multicultural society the United States has become, the tenets of one religion, the Protestant religion, will no longer be viewed as providing all the required elements of public faith, although some (increasingly marginalized) fundamentalists insist that they should be. But it is also true that the one group still looked upon with considerable suspicion by most Americans are those who profess to have no faith at all. Some Christians, certain that the public life of America is hostile to religion, conclude that we are no longer in any meaningful sense a devout society; but in fact the United States remains as true to its religious origin as ever.

To say that Americans continue to believe in God and to hope that their society is guided by religious principles, however, says little about the kind of God in which they believe and what the appropriate principles ought to be. There is much about religion that has changed little over the course of American history; populistic, personalistic, and anti-institutional instincts have been there since the Puritans began to lose control of the faithful in the seventeenth century. But it would be equally incorrect to argue that, when it comes to faith, everything is always as it has been, for there are aspects of American religion that have changed dramatically, even in the past decade or two, including a palpable increase in religious toleration that extends to non-Christians; a preference for personalized faith that has influenced all religions, not just Protestant and evangelical ones; a distrust of leadership that reflects similar crises of confidence involving business and politics; the acceptance by most Catholics of both American culture and modernity; and a rapid growth in the number of believers who are neither Protestant, Catholic, nor Jewish. Sociologists a few decades ago predicted the decline of religion in modern societies, but in the most modern society of all religion has neither declined nor advanced; it has been transformed.

There are forms of religion that evoke the magic and mystery, as well as the sectarianism and violence, of older forms of faith; they tend to be found, as a recent book argues, primarily throughout the Southern half of the globe, where one can witness the rapid rise of a form of Christianity that harkens back to the time before the Reformation, the Enlightenment, and the Second Vatican Council. Because a faith gap has developed between the rich nations and the poor nations that is as yawning as the wealth gap, the transformation of religion in modern societies like the United States is equally as significant; it is, in fact, the counterpart of, and in some ways a reaction against, the spread of fundamentalist forms of faith everywhere else. No one who practices their faith in the United States, even those who have recently arrived from Third World countries, can escape these modernizing forces. If this polarization continues, and there is every sign that it will, American Christians and Jews, soon to be joined by American Muslims and Buddhists, will have more in common with secular people in the societies in which they live and worship than they will have with coreligionists who live in countries where older forms of faith flourish.

BELIEVERS AS FULL CITIZENS

Somehow the news about the transformation of American religion has not been transmitted, at least to a significant number of intellectuals who write about the subject. As they advocate one position or another about the proper role of faith in American public life, it is as if Jonathan Edwards is still preaching and his congregation is still quaking in fear.

One side in this debate wants to insist that religious believers are still a people apart, their ways of life too austere and their beliefs too prophetic to be easily reconciled with contemporary American culture. Liberalism—not in the sense of the Democratic Party and its programs but in the more philosophical sense of a belief in individual freedom and scientific progress—is the name often given to American secular culture by those who view religious believers as alienated from it. To its advocates, liberalism means tolerance, respect, equality, and fairness. But to its critics, liberalism's claims are fraudulent; in reality, as one such critic argues, liberalism is a worldview in competition with religion—and one that will stop at nothing to win. For Stanley Fish, America's most provocative English professor, "broadmindedness is the opposite of what religious conviction enacts and requires." Religious believers should not be fooled by the sheep's clothing that liberal wolves so often adorn, especially the notion that we can rely on reason to iron out our differences. "There are no reasons you can give to the devout, not because they are the kind of people who don't listen to reason but because the reasons you might give can never be reasons for them unless either they convert to your faith or you convert to theirs." Because of their apocalyptic outlook on the world, religious people have no choice but to reject the secular world in which they find themselves. "To put the matter baldly, a person of religious conviction should not want to enter the marketplace of ideas but to shut it down, at least insofar as it presumes to determine matters that he believes have been determined by God and faith. The religious person should not seek an accommodation with liberalism; he should seek to rout it from the field."

Other writers of a similar disposition hold that practicing Christians have become "resident aliens" of the society in which they live. "We . . . bent over backward, in our illustrations and narratives . . . to use examples that were ordinary, local, and typical, so as to underscore that the sort of prophetic church we had in mind already exists, at least in glimpses," write Stanley Hauerwas and William Willimon in a book of that name, and for that reason, they insist that their book is not "'unrealistic' or 'idealistic' or 'sectarian.'" Yet sociologically speaking, *Resident Aliens* fails to capture much of the actual realities of American religious life, including the fact that untold numbers of religious conservatives are quite at home in the culture around them. The book is addressed specifically to Christians, yet of all the believers in the United States, Christians tend to jump on whatever cultural fad happens to be preoccupying secular people in their society, as their megachurches, which feature everything from state-of-the-art technology to shopping-mall conveniences, so often demonstrate. More than that, they have played a significant role in shaping culture, putting their imprint on the books Americans buy, the ideas they debate, the movies they watch, and the political candidates they elect. It is poor timing at best to portray Christians as seeking alienation from the world at the very moment they have chosen to reject a strategy of withdrawal from American culture in favor of a (rather successful) effort to influence it.

"Christians are now in the odd position of trying to destroy, or at least critique, the very culture we created in order that we may be more nearly faithful," writes Hauerwas, a theologian whose work is influential in conservative Christian circles. If Hauerwas sounds like a 1960s radical, that is because in many ways he is one; he calls C. Wright Mills, the very embodiment of 1960s radicalism, for example, "wonderful." This adulation of Mills offers a clue to this way of thinking. Once upon a time, the New Left and the counterculture dispensed with ideas about acting responsibly in favor of living authentically. Now the same idea, and even the same kind of language, has passed over to Christian theologians. Against the often intemperate, radically separatist movements of the 1960s, wiser voices spoke of the need for moderation and restraint, in the process pointing out that many a countercultural radical shared more with the culture he was protesting than he realized. The same lesson needs to be reinforced whenever those who speak on behalf of people of faith insist, in a rather perverse way, that believers have no place at the table of modernity. They do. And most likely they always will.

Oddly enough, those who presume to speak in the name of believers share the same image of them as those who distrust people of strong religious faith. After his extensive treatment of fundamentalist believers in the United States, one anthropologist found considerable reason for alarm. "One prerequisite for democracy is an openness to the position of the other," he writes. But "where we believe, as the Fundamentalists do, that we have special access to *the* truth, then we have no choice but a stubborn proclamation of that truth. Such a position is absolutist." For Vincent Crapanzano, there can be neither compromise nor dialogue with fundamentalists. They approach the world with an attitude of combat. Hence, politics with them will always be one-sided. "We see this, most dramatically, in the dispute over abortion, but it occurs frequently over other less dramatic issues in the United States today. I am speaking not just of school prayer, homosexuality, and the right to bear arms, but in the way these and other issues are argued by the absolutists. Theirs is simply an assertive discourse."

Distrust of strong religious believers can also be found among those contemporary political philosophers who have been influenced by the idea of "democratic discourse." Liberal values, they maintain, are best preserved when people who have radically different ideas about public policy agree to discuss their differences through appeals to reason. Strong religious believers, however, may prefer revelation over reason, and when they do, they alienate themselves from the rules by which liberal democratic society best organizes itself.

These liberal fears concerning strong religious belief are taken to their logical conclusion by Stephen Macedo, who aims to outline common principles of tolerance and respect on which everyone, or at least everyone who is reasonable, can agree. Toward that end, he distinguishes between those he calls "moderate" or "reasonable" fundamentalists and more conservative believers. Generous toward the one, he offers out few olive branches to the other. Arguing on behalf of a political liberalism with "spine," Macedo claims that "we should also be resolute in facing up to the fact that no version of liberalism can make everyone happy." When religious believers opt to reject the rules of the liberal game, their concerns can properly be ignored. As an example, he cites the case of Vicki Frost, a conservative Christian parent who wanted her child withdrawn from a public-school class in Tennessee when students were asked to read books to which she objected; since it is essential that a liberal society teach such values as tolerance, this liberal philosopher concludes, she has no valid basis on which to justify her unwillingness to have her children exposed to diverse ideas. Indeed, he would deny to fundamentalists the right to send their children to private schools if those schools also opted out of their civic duty to teach tolerance. "Liberal civic education," he writes, "is bound to have the effect of favoring some ways of life or religious convictions over others. So be it." Although he claims to want to avoid an all-out war between liberalism and faith, evidently one cannot do so: "Perhaps, in the end, our politics does come down to a holy war between religious zealots and proponents of science and public reason."

One problem with this way of thinking is that liberals often confuse what religious believers say about themselves with what they actually do. No better example is provided than by the question of biblical literalism. Conservative Christians tell everyone who will listen that they believe that guidelines for how to live are contained in the Bible, which must be read as the literal truth of what God commands. Liberal critics take them at their word, calling those who ascribe to principles of biblical inerrancy "totalistic" in their faith (since, for them, the Bible contains the whole truth). Others write that because fundamentalists adhere to a literal reading of Scripture, they "resist symbolic and allegorical interpretation." But no one lives this way. Christian worship, for one thing, is far more allegorical than it is literal; especially in their small groups, even those ostensibly devoted to Bible study, Christians tell stories about trauma and recovery capable of being interpreted in many different ways. And they do not consult the Bible seeking answers about the right way to live; on the contrary, their decisions are typically shaped by many factors, religious and nonreligious alike, after which they turn to the Bible for support. It makes little sense to argue that no text can actually be taken literally. So-called biblical literalists already know this in practice, their public rhetoric on the matter to the contrary.

If defenders of the faith run the risk of encouraging separatism in their defense of the devout, liberals threaten to undermine their own liberalism when they write about religion. A liberal temperament ought to be disposed to respect as many points of view as possible, including those that in turn have little respect for liberalism. Such a result is not achieved when liberals insist that everyone must conform to their principles, as if the world is simply a tough place and choices have to be made. One can rightly ask of religious believers who use the public schools, and are therefore supported by the taxes paid by everyone else, to abide by the common principles that govern those schools, even when they conflict with the worldview of those believers. But to deny those who care about their faith the ability to pass it on to their children through private education seems a needlessly illiberal response to a complicated issue. In terms made famous by the political philosopher Judith Shklar, liberals need not react out of fear, including fear of religious devotion, but should seek ways to accommodate those whose conception of the world shares little in common with their own.

Between one picture of religious believers as resident aliens and another as hostile to liberal values there is not much to choose. Fortunately, both pictures are inaccurate ones, at least insofar as they represent efforts at generalization. One can, of course, always find some religious believers in the United States who reject liberal society in favor of apocalyptic beliefs. But they are a small minority, and a shrinking one at that. Just as Americans tend to vote for politicians who move toward the middle of the road, they tend to be instinctive moderates when it comes to religion; we are, as is so often said, a religious people, but we are not a zealous one. Despite the attention they receive, religious extremists are often difficult to find in the United States: there has been a revival of fundamentalism but far less than one of more moderate forms of evangelicalism; Reform Jews continue to outnumber, and perhaps to outgrow, Orthodox Jews; and conservative Catholics, who often think of themselves as remaining steadfast to the core teachings of the Church, are a decided minority among all Catholics.

Nor are American religious believers imperialistic in their attitudes toward everyone else. The God in whom they believe is capacious and understanding of many different ways of life, one reason why Catholics are not happy believing that theirs is the one true church or why Jews worry about a God who strikes them as too Jewish. It is true that the United States has a strong commitment to the separation of church and state, but at least part of the reason for that commitment is due to what believers want and not what society imposes; few evangelicals actually go out and try to recruit people in public, and the rest are content with living a good life while hoping that others notice. If anything, the problem American believers have is lack of confidence rather than excessive arrogance. They have found their own comfortable niches in American society and instinctively risk aggressive strategies that would disturb the status quo.

Believers in America are neither an exotic nor an endangered species. They ought not to be treated as holding fast to ways of life that, if not faithfully recorded by anthropologists, will soon disappear, nor are they properly viewed as cabalists hiding from public scrutiny until the time is right to launch their efforts to shape the world in their image. They believe in a supernatural creator, but there is little supernatural about the ways in which they do so. Religious believers blend into the modern American landscape. They increasingly live in suburbs, send their children to four-year liberal-arts colleges, work in professional capacities, enjoy contemporary music, shop in malls, raise confused and uncertain children, and relate primarily to other people with whom they share common interests.

In his reflections on religion and modernity, Peter Berger proposes that religion can offer people a "sacred canopy" that protects them against the chaos of the unexplained. After studying contemporary religious believers, another sociologist, Christian Smith, suggests that they instead need "'sacred umbrellas,' small, portable, accessible relational worlds—religious reference groups—'under' which their beliefs can make complete sense." Smith's revised metaphor captures well the sense in which American religious believers maintain their distinctiveness even as they live in the same modern and pluralistic world lived in by everyone else.

There is, then, no reason to fear that the faithful are a threat to liberal democratic values. Unlike many liberal societies, such as the Netherlands or Great Britain, the United States continues to honor religion publicly. But unlike many deeply religious societies, such as Iran or Poland, it has had a long history of respect for individual rights. Americans love God and democracy and see no contradiction between the two, which is why they clothe their public life in the language of faith while they bring God down to earth and seek salvation through personal choice. Despite what both their friends and their critics often argue, believers are full citizens of the United States, and it is time to make peace between them and the rest of America.

RELIGION'S BAD YEAR

Questions about the proper role for religion in American life have been asked since the arrival of the Puritans and continue into the present time. When we discuss whether textbooks should teach evolution, prayers should be permitted at graduation ceremonies and football games, or parents should be allowed to use publicly financed vouchers to send their children to religious schools, we are engaged in a running controversy that probably will not, and certainly should not, stop. At the same time, our answers to those questions should begin to reflect the reality of religion as it is actually lived and not the imagined religion so often identified by self-proclaimed friends and antagonists of the faithful.

In its efforts to wrestle with the problem of what makes for good citizenship, the Supreme Court of the United States, starting with a case decided in 1973, established a test: Governmental assistance to religious organizations is permissible so long as those organizations are not pervasively sectarian. Yet whatever other charges one might wish to launch against the faithful in American society today, sectarianism, which is among the most common, is actually among the least appropriate. It is not just that Americans do not know much about the ideas of the sects they have presumably joined. The ways in which Americans approach religion with anti-institutional instincts mitigates against any kind of sectarian temperament. As believers switch from one denomination to another, search for ways to avoid the stiff formality of church attendance in favor of home worship, or join parachurch religious movements that meet in stadiums and hotels, they may be expressing a certain flightiness that is disturbing to those who believe that genuine religious fellowship requires a stable group of fellows. But they are also lacking in those characteristics that make for effective sectarianism. One cannot imagine them as avid defenders of a particular piece of religious turf because there is so little ground under their feet. A sectarian society requires sects, but the ways Americans actually practice their faith deprive sects of the doctrines, numbers, and legitimacy they need to flourish.

Growth is the enemy of sectarianism. Religions committed to the principle that the world is irredeemably corrupt and the sin of human beings deeply etched may be content to watch their membership numbers stagnate as they gather into sects, but just about all other religions in America want to be attractive to the uncommitted and to retain the already committed. This adherence to growth can have its frustrations; watching sermons reduced to PowerPoint presentations or listening to one easily forgettable praise song after another makes one long for an evangelical willing to stand up, Luther-like, and proclaim his opposition to the latest survey of evangelical taste. Tacky as evangelicalism can be, however, sectarian it is not. Its problem, in fact, is the opposite—so strong a desire to copy the culture of hotel chains and popular music that it loses what religious distinctiveness it once had.

Does this mean that we should conclude that religious believers are no longer hell-bent on prohibiting abortion, throwing Darwin out of public schools, denouncing homosexuals, and imposing their prayers on others? The answer—if, like me, you think some abortions should be legal, the theory of evolution true, gay marriage an idea worth considering, and the rights of minorities protected—is that we should not. But we should deal with them in a different way than we have. We ought, first, to recognize that in a democratic society those religious believers who insist that creation science should be given equal time with Darwin have the right to their opinion and can, like all other citizens, seek to influence public officials to adopt their point of view. Too often liberal critics of religion have sought to win their battles over the role of religion in the public square, not by engaging in politics but by appealing to courts. Lying behind that strategy is the twin sense that most Americans are people of strong faith and that the Reverend Jerry Falwell is a stand-in for a significant number of them. So powerful is the potential of the religious right, in the view of liberal critics, that only through strict application of First Amendment principles can the United States be saved from religious oppression. Democracy, liberals of this persuasion believe, is a wonderful form of government, but when it comes to protecting the rights of religious minorities or nonbelievers, a nondemocratic institution like the courts is required to keep it in check.

Once they begin to recognize that Jerry Falwell speaks for very few Christians, let alone the devout of other persuasions, liberals might find that it is possible to give reasons to the faithful through usual democratic venues. Ordinary evangelicals believe that abortion is wrong and homosexuality a sin, and many of them detest what their children learn in public school as well as the ways they learn it. They also believe that people deserve a second chance, that rules sometimes need to be bent under unusual circumstances, and that schools are essential to democracy and individual upward mobility. When the differences between them and liberal secularists are argued out in election campaigns or debated on talk shows, there is no necessary reason why liberal views should win; democracy does not determine the winners in advance. But if the arguments of liberals are good ones, they can make a dent, not necessarily by changing minds—again, there is no necessary reason why they should—but by leaving impressions. As much as evangelicals disagree with liberals, their culture, should liberals ever to care to look, is one of caring and concern (and increasingly one of social justice). And in the process, liberals might even find that they have something to learn from conservative Christians: Who these days does not believe that abortion is a morally problematic act, even if justified in some cases, or that Christian charity is a virtue worth protecting?

The need for the very religious, the moderately religious, and the nonreligious to find common ground has been exacerbated by the fact that, in an astonishingly concentrated one-year period starting in September 2001, all the world's major religions found themselves facing crises that raised the uncomfortable question of whether religion is compatible with modern liberal democracy after all.

Leading the list of those events, of course, would have to be the terrorist attack of September 11 itself, which was launched in the name of one religion, Islam, against all those who, because their faith happens to be different, are treated as infidels and therefore as people whose lives simply do not count. Some argue that the ideas of Osama bin Laden represent a political form of Islam that is, in many ways, a perversion of a faith that is much more peaceful than he and his followers make it out to be. But it is impossible to deny the appeal of militant forms of Islam to millions of people around the world, nor the fact that the terrorists who carried out the acts were inspired by religious visions. Time will tell whether the attacks on the World Trade Center and the Pentagon represented the last gasp of a political Islam that has steadily been losing its appeal in the Muslim world or whether it will kick off a new round of violence in the name of faith. For the moment, the attack stands as a reminder of the power of religion to fuel hatred and to justify extremism.

Determined to prove that extremist Muslims are not the only hateful people in the world, some conservative Christians in the United States—including Rev. Jerry Falwell, Rev. Jerry Vines of the Southern Baptist Convention, and Rev. Franklin Graham, son of Billy Graham—responded to the September 11 attack by denouncing Islam as a false faith, including charges that the Prophet was a pedophile and a terrorist. In so doing, they invoked the intolerance historically associated with their own Christian tradition, even if in some cases they found avid defenders. Vines and Graham were right to speak as they did, claimed R. Albert Mohler Jr., president of the Southern Baptist Theological Seminary of Louisville, Kentucky. "An Islam that settles for religious pluralism," he wrote, "is not authentic Islam, and Christianity without zeal for conversion is not authentic Christianity." If we believe, as Mohler does, that "religions stand or fall on the validity of their truth claims," there will inevitably be as many truths at war with each other as there are faiths. Some people, it would seem, lament the fact that the days of the Crusades are over.

Judaism has contributed its share to the zealotry and violence with which religion is so frequently associated. Faced with suicide bombings of civilians, Israel can hardly be expected to sit back and do nothing. But by taking actions above and beyond measures of self-defense or even justified retaliation, such as arresting and detaining Palestinian moderates or allowing settlements in the West Bank to continue, the government of Ariel Sharon, dependent on the votes of extreme right-wing religious parties, seems to prefer a situation of continued religious war to any realistic possibility for peace. American Jews are divided over their responses to what is happening in the Middle East, but all of them are made aware by those events of the existence within their religion of chiliastic tendencies unwilling to make accommodations to a world of religious pluralism. No matter how determined Jews in both Israel and the United States are to resist terrorist attacks, there will never be peace in the Middle East until both Jews and Muslims find a way to live together on land they both claim as their own.

The pedophilia crisis that broke out in the Catholic Church in 2002 is not an example of religious intolerance; on the contrary, despite a history of anti-Catholicism in Protestant America, there has been almost no gloating in Protestant circles about the troubles faced by the American Catholic hierarchy. That crisis, however, does serve as a reminder of another of religion's less than positive undemocratic legacies: a history of secrecy and an unwillingness to respond to legitimate criticism. The actions of Bernard Cardinal Law in Boston revealed a church leadership desperately out of touch with the sensibilities of its members. For years, the church denied that it had a serious problem of sexual abuse on its hands. Then it reached settlements in individual cases contingent upon confidentiality, which often left victims feeling as if they were the ones victimized. It then turned around and assigned abusive priests to other locations, rarely informing those at the new destination of any problems to which they ought to pay attention. And when the extent of the crisis was portrayed in the press, Church officials responded in legalistic terms that made them seem indistinguishable from corporation presidents or politicians seeking to explain away their own scandalous acts. If one needed evidence of why Americans so often make a distinction between their faith, which they treat with reverence, and the institutions within which faith is traditionally practiced, about which they are usually less enthusiastic, the pedophilia crisis provides it.

As these examples of strife and secrecy suggest, the first year of the twenty-first century has not been a good one for people of faith. For some, this may merely mean that religion is getting what it deserves. Religion, they would point out, has always been a force for discord and intolerance, and we can hardly be surprised when it reverts to form. As tragic as all these events are, they may have a positive outcome. By reminding us of the degree to which strong forms of faith are incompatible with liberal principles, September 11 and its aftermath, from this perspective, underscores the need to protect democratic societies against ways of life it is poorly prepared to accommodate. We should respond to all these events by strengthening the wall between church and state and by keeping the public square free of religious proselytizing so that we are not swept up in the new religious wars that threaten societies outside the United States and can easily spill over into our own society as well.

I believe that steps in this direction would be the wrong ones to take. Their consequence would be to persuade the faithful that they really are resident aliens of the society obligated to practice "exercises in resistance" against it. Fortunately, there is no reason to make them feel that way. Understanding how religion is actually practiced in the United States offers the more optimistic scenario that religion need not be an enemy of democracy and can in many cases be its friend.

Take the question of religious intolerance. When I visited the Cincinnati Vineyard Fellowship, its pastor Steve Sjogren told me that the message of his sermons is "love, love, love, love, love, truth." I think he may have his priorities wrong; love is something you get from your family, not your church. Still, believers who prefer a God of love to a God of truth are not going to kill for their beliefs—or to give their support to those who do. It is because Americans do not treat religion as a battle for the soul that the conservative Christians who denounced Islam as a false religion received very little hearing for their views; if anything, they embarrassed themselves and marginalized their message. Despite the enormous numbers left dead by the September 11 attack, and despite the fact that all the killers were believers in Islam, moreover, Americans did not engage in the religious war their enemies were trying to provoke. On the contrary, September 11 was met with official recognition by the president of the United States, and unofficial recognition by ordinary people, that Islam had become an important current in the domestic life of the United States. The American record on these matters looks especially positive in comparison with the record of countries like ours. The French typically lecture the United States on its moral failings, yet Jean-Marie Le Pen, an immigrant-bashing politician of decidedly anti-Muslim and anti-Semitic views, has a large following in France, while the only politician to speak in similar terms in the United States, Patrick Buchanan, has been effectively marginalized as a political force. And other countries in Europe widely praised for their tolerance, such as the Netherlands and Denmark, have also displayed far more religious intolerance in their electoral campaigns than one can find in the United States.

Similar conclusions follow from the widespread tendency of Americans to switch faiths. It is difficult for Protestants and Catholics to maintain their historic distrust of one another when so many Americans who were born in one religion now find themselves belonging to the other. The same now applies to Jews and will one day apply to all those outside the Judeo-Christian tradition. In the aftermath of September 11, there were incidents of anti-Semitism on

American campuses, but they were nothing like the attacks on synagogues and public sites heard in Western Europe. Anti-Semitism is tame in this country not because conservative Christians took the lead in defending Israel; in fact, their strong support was motivated by interpretations of Christian eschatology that contain anti-Semitic overtones. It is more likely due to widespread intermarriage between Christians and Jews and the increasingly similar practices both religions adopt. As much as we may be tempted to denounce as flighty Americans who change their faith as often as their cars, we ought to recognize that religious switching acts as a kind of insurance policy against bigotry. If you cannot be sure today what your faith will be tomorrow—let alone the faith of the people your son or daughter bring home for the weekend—you had better not say anything too nasty about any of them. Sometimes the more seemingly frivolous of the ways Americans practice their faith turn out to be blessings in disguise.

For all the ways in which the transformation of American religion disappoints those who long for more theologically informed faiths that take sin seriously and make the honoring of tradition obligatory, an often unnoticed success story lies behind the ways in which Americans practice their faith. In theory, religious differences ought to be more difficult to resolve than racial and ethnic ones. Faith, after all, is something that people have fought over the centuries, and even in the United States, the first society in the world to write freedom of religion into its constitution, Protestants typically treated their religion, the majority religion, as the guiding source of American values, whatever Catholics and Jews thought about the matter. Discrimination's original sin in the United States was religious discrimination. If you believed the wrong things, and even if you believed the right things but believed them the wrong way, you were treated as if you really belonged somewhere else.

Yet at a time when the United States still experiences serious legacies of racial discrimination, its record on religious pluralism is truly remarkable. Just as the September 11 attacks were met with relatively minimal outbreaks of Muslim bashing, the scandals facing the Catholic Church produced very little rejoicing in Protestant circles, even in those conservative Protestant denominations that once displayed a history of anti-Catholic bigotry. Even more remarkably, Americans not only welcome to their shores religious believers from non–Judeo-Christian traditions, they give them the higher compliment of converting to their traditions; nothing is more symbolic of the benefits of America's religious transformation than the fact that Buddhists from Asia convert to Christianity at the same time that Christians and Jews from the United States convert to Buddhism. It is true that, when it comes to issues involving racial diversity, Americans tend to disagree about affirmative action or the amount of progress the society has made in progressing toward greater racial equality. Lost in the somewhat depressing story about race is the fact that we disagree much less over questions such as whether one religion should be society's official religion, exactly the kind of issue that divides societies different from our own.

Understanding more about the ways Americans practice religion also helps put the pedophilia crisis of the Catholic church in perspective. Americans are more likely to identify with their faith, which they consider personal to them, than with the institutions, including denominations and congregations, that have historically represented their faith to them. This latent anti-institutionalization became particularly important in the pedophilia crisis because, of all religions in the United States, Catholics, in previous decades, were the most institutionally loyal—actively joining labor unions, supporting urban political machines, working for government, sponsoring their own system of schools, and sticking with their parish. All that has begun to change as Catholics become more like other religious believers in the United States. Now suburban and middle class, they work in companies in which women share power with men, CEOs are held accountable for their actions, people advance on the basis of talent rather than loyalty, and failure is punished by the marketplace. In their response to the sins of the hierarchy, American Catholics are unlikely to leave their faith behind; the most prominent organization to arise out of the crisis, on the contrary, is called the Voice of the Faithful. What they are seeking is a church that is more responsive and open, a church, in short, like the rest of America. Because they are, the pedophilia scandal could turn out to be a source of replenishment for American Catholicism rather than a nail in its coffin.

Religion, like the stock market, has its ups and downs, and there may occur a time when talk of jihad dies down, peace is achieved in the Middle East, and the Catholic Church becomes more democratic. But it is not the headline-grabbing events that will determine the future of American religion. American religion had already become more personalized and individualistic, less doctrinal and devotional, more practical and purposeful, and increasingly at home with the culture surrounding it long before September 11, suicide bombings, and the trials and tribulations of Bernard Cardinal Law. The events of religion's bad year may have sped them along, but whatever changes in religious practice they encourage would most likely have taken place in some form or other without them.

We can never predict what future decades will bring to the practice of American religion. But we can control the effects of those developments by narrowing the gap between the high expectations we often have for religion and the realities of ordinary people leading mundane lives. The more we refrain from treating religion as if it has some status that makes it different from everything else in the world—holier and more moral if you like it, more sectarian and divisive if you do not—the greater our chances of avoiding religion's ugly legacies while still being able to appreciate its benefits for the individuals who practice it and for the democratic society they inhabit. American religion has been so transformed that we have reached the end of religion as we have known it. This does not mean religion no longer has meaning. It means we will have to know it in new ways.

NOTES

INTRODUCTION: THE PASSING OF THE OLD-TIME RELIGION

1   "So . . . thus it is": Jonathan Edwards, "Sinners in the Hands of an Angry God," in John E. Smith, Harry S. Stout, and Kenneth P. Minkema, eds., *A Jonathan Edwards Reader* (New Haven: Yale University Press, 1995), 95.

1   Much ink: See, for example, George M. Marsden, *Jonathan Edwards: A Biography* (New Haven: Yale University Press, 2003).

3   as it is lived: Two attempts at providing an overview of recent research into lived religion are Colleen McDannell, ed., *Religions of the United States in Practice*, 2 vols. (Princeton: Princeton University Press, 2001), and David D. Hall, ed., *Lived Religion in America: Toward a History of Practice* (Princeton: Princeton University Press, 1997). Specific works dealing with various religious practices will be cited throughout these notes. This is perhaps the appropriate place to say that many students of lived religion alter the names of the churches and communities they study to provide protection against invasion of privacy, so that some of the names of churches and believers given throughout the text are disguised.

CHAPTER 1. WORSHIP

10   "was immutable": Jay P. Dolan, *In Search of American Catholicism: A History of Religion and Culture in Transition* (New York: Oxford University Press, 2002), 169.

10   Throughout Catholic America: Joseph Gremillion and Jim Castelli, *The Emerging Parish: The Notre Dame Study of Catholic Life Since Vatican II* (New York: Harper and Row, 1987), 120–31.

11 professional liturgists: Michael J. McCallion and David R. Maines, "The Liturgical Social Movement in the Vatican II Catholic Church," *Research in Social Movements* 21 (1999): 125–49.

11 Critics of: See, for example, David Torevell, *Losing the Sacred: Ritual, Modernity, and Liturgical Reform* (Edinburgh: T&T Clark, 2000), 145.

11 inner conviction: Mary Douglas, *Natural Symbols: Explorations in Cosmology* (New York: Pantheon, 1982), 51.

12 "When I walk": Michael J. McCallion, "Lay and Professional Views on Tabernacle Location in Catholic Parishes," *Journal of Contemporary Ethnography* 29 (December 2000): 725–33.

13 "The craziest time": Michael J. McCallion, David R. Maines, and Steven E. Wolfel, "Policy as Practice: First Holy Communion as a Contested Situation," *Journal of Contemporary Ethnography* 25 (October 1996): 312.

13 "public duty": *Catholic Encyclopedia,* www.newadvent.org/cathen/09306a.htm.

13 "Following Vatican II": Charles R. Morris, *American Catholic* (New York: Times Books, 1997), 308.

13 attendance at Mass: William V. D'Antonio, James D. Davison, Dean R. Hoge, and Katherine Meyer, *American Catholics: Gender, Generation, and Commitment* (Walnut Creek, Calif.: AltaMira, 2001), 52–53.

14 "feeling of meditating": Gremillion and Castelli, *The Emerging Parish,* 132.

14 "it was like": Dean R. Hoge, William D. Dinges, Mary Johnson, and Juan L. Gonzales, *Young American Catholics: Religion in the Culture of Choice* (Notre Dame, Ind.: University of Notre Dame Press, 2001), 161–62.

14 "Mary was the first": Mary Jo Neitz, *Charisma and Community: A Study of Religious Commitment within the Charismatic Renewal* (New Brunswick, N.J.: Transaction Books, 1987), 107, 164.

15 "The past five years": Peter McDonough and Eugene C. Bianchi, *Passionate Uncertainty: Inside the American Jesuits* (Berkeley and Los Angeles: University of California Press, 2002), 115.

15 While only 4 percent: Gremillion and Castelli, *The Emerging Parish,* 159.

15 "evangelical orientation": Hoge et al., *Young American Catholics,* 168–69, 170.

15 About one in twenty: Bernard J. Lee, S. M., with William V. D'Antonio, *The Catholic Experience of Small Christian Communities* (New York: Paulist Press, 2000), 6–7, 9, 10, 137.

16 "We're not a": Robert F. Keeler, *Parish!: The Pulitzer Prize–Winning Story of a Vibrant Catholic Community* (New York: Crossroad Publishing Company, 1997), 129, 137.

16 transubstantiation: D'Antonio et al., *American Catholics,* 54–55.

17 "individual emphasis": Sister Marie Augusta Neal, *Values and Interests in Social Change* (London: Prentice Hall, 1965), 26–27, cited in Douglas, 7.

17   "collective connection": Charles Taylor, *Varieties of Religion Today: William James Revisited* (Cambridge, Mass.: Harvard University Press, 2002), 24, 79–107.

18   *Adon Olam:* Lynn Davidman, "Beyond Synagogue Walls," in Michele Dillion, ed., *Handbook for the Sociology of Religion in America* (Cambridge, Mass.: Cambridge University Press, forthcoming).

18   25 percent: Personal discussion with Barry A. Kosmin, Washington, D.C., May 9, 2002.

18   "I think our kids": Quoted in Sylvia Barack Fishman, *Jewish Life and American Culture* (Albany: State University of New York Press, 2000), 134.

18   "I could do away": Frida Kerner Furman, *Beyond Yiddishkeit: The Struggle for Identity in a Reform Synagogue* (Albany: State University of New York Press, 1987), 80, 84.

19   "Prayer": L. A. Hoffman, "Creative Liturgy," *The Jewish Spectator* 40 (Winter 1975): 48, cited in Furman, 65.

19   "do not focus": Steven M. Cohen and Arnold M. Eisen, *The Jew Within: Self, Family, and Community in America* (Bloomington: Indiana University Press, 2000), 85.

19   Kehillat Kodesh: Samuel C. Heilman, *Synagogue Life: A Study in Symbolic Interaction* (New Brunswick, N.J.: Transaction, 1998 [1976]), 66–68.

20   Consider *nusach:* Jeffrey A. Summit, *The Lord's Song in a Strange Land: Music and Identity in Contemporary Jewish Worship* (New York: Oxford University Press, 2000), 107–25.

21   "During the Torah": Heilman, *Synagogue Life,* 148.

22   "Throughout the service": Nancy Tatom Ammerman, *Bible Believers: Fundamentalists and the Modern World* (New Brunswick, N.J.: Rutgers University Press, 1987), 37.

23   "Lord, give me": Diane Winston, "Answered Prayers: The Rockhaven House Fellowship," in Robert Wuthnow, ed., *"I Come Away Stronger": How Small Groups Are Shaping American Religion* (Grand Rapids: Eerdmans, 1994), 28.

23   old business: Natalie Searl, "The Women's Bible Study Group: A Thriving Evangelical Support Group," in Wuthnow, *"I Come Away Stronger,"* 97–124.

24   "Christian worship": Marva J. Dawn, *Reaching Out without Dumbing Down: A Theology of Worship for the Turn-of-the-Century Culture* (Grand Rapids: Eerdmans, 1995), 80, 108.

25   "wear their Sunday best": R. Stephen Warner, *New Wines in Old Wineskins: Evangelicals and Liberals in a Small-Town Church* (Berkeley and Los Angeles: University of California Press, 1988), 35–40.

26   worship wars: Thomas G. Long, *Beyond the Worship Wars: Building Vital and Faithful Worship* (Bethesda, Md.: Alban Institute, 2001).

26   "People today": Timothy Wright, *A Community of Joy: How to Create Contemporary Worship* (Nashville: Abington, 1994), 20–21, cited in Long, 28.

27   the resulting findings: Mark Chaves, *How Do We Worship?* (Bethesda, Md.: Albin Institute, 1999), 27–47.

27   "conservative": Conrad Cherry, Betty A. DeBerg, and Amanda Porterfeld, *Religion on Campus: What Religion Really Means to Today's Undergraduates* (Chapel Hill: University of North Carolina Press, 2001), 21.

28   "it is a misnomer": Dawn, *Reaching Out*, 81.

28   Janie Sjogren: Interview with Janie Sjogren, March 4, 2002.

28   About half of the time: Julie Ingersoll, "Contemporary Christian Worship Music," in McDannell, *Religions of the United States*, vol. 2, 123, and Donald E. Miller, *Reinventing American Protestantism: Christianity in the New Millennium* (Berkeley and Los Angeles: University of California Press, 1997), 85, 122.

28   a franchise: As, for example, at Brentwood Baptist Church in Houston; see Patricia Leigh Brown, "Megachurches as Minitowns," *New York Times*, May 9, 2002, D1.

28   one church: Ingersoll, "Christian Worship Music," 123.

29   to find out: Kimon Howland Sargeant, *Seeker Churches: Promoting Traditional Religion in a Nontraditional Way* (New Brunswick, N.J.: Rutgers University Press, 2000), 66.

29   "simplistic, repetitive": Long, *Beyond the Worship Wars*, 59.

29   "In my view": Martha Bayles, e-mail to author, August 21, 2002.

30   "I would not think": Stephen Haynes, e-mail to author, April 11, 2002.

32   "Would the guy": I listened to Workman's sermons on the church's website: www.vccproductions.com.

32   "Jesus will save": Randall Balmer, *Mine Eyes Have Seen the Glory: A Journey into the Evangelical Subculture in America* (New York: Oxford University Press, 1989), 231.

33   "I want to": Bruce Wilkinson, *The Prayer of Jabez: Breaking Through to the Blessed Life* (Sisters, Ore.: Multnomah Publishers, 2000), 19, 31.

34   Jon   from: prayerofjabez.com/JabezTestimonies/MoreBlessings Archive16.html#CancerPatientBlessings.

34   "I   was   pointed":   prayerofjabez.com/JabezTestimonies/More BlessingsArchive16.html#Sleeping.

35   At the height: See, for example, Samuel P. Huntington and Zbigniew Brzezinski, *Political Power USA/USSR* (New York: Viking Press, 1964).

35   "may be moving": Cohen and Eisen, *The Jew Within*, 190.

CHAPTER 2. FELLOWSHIP

37   in truth: Michael O. Emerson and Christian Smith, *Divided by Faith: Evangelical Religion and the Problems of Race in America* (New York: Oxford University Press, 2000); R. Stephen Warner, "The Place of the Contemporary

American Religious Congregation," in James P. Wind and James W. Lewis, *American Congregations*, vol. 2, *New Perspectives in the Study of Congregations* (Chicago: University of Chicago Press, 1994), 83.

38   a recent survey: Wade Clark Roof, *Spiritual Marketplace: Baby Boomers and the Remaking of American Religion* (Princeton: Princeton University Press, 1999), 85.

39   "denominational society": Andrew M. Greeley, *The Denominational Society: A Sociological Approach to Religion in America* (Glenview, Ill.: Scott Foresman, 1972).

39   "denominational barriers": Robert Wuthnow, *The Restructuring of American Religion: Society and Faith since World War II* (Princeton: Princeton University Press, 1988), 97.

39   has been challenged: Darren E. Sherkat, "Tracking the Restructuring of American Religion: Religious Affiliation and Patterns of Religious Mobility, 1973–1998," *Social Forces* 79 (June 2001): 1459–93, and Lyman A. Kellstedt and John C. Green, "Knowing God's Many People: Denominational Preference and Political Behavior," in David C. Leege and Lyman A. Kellstedt, eds., *Rediscovering the Religious Factor in American Politics* (Armonk, N.Y.: M. E. Sharpe, 1993), 65. Wuthnow maintains his thesis about the declining significance of denominations, but with some modifications, in "Restructuring of American Religion: Further Evidence," *Sociological Inquiry* 66 (August 1996): 324.

39   most studied community: For background, see Rita Caccamo, *Back to Middletown: Three Generations of Sociological Reflection* (Stanford: Stanford University Press, 2000), and Richard Wrightman Fox, "Epitaph for Middletown: Robert S. Lynd and the Analysis of Consumer Culture," in Richard Wrightman Fox and T. J. Jackson Lears, eds., *The Culture of Consumption: Critical Essays in American History 1880–1980* (New York: Pantheon, 1983), 101–41.

39   Daily prayer: Robert S. Lynd and Helen Merrell Lynd, *Middletown: A Study in Modern American Culture* (New York: Harcourt, Brace, and World, 1959 [1929]), 304, 334–35, 336, 337, 344, 353, 371.

41   "a loss in cooperation": Robert S. Lynd and Helen Merrell Lynd, *Middletown in Transition: A Study in Cultural Conflicts* (New York: Harcourt Brace, 1937), 304.

41   a Gallup Poll: Cited in Wuthnow, *The Restructuring of American Religion*, 88.

41   another Gallup Poll: Wuthnow, *The Restructuring of American Religion*, 88. For additional evidence, see Wade Clark Roof and Christopher Kirk Hadaway, "Shifts in Religious Preference: The Mid-Seventies," *Journal for the Scientific Study of Religion* 16 (1977): 409–12.

42   as much about choice: For examples, see Philip E. Hammond, *Religion and Personal Autonomy* (Columbia, S.C.: University of South Carolina Press, 1992); Bernard Lazerwitz, J. Alan Winter, Arnold Dashefsky, and Ephraim Tabory, *Jewish Choices: American Jewish Denominationalism* (Albany: State University of New York Press, 1998); and Roof, *Spiritual Marketplace*.

42   "The major denominational": Theodore Caplow, Howard M. Bahr, and Bruce A. Chadwick, *All Faithful People: Change and Continuity in Middletown's Religion* (Minneapolis: University of Minnesota Press, 1983), 126, 282–83.

43   "I am who I am": Joseph B. Tamney, *The Resilience of Conservative Religion: The Case of Popular, Conservative, Protestant Congregations* (New York: Cambridge University Press, 2002), 81, 92, 98.

44   having already invested: Rodney Stark and Roger Finke, *Acts of Faith: Exploring the Human Side of Religion* (Berkeley: University of California Press, 2000), 123.

44   "the circulation of the saints": Reginald Bibby and Merlin Brinkerhoff, "Circulation of the Saints 1966–1990: New Data, New Reflections," *Journal for the Scientific Study of Religion* 33 (1994): 273–80.

44   "felt dead": Tamney, *The Resilience of Conservative Religion*, 102–105, contains Teri's story.

45   "I haven't the": Roof, *Spiritual Marketplace*, 18.

46   a bit sobering: Sargeant, *Seeker Churches*, 141.

46   the "neutral environment": Nancy L. Eiesland, *A Particular Place: Urban Restructuring and Religious Ecology in a Southern Exurb* (New Brunswick, N.J.: Rutgers University Press, 2000), 57, 60.

46   "American religion": Robert Wuthnow, *Sharing the Journey: Support Groups and America's New Quest for Community* (New York: Free Press, 1994), 355.

47   85.1 percent of American Jews: Sherkat, "Tracking the Restructuring of American Religion," 1466.

47   only 56 percent: Lazerwitz et al., *Jewish Choices*, 80.

47   is "achieved": Chaim I. Waxman, *Jewish Baby Boomers: A Communal Perspective* (Albany: State University of New York Press, 2001), 129.

47   a physician named Molly: Cohen and Eisen, *The Jew Within*, 15–16, 19–21.

47   20 and 30 percent: Jack Wertheimer, *A People Divided: Judaism in Contemporary America* (New York: Basic Books, 1993), 52.

48   "Perhaps more": Fishman, *Jewish Life and American Culture*, 13.

48   Catholics have: Sherkat, "Tracking the Restructuring of American Religion," 1467.

48   Catholics remain Catholic: Andrew M. Greeley, *The Catholic Myth: The Behavior and Beliefs of American Catholics* (New York: Scribner's, 1990), 15–33; Andrew M. Greeley and Michael Hout, "Musical Chairs: Patterns of Denominational Change," *Sociology and Social Research* 72 (1988): 75–86.

48   the attraction of: Luís León, "Born Again in East LA: The Congregation as Border Space," in R. Stephen Warner and Judith G. Wittner, eds., *Gatherings in the Diaspora: Religious Communities and the New Immigration* (Philadelphia: Temple University Press, 1998), 163–96.

48   non-Latino Catholic: See, for example, Hoge et al., *Young American Catholics*, 46.

49   nearly every: For examples, see Sargeant, *Seeker Churches*, 30; Miller, 69; and Ammerman, *Bible Believers*, 30.

49   a sense of identity: Nancy Tatom Ammerman, *Congregation and Community* (New Brunswick, N.J.: Rutgers University Press, 1997), 330. See, as well, the examples in Wind and Lewis, *American Congregations*, vol. 1: *Portrait of Twelve Religious Communities* (Chicago: University of Chicago Press, 1994).

50   "It was so": Jenny Orr's comments can be found in her essays "When God Dries Up the Stream," at www.webcom.com/hchp/dryup.htm, and "Re-Entry into Real Life," at www.webcom.com/hchp/reallife.htm.

50   "Guardian, schoolmaster": Leta van Duin, "The Single Greatest Pitfall of Leadership," www.webcom.com/hchp/pitfall.htm.

50   the house church movement: For a movement manifesto, see Tom Begier, Tim Richey, Nick Vasiliades, and Frank Viola, *The House Church Movement* (Jacksonville, Fla.: SeedSowers, n.d.).

50   Although home churching: One exception is Stuart A. Wright, "Religious Innovation in the Mainline Church: House Churches, Home Cells, and Small Groups," in Nancy Tatom Ammerman and Wade Clark Roof, eds., *Work, Family, and Religion in Contemporary Society* (New York and London: Routledge, 1995), 261–81.

51   "there simply is no": Roger Upton, "Church House or House Church?," www.geocities.com/sovgracenet/housech.html.

51   "relational Christianity": Glenn Heller, "Accomplishment Christianity vs. Relational Christianity." www.webcom.com/hchp/accompli.htm.

51   many of whom: Mitchell L. Stevens, *Kingdom of Children: Culture and Controversy in the Homeschooling Movement* (Princeton: Princeton University Press, 2001), passim.

51   "pyramid structures": Mike Peters, "Organic Leadership = Jesus' Headship," www.webcom.com/hchp/orglead.htm.

51   "It seems that": Tracey Amino's comments were found in her essays "When the Old Testament Prophet Visits Your House Church" and "Do We Have to Have a Church Planter?," at www.webcom.com/hchp/planter.htm and www.webcom.com/hchp/prophet.htm.

53   "Your pathway": Matthew P. Lawson, "Accountability and Fellowship in an Assemblies of God Cell Group," in Wuthnow, *"I Come Away Stronger,"* 92–94.

53   "shul with a pool": David Kaufman, *Shul with a Pool: The "Synagogue-Center" in American Jewish History* (Hanover, N.H.: University Press of New England, 1999).

53   "might find a": Quoted in Jonathan Sarna and Karla Goldman, "From Synagogue-Community to Citadel of Reform: The History of K. K. Bene Israel (Rockdale Temple) in Cincinnati, Ohio," in Wind and Lewis, *American Congregations*, vol. 1, 185.

54   "Kelton Minyan": Riv-Ellen Prell, *Prayer and Community: The Havurah in American Judaism* (Detroit: Wayne State University Press, 1989), 143–49.

54   the experiences of: Robert C. Liebman, "Finding a Place: The Vision of Havurah," in Wuthnow, *"I Come Away Stronger,"* 300–21.

55   "An ongoing struggle": Tamney, *The Resilience of Conservative Religion,* 85–86.

56   "genuine Christian communities": Lee and D'Antonio, 126, 132–33.

56   "Church is a very big": Hoge et al., *Young American Catholics,* 80–84, 181, 185–86.

58   "I came back": His testimony is found at www.promisekeepers.org/test/test228.htm.

58   an extremely controversial: See, for example, Joe Conanson, Alfred Ross, and Lee Cokorinos, "The Promise Keepers Are Coming: The Third Wave of the Religious Right," *The Nation,* October 7, 1996, 11–12+. For essays on the movement, see Dane S. Claussen, ed., *Standing on the Promises: The Promise Keepers and the Revival of Manhood* (Cleveland: Pilgrim Press, 1999).

59   Appealing to charismatics: Stephen D. Johnson, "Who Supports the Promise Keepers?," in Rhys H. Williams, *Promise Keepers and the New Masculinity: Private Lives and Public Morality* (Lanham, Md.: Lexington Books, 2001), 101–102.

59   "We're trying to": Cited in Ken Abraham, *Who Are the Promise Keepers?: Understanding the Christian Men's Movement* (New York: Doubleday, 1997), 150.

59   "No one is": E. Glenn Wagner, *The Awesome Power of Shared Beliefs: Five Things Every Man Should Know* (Dallas: Word Publishing, 1995), 8, cited in Larry Dean Allen II, "A Comparative Analysis of the Men of Religion Forward Movement and Promise Keepers" (Ph.D. diss., Boston University, 2000), 218.

59   "generic, conservative": Melinda Bollar Wagner, "Generic Conservative Christianity: The Demise of Denominationalism in Christian Schools," *Journal for the Scientific Study of Religion* 36 (1997): 13–24.

59   McCartney himself: He tells his story in Bill McCartney, with Dave Diles, *From Ashes to Glory* (Nashville: Thomas Nelson, 1990), and Bill McCartney, with David Halbrook, *Sold Out: Becoming Man Enough to Make a Difference* (Nashville: Word Publishing, 1997).

60   a 1996 "perspective": United States Conference of Catholic Bishops' Committee on Marriage and Family, "A Perspective on Promise Keepers," www.nccbuscc.org/laity/marriage/promise.htm.

60   Mainline denominations: For the Methodists, see *United Methodist Daily News,* September 30, 1997, at www.umns.umc.org/news97/sep/gumen.htm, and for the Presbyterians, see Douglas DeCelle, "Presbyterians and the Promise Keepers," *Presbyterians Today Online,* December 1997, at www.pcusa.org/pcusa/today/features/feat9712g.htm.

60   "it is going": Ernest Pickering, *Promise Keepers and the Forgotten Promise* (Decatur, Ala.: Baptist World Mission, 1955), cited in Michael Ellsworth Eidenmuller, "A Rhetoric of Religious Order: The Case of Promise Keepers" (Ph.D. diss., Louisiana State University, 1998), at www.uttyler.edu/meidenmuller/scholarship/dissertation.htm.

61   "The goal of": Amy Schindler and Jennifer Carroll Lena, "Promise Keepers in Perspective: Organizational Characteristics of a Men's Movement," *Research in the Social Scientific Study of Religion* 11 (2000): 213.

61   "We can't compete": Abraham, *Who Are the Promise Keepers?*, 153.

61   "the moral aspect": George N. Lundskow, *Awakening to an Uncertain Future: A Case Study of the Promise Keepers* (New York: Peter Lang, 2002), 47.

62   any controversial topic: Sean F. Everton, "The Promise Keepers: Religious Revival or Third Wave of the Religious Right?," *Review of Religious Research* 43 (September 2001): 51–69.

62   "you've got to": Lundskow, *Awakening to an Uncertain Future*, 69.

62   At one such group: Bryan W. Brickner, *The Promise Keepers: Politics and Promises* (Lanham, Md.: Lexington Books, 1999), 21–24.

62   "muscular Christianity": For the history, see Clifford Putney, *Muscular Christianity: Manhood and Sports in Protestant America, 1880–1920* (Cambridge, Mass.: Harvard University Press, 2001). For the current situation, see Tony Ladd and James A. Mathisen, *Muscular Christianity: Evangelical Protestants and the Development of American Sport* (Grand Rapids, Mich.: Baker Books, 1999). An attempt to relate Promise Keepers to this tradition can be found in Dane S. Claussen, ed., *The Promise Keepers: Essays on Masculinity and Christianity* (Jefferson, N.C.: McFarland, 2000).

62   make up its mind: William H. Lockhart, "'We Are One Life,' But Not of One Gender Ideology: Unity, Ambiguity, and the Promise Keepers," in Williams, *Promise Keepers*, 73–92.

62   "the kind of thing": Lundskow, *Awakening to an Uncertain Future*, 76.

63   in one such group: John Bartkowsi, "Breaking Walls, Raising Fences: Masculinity, Intimacy, and Accountability among the Promise Keepers," *Sociology of Religion* 61 (2000): 48–49.

63   to avoid denominations: R. Marie Griffith, *God's Daughters: Evangelical Women and the Power of Submission* (Berkeley and Los Angeles: University of California Press, 1997), 67.

63   "We're not playin'": John P. Bartkowski, *The Promise Keepers: Servants, Soldiers, and Godly Men* (New Brunswick, N.J.: Rutgers University Press, forthcoming).

64   it is very much: The organization of Promise Keepers is described in Schindler and Lena.

65   "join churches": Will Herberg, *Protestant, Catholic, Jew: An Essay in American Religious Sociology* (Chicago: University of Chicago Press, 1983 [1955]), 41.

65   "a psychological anchor": Roof, *Spiritual Marketplace*, 135.

65   "Denominationalism is": Winthrop Hudson, *American Protestantism* (Chicago: University of Chicago Press, 1961), 34.

CHAPTER 3. DOCTRINE

67　"There was no": Vincent Crapanzano, *Serving the Word: Literalism in America from the Pulpit to the Bench* (New York: New Press, 2000), 87.

68　once accused: Richard Hofstadter, *Anti-Intellectualism in American Life* (New York: Knopf, 1963).

68　decidedly intellectual: The best histories are George M. Marsden, *Fundamentalism and American Culture: The Shaping of Twentieth-Century Evangelism, 1870–1925* (New York: Oxford University Press, 1980), and Joel Carpenter, *Revive Us Again: The Reawakening of American Fundamentalism* (New York: Oxford University Press, 1997).

69　"Bible roulette": Neitz, *Charisma and Community*, 28.

69　"Although they often": Ammerman, *Bible Believers*, 53.

69　descended from Jonathan Edwards: Carpenter, *Revive Us Again*, 113.

69　"The Bible can prove": Ammerman, *Bible Believers*, 54.

71　"Despite all the": Balmer, *Mine Eyes*, 156.

71　"many of the": Arlene Stein, *The Stranger Next Door: The Story of a Small Community's Battle over Sex, Faith, and Civil Rights* (Boston: Beacon Press, 2001), 86, 89, 217.

72　"most life-changing": Searl, "Women's Bible Study Group," in Wuthnow, *"I Come Away Stronger,"* 97–124.

73　"We don't really": George M. Thomas and Douglas S. Jardine, "Jesus and Self in Everyday Life: Individual Spirituality through a Small Group in a Large Church," in Wuthnow, *"I Come Away Stronger,"* 294.

73　"an argument culture": Deborah Tannen, *The Argument Culture: Moving from Debate to Dialogue* (New York: Random House, 1998).

73　"for the most part": Lawson, "Accountability and Fellowship," in Wuthnow, *"I Come Away Stronger,"* 92.

73　An evangelical fellowship: Winston, "Answered Prayers," in Wuthnow, *"I Come Away Stronger,"* 20.

74　those who said: Wuthnow, *Sharing the Journey*, 243.

74　Benjamin Franklin's: William D. Romanowski, *Eyes Wide Open: Looking for God in Popular Culture* (Grand Rapids, Mich.: Brazos, 2001), 119.

74　"a more plausible": Sargeant, *Seeker Churches*, 31, 101.

75　"a second reformation": Miller, *Reinventing American Protestantism*, 11.

75　Calvary Chapel: Miller, *Reinventing American Protestantism*, 34.

76　under the leadership: Robin Dale Perrin, "Signs and Wonders: The Growth of the Vineyard Christian Fellowship," Ph.D. diss., Department of Sociology, Washington State University, 1989, 58.

76　opened up: Stark and Finke, *Acts of Faith*, 151.

76　Greg Laurie: Robin D. Perrin, Paul Kennedy, and Donald E. Miller, "Examining the Sources of Conservative Church Growth: Where Are the New Evangelical Movements Getting Their Numbers?," *Journal for the Scientific Study of Religion* 36 (1997): 71–80.

76   its founding pastor: Interview with Steve Sjogren, Vineyard Community Church, Cincinnati, March 5, 2002.

76   "Some people really": Miller, *Reinventing American Protestantism*, 128.

77   "I have seen": Randall Balmer and Jesse T. Todd Jr., "Calvary Chapel, Costa Mesa, California," in Wind and Lewis, *American Congregations*, vol. 1, 678.

77   just under half: Miller, *Reinventing American Protestantism*, 93, 95.

77   From the start: Cheryl J. Sanders, *Saints in Exile: The Holiness-Pentecostal Experience in African American Religion and Culture* (New York: Oxford University Press, 1996), 6–9.

77   six hundred congregations: Omar M. McRoberts, *Streets of Glory: Church and Community in a Black Urban Neighborhood* (Chicago: University of Chicago Press, 2003), 161 n.3 (chapter 6).

78   fastest-growing religion: C. Eric Lincoln and Lawrence H. Mamiya, *The Black Church in the African American Experience* (Durham, N.C.: Duke University Press, 1990), 84, 335, 364, 385, 388.

78   "saw 'ring-shouts'": Lawrence H. Mamiya, "A Social History of the Bethel African Methodist Episcopal Church in Baltimore: The House of God and the Struggle for Freedom," in Wind and Lewis, *American Congregations*, vol. 1, 236, 264, 265, 274.

79   "rocking church": Mamiya, "A Social History," 264.

79   a fairly widespread occurrence: See, for example, David D. Daniels III, "'Ain't Gonna Let Nobody Turn Me "Round'": The Politics of Race and the New Black Middle-Class Religion," in Lowell W. Livesey, ed., *Public Religion and Urban Transformation: Faith in the City* (New York: New York University Press, 2000), 171–72, and Fredrick C. Harris, *Something Within: Religion in African-American Political Activism* (New York: Oxford University Press, 1999), 12–26.

80   "the end of evangelicalism": Interview with Alan Jacobs, Wheaton, Illinois, March 21, 2002.

80   "away from a": Alan Jacobs, e-mail to author, March 28, 2002.

81   "We're in the": Richard J. Mouw, *The Smell of Sawdust: What Evangelicals Can Learn from Their Fundamentalist Heritage* (Grand Rapids, Mich.: Zondervan, 2000), 66–67.

81   "If we use": Sargeant, *Seeker Churches*, 5.

81   "We agree with": Penny Edgell Becker, *Congregations in Conflict: Cultural Models of Local Religious Life* (New York: Cambridge University Press, 1999), 89, 110, 111, 140, 143.

82   It is common: See, for example, E. Digby Baltzell, *The Protestant Establishment: Aristocracy and Caste in America* (New York: Random House, 1964).

82   "so wedded were": Wade Clark Roof and William McKinney, *American Mainline Religion: Its Changing Shape and Future* (New Brunswick, N.J.: Rutgers University Press, 1987), 22.

83   two-party system: Martin Marty, *Righteous Empire: The Protestant Experience in America* (New York: Dial Press, 1970).

83   But such efforts: Romanowski, *Eyes Wide Open*, and William D. Romanowski, *Pop Culture Wars: Religion and the Role of Entertainment in American Life* (Downers Grove, Ill.: InterVarsity Press, 1996).

84   a "wasteland": The material in this and the next three paragraphs comes from Daniel V. A. Olson, "Making Disciples in a Liberal Protestant Church," in Wuthnow, *"I Come Away Stronger,"* 125–47.

86   "everyone agrees": Jody Shapiro Davie, *Women in the Presence: Constructing Community and Seeking Spirituality in Mainline Protestantism* (Philadelphia: University of Pennsylvania Press, 1995), 52.

86   "may in fact be": Nancy T. Ammerman, "Golden Rule Christianity: Lived Religion in the American Mainstream," in Hall, *Lived Religion in America*, 199, 201.

87   "our membership": Randall Balmer, *Grant Us Courage: Travels Along the Mainline of American Protestantism* (New York: Oxford University Press, 1996), 14.

87   Once dismissed by: John T. McGreevy, "Thinking on One's Own: Catholicism in the American Intellectual Imagination, 1928–1960," *Journal of American History* 84 (June 1997): 97–131.

88   Asked by pollsters: D'Antonio et al., *American Catholics*, 42, 43–49.

88   Asked a number: Hoge et al., *Young American Catholics*, 16, 60, 61.

89   "God has sent": Gremillion and Castelli, *The Emerging Parish*, 154, 155.

89   "Catholic mind": Joseph Fichter, S. J., *Southern Parish: Dynamics of a City Church* (Chicago: University of Chicago Press, 1951), 270.

90   "the Catholic faithful": www.vatican.va/roman_curia/congregations/cfaith/documents/rc_con_cfaith_doc_20000806_dominus-iesus_en.html.

90   "I just feel": Hoge et al., *Young American Catholics*, 57, 171, 221, 223–24; D'Antonio et al., *American Catholics*, 45.

90   "are not doctrinal": Greeley, *The Catholic Myth*, 44.

91   the evangelical kaleidoscope: I have borrowed this term from Timothy L. Smith, "The Evangelical Kaleidoscope and Call to Christian Unity," *Christian Scholar's Review* 15 (1986): 125–40.

91   "They told us": Cohen and Eisen, *The Jew Within*, 155, 162.

92   Asked whether: Samuel Heilman and Stephen M. Cohen, *Cosmopolitans and Parochials: Modern Orthodox Jews in America* (Bloomington: Indiana University Press, 1989), 89.

92   "Oh, man": Cohen and Eisen, *The Jew Within*, 162–64.

93   "I'm doing vacation": Dean R. Hoge, Benton Johnson, and Donald A. Luidens, *Vanishing Boundaries: The Religion of Mainline Protestant Baby Boomers* (Louisville: Westminster/John Knox Press, 1994), 103–105.

94   "Our government makes": Will Herberg, *Protestant, Catholic, Jew*, 84, 260.

95   what has (confusingly): Robert W. Fogel, *The Fourth Great Awakening and the Future of Egalitarianism* (Chicago: University of Chicago Press, 2000).

95   "so innocently": Herberg, *Protestant, Catholic, Jew*, 268.

CHAPTER 4. TRADITION

97   "The feeling one gets": Quoted in Stuart Schoenfeld, "Ritual and Role Transition: Adult Bat Mitzvah as a Successful Rite of Passage," in Jack Wertheimer, ed., *The Uses of Tradition: Jewish Continuity in the Modern Era* (Cambridge, Mass.: Harvard University Press, 1992), 358.

98   There is, for one thing: Schoenfeld, "Ritual and Role Transition," 350; Barry A. Kosmin, "Coming of Age in the Conservative Synagogue: The Bar/Bat Mitzvah Class of 5755," in Jack Wertheimer, ed., *Jews in the Center: Conservative Synagogues and Their Members* (New Brunswick, N.J.: Rutgers University Press, 2000), 234.

98   "quiet, humble": Jenna Weissman Joselit, *The Wonders of America: Reinventing Jewish Culture, 1880–1950* (New York: Hill and Wang, 1994), 90.

98   "Maintenance of the bar": Kosmin, "Coming of Age," 265.

98   only to 1922: Schoenfeld, "Ritual and Role Transition," 350.

99   buy Kosher: Etan Diamond, *And I Will Dwell in Their Midst: Orthodox Jews in Suburbia* (Chapel Hill and London: University of North Carolina Press, 2000), 118–25.

100   "Is Club Med Kosher?": *Tradition* 21 (Fall 1985): 27–36, cited in Diamond, *And I Will Dwell,* 129.

100   "when we certify": Wertheimer, *A People Divided,* 129.

100   a slaughterhouse: Stephen G. Bloom, *Postville: A Clash of Cultures in Heartland America* (New York: Harcourt, 2000).

100   bitterly ugly conflicts: Samuel G. Freedman, *Jew vs. Jew: The Struggle for the Soul of American Jewry* (New York: Simon & Schuster, 2000), and Phil Zuckerman, *Strife in the Sanctuary: Religious Schism in a Jewish Community* (Walnut Creek, Calif.: AltaMira, 1999).

100   recent historical vintage: Michael K. Silber, "The Emergence of Ultra-Orthodoxy: The Invention of a Tradition," in Wertheimer, *The Uses of Tradition,* 23.

101   in the interwar period: Herbert Danzger, *Returning to Tradition: The Contemporary Revival of Orthodox Judaism* (New Haven: Yale University Press, 1989), 143.

101   Traditions, it has been said: Eric Hobsbawm, "Mass-Producing Traditions: Europe, 1870–1914," in Eric Hobsbawm and Terence Ranger, *The Invention of Tradition* (Cambridge: Cambridge University Press, 1984), 263–307.

102   "Spirituality does not": Summit, *The Lord's Song,* 89.

102   *shokeling,* in Yiddish: Heilman, *Synagogue Life,* 218.

102   "explicit desire to get married": Lynn Davidman, *Tradition in a Rootless World: Women Turn to Orthodox Judaism* (Berkeley and Los Angeles: University of California Press, 1999), 114.

102   "You mean there": Rivka Zakutinsky and Yaffa Leba Gottlieb, *Around Sarah's Table: Ten Hasidic Women Share Their Stories of Life, Faith, and Tradition* (New York: Free Press, 2001), 63.

103   In a study: Debra Renee Kaufman, *Rachel's Daughters: Newly Orthodox Jewish Women* (New Brunswick, N.J.: Rutgers University Press, 1991), 17, 32, 118.

103   "several viable choices": Danzger, *Returning to Tradition*, 81.

104   choosing chosenness: The phrase comes from Cohen and Eisen, *The Jew Within*, 22.

105   "exaggerated conformity": Danzger, *Returning to Tradition*, 270–72.

105   "over justify": Silber, "Ultra-Orthodoxy," 53.

105   "peculiarly modern notion": Charles S. Liebman, "The Reappropriation of Jewish Tradition in the Modern Era," in Wertheimer, *The Uses of Tradition*, 474.

106   "helps set my": Samuel C. Heilman, "Holding Firmly with an Open Hand: Life in Two Conservative Synagogues," in Wertheimer, *Jews in the Center*, 139, 174, 176.

107   "We have found": Paul Ritterband, "Public Worship: The Partnership between Families and Synagogues," in Wertheimer, *Jews in the Center*, 226.

107   47 percent of all: Jack Wertheimer, "Introduction," in Wertheimer, *Jews in the Center*, 226.

107   "mindless traditionalism": Furman, *Beyond Yiddishkeit*, 53–56.

107   "the commitment of": Ibid., 45, 49.

108   Suzanne: Cohen and Eisen, *The Jew Within*, 91.

109   In March 2000: Denise L. Eger, "Embracing Lesbians and Gay Men: A Reform Jewish Innovation," in Dana Evan Kaplan, ed., *Contemporary Debates in American Reform Judaism: Conflicting Visions* (New York: Routledge, 2001), 180–92.

109   "Over the next few": Dana Evan Kaplan, "Introduction," in Kaplan, *Contemporary Debates*, 3.

109   "the new is prohibited": Cited in Samuel C. Heilman, *Defenders of the Faith: Inside Ultra-Orthodox Jewry* (Berkeley and Los Angeles: University of California Press, 2000 [1992]), 20.

109   San Francisco's: Kaplan, "Introduction," 14.

109   persists, and even grows: Bernard M. Lazerwitz and Ephraim Tabory, "A Religious and Social Profile of Reform Judaism in the United States," in Kaplan, *Contemporary Debates*, 21.

109   the dinner celebrating: Debra Nussbaum Cohen, "A Menu for Reform," *Wall Street Journal* July 6, 2001, W11.

109   at the beginning: Michael A. Meyer, "Tradition and Modernity Reconsidered," in Wertheimer, *The Uses of Tradition*, 468.

109   the 1999 Statement: A Statement of Principles for Reform Judaism, Adopted at the 1999 Pittsburgh Convention, Central Conference of American Rabbis, May 1999/Sivan 5759, www.ccarnet.org/platforms/principles.html.

110   "traditioning": Samuel Heilman, *The People of the Book: Drama, Fellowship, and Religion* (Chicago: University of Chicago Press, 1983), 62–65.

111 "mavericks at heart": Grant Wacker, *Heaven Below: Early Pentecostals and American Culture* (Cambridge, Mass.: Harvard University Press, 2001), 28.

111 traditional ways of life: See, for example, James Penning and Corwin Smidt, *Evangelicalism: The Next Generation* (Grand Rapids, Mich.: Baker Books, 2002).

111 too-easy association: See Christian Smith, *American Evangelicalism: Embattled and Thriving* (Chicago: University of Chicago Press, 1998); Christian Smith, *Christian America?: What Evangelicals Really Want* (Berkeley and Los Angeles: University of California Press, 2000); Emerson and Smith, *Divided by Faith*.

112 "included Christian": Eiesland, *A Particular Place,* 49, 103.

113 most famous megachurch: Charles Trueheart, "Welcome to the Next Church," *The Atlantic Monthly* (August 1996): 37–58.

113 "We do have": Stewart M. Hoover, "The Cross at Willow Creek: Seeker Religion and the Contemporary Marketplace," in Bruce David Forbes and Jeffrey H. Mahan, eds., *Religion and Popular Culture in America* (Berkeley and Los Angeles: University of California Press, 2000), 145.

113 one survey of: Sargeant, *Seeker Churches,* 61.

114 "Tradition": Sargeant, *Seeker Churches,* 63.

114 "In doing this": Eiesland, *A Particular Place,* 58.

115 "We have people": Gerardo Marti, "Mosaic on Mission: Creativity, Community, and Catalytic Leadership in a Los Angeles, Multi-ethnic Church" (Ph.D. diss., University of Southern California, 2002), 82, 197–98, 202–03.

117 "No church, according to my research": Sargeant, *Seeker Churches,* 183.

118 "Catholicism, for reasons": Peter L. Berger, *The Sacred Canopy: Elements of a Sociological Theory of Religion* (Garden City, N. Y.: Anchor Books, 1967), 169.

118 "Catholics, more than": Stanley Hauerwas, *In Good Company: The Church as Polis* (Notre Dame, Ind.: University of Notre Dame Press, 1995), 105.

118 Whether described as: William I. Thomas and Florian Znaniecki, *The Polish Peasant in Europe and America* (Urbana, Ill.: University of Illinois Press, 1984), and Herbert Gans, *The Urban Villagers: Group and Class in the Life of Italian Americans,* 2nd ed. (New York: Free Press, 1982).

118 "Archdiocesan attempts": Paul Wrobel, *Our Way: Family, Parish, and Neighborhood in a Polish-American Community* (Notre Dame, Ind.: University of Notre Dame Press, 1979), 95. See also Timothy Meagher, *Inventing Irish America: Generation, Class, and Ethnicity in a New England City, 1880–1928* (Notre Dame, Ind.: University of Notre Dame Press, 2001).

119 Catholic conservatives: Michele Dillon, *Catholic Identity: Balancing Reason, Faith, and Power* (New York: Cambridge University Press, 1999).

119 "by no means": Gremillion and Castelli, *The Emerging Parish,* 31.

120 "intense devotional": Robert A. Orsi, "'Mildred, Is It Fun to Be a Cripple?': The Culture of Suffering in Mid-Twentieth-Century American

Catholicism," in Thomas J. Ferraro, ed., *Catholic Lives, Contemporary America* (Durham: Duke University Press, 1997), 47.

120   one study found: Gremillion and Castelli, *The Emerging Parish,* 145.

120   far more Catholics: D'Antonio et al., *American Catholics,* 60.

120   among younger Catholics: Hoge et al., *Young American Catholics,* 156.

120   According to one estimate: James O'Toole, "Empty Confessionals: Where Have All the Sinners Gone?" *Commonweal* (February 23, 2001): 10–12.

120   "walking into": Hoge et al., *Young American Catholics,* 82.

120   "the scariest sacrament": Keeler, *Parish!,* 78, 83.

121   "There seems to be": Gremillion and Castelli, *The Emerging Parish,* 147.

121   "endangered species list": Thomas Beaudoin, e-mail to author, August 15, 2002.

121   Many older Catholics: The writer Garry Wills does; see Garry Wills, "Priests and Boys," *New York Review of Books* XLIV (July 13, 2002): 12.

121   "It seemed like": Keeler, *Parish!,* 68.

122   "We did not put": Keeler, *Parish!,* 73.

122   Among Catholics who: James O'Toole, letter to the author, September 20, 2002.

122   "greater participation": Hoge et al., *Young American Catholics,* 118.

123   "This is an": Jeffrey M. Burns, "*¿Qué es esto?:* The Transformation of St. Peter's Parish, San Francisco, 1913–1990," in Wind and Lewis, *American Congregations,* vol. 1, 418, 442, 445–46.

123   Tagalog-speaking: Filipinos are among the most understudied of American immigrants; for an exception, see Steffi San Buenaventura, "Filipino Religion at Home and Abroad: Historical Roots and Immigrant Transformations," in Pyong Gap Min and Jung Ha Kim, eds., *Religions in Asian America: Building Faith Communities* (Walnut Creek, Calif.: AltaMira, 2002), 143–83.

124   "political activism": Mark R. Warren, *Dry Bones Rattling: Community Building to Revitalize American Democracy* (Princeton: Princeton University Press, 2001), and Richard L. Wood, *Faith in Action: Religion, Race, and Democratic Organizing in America* (Chicago: University of Chicago Press, 2002).

124   "not only": Paul Wilkes, *Excellent Catholic Parishes: The Guide to Best Places and Practices* (New York: Paulist Press, 2001), 21, 30, 36, 38.

125   "The single greatest": Cited in Adrian Wooldridge, "As Labor Lost Ideology, U. S. Parties Found It," *New York Times,* July 22, 2001, section 4, 4.

125   "There is no": William G. McLoughlin, *Revivals, Awakenings, and Reform: An Essay on Religion and Social Change in America, 1607–1977* (Chicago: University of Chicago Press, 1978), 18.

CHAPTER 5. MORALITY

127   "Citizens who are": William E. Simon Jr., "Why America Needs Religion," www.heritage.org/library/lecture/hl687.html.

128   "The woman in": Phyllis Schlafly, *The Power of the Christian Woman* (Cincinnati: Standard, 1981), cited in Michael Lienesch, *Redeeming America: Piety and Politics in the New Christian Right* (Chapel Hill: University of North Carolina Press, 1993), 71.

128   "Much of the": Cited in Christel J. Manning, *God Gave Us the Right: Conservative Catholic, Evangelical Protestant, and Orthodox Jewish Women Grapple with Feminism* (New Brunswick, N.J.: Rutgers University Press, 1999), 35.

128   "insulate the Christian": Tim LaHaye, *Battle for the Family*, 206, cited in Lienesch, *Redeeming America*, 92.

128   In June 1998: For the relevant sections, see www.sbc.net/bfm/bfm2000.asp#xviii.

129   "We have a": Brenda Brasher, *Godly Women: Fundamentalism and Female Power* (New Brunswick, N.J.: Rutgers University Press, 1998), 63.

129   "We believe that": Manning, *God Gave Us the Right*, 111.

130   "The male ego": John P. Bartkowski, *Remaking the Godly Marriage: Gender Negotiation in Evangelical Families* (New Brunswick, N.J.: Rutgers University Press, 2001), 102.

130   "Many of the": Ibid., 101.

130   "Shoot, we do": Manning, *God Gave Us the Right*, 113.

131   When Gilligan: Carol Gilligan, *In a Different Voice: Psychological Theory and Women's Development* (Cambridge, Mass.: Harvard University Press, 1982).

131   "It's emotional": Brasher, *Godly Women*, 108–109.

132   "Jugglers for Jesus": Lori G. Beaman, *Shared Beliefs, Different Lives: Women's Identities in Evangelical Context* (St. Louis: Chalice Press, 1999), 77.

132   "My self-esteem": Searl, "Women's Bible Study Group," in Wuthnow, *"I Come Away Stronger,"* 113.

132   a single instance: Bartkowski, *Remaking the Godly Marriage*, 126.

132   "gender inerrancy": Nancy Nason-Clark, "Conservative Protestants and Violence against Women," in Mary Jo Neitz and Marion S. Goldman, eds., *Sex, Lies and Sanctity: Religion and Deviance in Contemporary North America* (Greenwich, Conn.: JAI Press, 1995), 112.

132   "to live up to": Bartkowski, *Remaking the Godly Marriage*, 130.

133   "Marabel Morgan became": Peter Gardella, "Sex and Submission in the Spirit," in McDannell, *Religions of the United States*, vol. 2, 173.

133   Her book: Marabel Morgan, *The Total Woman* (Old Tappan, N.J.: Fleming H. Revell, 1973).

133   "is a beautiful": Bartkowski, *Remaking the Godly Marriage*, 95–96.

133   "I've heard from": Janet Stocks, "To Stay or to Leave?: Organizational Legitimacy in the Struggle for Change among Evangelical Feminists," in Penny

Edgell Becker and Nancy L. Eiesland, eds., *Contemporary American Religion: An Ethnographic Reader* (Walnut Creek, Calif.: AltaMira, 1997), 105, 106.

134 "Homosexuality is not": Telephone interview with Mimi Haddad, August 4, 2002.

134 "There are lots": Telephone interview with Linda Bieze, April 3, 2002.

134 "spend little": Jerry Falwell, *Listen America!* (Garden City, N.Y.: Doubleday, 1980), 150, cited in Lienesch, *Redeeming America,* 59.

135 whose 1941 book: John R. Rice, *Bobbed Hair, Bossy Wives, and Women Preachers* (Murfreesboro, Tenn.: Sword of the Lord Publishers, 1941).

135 "calling on": Susan Friend Harding, *The Book of Jerry Falwell: Fundamentalist Language and Politics* (Princeton: Princeton University Press, 2000), 173.

135 "The decision:" James Dobson, *Marriage and Sexuality: Dr. Dobson Answers Your Questions* (Wheaton, Ill.: Tyndale House, 1982), 47–49, cited in Manning, *God Gave Us the Right,* 57.

135 "There is a": James C. Dobson, *Love Must Be Tough* (Waco, Tex.: Word Books, 1983), 25, cited in Judith Stacey and Susan Elizabeth Gerard, "'We are Not Doormats': The Influence of Feminism on Contemporary Evangelicals in the United States," in Faye Ginsburg and Anna Lowenhaupt Tsing, eds., *Uncertain Terms: Negotiating Gender in American Culture* (Boston: Beacon Press, 1990), 104.

136 "are more spiritual": Manning, *God Gave Us the Right,* 109.

136 "a tradition of": Kaufman, *Rachel's Daughters,* 76–78, 82, 126.

137 "*mikvah* was the": Rivka Zakutinsky and Yaffa Leba Gottlieb, *Around Sarah's Table, Ten Hasidic Women Share Their Stories of Life, Faith, and Tradition* (New York: Free Press, 2001), 105.

138 "If government": Stephen Goldsmith, "Having Faith in Our Neighborhoods," in E. J. Dionne and John J. Dilulio Jr., *What's God Got to Do with the American Experiment?* (Washington, D.C.: Brookings Institution, 2000), 78.

138 "And the sad": Timothy J. Nelson, "The Church and the Street: Race, Class, and Congregation," in Becker and Eiesland, *Contemporary American Religion,* 182–83, 184.

139 "the ministers advocate": Jenny Berrien, Omar McRoberts, and Christopher Winship, "Religion and the Boston Miracle: The Effect of Black Ministry on Youth Violence," in Mary Jo Bane, Brent Coffin, and Ronald Thiemann, eds., *Who Will Provide? The Changing Role of Religion in American Social Welfare* (Boulder, Colo.: Westview Press, 2000), 275.

140 one of the activists: The quotes in this and the next two paragraphs come from McRoberts, *Streets of Glory,* 91–94, 97, 109.

142 "The devil hates": Arlene M. Sanchez Walsh, "El Aposento Alto: Searching for a Latino Pentecostal Identity" (Ph.D. diss., Claremont Graduate University, 2001), 258.

142 "the strongest is": Robert Dannin, *Black Pilgrimages to Islam* (New York: Oxford University Press, 2002), 166, 176, 182.

143   the Revival Center Church: Isaac B. Laudarji and Lowell W. Livezey, "The Churches and the Poor in a 'Ghetto Underclass' Neighborhood," in Livezey, *Public Religion and Urban Transformation,* 101.

143   as a best-selling: Alex Kotlowitz, *There Are No Children Here: The Story of Two Boys Growing Up in the Other America* (New York: Doubleday, 1991).

144   "returned home": Courtney J. Bender, "Praying for the Saints: Mennonite Charismatics and the Conundrum of Community," in Wuthnow, *"I Come Away Stronger,"* 242.

144   There are more: Jan Shipps, *Sojourner in the Promised Land: Forty Years among the Mormons* (Urbana, Ill.: University of Illinois Press, 2000), 37.

145   "more so than": Tim B. Heaton, Kristen L. Goodman, and Thomas B. Holman, "In Search of a Peculiar People: Are Mormon Families Really Different?" in Marie Cornwall, Tim B. Heaton, and Lawrence A. Young, eds., *Contemporary Mormonism: Social Science Perspectives* (Urbana, Ill.: University of Illinois Press, 1994), 113.

145   one study showed: Bruce A. Chadwick and H. Dean Garrett, "'Choose Ye this Day Whom Ye Will Serve': LDS Mother's Reaction to Church Leader's Instructions to Remain in the Home," in Douglas J. Davies, ed., *Mormon Identities in Transition* (London and New York: Cassell, 1996), 166–79.

145   to smoke: Stephen J. Bahr, "Religion and Adolescent Drug Use: A Comparison of Mormons and Other Religions," in Cornwall et al., *Contemporary Mormonism,* 118–37.

145   Mormonism is, theologically: An excellent, if controversial, treatment is John L. Brooke, *The Refiner's Fire: The Making of Mormon Cosmology, 1644–1811* (Cambridge: Cambridge University Press, 1994).

146   Mormonism began: Shipps, *Sojourner in the Promised Land,* 38–39, 140.

146   "I wouldn't say that": *San Francisco Chronicle,* June 6, 1998, A6, cited in ibid., 123, n.46.

146   "is all but creedless": This quotation and those in the following two paragraphs come from Mark P. Leone, *Roots of Modern Mormonism* (Cambridge, Mass.: Harvard University Press, 1979), 181, 187–89, 190.

148   "there's never": Jana Kathryn Riess, "Mormon Fast and Testimony Meetings," in McDannell, *Religions of the United States,* vol. 2, 70.

148   "felt very comfortable": Susan Buhler Taber, *Mormon Lives: A Year in the Elkton Ward* (Urbana, Ill.: University of Illinois Press, 1993), 101, 278, 314.

149   "In direct contrast": Shipps, *Sojourner in the Promised Land,* 259.

149   Polynesian wards: Jessie L. Embrie, "Ethnic American Mormons: The Development of a Community," in Davies, *Mormon Identities in Transition,* 64.

149   "too much assimilation": Armand L. Mauss, "Identity and Boundary Maintenance: International Prospects for Mormonism at the Dawn of the Twenty-First Century," in Davies, *Mormon Identities in Transition,* 10.

150   "both a reflection": Shipps, *Sojourner in the Promised Land,* 271, 272.

150   "inexorably (if slowly)": Mauss, "Identity and Boundary Maintenance," 11.

150   "I went to": Taber, *Mormon Lives*, 71.

151   "I can communicate": Embrie, "Ethnic American Mormons," 64.

151   an experiment: Robin D. Perrin, "Religiosity and Honesty: Continuing the Search for the Consequential Dimension," *Review of Religious Research* 41 (2000): 534–44.

152   a widely cited: Travis Hirschi and Rodney Stark, "Hellfire and Delinquency," *Social Problems* 17 (1969): 202–13.

152   greater amounts: Robert D. Plotnick, "The Effects of Attitudes on Teenage Premarital Pregnancy and Its Resolution," *American Sociological Review* 57 (December 1992): 800–11; www.barna.org/cgi-in/PagePress Release.asp?PressReleaseID=39&Reference=D; Blaine Harden, "Bible Belt Couples 'Put Asunder' More, Despite New Efforts," *New York Times*, May 18, 2001, A1. For helpful background on this issue, see W. Bradford Wilcox, "Religion, the Marriage Movement and Marriage Policy," a report presented by the Pew Forum on Religion and Public Life, May 2002, Washington, D.C.

152   many studies: For a sample, see John P. Hoffman, "Religion and Problem Gambling in the U.S.," *Review of Religious Research* 41 (2000): 488–509; John K. Cochran and Ronald L. Akers, "Beyond Hellfire: An Exploration of the Variable Effects of Religiosity on Adolescent Marijuana and Alcohol Use," *Journal of Research in Crime and Delinquency* 26 (August 1989): 198–225; Harold G. Grasmick, Robert J. Bursik Jr., and John K. Cochran, "Render unto Caesar What Is Caesar's: Religiosity and Taxpayer's Inclination to Cheat," *Sociological Quarterly* 32 (1991): 251–66; Christopher G. Ellison and Kristin L. Anderson, "Religious Involvement and Domestic Violence Among U.S. Couples," *Journal for the Scientific Study of Religion* 40 (2001): 269–86.

152   it has been: Alan J. Richard, David C. Bell, and Jerry W. Carlson, "Individual Religiosity, Moral Community, and Drug User Treatment," *Journal for the Scientific Study of Religion* 39 (2000): 240–46.

CHAPTER 6. SIN

156   "is not only": Cornelius Plantinga Jr., *Not the Way It's Supposed to Be: A Breviary of Sin* (Grand Rapids, Mich: Eerdmans, 1995), 12.

157   the leading historian: Wacker, *Heaven Below*, 128, 136.

158   "We wanted to": Griffith, *God's Daughters*, 104, 105.

159   "Food has long": Roof, *Spiritual Marketplace*, 106.

159   "Did you ever": Patricia B. Kreml, *Slim for Him* (Plainfield, N.J.: Logos International, 1978), 9, cited in Griffith, *God's Daughters*, 145.

159   the past few years: Don Colbert, *What Would Jesus Eat?: The Ultimate Program for Eating Well, Feeling Great, and Living Longer* (Nashville: Thomas Nelson, 2002); Colleen Zuck and Elaine Meyer, *Daily Word for Weight Loss: Spiritual Guidance to Give You Courage on Your Journey* (Emmaus, Pa.: Rodale Press, 2002); Matthew Anderson, *The Prayer Diet: The Unique Physical, Mental, and*

Spiritual Approach to Healthy Weight Loss (New York: Kensington, 2001); and Jan Christiansen, *More of Him Less of Me: My Personal Thoughts, Inspirations, and Meditations on the Weigh Down Diet* (Lancaster, Pa.: Starburst Publishers, 1999).

159   by one estimate: Michelle Mary Lelwica, *Starving for Salvation: The Spiritual Dimensions of Eating Problems among American Girls and Women* (New York: Oxford University Press, 1999), 76.

160   "The diet is": Lelwica, 77.

161   "to stop perceiving": Davie, *Women in the Presence*, 63, 94, 96.

161   "Americans may be drawn": Wuthnow, *After Heaven*, 129–31, 133.

162   "culture of suffering": Orsi, "'Mildred, Is It Fun to Be a Cripple?'", in Ferraro, *Catholic Lives, Contemporary America*, 19–64.

162   fears of: Wrobel, *Our Way*, 92–93.

162   "first half of": D'Antonio et al., *American Catholics*, 12–13, 72.

163   "quasi-scientific character": Hoge et al., *Young American Catholics*, 150, 156–58.

164   "God who hears": Cohen and Eisen, *The Jew Within*, 95, 156–57.

164   "marketed the": Davidman, *Tradition in a Rootless World*, 138–40.

165   "is a God of": Wuthnow, *Sharing the Journey*, 7.

165   "I was more": Tamney, *The Resilience of Conservative Religion*, 103.

166   "discussion in terms": Sargeant, *Seeker Churches*, 95.

166   "believe that": Ibid. 87, 89.

166   "too much self-discipline": author visit to Saddleback Church, August 4, 2002.

167   A 1986 survey: Nancy Tatom Ammerman, *Baptist Battles: Social Change and Religious Conflict in the Southern Baptist Convention* (New Brunswick, N.J.: Rutgers University Press, 1990), 107.

168   "The wages of sin": The material in this paragraph is from Marsha Witten, *All Is Forgiven: The Secular Message in American Protestantism* (Princeton: Princeton University Press, 1993), 50, 84–88, 92, 96, 99.

168   "I think I've learned": Winston, "Answered Prayers," in Wuthnow, *"I Come Away Stronger,"* 18.

169   fundamentalist leaders: Ammerman, *Baptist Battles*, 225.

169   "the group made": Winston, "Answered Prayers," 24.

170   "Christianese": Paul A. Bramadat, *The Church on the World's Turf: An Evangelical Christian Group at a Secular University* (New York: Oxford University Press, 2000), 56, 61–62.

171   "I discovered that": Witten, *All Is Forgiven*, 100.

171   "has all too often": Theodore W. Jennings Jr., "Reconstructing the Doctrine of Sin," in Andrew Sung Park and Susan L. Nelson, eds., *The Other Side of Sin: Woundedness from the Perspective of the Sinned-Against* (Albany: State University of New York Press, 2001), 121. See also Stephen Gene Ray Jr., "Silenced by the Night: A Constructive Reconstrual of the Protestant Doctrine of Sin" (Ph.D. diss., Yale University, 2000).

171 "the very idea": Donald Capps, *The Depleted Self: Sin in a Narcissistic Age* (Minneapolis: Fortress Press, 1993), 2.

172 "Many participants": Olson, "Making Disciples," in Wuthnow, *"I Come Away Stronger,"* 139.

172 "This is for me": Davie, *Women in the Presence*, 73.

172 "a judgmental overlord": Mark Oppenheimer, "Folk Music in the Catholic Mass," in McDannell, *Religions of the United States*, vol. 2, 106.

172 "they are not": D'Antonio et al., *American Catholics*, 59.

173 "non-judgmental Judaism": Liebman, "Finding a Place," in Wuthnow, *"I Come Away Stronger,"* 301.

173 "My way is": Cohen and Eisen, *The Jew Within*, 36.

174 "sinning and going": McRoberts, *Streets of Glory*, 63–64.

174 contact the police: Berrien, McRoberts, and Winship, "Religion and the Boston Miracle," 277.

174 "It's so easy to condemn": McRoberts, *Streets of Glory*, 95.

175 "not really a sin": León, "Born Again in East LA," in Warner and Wittner, *Gatherings in the Diaspora*, 181.

175 "holier than thou": For examples, see Sargeant, *Seeker Churches*, 89, and Tamney, *The Resilience of Conservative Religion*, 178–79.

176 It has been a: Martin E. Marty, *The Irony of It All 1893–1919*, vol. 1 of *Modern American Religion* (Chicago: University of Chicago Press, 1986), 258.

176 "Low self-esteem": These two paragraphs are indebted to James Davison Hunter, *The Death of Character: Moral Education in an Age without Good or Evil* (New York: Basic Books, 2000), 134, 141.

177 "a non-profit religious": www.psychoheresy-aware.org/ministry .html.

178 founded in 1948: George M. Marsden, *Reforming Fundamentalism: Fuller Seminary and the New Evangelicalism* (Grand Rapids, Mich.: Eerdmans, 1987).

179 Peck's most famous: M. Scott Peck, *The Road Less Traveled: A New Psychology of Love, Traditional Values, and Spiritual Growth* (New York: Simon & Schuster, 1978).

179 "clashes with Christianity": www.psychoheresy-Aware.org/mspeck 44.html

179 "Even Peck's most": Wendy Kaminer, *I'm Dysfunctional, You're Dysfunctional: The Recovery Movement and Other Self-Help Fashions* (Reading, Mass.: Addison-Wesley, 1992), 127.

180 "Jesus Christ": Richard J. Mouw, *Political Evangelism* (Grand Rapids, Mich.: Eerdmans, 1973), 13, 14.

180 "sin does afflict": Mouw, *The Smell of Sawdust*, 124–25.

180 "The word is": Cited in A. James Reichley, *Religion in American Public Life* (Washington, D.C.: The Brookings Institution, 1985), 69.

181 "is a moral corruption": Balmer, *Mine Eyes*, 201.

182 "theologically and morally": Hunter, *The Death of Character*, 133.

182   a brief look: recoverybooks.com/xesteem.html.

182   including: Charles Gerber, *Christ-Centered Self-Esteem: Seeing Ourselves Through God's Eyes* (Joplin, Mo.: College Press Publishing Co., 2001), and Tamyra Horst, *A Woman of Worth: Living as a Daughter of the King* (Nampa, Idaho: Pacific Publishers Association, 2002).

182   "almost   every   one":   www.amazon.com/exec/obidos/ISBN%3 D0899007643/christiansinrecoA/104-8320125-1821518.

183   Some writers: Robert C. Fuller, *Spiritual but Not Religious: Understanding Unchurched America* (New York: Oxford University Press, 2001).

183   "spiritual junkie": Wuthnow, *After Heaven*, 154, 164.

183   "Avoid arrogance": Wuthnow, *Sharing the Journey*, 200–201.

CHAPTER 7. WITNESS

185   America's religions: A helpful introduction to this topic can be found in Martin E. Marty and Frederick E. Greenspahn, eds., *Pushing the Faith: Proselytism and Civility in a Pluralistic World* (New York: Crossroad, 1988).

185   freedom of public religion: For this turn of phrase, I am indebted to John Witte Jr., *Religion and the American Constitutional Experiment: Essential Rights and Liberties* (Boulder: Westview, 2000), 238.

186   one survey: Smith, *American Evangelicalism*, 38.

186   "I love Christ": Beaman, *Shared Beliefs, Different Lives*, 38.

187   "What am I": Bramadat, *The Church on the World's Turf*, 129.

187   "I'm willing": Beaman, *Shared Beliefs*, 38.

187   "It's our duty": Ibid.

188   efforts by: Stark and Finke, *Acts of Faith*, 135.

188   "I went to": Brasher, *Godly Women*, 41, 55.

189   "shoving": Beaman, *Shared Beliefs*, 39.

189   "really witnessing": Ammerman, *Bible Believers*, 91, 93–95.

190   Studies of converts: Kaufman, *Rachel's Daughters*, 120.

190   "When people become": Ammerman, *Bible Believers*, 95–96.

190   groups ranging from: For an example of how Promise Keeper members resist witnessing in favor of talking to the already saved, see Lundskow, *Awakening to an Uncertain Future*, 47–48. For examples of "friendship evangelizing" among college students, see Bramadat, *The Church on the World's Turf*, 124.

191   some such contact: Melinda Bollar Wagner, *God's Schools: Choice and Compromise in American Society* (New Brunswick, N.J.: Rutgers University Press, 1990).

191   "limited contact": Alan Peshkin, *God's Choice: The Total World of a Fundamentalist Christian School* (Chicago: University of Chicago Press, 1986), 271.

191   "It's . . . like when": Ammerman, *Bible Believers*, 101.

191   "Whenever I hear": Beaman, *Shared Beliefs*, 39.

192   "lifestyle evangelism": Tamney, *The Resilience of Conservative Religion*, 84, 87.

192   "living . . . an": Ammerman, *Bible Believers,* 91.

193   "ask people to": Steve Sjogren, *Conspiracy of Kindness: A Refreshing New Approach to Sharing the Love of Jesus with Others* (Ann Arbor, Mich.: Vine Books, 1993), 68.

193   "You can't be": Interview with Steve Sjogren, March 4, 2002.

193   "Just to show": This quotation and those in the next paragraph come from Sjogren, *Conspiracy of Kindness,* 43, 44, 103, 180–81.

195   "Jesus was": Sjogren Interview, March 4, 2002.

195   "I take what is worldly": Sargeant, *Seeker Churches,* 4, 5.

197   inner-city Philadelphia: Lee R. Cooper, "Publish or Perish: Negotiating Jehovah's Witness Adaptation in the Ghetto," in Irving L. Zaretsky and Mark P. Leone, eds., *Religious Movements in Contemporary America* (Princeton: Princeton University Press, 1974), 713.

197   "Once you understand": McRoberts, *Streets of Glory,* 88–90.

198   While sociologists: William Julius Wilson, *When Work Disappears: The World of the New Urban Poor* (New York: Knopf, 1996).

198   Jews and Catholics: Gerald H. Gamm, *Urban Exodus: Why the Jews Left Boston and the Catholics Stayed* (Cambridge, Mass.: Harvard University Press, 1999); Hillel Levine and Lawrence Harmon, *The Death of an American Jewish Community: A Tragedy of Good Intentions* (New York: Free Press, 1992).

198   "Those who": James Hudnut-Beumler, *Looking for God in the Suburbs: The Religion of the American Dream and Its Critics* (New Brunswick, N.J.: Rutgers University Press, 1994), 6.

199   social critics: Herberg, *Protestant, Catholic, Jew,* and Gibson Winter, *The Suburban Captivity of the Churches: An Analysis of Protestant Responsibility in the Expanding Metropolis* (Garden City, N.Y.: Doubleday, 1961).

199   "the suburban frontier": Marshall Sklare and Joseph Greenblum, *Jewish Identity on the Suburban Frontier: A Study of Group Survival in the Open Society,* 2nd ed.; (Chicago: University of Chicago Press, 1979).

199   most reluctant: John T. McGreevy, *Parish Boundaries: The Catholic Encounter with Race in the Twentieth-Century Urban North* (Chicago: University of Chicago Press, 1996). See also Eileen M. McMahon, *What Parish Are You From?: A Chicago Irish Community and Race Relations* (Lexington: University Press of Kentucky, 1995).

199   mid-1990s: Smith, *American Evangelicalism,* 77–78.

200   "Six Flags over": Breakfast discussion with Memphis clergy, April 10, 2002.

200   "Lots of people": Balmer, *Grant Us Courage,* 82.

201   "the power of God": Breakfast meeting with Memphis clergy, April 10, 2002.

202   as it recently: *Good News Club v. Milford Central School,* 121 S. Ct. 2093 (2001).

202   on fairgrounds: *Heffron v. International Society for Krishna Consciousness,*

452 U.S. 640 (1981); *Airport Commissioners of Los Angeles v. Jews for Jesus*, 482 U.S. 569 (1987).

202 With similarly: *Lloyd Corp. v. Tanner*, 407 U.S. 551 (1972); *Pruneyard Shopping Center v. Robings*, 447 U.S. 74 (1980).

202 Hope Evangelical: Francine Parnes, "Yes, God Is Everywhere, Even at the Local Mall," *New York Times*, March 2, 2002, B7.

202 "Hebron has": Eiesland, *A Particular Place*, 59, 61, 74.

203 "family congregation": Becker, *Congregations in Conflict*, 82.

203 a good job: Breakfast meeting with Memphis clergy, April 10, 2002.

205 in a 1994 survey: Cited in Dawn, *Reaching Out*, 152.

205 "If you put on": Breakfast meeting with Memphis clergy, April 10, 2002.

206 "Sometimes people": Marsden, *Fundamentalism and American Culture*, 157.

206 "cannot believe": Romanowski, *Pop Culture Wars*, 38.

207 vaudeville, magic shows: Kathryn J. Oberdeck, *The Evangelist and the Impresario: Religion, Entertainment, and Cultural Politics in America, 1884–1914* (Baltimore: Johns Hopkins University Press, 1999). See also Colleen McDannell, *Material Christianity: Religion and Popular Culture in America* (New Haven: Yale University Press, 1995); R. Laurence Moore, *Selling God: American Religion in the Marketplace of Culture* (New York: Oxford University Press, 1994); and Leigh Eric Schmidt, *Consumer Rites: The Buying and Selling of American Holidays* (Princeton: Princeton University Press, 1995).

207 proliferation of: Jan Blodgett, *Protestant Evangelical Literary Culture and Contemporary Society* (Westport, Conn.: Greenwood Press, 1997).

207 not sufficient for: For the material in this paragraph, I am indebted to Douglas Carl Abrams, *Selling the Old-Time Religion: American Fundamentalists and Mass Culture, 1920–1940* (Athens and London: University of Georgia Press, 2001), 28, 32, 59, 84, 97, 101.

208 "Born again adults": Cited in Romanowski, *Eyes Wide Open*, 12.

208 "Reaching Hollywood": Marti, "Mosaic on Mission," 194.

208 "The subtleties": Jeffrey K. Hadden and Anson Shupe, *Televangelism: Power and Politics on God's Frontier* (New York: Henry Holt and Co., 1988), 133. See also Razelle Frankl, "Television and Popular Religion: Changes in Church Offerings," in David G. Bromley and Anson Shupe, eds., *New Christian Politics* (Macon, Ga.: Mercer University Press, 1984), 129–38.

209 "What are the": www.av1611.org/othpubls/teenidol.html.

209 In a 1983 survey: William D. Romanowski, "Evangelicals and Popular Music: The Contemporary Christian Music Industry," in Forbes and Mahan, *Religion and Popular Culture in America*, 106–07, 116, 120.

210 conservative Christian watchdogs: See, for example, Texe Marrs, "The Dragon's Hot Breath: Unmasking the Awful Truth about Christian Rock," logosresourcepages.org/chr-rock.htm.

210 After Grant received: Steve Rabey, "A Singer Returns to Christian Basics," *New York Times*, May 11, 2002, A14.

211   none of them: Romanowski, *Eyes Wide Open,* 71.

211   "astounded at": Balmer, *Mine Eyes,* 231.

212   "Turning mass recordings": Romanowski, "Evangelicals and Popular Music," 112.

213   "it says in": Bramadat, *The Church on the World's Turf,* 127.

CHAPTER 8. IDENTITY

215   Religious identity: Clifford Geertz, *Islam Observed* (Chicago: University of Chicago Press, 1971), 56.

216   Christians compose: For the statistics in this paragraph, see Kwang Chung Kim, R. Stephen Warner, and Ho-Youn Kwon, "Korean American Religion in International Perspective," in Ho-Youn Kwon, Kwang Chung Kim, and R. Stephen Warner, eds., *Korean Americans and Their Religions: Pilgrims and Missionaries from a Different Shore* (University Park, Pa.: Pennsylvania State University Press, 2001), 3–24.

216   "I never went": Victoria Hyonchu Kwon, "Houston Korean Ethnic Church: An Ethnic Enclave," in Helen Rose Ebaugh and Janet Saltzman Chafetz, eds., *Religion and the New Immigrants: Continuities and Adaptations in Immigrant Congregations* (Walnut Creek, Calif.: AltaMira, 2000), 116.

216   According to a: Kwang Chung Kim and Shin Kim, "The Ethnic Roles of Korean Immigrant Churches in the United States," in Kwon et al., *Korean Americans,* 71–94.

217   Sociologists suggest: Won Moo Huhr and Kwang Chung Kim, "Religious Participation of Korean Immigrants in the United States," *Journal for the Scientific Study of Religion* 29 (1990): 19–34.

217   "Many contemporary": Fenggang Yang, *Chinese Christians in America: Conversion, Assimilation, and Adhesive Identities* (University Park, Pa.: Pennsylvania State University Press, 1999), 94.

218   "I felt like": Peter T. Cha, "Ethnic Identity Formation and Participation in Immigrant Churches: Second-Generation Korean American Experiences," in Kwon et al., *Korean Americans,* 152.

218   "silent exodus": Helen Lee, "Silent Exodus," *Christianity Today,* August 12, 1996, 51–52, cited in Karen J. Chai, "Beyond 'Strictness' to Distinctiveness," in Kwon et al., *Korean Americans,* 158.

218   "might be more": Cha, "Ethnic Identity Formation," 155.

218   suburban Boston: Karen J. Chai, "Competing for the Second Generation: English-Language Ministry at a Korean Protestant Church," in Warner and Wittner, *Gatherings in the Diaspora,* 295–331, and Karen J. Chai, "Beyond 'Strictness,'" 157–80.

218   No mention of: Chai, "Beyond 'Strictness,'" 172.

219   "American-born": Russell Jeung, "Asian American Pan Ethnic Formation and Congregational Culture," in Min and Kim, *Religion in Asian America,* 235.

219 "I am Christian": Soyoung Park, "The Intersection of Religion, Race, Ethnicity, and Gender in the Identity Formation of Korean American Evangelical Women," in Kwon et al., *Korean Americans*, 196.

219 "troubled by": Antony W. Alumkal, "Being Korean, Being Christian: Particularism and Universalism in a Second-Generation Congregation," in Kwon et al., *Korean Americans*, 187.

219 as one sociologist: The material in this paragraph is indebted to Carolyn Chen, "Getting Saved in America: Immigrants Converting to Evangelical Christianity and Buddhism" (Ph.D. Diss., University of California, Berkeley, 2002), 2, 50.

220 "These immigrants": Yang, *Chinese Christians*, 4, 192.

220 "Many Confucian": Rudy V. Buston, "The Gospel According to the Model Minority?: Hazarding an Interpretation of Asian American Evangelical College Students," in David K. Yoo, ed., *New Spiritual Homes: Religion and Asian Americans* (Honolulu: University of Hawaii Press, 1999), 178.

221 One minister: Yang, *Chinese Christians*, 147.

221 tapered off: Larry L. Hunt, "Hispanic Protestantism in the United States: Trends by Decade and Generation," *Social Forces* 77 (June 1999): 1616.

221 the staging of: Arlene M. Sanchez Walsh, "El Aposento Alto," 118.

222 "The change": León, "Born Again in East LA," in Warner and Wittner, *Gatherings in the Diaspora*, 177.

222 preaches a message: See, for example, Michael Frederick Kozart, "Practice, Meaning, and Belief in Latino Pentecostalism: A Study in the Dynamics of Religious Healing, Theology, and Social Order" (Ph.D. diss., University of California Berkeley, 1999).

222 "My relatives": Kathleen Sullivan, "Iglésia de Dios: An Extended Family," in Ebaugh and Chafetz, *Religion and the New Immigrants*, 145.

222 among a sample: Edwin David Aponte, "Latino Protestant Identity and Empowerment: Hispanic Religion, Community, Rhetoric, and Action in a Philadelphia Case Study" (Ph.D. diss., Temple University, 1998), 173.

223 "weird doctrines": Walsh, "El Aposento Alto," 211.

224 traveled to: Ibid., 238.

224 "a relationship with": León, "Born Again in East LA," in Warner and Wittner, *Gatherings in the Diaspora*, 184.

224 "various stages": Allan Figueroa Deck, S. J., "The Challenge of Evangelical/Pentecostal Christianity to Hispanic Catholicism," in Jay P. Dolan and Allan Figueroa Deck, eds., *Hispanic Catholic Culture in the U.S.: Issues and Concerns* (Notre Dame, Ind.: University of Notre Dame Press, 1994), 425.

225 Ryan DeLaTorre: Walsh, "El Aposento Alto," 279–80, 300.

225 "Harvest leaves": Walsh, "El Aposento Alto," 282.

226 more than sixty: Yvonne Yazbeck Haddad, "The Dynamics of Islamic Identity in North America," in Yvonne Yazbeck Haddad and John L. Esposito, eds., *Muslims on the Americanization Path?* (New York: Oxford University Press, 2000), 20.

226   "[Our] common tie is": Elise Goldwasser, "Economic Security and Muslim Identity: A Study of the Immigrant Community in Durham, North Carolina," in Haddad and Esposito, *Muslims on the Americanization Path?*, 310.

226   "The children": Ibid., 311–12.

227   Orange County: Visit to the Islamic Society of Orange County, October 4, 2002; interview with Musammil H. Siddiqi, director.

227   347 frequent: Yvonne Yazbeck Haddad and Adair T. Lummis, *Islamic Values in the United States: A Comparative Study* (New York: Oxford University Press, 1987), 42.

228   his "congregation": Siddiqi interview.

228   "the Sunday service": Linda S. Walbridge, *Without Forgetting the Imam: Lebanese Shi'ism in an American Community* (Detroit: Wayne State University Press, 1997), 101.

229   "The role of": Haddad and Lummis, *Islamic Values,* 59.

230   In a city like: Hoda Badr, "Al-Noor Mosque: Strength Through Unity," in Ebaugh and Chafetz, *Religion and the New Immigrants,* 195.

230   "It is hard": Nimat Hafez Barazangi, "Islamic Education in the United States and Canada: Conception and Practice of the Islamic Belief System," in Yvonne Yazbeck Haddad, ed., *The Muslims of America* (New York: Oxford University Press, 1991), 166.

230   they are hardly likely: John O. Voll, "Islamic Issues for Muslims in the United States," in Haddad, *The Muslims of America,* 207.

231   approaching *salat*: Walbridge, *Without Forgetting the Imam,* 136–39.

231   in Raleigh: Goldwasser, "Economic Security," 307.

231   "perhaps more than half": Walbridge, *Without Forgetting the Imam,* 147.

232   that Pakistanis: Haddad and Lummis, *Islamic Values,* 34.

232   holiday begins: Walbridge, *Without Forgetting the Imam,* 140.

232   Farrukh Siddiqui: Susan Sachs, "Pursuing an American Dream While Following the Koran," *New York Times,* July 5, 2001, C1.

233   informal rules: See Sachs, "Pursuing an American Dream," and Haddad and Lummis, *Islamic Values,* 100.

233   "So many times": Haddad and Lummis, *Islamic Values,* 100–01.

233   in 1984: Ruholla Khomeini, *A Clarification of Questions: An Unabridged Translation of Rasaleh Towzih al-Masael* (Boulder: Westview Press, 1984).

234   "The Prophet": Haddad and Lummis, *Islamic Values,* 27–28.

234   "Actually": Badr, "Al-Noor Mosque," 217.

235   Arranged marriages: Haddad and Lummis, *Islamic Values,* 110, 141, 143, 151.

235   "the standard of": Goldwasser, "Economic Security," 309.

237   "I've lived in": Wendy Cadge, "Seeking the Heart: The First Generation Practices Theravada Buddhism in America" (Ph.D. diss., Princeton University, 2002), 169.

237   "Becoming Christian": Chen, "Getting Saved," 104.

238   at Wat Dhammaran in Chicago: Paul David Numrich, *Old Wisdom in the New World: Americanization in Two Immigrant Theravada Buddhist Temples* (Knoxville: University of Tennessee Press, 1996), 7–9.

238   although not: Penny Van Esterik, *Taking Refuge: Lao Buddhists in North America* (Tempe, Ariz.: Arizona State University Press, 1992), 111.

238   "rather silly": Numrich, *Old Wisdom*, 50.

238   Three-day rituals: Van Esterik, *Taking Refuge*, 115.

238   opt for: Janet McLellan, *Many Petals of the Lotus: Five Asian Buddhist Colonies in Toronto* (Toronto: University of Toronto Press, 1999), 46.

239   "I do not see": Cadge, "Seeking the Heart," 218.

239   survey of "new Buddhists": James William Coleman, *The New Buddhism: The Western Transformation of an Ancient Tradition* (New York: Oxford University Press, 2001), 119–20.

239   only 11.5 percent: Numrich, *Old Wisdom*, 123.

240   American converts to Buddhism: Descriptions of the religious practices of American-born converts can be found in Charles S. Prebish, *Luminous Passage: The Practice and Study of Buddhism in the United States* (Berkeley and Los Angeles: University of California Press, 1999); Coleman, *The New Buddhism;* and Cadge, "Seeking the Heart." See also David L. Preston, *The Social Organization of Zen Practice: Constructing Transcultural Reality* (New York: Cambridge University Press, 1988).

240   one popular book: Stephen Batchelor, *Buddhism without Beliefs: A Contemporary Guide to Awakening* (New York: Riverhead Books, 1997).

240   an intellectual approach: Numrich, p. 124.

240   "It seems pretty much": Cadge, "Seeking the Heart," 134.

241   relative lack: Numrich, *Old Wisdom*, 121.

241   "expressive" ethic: Cadge, "Seeking the Heart," 137, citing Steven Tipton, *Getting Saved from the Sixties: Moral Meaning in Conversion and Cultural Change* (Berkeley and Los Angeles: University of California Press, 1982).

242   "If Buddhists propagate": The practitioner is Stan Levinson, cited in Numrich, *Old Wisdom*, 123.

242   "Our era": Prebish, *Luminous Passage*, 90.

243   have questioned: Diana Eck, *A New Religious America: How "A Christian Country" Has Become the World's Most Religiously Diverse Nation* (San Francisco: HarperCollins, 2001).

CONCLUSION: IS DEMOCRACY SAFE FROM RELIGION?

245   "as 'sticking out'": Berger, *The Sacred Canopy*, 26.

246   Social scientists: A good overview can be found in Stark and Finke, *Acts of Faith*.

247   In politics: For an account of what Americans know about politics,

see Michael X. Delli Carpini and Scott Keeter, *What Americans Know about Politics and Why It Matters* (New Haven: Yale University Press, 1996).

247 just under half: George D. Gallup Jr. and D. Michael Lindsay, *Surveying the Religious Landscape: Trends in U.S. Beliefs* (Harrisburg, Pa.: Morehouse Publishing, 1999), 49. See also Bill Broadway, "Are the Faithful Misinformed? Americans Hold 'Errant' Theological Positions, Survey Finds," *Washington Post,* August 5, 2000, B9. I am grateful to Peter Schuck for this reference.

248 Some Christians: Stephen Carter, *The Culture of Disbelief: How American Law and Politics Trivialize Religious Devotion* (New York: Basic Books, 1993).

248 a recent book: Philip Jenkins, *The Next Christendom: The Coming of Global Christianity* (New York: Oxford University Press, 2002).

250 "There are no": Stanley Fish, *The Trouble with Principle* (Cambridge, Mass.: Harvard University Press, 1999), 209, 250.

250 "resident aliens": Stanley Hauerwas and William Willimon, *Resident Aliens: A Provocative Christian Assessment of Culture and Ministry for People Who Know That Something Is Wrong* (Nashville: Abingdon Press, 1989).

250 "We . . . bent over backward": Stanley Hauerwas and William H. Willimon, *Where Resident Aliens Live: Exercises for Christian Practice* (Nashville: Abingdon Press, 1996), 17, 18.

250 "Christians are now": Hauerwas, *In Good Company,* 55–56. Hauerwas identifies Mills with Harvard, but he actually taught at Columbia.

251 "One prerequisite": Crapanzano, *Serving the Word,* 336.

252 "we should also be": Stephen Macedo, "Liberal Civic Education and Religious Fundamentalism: The Case of God v. John Rawls?" *Ethics* 105 (April 1995): 468–96.

252 Vicki Frost: Her story is told in Stephen Bates, *Battleground: One Mother's Crusade, the Religious Right, and the Struggle for Control of Our Classrooms* (New York: Poseidon Press, 1993).

253 "totalistic": Macedo, "Liberal Civic Education," 478.

253 "resist symbolic": Crapanzano, *Serving the Word,* 65.

253 out of fear: Judith Shklar, *Ordinary Vices* (Cambridge, Mass.: Harvard University Press, 1984), 237–49.

255 "'sacred umbrellas'": Smith, *American Evangelicalism,* 106.

256 decided in 1973: *Hunt v. McNair,* 413 U.S. 734 (1973). For additional decisions using the standard, see *Roemer v. Board of Education,* 426 U.S. 736 (1976); *School District of the City of Grand Rapids v. Ball,* 473 U.S. 373 (1985); *Bowen v. Kendrick,* 487 U.S. 589 (1988); and *Mitchell v. Helms,* 120 S. Ct. 2738 (2000). A helpful overview is offered in Stephen V. Monsma, "The 'Pervasively Sectarian' Standard in Theory and Practice," *Notre Dame Journal of Law, Ethics & Public Policy* 13 (1999): 321–40.

258 Some argue that: John L. Esposito, *Holy War: Terror in the Name of Islam* (New York: Oxford University Press, 2002).

258 Rev. Jerry Falwell: For a sample of articles, see "Muhammad a Terrorist to Falwell, *New York Times,* October 4, 2002, 17; and Gustav Niebuhr, "Mus-

lim Group Seeks to Meet Billy Graham's Son," *New York Times*, November 20, 2001, B5.

259 "An Islam that": Letter to the editor, *New York Times*, July 15, 2002, A20.

260 "exercises in resistance": David Tracey, *Plurality and Ambiguity: Hermeneutics, Religion, Hope* (Chicago: University of Chicago Press, 1987), 84, cited in Carter, *The Culture of Disbelief,* 41.

261 "love, love, love": Interview with Steve Sjogren, March 4, 2002.

INDEX

abortion, 4, 117, 257
accountability groups, 61–62
African Methodist Episcopal (A.M.E.) Church, 77–79, 112, 138
African Americans, 29–30, 114, 115, 159, 173–75, 198, 217; Baptist, 8–9; faith-based initiatives of, 138–41; Mormon, 146; Muslim, 142–43; Pentecostal, 77–80, 131, 139, 200
Aglow International Fellowship, 63, 157–58, 160, 202
Ahmad, Latifa, 226, 235
AIDS, 122, 124, 181, 184
Akers, Ronald L., 284n
Alcance Victoria (Los Angeles), 141–42, 221, 223–24
Alinsky, Saul, 124
Allen, Larry Dean, II, 272n
Allen Temple Baptist Church (Oakland, California), 8–9, 22
Al-Noor mosque (Houston), 230, 234
Alumkal, Antony W., 291n
Ambrose, St., 133
American Baptist Seminary of the West, 9
American Family Association, 207
American Psychological Association, 170, 178
Amish, 143–44
Ammerman, Nancy Tatom, 69, 86–87, 267n, 271n, 274n, 276n, 285n, 287n, 288n
Anderson, Kristin L., 284n

Anderson, Matthew, 159, 284n
Anglicans, 112
Anti-Defamation League, 47
anti-Semitism, 116, 153, 261–62
Aponte, Edwin David, 291n
Arguinzoni, Sonny, 223, 225
Arguinzoni, Sonny, Jr., 224
Ashcroft, John, 157
Asian immigrants, 115, 149, 198, 216–21, 225, 237, 238, 240, 263
Assemblies of God, 9, 53, 54, 59, 70, 73, 112, 156
Auden, W. H., 80
Augsburg Confession, 71
Augustine, St., 127, 133
Azusa Christian Community (Boston), 140–41

Bach, Johann Sebastian, 28, 29
Badr, Hoda, 292n
Bahr, Howard M., 270n
Bahr, Stephen J., 283n
Bakker, Jim, 153, 208
Bakker, Tammy Faye, 153
Balmer, Randall, 32, 211, 268n, 274n, 275n, 276n, 286n, 288n, 290n
Baltzell, E. Digby, 275n
Bane, Mary Jo, 282n
Bañuelas, Arturo, 124
Baptists, 22, 23, 44, 45, 82, 115, 169–70, 183, 195; African American, 8–9, 77, 78; Southern, 42, 46, 70, 51, 59, 80, 81, 112, 114, 165–69, 172, 200–202, 258

Baptist World Mission, 60
Barazangi, Ninat Hafez, 292n
bar and bat mitzvah, 98–99
Bartkowski, John P., 273n, 281n
Batchelor, Stephen, 293n
Bates, Stephen, 294n
Bayles, Martha, 29, 268n
Beaman, Lori G., 281n, 287n
Beaudoin, Thomas, 280n
Becker, Penny Edgell, 275n, 282n, 289n
Begier, Tom, 271n
Belgic Confession, 71
Bell, David C., 284n
Bell, E. N., 156, 158
Bellevue Baptist Church (Memphis), 200–201
Bender, Courtney J., 283n
Berger, Peter L., 118, 245, 255, 279n, 293n
Berrien, Jenny, 282n, 286n
Beth Israel (Hartford, Connecticut), 109
Beth Pinchas, 21
Bethel A.M.E. Church (Baltimore), 78, 79, 81
Bianchi, Eugene C., 266n
Bias Chana (Minnesota), 102, 103
Bibby, Reginald, 270n
Bible, 10, 22, 25, 33, 39, 67–69, 87, 114, 129, 148, 171, 177, 194, 208, 213, 216–21, 252–53; Acts, 74, 85; Corinthians, 67, 182; Ephesians, 182; Exodus, 85; Galatians, 182; Genesis, 85, 247; Hebrews, 9, 85; John, 205; Luke, 85, 115–16, 182; Matthew, 205; Psalms, 9, 24; Timothy, 183; see also New Testament; Old Testament
Bible Institute of Los Angeles, 179
Bible-study groups, 52, 76, 84–86, 94, 130, 132, 136, 161, 216, 218, 220
Bieze, Linda, 134, 282n
Biola University, 179
Blodgett, Jan, 289n
Bloom, Stephen G., 277n
Bly, Robert, 62
Bob Jones University, 48, 206

born-agains, see evangelicals
Boston University, 176
Bramadat, Paul A., 285n, 287n, 290n
Brasher, Brenda, 281n, 287n
Brickner, Bryan W., 273n
Brigham Young University, 150; Charles Redd Center for Western Studies, 151
Brinkerhoff, Merlin, 270n
Broadway, Bill, 294n
Bromley, David G., 289n
Brooke, John L., 283n
Brown, Patricia Leigh, 268n
Brownsville Assembly of God Church (Pensacola), 80
Bryant, John, 79
Brzezinski, Zbigniew, 268n
Buddhists, 183, 216, 237–43, 263
Buenaventura, Steffi San, 280n
Burns, Jeffrey M., 280n
Bursik, Robert J., Jr., 284n
Bush, George W., 117, 157
Buston, Rudy V., 291n

Caccamo, Rita, 269n
Cadge, Wendy, 292n, 293n
Calvary Chapel, 75–76, 80, 81, 224
Calvary Church (Memphis), 203
Calvin, John, 45, 84, 150
Calvin College, 70–71, 180, 212
Calvinism, 86, 146, 181, 184
Cambridge Insight Meditation Center (CIMC), 239
Cana Conferences, 121
Caplow, Theodore, 270n
Capps, Donald, 286n
Carlson, Jerry W., 284n
Carpenter, Joel, 274n
Carter, Stephen, 294n, 295n
Castelli, Jim, 265n, 276n, 279n, 280n
Catholics, 23, 41, 42, 46, 80, 82, 92, 111, 112, 150, 183, 185, 198, 199, 248, 261, 262, 264; attitudes toward tradition of, 117–25; charismatic, 14–15, 60; conservative, 1, 254; doctrine of, 87–91; elitism of, 93; fellowship among, 37, 55–57; Latino, 221–24, 238, 243; liturgy

of, 10–18, 21, 22, 25, 27, 35; Luther and, 51, 71; moral views of, 127; Mormons and, 146, 148; parachurch organizations of, 58–59; pedophilia scandals of, 57, 87, 153–54, 259–60, 262–63; popular entertainment and, 206; prejudice against, 116, 263; sin and, 162–63, 170, 172–73, 177; switching to Protestantism by, 48–49, 53, 59, 169

Center for Christian Leadership, 33

Central Conference of American Rabbis, 109

Cha, Peter T., 290n

Chadwick, Bruce A., 270n, 283n

Chafetz, Janet Saltzman, 290–92n

Chai, Karen J., 290n

charismatics, 26, 59, 75, 81, 113, 144; Catholic, 14–15, 60

Chaves, Mark, 268n

Chen, Carolyn, 291n, 292n

Cherry, Conrad, 268n

Chicago, University of, 45, 176

Chicago Gospel Tabernacle, 207

Chinese, 219–21, 225, 243

Chinese Christian Church (CCC; Washington, D.C.), 220–21

Christian Century, 200

Christian Reformed Church, 70–71, 74, 180

Christian Science, 112

Christians, 2, 31, 53, 92, 126, 136, 215, 236, 248–51; Asian, 216–21, 225, 263; born-again, 3, 14, 167 (see also evangelicals); Buddhism and, 237, 238, 242; charity of, 41; conservative, 251, 252, 258, 261, 262; denominational switching by, 44–46, 109; doctrinal uncertainty of, 72, 74; early, 16, 50; Eastern Orthodox, 3, 112; feminism and, 129–35; Golden Rule, 86–87, 90; Jews and, 110, 239; moral views of, 127–29, 151–53; multiculturalism and, 225; Muslims and, 194, 227–32, 236, 258–59; in parachurch organizations, 58–64; popu-

lar culture and, 27, 28, 30, 141–42, 206–12; proselytizing by, 187–88, 191; psychology and, 177, 179, 182; relational, 51; sin and, 157–59, 163, 164, 166, 168, 177; worship by, 21, 23–24, 253; see also Catholics; Protestants

Christians for Biblical Equality (CBE), 134

Christiansen, Jan, 159, 285n

Church of the Brethren, 143–44

Church of Christ, 112

Church of God, 42, 59, 181

Church of God in Christ, 77–78, 141, 159, 200

Church of Jesus Christ of Latter-day Saints, see Mormons

Church of the Nazarene, 42, 112, 181

Church of the Redeemer (Chestnut Hill, Massachusetts), 7–8

Cincinnati Vineyard Fellowship, 28, 31–32, 76, 193, 203, 261

Claussen, Dane S., 272n, 273n

Clinton, Bill, 173–74

Cochran, John K., 284n

Coffin, Brent, 282n

Cohen, Debra Nussbaum, 278n

Cohen, Steven M., 267n, 268n, 270n, 276n, 278n, 285n, 286n

Colbert, Don, 159, 284n

Coleman, James William, 293n

Columbia Broadcasting System (CBS), 209

Communion, First, 162

Conanson, Joe, 272n

confession, sacrament of, 120–21, 172

Confucianism, 220, 221

Congregation for the Doctrine of the Faith, 89, 91

Congregation Emanuel (San Francisco), 109

Cooper, Lee R., 288n

Cornwall, Marie, 283n

Cortes, Ernesto, 124

Crapanzano, Vincent, 251, 274n, 294n

Dallas Theological Seminary, 33

Daniels, David D., III, 275n

Dannin, Robert, 282n
D'Antonio, William V., 266n, 272n, 276n, 280n, 285n, 286n
Danzger, Herbert, 277n, 278n
Darwinism, 116, 177, 257
Dashefsky, Arnold, 269n
Davidman, Lynn, 102, 267n, 277n, 285n
Davidson, James D., 266n
Davie, Jody Shapiro, 276n, 285n, 286n
Davies, Douglas J., 283n
Dawn, Marva J., 24, 28, 33, 267n, 289n
DeBerg, Betty A., 268n
DeCelle, Douglas, 272n
Deck, Allan Figueroa, 291n
Delli Carpini, Michael X., 294n
Democratic Party, 42, 123, 249
denominationalism, 38–49, 65–66; parachurch movement and, 59, 60, 63; switching and, 41–48, 59, 66; see also specific denominations
Dharma Sisters, 241
Dharma Vijaya Buddhist Vihara (Los Angeles), 238
Dial-the-Truth Ministries, 209
Diamond, Etan, 277n
Dick Van Dyke Show, The, 99
dietary practices: Islamic, 231–32; Orthodox Jewish, 99–101
Diles, Dave, 272n
Dillon, Michele, 267n, 279n
Dilulio, John J., Jr., 282n
Dinges, William D., 266n
Dionne, E. J., 282n
Disciples of Christ, 144
dispensationalism, 68, 69
divorce, 44, 117, 126, 152, 165, 167, 169
Dobson, James C., 33, 135, 282n
doctrine, 3, 40, 67–95; Catholic, 87–91, 93; denominational, 40; evangelical, 69–77, 80; fundamentalist, 67–70, 80, 94–95; Jewish, 90–94; mainline Protestant, 81–87, 93; Mormon, 146–48; Pentecostal, 77–81
Dolan, Jay P., 265n, 291n
Dooley, Thomas, 162

Dordt, Canons of, 71
Douglas, Mary, 266n
Downes, Richard H., 7–8

Ebaugh, Helen Rose, 290–92n
Eck, Diana, 293n
Edwards, Jonathan, 1–3, 36, 69, 178, 180
Eger, Denise L., 278n
Eidenmuller, Michael, 272n
Eiesland, Nancy L., 270n, 279n, 282n, 289n
Eisen, Arnold M., 268n, 269n, 271n, 276n, 278n, 285n, 286n
Eisenhower, Dwight D., 94
Elliott, Cheryl, 8–9
Ellison, Christopher G., 284n
Embrie, Jessie L., 283n, 284n
Emerson, Michael O., 268n, 279n
Emory University, 29
Episcopalians, 7–8, 22, 41, 76, 80, 82, 90, 144, 179, 203
Equal Rights Amendment, 137
Esposito, John L., 291n, 292n, 294n
Eucharist, 120
Evangelical and Ecumenical Women's Caucus (EEWC), 134
evangelicals, 1, 14, 76, 77, 83, 86–88, 91–93, 102, 130, 181, 161, 248, 254, 258; Asian American, 217, 218, 220, 221; doctrine of, 69–75, 80–82, 87; formerly in mainline denominations, 42; gender roles among, 129, 130, 132–34; Latino, 48, 222–25; lifestyle, 192–93; megachurch, 26–29, 34, 36, 74, 113–14, 202–5, 216; morality of, 152; Mormons and, 145, 147; nonjudgmentalism of, 170, 175; parachurch organizations of, 59, 63; popular culture and, 83–84, 206–13, 256–57; witnessing by, 185–87, 189, 194–97, 199, 205–6; psychology and, 178–82; servant, 193–94; tradition and, 111–12, 116–17; weight-loss groups for, 159–60; worship of, 23–36
Evans, John H., 206–7

Everton, Sean F., 273n
Extreme Unction, 122

faith-based initiatives, 138–43, 153
faith statements, 70, 71
Falwell, Jerry, 134–35, 257, 258, 282n
fellowship, 37–66; anti-institutional,
    37–38, 49–58; denominationalism
    and, 38–49, 65–66; parachurch,
    58–64
feminism, 128–35, 137, 172; biblical,
    133–34
Ferraro, Thomas J., 280n, 285n
Fichter, Joseph, 276n
Finke, Roger, 270n, 274n, 287n, 293n
Finney, Charles Grandison, 206, 207
First Community Church (Columbus,
    Ohio), 87
First Presbyterian Church (Lexington,
    Kentucky), 87
First Things magazine, 80
Fish, Stanley, 250, 294n
Fishman, Sylvia Barack, 267n, 271n
Flake, Rev. Floyd, 78
Focus on the Family, 33, 34, 135
Fogel, Robert W., 276n
Fong, Oden, 77
Forbes, Bruce David, 279n, 289n
Foucault, Michel, 171
Fox, Everett, 85
Fox, Richard Wrightman, 269n
Frankl, Razelle, 289n
Freedman, Samuel G., 277n
Freud, Sigmund, 177, 178
Frost, Vicki, 252
Fuller, Charles, 178
Fuller, Robert C., 287n
Fuller Theological Seminary, 81,
    178–80
fundamentalists, 60, 74, 94–95, 112,
    135, 233–34, 249, 251–54; antili-
    turgical worship of, 22; challenge
    to mainline Protestantism of, 198;
    doctrine of, 67–70, 80, 81; divorce
    opposed by, 169; psychology and,
    177, 178; popular culture and,
    206–7, 209, 210; traditional values
    of, 117; withdrawal from family by

converts to, 190; witnessing by,
    185, 186, 189
Furman, Frida Kerner, 267n, 278n

Gaeta, Francis X., 121
Gallup, George D., Jr., 294n
Gamm, Gerald H., 288n
Gans, Herbert, 279n
Gardella, Peter, 281n
Garrett, H. Dean, 283n
Geertz, Clifford, 215, 290n
General Social Survey, 45
Gerard, Susan Elizabeth, 282n
Gilligan, Carol, 131, 281n
Ginsburg, Faye, 282n
Golden Rule Christians, 86–87, 90
Goldman, Karla, 271n
Goldman, Marion S., 281n
Goldsmith, Stephen, 138, 282n
Goldwasser, Elise, 292n
Gonzales, Juan L., 266n
Goodman, Kristen L., 283n
Gottlieb, Yaffa Leba, 277n, 282n
"Grace Abounding" website, 51
Graham, Billy, 60, 80, 258
Graham, Franklin, 258, 259
Grant, Amy, 209–11
Grasmick, Harold G., 284n
Great Commission, 205, 208
Great Depression, 40–41
Greeley, Andrew M., 39, 90, 269n,
    270n, 276n
Green, John C., 269n
Greenblum, Joseph, 288n
Greenspahn, Frederick E., 287n
Gremillion, Joseph, 265n, 276n, 279n,
    280n
Griffith, R. Marie, 273n, 284n
Guy, James D., 179–80

Hadassah Southern California, 18
Hadaway, Christopher Kirk, 269n
Haddad, Mimi, 134, 281n
Haddad, Yvonne Yazbeck, 291n, 292n
Hadden, Jeffrey K., 289n
Halbrook, David, 272n
Hall, David D., 265n
Hammond, Philip E., 269n

Handel, George Frideric, 29
Hansel, Bob, 203
Harden, Blaine, 284*n*
Harding, Susan Friend, 282*n*
Hare Krishnas, 214
Harmon, Lawrence, 288*n*
Harrelson, Walter, 85
Harris, Fredrick C., 275*n*
Hartford Seminary, 176
Harvest Bible College, 225
Harvest Christian Fellowship (River-side, California), 31, 76
Hasidim, 99, 103
Hassan, Hathout, 236
Hauerwas, Stanley, 118, 250–51, 279*n*, 294*n*
havurot, 54, 58, 173
Haynes, Stephen, 30–31, 268*n*
Heaton, Tim B., 283*n*
Hebron Baptist Church (Dacula, Georgia), 46, 113, 114, 202, 203
Heidelberg Catechism, 71
Heilman, Samuel C., 267*n*, 276–78*n*
Herberg, Will, 64–65, 94, 95, 273*n*, 276*n*, 288*n*
Heritage Foundation, 127
Hinckley, Gordon, 146, 148
Hindus, 3, 112
Hirschi, Travis, 284*n*
Hispanics, *see* Latinos
Hobsbawm, Eric, 277*n*
Hoffman, John P., 284*n*
Hoffman, L. A., 19, 267*n*
Hofstadter, Richard, 274*n*
Hoge, Dean R., 266*n*, 270*n*, 272*n*, 276*n*, 280*n*, 285*n*
Holman, Thomas B., 283*n*
holiness churches, 42, 181
home fellowship, 52–55
homosexuality, 60, 109, 114, 181, 184, 217, 257
Hoover, Stewart M., 279*n*
Hope Evangelical Covenant Church (Grand Forks, North Dakota), 202
Hope Presbyterian Church (Memphis), 30–31
Horowitz, Rav Naftali, 21
house church movement, 50–52, 58

Hout, Michael, 270*n*
Howard University, 8
Hudnut-Beumler, James, 288*n*
Hudson, Winthrop, 65, 273*n*
Huhr, Won Moo, 290*n*
Hunt, Larry L., 291*n*
Hunter, James Davison, 182, 286*n*
Huntington, Samuel P., 268*n*

Idlewild Presbyterian Church (Memphis), 30, 31, 201
immigrants, 215, 242–44; Asian, 115, 149, 198, 216–21, 225, 237–42, 263; European, 123; Latin American, *see* Latinos; Muslim, 226–36, 238, 239
individualism, 66, 167; Catholic, 14, 17; Jewish, 18, 48; Protestant, 11, 17, 24, 35, 51, 220
inerrancy, biblical, 68, 177, 217, 253
Ingersoll, Julie, 268*n*
inner-city churches: faith-based initiatives of, 138–43; immigrants in, 221–24; nonjudgmentalism of, 173–75; witnessing by, 196–200
intermarriage, 41, 47, 109, 218, 262
Irish Americans, 123
Irwin, Jeff, 201
Islam, *see* Muslims
Islamic Center of Orange County, 227, 228
Islamic Center of Southern California, 236
Italian Americans, 123

Jabez, Prayer of, 33–35
Jacobs, Alan, 80–81, 275*n*
James, William, 17
Japanese, 238, 239
Jardine, Douglas S., 274*n*
Jehovah's Witnesses, 186, 197, 214
Jenkins, Philip, 294*n*
Jennings, Theodore W., Jr., 285*n*
Jerusalem Talmud, 101
Jesuits, 14–15
Jesus First practices, 15
Jesus People, 75
Jeung, Russell, 290*n*

Jews, 27, 87, 112, 185, 198, 199, 215, 228, 237, 239, 263; Conservative, 19, 91, 98, 105–7; conversion to Christianity of, 31, 242; doctrine of, 90–94; fellowship among, 37, 53–55; for Jesus, 214; liturgy of, 17–22, 25; Muslims and, 229, 230, 259; nonjudgmentalism and, 172, 173; nonobservant, 17–18; Orthodox, 1, 19–21, 99–107, 110, 111, 117, 136–37, 157, 164, 173, 185, 190, 232, 234, 254; parachurch organizations of, 58–59; prejudice against, *see* anti-Semitism; traditions of, 97–99; Reconstructionist, 53, 98; Reform, 18–19, 21, 47–48, 54, 56, 82, 91, 98, 100, 105, 107–10, 176–77, 254; sin and, 163–65
John Paul II, Pope, 88, 121
Johnson, Benton, 276n
Johnson, Mary, 266n
Johnson, Stephen D., 272n
Jones, Bob, Jr., 207
Jones, Bob, Sr., 207
Joselit, Jenna Weissman, 277n
Judeo-Christian tradition, 215, 243, 261

Kabbalah, 101
kaddish, 105–6
Kaminer, Wendy, 179, 286n
Kaplan, Dana Evan, 278n, 280n
Kaplan, Mordecai, 53, 98
Kaufman, David, 271n
Kaufman, Debra Renee, 278n, 282n, 287n
Keach's Catechism, 71
Keeler, Robert F., 16, 120, 266n, 280n
Keeter, Scott, 294n
Kellstedt, Lyman A., 269n
Kennedy, Paul, 274n
Kenneth Hagin Ministries, 32
Khomeini, Ayatollah Ruholla, 233, 292n
Kim, Jung Ha, 280n, 290n
Kim, Kwang Chung, 290n
Kim, Shin, 290n
King, Martin Luther, Jr., 200

Knox, John, 241
Kohen, Elissa, 109
Koran, 229, 232
Koreans, 216–19, 225
Kosmin, Barry A., 267n, 277n
Kotlowitz, Alex, 283n
Kozart, Michael Frederick, 291n
Kreml, Patricia B., 159, 284n
Kwon, Ho-Youn, 290n, 291n
Kwon, Victoria Hyonchu, 290n

Ladd, Tony, 273n
LaHaye, Tim, 69, 128, 281n
Laotians, 238
Lasseigne, Jeff, 31
Latinos, 9, 15, 115, 120, 122–25, 141, 149, 175, 198, 217, 221–25, 238, 243
Laudarji, Isaac B., 283n
Laurie, Greg, 76
Lausanne Covenant, 71
Law, Bernard Cardinal, 57, 259–60, 264
Lawson, Matthew P., 271n, 274n
Lazerwitz, Bernard, 269n, 278n
Lears, T. J. Jackson, 269n
Lee, Bernard J., 55–56, 266n, 272n
Lee, Helen, 290n
Leege, David C., 269n
Lelwica, Michelle Mary, 285n
Lena, Jennifer Carroll, 273n
Léon, Luís, 271n, 286n, 291n
Leone, Mark P., 147, 283n, 288n
Levine, Hillel, 288n
Levinson, Stan, 293n
Lewis, James W., 269n, 271n, 275n, 280n
liberalism, 249–53, 255, 257–58; Catholic, 172; feminism and, 129; Ultra-Orthodox Judaism as reaction against, 101, 104
Liebman, Charles S., 278n
Liebman, Robert C., 272n, 286n
Lienesch, Michael, 281n, 282n
lifestyle evangelism, 192–93
Lincoln, C. Eric, 275n
Lincoln Square Synagogue (New York City), 164–65

Lindsay, D. Michael, 294n
Lindsey, Hal, 69
Lister, Isabel, 16
liturgy, 3, 35; Catholic, 10–13, 16, 21, 22, 25, 27, 35, 119; Jewish, 17–22, 25, 27; mainline Protestant, 22, 24–26
Livesey, Lowell W., 275n, 283n
Lockhart, William H., 273n
Long, Thomas G., 267n
Lubavitchers, 99, 101, 102, 185
Luidens, Donald A., 276n
Lummis, Adair T., 292n
Lundskow, George N., 273n, 287n
Luther, Martin, 45, 51, 67, 71, 84, 150, 256
Lutherans, 22, 24, 41, 46, 150, 185; Missouri Synod, 70
Lynd, Helen Merrell, 39–41, 269n, 270n
Lynd, Robert S. 39–41, 269n, 270n

Macedo, Stephen, 252, 294n
Machen, J. Gresham, 68
Magruder, Jeb Stuart, 87
Mahan, Jeffrey H., 279n, 289n
Maines, David R., 266n
Mallozzi, Mary, 56
Mamiya, Lawrence H., 275n
Manning, Christel J., 281–82n
marriage: arranged, 102–3, 226; Catholic, 121–22; gender roles in, 132–37, 145; nontraditional, 109; see also intermarriage
Marrs, Texe, 289n
Marsden, George M., 265n, 274n, 286n, 289n
Marti, Gerardo, 279n, 289n
Marty, Martin E., 275n, 286n, 287n
Mason, Charles Harrison, 77
Mass, Catholic, 11, 13–14, 16, 18, 56, 88, 89, 122; Tridentine, 10, 21
Mathisen, James A., 273n
Mauss, Armand L., 283n
McCallion, Michael J., 266n
McCartney, Bill, 58–60, 62, 272n
McDannell, Colleen, 265n, 268n, 281n, 283n, 286n, 289n

McDonough, Peter, 266n
McGreevy, John T., 276n, 288n
McKinney, William, 275n
McLellan, Janet, 293n
McLoughlin, William G., 125–26, 280n
McMahon, Eileen M., 288n
McManus, Erwin, 115
McMaster University, 170–71
McPherson, Aimee Semple, 131
McRoberts, Omar Maurice, 275n, 282n, 286n, 288n
Meagher, Timothy, 279n
meditation, 237, 239–40
megachurches, 34, 36, 45–46, 59, 63, 166, 216, 224, 250; doctrine and, 74, 76; music in, 28–29; tradition absent from, 113–14, 117; witnessing in, 202–5; worship in, 26–28
Mendelssohn, Felix, 28, 238
Mendocino Presbyterian Church, 24–26
Mennonites, 143–44
Methodists, 22, 40, 41, 43, 45, 60, 76, 82, 84–87, 93, 112, 119, 172, 176, 201
Meyer, Elaine, 159, 284n
Meyer, Katherine, 266n
Meyer, Michael A., 278n
Midrash, 101
mikveh, 136–37
Miller, Donald E., 268n, 274n, 275n
Mills, C. Wright, 251, 294n
Min, Pyong Gap, 280n, 290n
Minkema, Kenneth P., 265n
Minow, Newton, 84
"Misericordia Dei" (John Paul II), 121
missionaries, Mormon, 149, 150, 188, 193
Mohler, R. Albert, Jr., 259
Monsma, Stephen V., 294n
Moody, Jess, 81
Moore, R. Laurence, 289n
morality, 127–55; gender roles and, 128–37; inner-city poverty and, 138–43; Mormon, 144–51; tradition and, 125; see also sin
Morgan, Marabel, 133, 281n

Mormons, 1, 47, 48, 144–52, 186, 188, 193, 239
Morris, Charles R., 13, 266n
Mosaic (Los Angeles), 114–17
Mouw, Richard, 81, 180–81, 275n, 286n
Movie Morality Ministries, 207
multiculturalism, Mormon, 149–51
music: in Catholic liturgy, 10; classical, 29, 30, 238–39; contemporary Christian, 28–29, 32, 115, 209–12; folk, 172; gospel, 8, 29–30, 3; in Jewish liturgy, 20–21; rap, 141–42
Muslims, 142–43, 194, 226–36, 238, 258, 259–61, 262

narcissism, 23–24, 33–34, 170
Nason-Clark, Nancy, 281n
National Association of Evangelicals, 69
National Association of Religious Broadcasters, 209
National Baptist Convention, 77
National Council of Churches, 233
National Organization for Women, 137
Native Americans, 58
Neal, Marie Augusta, 17, 266n
Neitz, Mary Jo, 266n, 274n, 281n
Nelson, Susan L., 285n
Nelson, Timothy J., 282n
New Age spirituality, 62, 178, 183, 223, 240
New Left, 251
Newsday, 16
New Testament, 2, 52
Nicene Creed, 70, 88
Niebuhr, Gustav, 294n
Niebuhr, H. Richard, 2
nonjudgmentalism, 3, 165–76, 187
Notre Dame Study of Catholic Life, 89, 119, 121
Numrich, Paul David, 293n
nusach, 20–21

Oberdeck, Kathryn J., 289n
Old Testament, 14, 52, 74, 108, 146, 164

Olson, Daniel V. A., 276n, 286n
Oppenheimer, Mark, 286n
Orsi, Robert A., 120, 162, 279n, 285n
O'Toole, James, 280n
Ovalle, Rogelio, 9

Pakistanis, 226, 229, 230, 232, 235
Palestinians, 259
parachurch movements, 58–64, 157–59
Park, Andrew Sung, 285n
Park, Soyoung, 291n
Parkwood Community Church (Glen Ellyn, Illinois), 218
Parnes, Francine, 289n
Payne, Daniel, 78–79
Peck, M. Scott, 178–80, 182, 286n
Penning, James, 279n
Pentecostals, 27, 50, 55, 75–81, 102, 111, 113, 166, 185; African American, 77–80, 139; formerly in mainline denominations, 42, 45, 53; Latino, 141–42, 175, 221–24; self-help oriented, 63; sin and, 156–58, 173; women leaders among, 131
People magazine, 210
Perrin, Robin Dale, 274n, 284n
Peshkin, Alan, 287n
Peters, Mike, 272n
Pickering, Ernest, 60, 272n
Plantinga, Cornelius, Jr., 156, 284n
Pledge of Allegiance, 247
Plotnick, Robert D., 284n
pluralism, 38, 46
Polish Americans, 123, 162
politics, 154, 247–48, 257–58; African American, 174; conservative Christian, 117; see also social justice
Polynesians, 149
popular culture: evangelicals and, 83–84, 115–17, 206–13, 256–57; in faith-based initiatives, 141–42
Porterfield, Amanda, 268n
Prebish, Charles S., 293n
Prell, Riv-Ellen, 271n
premillennialism, 68, 76
Presbyterians, 24–26, 40, 45, 60, 82,

86, 87, 93, 112, 144, 150, 161, 164, 168, 171, 201, 216–17, 219

Preston, David L., 293n

Princeton Theological Seminary, 68

Promise Keepers, 58–64, 190, 202

proselytizing, see witnessing

prosperity theology, 32–33

Protestants, 22–36, 45–46, 48, 243, 248, 262; Catholicism and, 11–12, 15, 16, 57, 88, 89, 117, 259, 261; conservative, 22, 31, 48–49, 81, 114, 117, 129, 131, 133, 156, 169–71, 177, 191, 217 (see also evangelicals; fundamentalists; Pentecostals); individualism of, 11, 17, 24, 51, 220; liberal, 216, 218; mainline, 24–25, 39–40, 42, 49, 70, 81–87, 161, 170, 171, 185, 186, 198, 199, 201, 203; moral views of, 127; Mormons and, 146, 149; parachurch organizations of, 59; popular culture and, 207; see also specific denominations

psychology, 170, 176–84

Puerto Ricans, 222

Puritans, 157, 248, 255

Putney, Clifford, 273n

Quakers, 22, 40

Rabey, Steve, 289n

racism, 153, 262

Rader, Paul, 207

Ramadan, 226, 230, 232

Ranger, Terence, 277n

Ratzinger, Joseph Cardinal, 89–90

Ray, Stephen Gene, Jr., 285n

Reagan, Ronald, 126

Recovery-Books.com, 182

Reformation, 248

Reform Seminary of Cincinnati, 109

Reichley, A. James, 286n

relativism, 89–90

Republican Party, 42, 117, 123, 126

Rhodes College, 30

Rice, John R., 135, 282n

Richard, Alan J., 284n

Richey, Tim, 271n

Riess, Jana Kathryn, 283n

Ritterband, Paul, 278n

Rivers, Eugene, 140–41, 174

Rodeheaver, Homer, 207

Roe v. Wade, 117

Rogers, Adrian, 200

Romanowski, William D., 274n, 276n, 289n, 290n

Roof, Wade Clark, 269–71n, 273n, 275n, 284n

Ross, Alfred, 272n

Ryrie Reference Bible, 68

Sabbath, Jewish observance of, 18, 53, 98, 99, 101, 110, 165

Sachs, Susan, 292n

Saddleback Church (Orange County, California), 29, 166–67

St. Brigid's parish (Long Island), 16, 120–22

St. Catherine's parish (Detroit), 12–13

St. Paul's A.M.E. Church (Cambridge), 79

St. Peter's parish (San Francisco), 123, 124

St. Pius X parish (El Paso), 124, 125

St. Thaddeus parish (Detroit), 118–19

Salvation Army, 214

Sanders, Cheryl J., 275n

Sargeant, Kimon Howland, 117, 268n, 270n, 271n, 274n, 275n, 279n, 285n, 286n, 288n

Sarna, Jonathan, 271n

Schindler, Amy, 273n

Schlafly, Phyllis, 128, 281n

Schmidt, Leigh Eric, 289n

Schoenfeld, Stuart, 277n

school prayer, 4, 230, 257

Schuck, Peter, 294n

Schuller, Robert, 32, 208

Scientologists, 214

Scofield Reference Bible, 68

Scopes trial, 112

Searl, Natalie, 267n, 274n, 281n

self-help movement, 32, 83, 93, 182–83; parachurch organizations and, 63

September 11 terrorist attacks, 7–8, 247, 258–59, 261, 262
servant evangelism, 193–94
Seventh-Day Adventists, 150
Shamblin, Gwen, 159–60
Sherkat, Darren E., 269n, 270n
Shipps, Jan, 149, 150, 283n
Shklar, Judith, 253, 294n
Shupe, Anson, 289n
Siddiqi, Musammil H., 292n
Silber, Michael K., 277n, 278n
Simon, William E., Jr., 127, 281n
sin, 155–84; changing conceptions of, 156–65; denominationalism and, 44; nonjudgmentalism toward, 165–76, 184; psychologizing of, 170, 176–84
Sjogren, Janie, 28, 268n
Sjogren, Steve, 76, 193–94, 203, 261, 275n, 288n, 295n
Sklare, Marshall, 288n
small-group activities, 59, 152–53, 167, 182; of Asian Americans, 218; Catholic, 15–16, 55–56; evangelical, 72–74; Jewish, 53–55, 173; of Latinos, 224; mainline Protestant, 46, 172; parachurch, 61–63; Southern Baptist, 168–69, 172; *see also* Bible-study groups
Smidt, Corwin, 279n
Smith, Christian, 254, 268n, 279n, 287n, 288n, 294n
Smith, Chuck, 75–77
Smith, J. Alfred, Sr., 9
Smith, John E., 265n
Smith, Joseph, 147–48, 150
Smith, Lucy, 131
Smith, Michael W., 209
Smith, Timothy L., 276n
social justice, 86, 199; Catholics and, 88; evangelicals and, 116; faith-based initiatives and, 139–41; Jews and, 92, 107–8
Society of Friends (Quakers), 22, 40
Southern Baptist Convention (SBC), 46, 59, 114, 169, 258
Southern Baptist Theological Seminary, 259

Stacey, Judith, 282n
Stark, Rodney, 270n, 274n, 284n, 287n, 293n
Stations of the Cross, 120, 122, 124
Stein, Arlene, 274n
Stevens, Mitchell L., 272n
Stocks, Janet, 281n
Stoddard, Solomon, 180
Stout, Harry S., 265n
Sullivan, Kathleen, 291n
Summit, Jeffrey A., 267n, 277n
Sunday, Billy, 59, 207
Supreme Court, U.S., 202, 256
Swaggert, Jimmy, 153, 208
switching, religious, 41–48, 59, 66, 148, 204, 256, 261; by immigrants, 216, 218, 219, 225, 243

Taber, Susan Buhler, 283n, 284n
Tabory, Ephraim, 269n, 278n
Talmud, 91, 101, 136
Tamney, Joseph B., 270n, 272n, 285n, 286n, 287n
Tannen, Deborah, 274n
Taylor, Charles, 17, 267n
televangelists, 32, 208–9
Temple Israel, 21
Temple Shalom, 18–19, 107, 108
Ten Point Coalition, 139, 140, 174
Theravada Buddhism, 238
Thich Nhat Hanh, 241
Thiemann, Ronald, 282n
Thomas, George M., 274n
Thomas, William I., 279n
Tipton, Steven, 293n
Tocqueville, Alexis de, 196, 220
Todd, Jesse T., Jr., 275n
Torah, 18, 21, 92, 94, 97, 104, 109, 110
Torevell, David, 266n
Tracey, David, 295n
tradition, 97–126; Catholic, 117–25; evangelical break with, 111–17; Jewish, 47, 91–110
Tradition magazine, 100
Tridentine Latin Mass, 10, 21
Trueheart, Charles, 279n
Tsing, Anna Lowenhaupt, 282n

Union of American Hebrew Congregations, 19, 54
Unitarians, 87, 112, 148, 213
United Church of Christ, 144
United Methodist Church, 84, 201; Board of Disciples of, 85
United States Conference of Catholic Bishops, 60
Upton, Roger, 51, 271*n*
usury, Islamic laws on, 232–33

Van Esterik, Penny, 293*n*
Van Osdel, Oliver W., 206
Vatican II, 10, 11–14, 17, 21, 88, 90, 118–20, 122–25, 172, 199, 248
Vaughn, Billy, 201
Vines, Rev. Jerry, 258, 259
Vineyard Fellowship, 28, 31–32, 60, 75–76, 193, 203, 224–25, 261
Vipassana Buddhism, 239, 240
Voice of the Faithful, 263
Voll, John O., 292*n*

Wacker, Grant, 279*n*, 284*n*
Wagner, Melinda Bollar, 272*n*, 287*n*
Walbridge, Linda S., 292*n*
Walk Thru the Bible Ministries, 33
Walsh, Arlene M. Sanchez, 282*n*, 291*n*
Warner, R. Stephen, 267*n*, 269*n*, 270*n*, 290–91*n*
Warren, Mark R., 280*n*
Warren, Rick, 166–67
Wat Dhammaran (Chicago), 238, 241
Wat Phila (Philadelphia), 240
Watch Tower Society, 197
Waxman, Chaim, 271*n*
Weekly Standard (magazine), 80
weight-loss programs, evangelical, 159–60
Wertheimer, Jack, 271*n*, 277–78*n*
Wesleyan Church, 181
Westminster Confession, 74
Wheaton College, 80, 179
Whitefield, George, 212
Wiccans, 112
Wilberforce University, 78
Wilcox, W. Bradford, 284*n*
Wildmon, Donald, 207

Wilkes, Paul, 124, 125, 280*n*
Wilkie, Richard, 84, 85, 87, 93
Wilkinson, Bruce, 33–34, 268*n*
Williams, Rhys H., 272*n*
Williams-Bryant, Cecelia, 79
Willimon, William H., 250, 294*n*
Willow Creek Church, 113, 166, 200, 224
Wills, Garry, 280*n*
Wilson, William Julius, 198, 288*n*
Wimber, John, 76
Wind, James P., 269*n*, 271*n*, 275*n*, 280*n*
Winona Lake Bible Conference, 207
Winship, Christopher, 282*n*, 286*n*
Winston, Diane, 267*n*, 274*n*, 285*n*
Winter, Gibson, 288*n*
Winter, J. Alan, 269*n*
witnessing, 3, 186–214; discomfort with, 187–90; by example, 191–95; in inner cities, 196–200, 224; among Latinos, 224–25; in megachurches, 202–5; popular culture and, 206–13; suburban, 200–202; withdrawal from world and, 190–91
Witte, John, Jr., 287*n*
Witten, Marsha, 285*n*
Wittner, Judith G., 270*n*, 290*n*, 291*n*
Wolfel, Steven E., 266*n*
women: Baptist, 114; Catholic, 88; Jewish, 101–4, 108–9; Muslim, 226–27, 234–35; parachurch movement and, 60, 62; personal appearance of, 157–60; submission versus empowerment of, 128–37; witnessing by, 186–89
Wood, Richard L., 280*n*
Wooldridge, Adrian, 280*n*
Workman, Dave, 31–32, 34, 268*n*
worship, 3, 7–36; Catholic, 10–17; evangelical, 23–36; fundamentalist, 22–23; Islamic, 227–31; Jewish, 17–22; mainline Protestant, 22, 24–28; Mormon, 147–49; small-group, *see* small-group activities
Wright, Stuart A., 271*n*
Wright, Timothy, 267*n*

Wrobel, Paul, 279n, 285n
Wuthnow, Robert, 39, 46, 165, 267n, 269–72n, 274n, 276n, 281n, 283n, 285–87n

Yang, Fenggang, 290n, 291n
Yom Kippur, 163–64
Yoo, David K., 291n

Young, Lawrence A., 283n

Zakutinsky, Rivka, 277n, 282n
Zaretsky, Irving L., 288n
Zen Buddhism, 239, 240
Znaniecki, Florian, 279n
Zuck, Colleen, 159, 284n
Zuckerman, Phil, 277n

ABOUT THE AUTHOR

Alan Wolfe is director of the Boisi Center for Religion and American Public Life at Boston College. He is author of *One Nation, After All* and *Moral Freedom* and a contributing editor of *The New Republic* and *The Wilson Quarterly*.